*DECIPHERING CAPITAL*

*Marx's Capital and its destiny*

Alex Callinicos

In memoriam

John Callinicos
(1920-2012)

# DECIPHERING CAPITAL

## Marx's Capital and its destiny

Alex Callinicos

Bookmarks Publications

*Deciphering Capital: Marx's Capital and its destiny*
Alex Callinicos

Published 2014 by Bookmarks Publications
c/o 1 Bloomsbury Street, London WC1B 3QE
Copyright © Bookmarks Publications
Typeset by Peter Robinson
Cover image: Shabolovka Radio Tower (1998)
by Richard Pare ©
Printed by Halstan UK

ISBN print edition: 978 1 909026 68 1
Kindle: 978 1 909026 69 8
ePub: 978 1 909026 70 4
PDF: 978 1 909026 71 1

# Table of contents

'Why then did I not answer you? Because I was the whole time at death's door. I thus had to make use of every moment when I was capable of work to complete my book to which I have sacrificed my health, happiness, and family. I hope this explanation suffices. I laugh at the so-called "practical" men and their wisdom. If one wanted to be an ox, one could, of course, turn one's back on the sufferings of humanity and look after one's own hide. But I should really have thought myself *unpractical* if I had pegged out without finally completing my book, at least in manuscript.'

*Karl Marx to Sigfrid Meyer, 30 April 1867*

**About the author**

Alex Callinicos is professor of European Studies at King's College London. He has written widely on Marxist theory. His books include *The Revolutionary Ideas of Karl Marx* (Bookmarks 1983), *Imperialism and Global Political Economy* (Polity 2009) and *Bonfire of Illusions* (Polity 2010). He is the editor of the journal *International Socialism*.

# Preface

I feel I have been writing this book all my adult life. It originates in the challenge that Imre Lakatos threw down at me in the summer of 1973 to pursue a doctoral thesis under his supervision on the scientificity of Marxism. Alas, he died a few months later so I had only a brief, glancing encounter with this brilliant personality. But I wrote my thesis on Marx's method in *Capital* between 1974 and 1978 at Balliol College, Oxford, under the supervision of, first, Paul Streeten and then Frances Stewart. Elements of this thesis survive in this book. So I must thank my supervisors here, and also Leszek Kolakowski, with whom I enjoyed exchanging ironies in his rooms at All Souls. As he was throughout my time at Balliol, Alan Montefiore was a benign and supporting presence.

During my doctoral research I was in receipt of a fellowship from the Beit Trust. I am happy (as required under the terms of the fellowship) finally to acknowledge this support. The Trust's founder Alfred Beit was a close ally of Cecil Rhodes in his efforts to conquer southern Africa and its mineral wealth for British imperialism. As another Beit Fellow, Charles van Onselen, wrote at the beginning of *Chibaro*, his study of the exploitation of African mine labour under Rhodes's and Beit's successors in colonial Zimbabwe, this kind of support for Marxists 'is further evidence of the fact that there is no simple relationship between base and superstructure'. The Marikana massacre in South Africa has shown that the black mineworkers' struggle continues even under regimes that claim to have brought 'national liberation'.

The outbreak of the Asian economic crisis in 1997-98 returned me to my studies of *Capital* as part of the effort led by my much missed friend and comrade Chris Harman to understand the dynamics of contemporary capitalism. Amid many other projects, writing this book for a long time hovered as an all too distant goal. I was lucky that I revisited *Capital* at a time when there has been a much broader renaissance of the Marxist critique of political economy. I have more to say about this renaissance and the intellectual influences from which I have benefitted in the

Introduction. Here I would to thank those who have given me more direct help. In particular, I am grateful to Sally Campbell, Joseph Choonara, Martin Empson, Fred Moseley, and Lucia Pradella, who all read the book in draft and made many valuable suggestions for its improvement. It is entirely my fault that I haven't always taken their advice. I have learned especially from Lucia Pradella, both in her comments on my manuscript and in the insights I have gained from her own research.

Finally, I must remember my father. My original research in the 1970s took place with my parents' somewhat bemused but always loving support. My father's long life drew to a close as I was working on this book. In my memory, rereading the crowning part of Marx's work, *Capital*, Volume III, is inextricably interwoven with my vigil at my father's bedside during his last illness. It is therefore only right that I should dedicate *Deciphering Capital* to his memory.

**Guide to Citations**

To simplify citations, the following works are referred to as follows in the text:

*C*I: Karl Marx, *Capital*, I (Harmondsworth, 1976)
*C*II: Karl Marx, *Capital*, II (Harmondsworth, 1978)
*C*III: Karl Marx, *Capital*, III (Harmondsworth, 1981)
*Con*: Karl Marx, *A Contribution to the Critique of Political Economy* (London, 1971)
*CW*: Karl Marx and Friedrich Engels, *Collected Works* (50 vols, Moscow, 1975-2005)
*EW*: Karl Marx, *Early Writings* (Harmondsworth, 1975)
*G*: Karl Marx, *Grundrisse* (Harmondsworth, 1973)
*GL*: G W F Hegel, *The Science of Logic* (Cambridge, 2010)
*MEGA²*: Karl Marx and Friedrich Engels, *Gesamtausgabe* (Berlin, 1975-)
*R*: *The Works and Correspondence of David Ricardo* (Piero Sraffa, ed, 11 vols, Cambridge, 1951-2)

The Penguin editions of the *Grundrisse* and *Capital* have become the standard translations of these works in English. Despite the high quality of the translations, I have sometimes felt it necessary to correct them, particularly to bring out more clearly the conceptual distinctions on which Marx is relying. This was also sometimes necessary for other translations, and particularly for the portions of the *Economic Manuscript of 1861-63* that were originally translated for the old Moscow edition of *Theories of Surplus Value*. When doing so I have normally relied on the online version of the Marx-Engels *Werke*, available online at http://www.dearchiv.de/php/mewinh.php. I should also pay tribute to the immense scholarly resource offered by the Marxists Internet Archive at http://www.marxists.org/.

When, very occasionally, I have preferred the older translations of *Capital* by Progress Publishers, I have cited them as follows:

MI: Karl Marx, *Capital*, I (Moscow, 1970)
MII: Karl Marx, *Capital*, II (Moscow, 1970)
MIII: Karl Marx, *Capital*, III (Moscow, 1971)

I have made heavy use of Marx's correspondence and manuscripts. When, as so often, he breaks into English, I have indicated this by putting these words in bold. Interpolations of the German original are put in round brackets when they have been placed there by the translator and in square brackets when I have put them there.

# Introduction

## The return to *Capital*

Marx's *Capital* is back where it belongs, at the centre of debate about Marxism and its purchase on the contemporary world. Of course, this isn't the first time this has happened. The renaissance of Marxism in the 1960s and early 1970s was the product of a profound political radicalisation whose high points were marked by the worker and student revolts of May-June 1968 in France and the hot autumn of 1969 in Italy.[1] It involved an intense engagement with *Capital*, and not as a pious or scholarly exercise, but as a means of better understanding both the nature of the Marxist project and the dynamics of capitalism. The collective undertaking by Louis Althusser and his students at the École normale supérieure that produced *Reading Capital* (1965) was merely the tip of a much larger iceberg.[2]

Althusser laid out a strenuous reading programme:

> But some day it is essential to read *Capital* to the letter. To read the text itself, complete, all four volumes, line by line, to return ten times to the first chapters, or to the schemes of simple reproduction and reproduction on a large scale, before coming down from the arid table-lands and plateaus of Volume Two to the promised land of profit, interest and rent. And it is essential to read *Capital* not only in its French translation (even Volume One in Roy's translation, which Marx revised, or rather, rewrote), but also in the German original, at least for the fundamental theoretical chapters and all the key passages where Marx's key concepts come to the surface.[3]

Rather surprisingly, Althusser later claimed that, when he wrote these words, he 'knew...nearly nothing of Marx', and indeed only read

---

1   Chris Harman, *The Fire Last Time* (London, 1988).
2   David Harvey, *Spaces of Hope* (Edinburgh, 2000), ch 1.
3   Louis Althusser, 'From Capital to Marx's Philosophy', in Louis Althusser and Étienne Balibar, *Reading Capital* (London, 1970), pp13-14. Althusser is including *Theories of Surplus Value*, sometimes identified with Marx's planned fourth book of *Capital*.

Volume I of *Capital* in 1964 for the seminar that resulted in *Reading Capital*.[4] But many others (myself included) did their best to follow his injunction, and the understanding of *Capital* was a main reference point in the Marxist debates of the time—not just in the immense controversy provoked by Althusser's reinterpretation of Marx, but also, for example, in the discussions among German and British Marxists about how to 'derive' the state from the capital relation.[5]

But, as the tide of reaction swept the political and intellectual scene in the second half of the 1970s, the debate on *Capital* largely fell silent (a fate suffered by Marxist intellectual work more generally). The study of Marx's economic writings didn't cease altogether, but heroically continued in some relatively specialised scholarly circles. Marxist economists discussed the so-called 'new interpretation' of the famous problem of how to transform values into prices of production first put forward in the early 1980s.[6] A small group of economists and philosophers got together as the International Symposium on Marxian Theory (ISMT), and came to produce in the 1990s a series of important collective volumes on *Capital*.[7]

And most significant in the long run is the *MEGA*—the vast project that David Ryazanov began in Russia after the October Revolution of publishing Marx's and Engels's complete writings. This was cut short when Ryazanov was murdered by Stalin during the 1930s, but taken up again by scholars in East Berlin during the 1970s. The Marx-Engels *Gesamtausgabe* (Complete Works, generally known as *MEGA²* in acknowledgement of Ryazanov's earlier efforts) survived the collapse of

4   Louis Althusser, *L'Avenir dure longtemps, suivi de Les Faits* (rev edn, Paris, 1994), p168. How much weight we can place on a text written after Althusser had murdered his wife that is a symptom of the psychological condition it seeks to analyse is an open question.

5   See, for example, John Holloway and Sol Picciotto, eds, *State and Capital* (London, 1978), and Simon Clarke, ed, *The State Debate* (Basingstoke, 1991).

6   The 'new interpretation' was first put forward in Gérard Duménil, *De la valeur aux prix de production* (Paris, 1980), and Duncan Foley, 'The Value of Money, the Value of Labour Power, and the Marxian Transformation Problem', *Review of Radical Political Economics*, 14:2 (1982).

7   ISMT volumes: Fred Moseley, ed, *Marx's Method in Capital: A Re-examination* (Atlantic Highlands NJ, 1993), Fred Moseley and Martha Campbell, eds, *New Investigations of Marx's Method* (Atlantic Highlands NJ, 1997), Christopher Arthur and Geert Reuten, eds, *The Circulation of Capital: Essays on Volume Two of Marx's Capital* (Basingstoke, 1997), Martha Campbell and Geert Reuten, eds, *The Culmination of Capital: Essays on Volume Three of Marx's Capital* (Basingstoke, 2001), Riccardo Bellofiore and Nicola Taylor, eds, *The Constitution of Capital: Essays on Volume One of Marx's Capital* (Basingstoke, 2004), Fred Moseley, ed, *Marx's Theory of Money: Modern Appraisals* (Basingstoke, 2005), and Riccardo Bellofiore and Roberto Fineschi, eds, *Rereading Marx: New Perspectives after the Critical Edition* (Basingstoke, 2009).

its original sponsor, the East German regime, in 1989, though it faces considerable difficulties in finishing what seems like an endless work. As a result, we now have available not only the crucial *Economic Manuscript of 1861-63* but also the various drafts from which Engels edited the second and third volumes of *Capital* after Marx's death in 1883 as well as many of the notebooks in which Marx excerpted from his vast reading and developed his ideas.[8]

In recent years, however, there has been an explosion of much wider interest in *Capital*. Two interconnected factors are involved here. The first is the gradual dispersal of the euphoria surrounding triumphant neoliberal capitalism after the collapse of the Stalinist regimes between 1989 and 1991. Financial and economic crises—first in East Asia in 1997-8 but then on a global scale following the financial crash of 2008— have played a crucial role here. One symptom of how these events have redirected attention back to *Capital* is the regular, indeed somewhat ritualistic, appearance of articles in mainstream journals announcing that, because of capitalism's latest difficulties, 'Marx is back'. Secondly, there has been a renewed contestation of capitalism, beginning with the protests at the World Trade Organization summit in Seattle in November 1999, reaching a temporary peak with the anti-war demonstrations of March 2003, but gaining renewed vigour since the outbreak of the global crisis, in the shape of the Arab revolutions, the 15 May movement in the Spanish state, and Occupy Wall Street and its numerous imitators.[9]

As in the 1960s, political radicalisation has stimulated intellectual investment in *Capital*. The most visible sign of this has been the immense audience for David Harvey's online lectures on *Capital*. But, as a broader interest in Marxist theory has re-emerged, so too has a focus on the interpretation of *Capital*. It is emblematic of this development that two of the premier English-speaking Marxist theorists, Harvey himself and Fredric Jameson, should both have recently published studies of *Capital*, I, followed now by another book by Harvey on Volume II.[10]

---

8  See the information about the *MEGA²* in the editors' Introduction to Bellofiore and Fineschi, eds, *Rereading Marx*, a volume devoted to assessing its significance to the understanding of *Capital*.

9  For assessments of different phases of this radicalisation, see Alex Callinicos, *An Anti-Capitalist Manifesto* (Cambridge, 2003), and Paul Mason, *Why It's Kicking Off Everywhere* (London, 2012).

10  David Harvey, *A Companion to Marx's Capital* (London, 2010), Fredric Jameson, *Representing Capital* (London, 2011), and David Harvey, *A Companion to Marx's Capital, Volume 2* (London, 2013).

In *The Limits to Capital*, a much earlier work that was one of the main fruits of the 1960s and 1970s wave of *Capital* studies, Harvey wrote: 'Everyone who studies Marx, it is said, feels compelled to write a book about the experience'.[11] This book is my own surrender to this compulsion. Harvey is right to suggest that studies of *Capital* are in part a struggle with the text. The passage from *Reading Capital* that I quoted earlier implies the same. Today, thanks to the much greater volume of Marx's economic manuscripts that are now available, wrestling with his writings has become an ever more strenuous undertaking.

## The problem of relations

But there has to be a better (and less narcissistic) reason for writing another book on *Capital* than paying tribute to one's time in the library. My excuses are both theoretical and political. Michael Heinrich, one of the most influential contemporary Marxists working on *Capital*, has pointed to the tendency in what he calls 'traditional Marxism' towards 'the substantialist misunderstanding of Marx's value theory'.[12] In other words, Marx's version of the labour theory of value is misinterpreted as being in essence the same as that developed by David Ricardo in *On Principles of Political Economy and Taxation* (first published in 1817). According to Ricardo, commodities exchange in proportion to the physical amounts of labour performed on them. Maurice Dobb is a sophisticated representative of this approach, presenting Marx, along with Ricardo and the other classical political economists before him, and the theorists of marginal utility who came to dominate mainstream economics from the 1870s onwards, as all offering versions of 'that unifying quantitative principle which enabled...['Political Economy'] to make postulates in terms of the general equilibrium of the economic system'.[13] Marx himself, by contrast, tended to stress the discontinuities between his own approach and that of his predecessors, arguing that, in focusing on 'the magnitude of value', Ricardo, like Adam Smith before him, ignored 'the form of value' (*CI*: 174 n 34); the problem of the form of value highlighted the peculiarity of the capitalist mode of production that the products of labour take the form of commodities that exchange

---

11  David Harvey, *The Limits to Capital* (Oxford, 1982), p xiii.
12  Michael Heinrich, *An Introduction to the Three Volumes of Karl Marx's Capital* (New York, 2012), p 49.
13  Maurice Dobb, *Political Economy and Capitalism* (London, 1937), p 5. Ronald L Meek, *Studies in the Labour Theory of Value* (London, 1956), is another distinguished and historically erudite version of the substantialist approach.

on the market according to their values, which in turn requires that these values are expressed in money.

The importance of the value form, first thematised by the Russian Marxist Isaak Rubin (another victim of Stalin) in the late 1920s, has informed much discussion of *Capital*, particularly since the problem was rediscovered by a number of German theorists in the 1960s. But in my view focus on the value form can give rise to another 'misunderstanding of Marx's value theory', what is best described as 'etherealism'. This is the mirror image of substantialism, in which any sense of Marx seeking to develop an empirical and quantitative theory of capitalist development vanishes. As I try to show in what follows, Heinrich himself, among many other contemporary *Capital* scholars, falls into this error. What both etherealism and substantialism have in common is a failure to grasp the centrality of the idea of capital as a relation (or rather as a nexus of relationships) to Marx's project.[14]

One way of understanding the trajectory of Marx's critique of political economy is to see it as a movement from substance—not to function (to echo the title of a famous essay of Ernst Cassirer's), but to relation. Marx's writings of the 1840s—*The German Ideology*, for example—often involve, as Jacques Derrida points out in *Spectres of Marx*, a substantialist problematic that counterposes to the institutions and ideologies of bourgeois society the struggles of 'real, living individuals'.[15] The formulation of the concept of the relations of production, which first becomes fully visible in *The Poverty of Philosophy* (1847), offered a means of escape, but the refinement of this concept became imbricated in the tortuous process through which Marx painfully constructed, and constantly reconstructed, his theory of the capitalist mode of production.

One central theme of the final product of this arduous struggle, *Capital* itself, is the way in which capitalist relations of production are systematically occluded by the functioning of the economic system as a whole. Thus Marx observes in a passage to which we return in chapter 3:

> the actual production process, as the unity of the immediate production process and the process of circulation, produces new configurations in which the threads of the inner connection get more and more lost, the

14  The most important discussion of relations in Marxism is provided by Althusser, despite his professed ignorance of *Capital*. Those interested in the philosophical background should take a look at the paper on Althusser reprinted as the Appendix to this book. See also Alex Callinicos, *Imperialism and Global Political Economy* (Cambridge, 2009), pp11-14.

15  Ernst Cassirer, *Substance and Function and Einstein's Theory of Relativity* (Chicago, 1923); Jacques Derrida, *Spectres de Marx* (Paris, 1993).

relations of production becoming independent of one another and the components of value ossifying into independent forms. (*C*III: 967)

The name that Marx gives for the process through which 'the threads of the inner connection get more and more lost' is, of course, fetishism, the naturalisation and fragmentation of social relations thanks to the production and circulation of use values as commodities. But what gets lost is the relationality of capital. And this itself must be conceived as consisting in a double relation—first, the exploitive relationship between wage-labour and capital, and, second, the dynamic, competitive relationship among capitals themselves, which does not simply serve to obscure the 'inner connection' but allows it to function, since it is through the interaction of 'many capitals' in competition that the imperative to accumulate is transmitted.

Yet if Marx's own discourse in *Capital* gives primacy to relations, it is striking how often in contemporary radical thought it is rather subjects that are given primacy over relations. For example, Toni Negri's *Marx beyond Marx* uses a particular reading of the *Grundrisse* to reduce the capital-relation to a relationship of force between two subjects—social capital and social labour. At one level, Negri's later books with Michael Hardt, *Empire*, *Multitude* and *Commonwealth*, represent a retreat from this position, since capital is dispersed, desubjectified, relativised into the network power of Empire. But the corollary is to enthrone one 'active social subject' of the contemporary capitalist process, the multitude, whose productive vitality simultaneously fuels the machines of Empire and prefigures the liberated 'joy of being communist'.[16] Though Hardt and Negri do occasionally register the interdependence of Empire and multitude, the extent of the disconnect between contemporary labour and capital, as they conceive it, is indicated by their employment of the metaphors of exodus and desertion to evoke the subversion of the capital relation—as if spatial displacement could somehow substitute for socio-political transformation.

In my view Marx offers the basis of an alternative approach. He himself complains that the political economist 'knows of nothing but either tangible objects or ideas—relations do not exist for him' (*CW*30: 150). I shall try to show how an understanding of capital as a nexus of relations allows us to gain a better grasp of Marx's argument. But this way into *Capital* is also politically important. In the first place, it allows us a better understanding of the dynamics of the global economic and

---

16    Michael Hardt and Toni Negri, *Multitude* (London, 2004), p100; *Empire* (Cambridge MA, 2000), p413.

financial crisis that began in 2007-8. As I show in chapter 6, Marx was particularly interested in the interaction between the tendency of the rate of profit to fall and the way the financial markets of his day (like those of our own) oscillated between bubble and panic. This is a relationship that is particularly relevant to making sense of what is happening to contemporary capitalism. Secondly, partly under the influence of the kind of philosophical conception to which I have just referred but also by misinterpretations of Marx's analysis of primitive accumulation, much contemporary radical thought tends to absolutise resistance to capital and to portray it as external to the capital relation. I try to show in chapters 5 and 7 why Marx in *Capital* provides a superior starting point for understanding the nature of revolutionary subjectivity.

**How to read Marx**

Anyone studying *Capital* and its precursors today can draw on plenty of support from other Marxists. There is now a wealth of commentaries. Among the older, three stand out—those by Evald Ilyenkov, Roman Rosdolsky, and Isaak Rubin have passed the test of time, setting standards for their successors to match up to. It is interesting that all are products of a distinctive central European culture of scholarship, and all were victims of the disasters of the 20th century—Rubin murdered under the Stalinist Terror, Ilyenkov driven to suicide by the forces of late-Soviet conformism, Rosdolsky taking refuge from the martyrdom of mid-century *Mitteleuropa* in Detroit (which in the year of his death, 1967, reverberated to the sounds of proletarian revolt).[17]

My understanding of *Capital* and capitalism is profoundly shaped by the influence of my teachers in the International Socialist tradition—Tony Cliff, Mike Kidron and Chris Harman, all, alas, no longer with us. I have also learned much from my contemporaries—Jacques Bidet, whose fine book *Que faire de Capital?* continues nearly 30 years after its publication to cast a long shadow, but also Chris Arthur, Gérard Duménil, Enrique Dussel, Ben Fine, David Harvey, Michael Krätke, Fred Moseley, Lucia Pradella, Alfredo Saad-Filho and John Weeks. The larger renewal of dialectical thought—represented above all in Fredric Jameson's magisterial work but also by Slavoj Žižek's provocations—is

---

17   E V Ilyenkov, *The Dialectic of the Abstract and Concrete in Marx's Capital* (Moscow, 1982), Roman Rosdolsky, *The Making of Marx's Capital* (London, 1977), and I I Rubin, *Essays on Marx's Theory of Value* (Detroit, 1972). The classic account of Detroit in revolt is Dan Georgakas and Marvin Surkin, *Detroit: I Do Mind Dying* (rev edn; London, 1999).

also an aid in studying *Capital*, the main site of controversy over Marx's relationship to the Hegelian dialectic.[18]

While, as will become clear, I don't believe the conceptual structure of *Capital* somehow mirrors that of Hegel's *Science of Logic*, I bow to no one in my admiration for Hegel. Not only is Marx heavily indebted to him for the conception of science that he develops in *Capital*, but Hegel to my mind remains the most advanced bourgeois thinker, who at the very dawn of industrial capitalism grasped the inherent limits of this mode of production and of political interventions aimed at managing its inner contradictions.[19] To deny that Marx somehow actualised the *Logic* in *Capital* is in no sense necessarily to be 'anti-Hegelian' or to diminish Hegel's sheer philosophical greatness. This greatness constantly seduces non-idealist thinkers into playing down the metaphysical extravagance that is central to his achievement, and Marxists into assimilating Marx to Hegel. One can acknowledge the force of this seductive power while refusing to give way to it.

Increasingly the question of the Marx-Hegel relationship has come to focus on the extent to which the system of categories that Hegel elaborates in the Logic influenced Marx's conceptual construction. In a famous letter to Friedrich Engels of 16 January 1858 Marx explained how he was getting on with his first major economic manuscript, the *Grundrisse*:

> What was of great use to me as regards method of treatment was Hegel's *Logic* at which I had taken another look **by mere accident**, Freiligrath having found and made me a present of several volumes of Hegel, originally the property of Bakunin. If ever the time comes when such work is again possible, I should very much like to write 2 or 3 sheets making accessible to the common reader the *rational* aspect of the method which Hegel not only discovered but also mystified. (CW40: 249)

One of the most recent attempts to write those sheets, which Marx of course never got round to (like so much else), has been taken by a current of Marxists working on *Capital* whose approach they describe as 'systematic dialectics'. Marx's Hegelianism, they argue, did not involve adhesion to a broad philosophy of history, but the development of a method of categorial construction. As Chris Arthur puts it, 'it is concerned with the articulation of categories designed to conceptualise an

---

18 See especially Fredric Jameson, *Valences of the Dialectic* (London, 2009), and Slavoj Žižek, *Less than Nothing: Hegel and the Shadow of Dialectical Materialism* (London, 2012).

19 See Lucia Pradella, 'Hegel, Imperialism, and Universal History', *Science & Society*, 78 (2014).

existent concrete whole'.[20] In Marx's case, this 'whole' was the capitalist mode of production. His preoccupation with the problem, and its interrelation with his substantive analysis, is indicated by a slightly later letter to Ferdinand Lassalle (22 February 1858): 'The work I am presently concerned with is a *Critique of Economic Categories* or, **if you like**, a critical exposé of the system of the bourgeois economy. It is at once an exposé and, by the same token, a critique of the system.' (*CW*40: 270)

While I disagree with Arthur and his co-thinkers that Hegel's *Logic* provides the template for *Capital*, they are right to highlight Marx's concern with constructing and ordering the concepts he used to analyse capitalism. But all this is swept aside by Harvey, the most influential contemporary commentator on *Capital*. In his 2011 Deutscher Memorial Lecture, Harvey argues that Marx in his economic writings was 'rigidly' guided by a passage from the 1857 Introduction to the *Grundrisse*: 'Thus production, distribution, exchange and consumption form a regular syllogism [for the political economists]; production is the generality, distribution and exchange the particularity, and consumption the singularity in which the whole is joined together. This is admittedly a coherence, but a shallow one' (*G*: 89). According to Harvey, 'he sticks as closely as he can to the bourgeois conception of a law-like level of generality—of production—and excludes the "accidental" and social particularities of distribution and exchange and even more so the chaotic singularities of consumption from his political-economic enquiries'.[21]

Harvey goes on at some length to illustrate Marx's exclusions (for example of supply and demand and of the credit system) and to document the difficulties that he believes this creates for Marx, difficulties that he claims express a polarisation between theory and history in which empirical detail is excluded from theoretical 'generality'. Now, as we shall see, Marx indeed struggles with the problem of what to include in and what to exclude from his analysis of capitalism. But this is inseparable from the problem of the construction and ordering of the categories that form this analysis, which Harvey completely ignores. Further, he argues that 'the three levels of generality, particularity and singularity are not the whole story. There is a fourth level—that of universality—which concerns the metabolic relation to nature'.[22]

---

20  Christopher J Arthur, *The New Dialectic and Marx's Capital* (Leiden, 2003), p4.
21  David Harvey, 'History versus Theory: A Commentary on Marx's Method in Capital', *Historical Materialism*, 20.2 (2012), pp6, 10. Harvey restates this interpretation in his Introduction to *A Companion to Marx's Capital, Volume 2*.
22  Harvey, 'History versus Theory', p12.

Harvey's source here is the famous passage when Marx calls the labour process 'the universal condition for the metabolic interaction (*Stoffwechsel*) between man and nature' (CI: 290). The trouble is that the word translated as 'universal' here is '*allgemeine*', while the original of 'generality' in the *Grundrisse* passage on which Harvey relies so heavily is '*Allgemeinheit*'. The same word may, of course, express two different concepts, but one can't help feeling that Harvey is ignoring the requirements of philological care in interpreting texts as complex and as sedimented as Marx's, particularly when these passages are then melded together to support the claim that 'the focus of Marx's scientific enquiry is to uncover how the general laws of capitalist political economy came to be, how they actually function, and why and how they might be changed. And he wants to do this without invoking the universality that describes our ever-evolving metabolic relation to nature'.[23]

Although Marx's treatment of nature is not the subject of this book, it worth saying that Harvey's last assertion is absolutely without warrant. As Paul Burkett shows in his definitive study:

> The power of Marx's approach [to nature] stems…from its consistent treatment of human production in terms of the mutual constitution of its social form and its material content. While recognising that production is structured by historically developed relations among producers and between producers and appropriators of the surplus product, Marx also insists that production as both a social and a material process is shaped and constrained by natural conditions, including, of course, the natural condition of human bodily existence.[24]

The trick in reading *Capital* is to track Marx's formulation and reformulation, his orderings and reorderings of categories, while not losing sight of the big picture that Harvey commands with such panache. In attempting to do this I have tried to follow a method that treats texts as products of history.[25] Setting them into their context while not allowing them to disappear into that context requires, in my

---

23  Harvey, 'History versus Theory', p13. Why Harvey should make this claim just after citing passages that contradict it is beyond me.

24  Paul Burkett, *Marx and Nature* (New York, 1999), p1. See, for a recent application of this approach, Martin Empson, *Land and Labour: Marxism, Ecology and Human History* (London, 2014).

25  This method, which draws rather eclectically on a variety of sources (including Althusser, R G Collingwood, Imre Lakatos and Quentin Skinner) is elaborated on in the Introduction to Alex Callinicos, *Social Theory: A Historical and Critical Introduction* (2nd edn; Cambridge, 2007).

view, paying attention to the problems they seek to address, as well as their interlocutors. The historian of economic thought J M Clark offers the following maxim: 'To understand any forceful writer and to make the necessary allowances, find out what it was against which he was reacting'.[26] One virtue of this method is that focusing on problems allows one to transcend the distinction between text and context. For the problem(s) that constitute a given text at once serve implicitly to order that text internally, but at the same time point outwards to the debates to which it is a contribution. Thus Marx's correspondence and, during the 1850s and early 1860s, his journalism are extremely valuable in allowing us to reconstruct the problems with which he was struggling. It is surprising how little even the best commentaries explore the context these writings (and Marx's notebooks) reveal.[27] They can help us at once to recover Marx as a historical subject and to render more intelligible the vast enterprise that is *Capital*.

The order of my argument therefore begins in chapter 1 with an examination of Marx's manuscripts and of the process through which they were written; this involves confronting some of the controversy about whether or not he revised the famous 'six-book plan' developed in 1858-9. Chapters 2 and 3 form in many ways the heart of the book, examining and seeking to clarify the problem of Marx's method. Of course, this requires confronting the question of Marx's relation to Hegel, which I believe is most fruitfully addressed if one follows Antonio Gramsci's cue and triangulates by adding Ricardo to the dialogue: Marx struggles at once to learn from and to transcend both. Chapter 4 seeks to address more directly some of the issues raised in contemporary debates about Marx's value theory while chapter 5 looks at the place of labour in *Capital*. Chapter 6 is devoted to a detailed study of Marx's thinking (never elaborated into a systematic theory) on capitalist crises. This is, as I have already suggested, an issue of pressing contemporary importance; I return to the actuality of Marx's thought more generally in the concluding chapter 7.

A final word is in order on the intellectual status of this book. More than anything else it is a work of philosophy, which focuses on the

26  Quoted in G S L Tucker, *Progress and Profits in British Economic Thought 1650-1850* (Cambridge, 1960), p5.
27  For a study that makes extensive use of the notebooks, see Lucia Pradella, 'Mondializzazione e critica dell'economia alla luce della nuova edizione storico-critica degli scritti di Marx ed Engels (*MEGA²*)' (PhD Thesis, Università degli Studi di Napoli 'Frederico II' and Université Paris-Ouest Nanterre La Défense, 2011), forthcoming in English as *Globalisation and the Critique of Political Economy: New Insights from Marx's Writings* (London, 2014).

clarification of concepts rather than on substantive analysis. But the boundary between the two is particularly blurred when one is dealing with Marx's critique of political economy, where what he calls the *'Critique of Economic Categories'* supports the effort, as he puts it in the Preface to the First Edition of *Capital*, I, 'to reveal the economic law of motion of modern society' (*CI*: 92). This book, as should already be clear, is not a basic introduction to *Capital*: there are some excellent ones already available, and I've tried my hand at presenting Marx's economic ideas simply elsewhere.[28] Nevertheless I try here to avoid more technical questions in value theory—above all, the perennial transformation problem, though I'm broadly sympathetic to Fred Moseley's approach to these issues.[29] But clarifying what Marx says in *Capital* also helps to clarify our understanding of capitalism itself.[30] This isn't because Marx was always right: I make plenty of criticisms in what follows. But after all my labours on his writings, what strikes me is their astonishing freshness and relevance to our times. Thomas Piketty's *Capital in the 21st Century*, both in its very title and in its claim that growing economic inequality is a consequence of a 'fundamental law of capitalism', pay indirect tribute to Marx's great work. Despite Piketty's disparaging comments on Marx and Marxism, the enormous impact his book has had has confirmed the actuality of the critique of, not of this or that aspect of capitalism, but of the system itself.

Jameson expresses very well Marx's fundamental intuition about capitalism:

> what the Marxist dialectic enjoins, as a historically new and original thought mode, is the conflation of Good and Evil, and the grasping of the historical situation as unhappiness and happiness all at once. The *Manifesto* proposes to see capitalism as the most productive moment of history and the most destructive one at the same time, and issues the

---

28  Alex Callinicos, *The Revolutionary Ideas of Karl Marx* (London, 1983), Joseph Choonara, *Unravelling Capitalism: A Guide to Marxist Political Economy* (London, 2009), Ben Fine and Alfredo Saad-Filho, *Marx's 'Capital'* (5th edn; London, 2010), and Duncan Foley, *Understanding Capital: Marx's Economic Theory* (Cambridge MA, 1986).

29  I'm grateful to Fred for letting me see parts of the draft of his forthcoming book, *Money and Totality: A Macro-Monetary Interpretation of Marx's Logic in Capital and the Transformation Problem*.

30  Incidentally, Fernand Braudel is wrong when he says Marx never used the word 'capitalism': *Civilisation and Capitalism 15th-18th Century*, Volume II (London, 1982), p237. Although Marx usually refers to bourgeois society or the capitalist mode of production, *'Kapitalismus'* occurs a couple of times in correspondence and very occasionally in the 1861-63 *Manuscript*: thus see *CW*32: 124, 34: 124, 43: 449, 45: 356. I'm grateful to Hiroshi Uchida for information on this subject.

imperative to think Good and Evil simultaneously, and as inseparable and inextricable dimensions of the same present of time.[31]

Jameson cites the *Communist Manifesto* here, but the same intuition is restated brilliantly in the *Grundrisse* and it continues to inform *Capital* (see especially G: 487-8). What Marx gains across his successive drafts is simultaneously analytical precision and empirical depth. His labours, as I discuss in chapter 1, were incomplete, but they left behind a critique, not just of political economy but of the mode of production that the '*Economic Categories*' simultaneously reveal and conceal that holds true in some ways more strongly today than when it was written. *Capital* and capitalism are chained together, antagonists in perennial combat. As long as the system whose logic Marx exposed survives, his great work will continue to repay study.

---

31   Jameson, *Valences of the Dialectic*, p551.

1

# Composition

## The Marx problem

The idea of someone who devotes their life to a work of art that turns out not to exist is a recurring one: it is, for example, the theme of Henry James's short story 'The Madonna of the Future'. In a very obvious sense this isn't the problem with Marx. What we have is not the absence of a work, but a profusion of them. Enrique Dussel has written about the 'four drafts of *Capital*', but this is an underestimate.[1] One can indeed identify the following economic manuscripts that form parts of the vast project that is best named by their recurring title or subtitle as Marx's critique of political economy:

1  The *Grundrisse*, written between July 1857 and May 1858; first published in 1939
2  The so-called *Urtext*, fragments of a draft of the *Contribution to a Critique of Political Economy*, written between August and October 1858 and first published in 1941
3  *A Contribution to the Critique of Political Economy*, written between November 1858 and January 1859; published in June 1859 as 'Part One' of Marx's intended *Critique of Political Economy*
4  *The Economic Manuscript of 1861-63*, written between August 1861 and July 1863 and intended as the continuation of the *Contribution*; published in part by Karl Kautsky as *Theories of Surplus Value* between 1905 and 1910 and in full only in 1982
5  *The Economic Manuscript of 1863-5*: Marx's draft of the three volumes of *Capital*, written between July 1863 and December 1865; from this friend and collaborator Friedrich Engels edited *Capital*, Volume III, published in 1894; the so-called 'Sixth Chapter' of *Capital*, Volume I, 'The Results of the Immediate Process of Production', was published in 1933, and the entire manuscript in 1988 and 1992

---

1  Enrique Dussel, 'The Four Drafts of *Capital*', *Rethinking Marxism*, 13:1 (2001).

6   *Capital*, Volume I, published in September 1867
7   *Le Capital*, the French edition of *Capital*, Volume I, published between 1872 and 1875 and increasingly treated as a separate text by scholars because of the substantial changes Marx made to it, not all of which were carried over into the second German edition (1873) or the third, published a few months after Marx's death in March 1883[2]
8   Smaller manuscripts written between the late 1860s and late 1870s in which Marx sought to address issues, particularly with respect to surplus value and profit, that he had broached in the 1863-5 *Manuscript*[3]
9   The manuscripts from which Engels edited *Capital*, Volume II (first published in 1885), which is a complex palimpsest of texts written at different times (see Table 1).

Table 1

*Manuscripts from which Capital, II, was compiled (page references to Penguin edition)*

|  | Pages | Manuscript | Date |
|---|---|---|---|
| Part One | 109 | II | 1870 |
|  | 110-120 | VII | 1878 |
|  | 120-123 | VI | 1877-8 |
|  | 123-196 | V | 1877 |
|  | 196-199 | notes found among extracts from books | 1877-8 |
|  | 200-206 | IV | before 1870 |
|  | 207-208 | VIII | after 1878 |
|  | 208-209 | IV | before 1870 |
|  | 211-212, 218 | notes from Ms II | 1870 |
| Part Two | 233-242 | IV | before 1870 |
|  | 242-424 | II | 1870 |
| Part Three | 427-434 | II | 1870 |
|  | 435-465 | VIII | 1878 |
|  | 465-470 | II | 1870 |
|  | 470-471 | VIII | 1878 |
|  | 471-474 | II | 1870 |
|  | 474-497 | VIII | 1878 |
|  | 498-513 | II | 1870 |
|  | 513-556 | VIII | 1878 |
|  | 556-564 | II | 1870 |
|  | 565-599 | VIII | 1878 |

*Source: C*II: 103

2   Karl Marx, 'Ergänzungen und Veränderungen zum ersten Band des *Kapitals*', a list of amendments and additions to Volume I, drafted in 1871-2 and again not all included in the published edition, have now been published in *MEGA*[2] II/6.
3   See Regina Roth, 'Karl Marx's Original Manuscripts in the Marx-Engels-Gesamtausgabe (MEGA): Another View on *Capital*', in Riccardo Bellofiore and Roberto Fineschi, eds, *Rereading Marx: New Perspectives after the Critical Edition* (Basingstoke, 2009), p33.

The problem then with *Capital* is not so much that Marx laboured without result, but that his efforts were so vast and incomplete that his work dissolves into the multiplicity of fragmentary texts that he left behind. The immense achievement of *MEGA²* in publishing the bulk of these manuscripts means that it is easy now for the apparently determinate structure of *Capital* to liquefy before our eyes. Dussel in his excellent study of the 1861-63 *Manuscript* expresses the view of a number of scholars:

> It is well known that Marx only wrote Volume I (Book I) for publication. Hence, all the other volumes should be methodologically considered as non-existent and one should make references in the future, exclusively to the *Manuscripts* of Marx themselves. Engels and Kautsky's editions (of Volumes II and III of *Capital*, edited in the 19th century, and the old *Theories of Surplus Value*) should be studied in order to know the thoughts of these two authors, but not Marx's own.[4]

This is an extreme reaction, to which I return below when discussing Engels's supposedly malign role in editing *Capital*, II and III. But in the meantime there is Marx himself to be dealt with. No one can dispute that, despite labours spanning more than 20 years, he left *Capital* unfinished. Michael Howard and John King in their outstanding history of Marxist economics take him to task for this:

> In view of the central political importance that he assigned to the economic analysis of capitalism, Marx's lethargy was most unfortunate. Even allowing for the effects of ill health, it is difficult not to convict him of neglecting his responsibilities, both to the international socialist movement whose mentor he aspired to be, and more especially to his lifelong friend Friedrich Engels, who was left to pick up the pieces.[5]

'Lethargy' is definitely not the right word. It is becoming increasingly clear thanks to the research conducted as part of *MEGA²* that Marx continued to work intensively (although not always continuously because of the interruptions caused by political activity and ill health) till not long before his death. For example, in 1879-81, before the hammer blow struck Marx by his wife Jenny's death in December 1881, he worked

---

4  Enrique Dussel, *Towards an Unknown Marx: A Commentary on the Manuscripts of 1861-63* (London, 2001), p164.
5  M C Howard and J E King, *A History of Marxian Economics* (2 vols, London, 1989, 1992), I, p3.

on world history, devoting five notebooks to the subject, which related to his efforts to broaden the scope of *Capital*.[6]

The problem rather is something much more mundane: Marx's inability to finish anything, which was often accompanied by announcements of imminent completion. For example, he wrote to Engels optimistically on 2 April 1851: 'I am so far advanced that I will have finished with the whole economic stuff in 5 weeks' time. *Et cela fait* [And that done] I shall complete the political economy at home and apply myself to another branch of learning at the Museum' (*CW*38: 325). The fact that he died nearly 32 years later leaving *Capital* unfinished is sometimes put down to his reaching some deep intellectual impasse. For example, Tristram Hunt speculates the problem might have been that 'the economics of *Das Kapital* no longer appeared credible or the political possibilities of communism unrealistic'.[7] Though Marx left behind him many unresolved problems, this kind of explanation is nonsense. His sometime Young Hegelian collaborator Arnold Ruge had identified the real problem as early as 1844, writing about Marx to Ludwig Feuerbach: 'He reads a lot; he works with uncommon intensity and has a critical talent...but he completes nothing, he always breaks off and plunges anew into an endless sea of books'.[8] Responding to Engels's chivvying to finish *Capital*, I, Marx sought (31 July 1865) to make a virtue of his perfectionism: '**Whatever shortcomings they may have**, the advantage of my writings is that they are an artistic whole, and can only be achieved through my practice of never having things printed until I have them in front of me *in their entirety*' (*CW*42: 173). The weary Engels replied rather crushingly (5 August 1865): 'I was greatly amused by the part of your letter which deals with the "work of art" **to be**' (*CW*42: 174).

The *1861-63 Manuscript*, the most important of the recently published drafts, provides an excellent insight into Marx's working method. He starts off as planned, writing a continuation of the 1859 *Contribution*: having dealt with the commodity and money in the two chapters of the earlier work, Marx now directly broaches 'capital in general'. For nearly 350 pages he writes what is recognisably an early version of *Capital*, I, before breaking off in March 1862 midway through his analysis of relative surplus value and machinery to discuss theories of surplus value (presumably to mirror the procedure he used in the *Contribution* of

---

6    Michael Krätke, 'Capitalism and World History: Marx's Unpublished Studies', paper
     delivered at *Historical Materialism* conference, London, November 2011.
7    Tristram Hunt, *The Frock-Coated Communist: The Revolutionary Life of Friedrich Engels*
     (London, 2009), p277.
8    Quoted in Jonathan Sperber, *Karl Marx: A Nineteenth Century Life* (New York, 2013), p487.

critically examining the political economists' treatment of value and money in respectively chapters 1, 'The Commodity' and 2, 'Money'). But then, while discussing Adam Smith's theory of profits, he confronts the problem of reproduction that will become one of the main subjects of *Capital*, II, and particularly the puzzle of how, in the circulation of commodities, the value of constant capital (invested in means of production) is replaced. Marx rather airily acknowledges that he has skidded off-piste: 'The question of the reproduction of the constant capital clearly belongs to the section on the reproduction process or circulation process of capital—which however is no reason why the kernel of the matter should not be examined here' (*CW*30: 414).

This first discussion of reproduction illustrates another of Marx's tendencies, which is to think on paper, trying to resolve a problem by writing about it. Here (as elsewhere) this involves plentiful calculations before he reins himself in: 'So much for this question, to which we shall return in connection with the circulation of capital' (*CW*30: 449). Marx then dives into a discussion of the problem of productive and unproductive labour, which at least is related to Smith, before digressing out of chronological sequence for 40 pages on John Stuart Mill. Then it's back to productive and unproductive labour, which slips into a further discussion of reproduction. At the end of this Marx acknowledges that he has not considered the case of extended reproduction (where the money generated by the cycle of production has to cover additional workers and means of production): 'This intermezzo has therefore to be completed in this historico-critical section, as occasion warrants' (*CW*31: 151). And then Marx returns to the chronology of his 'historico-critical' survey of the political economists, though not for long, since Marx inserts into the manuscript a 'digression' on the *Tableau Économique* of François Quesnay (leader of the 18th French school of Physiocratic economists), which greatly influenced the reproduction schemes in *Capital*, II, Part 3.

Although Marx then returns to the chronological track, he soon slides into his most fertile digression, on the theory of rent. This was apparently prompted by the German socialist leader Ferdinand Lassalle's request in June 1862 that he return the book on rent by the Ricardian economist Johan Karl Rodbertus that Lassalle had lent Marx (see Marx to Lassalle, 16 June 1862: *CW*41: 376-9). The result was what Dussel calls 'the central moment of all the *Manuscripts of 1861-63*', and 'the beginning of the confrontation with Ricardo'.[9] As we explore in more length in the

---

9   Dussel, *Towards an Unknown Marx*, p83. See also V S Vygodski, *The Story of a Great Discovery: How Karl Marx Wrote 'Capital'* (Tunbridge Wells, 1974), chs 5-7.

next chapter, ground rent is an obvious anomaly for the labour theory of value, since the landowner obtains a revenue thanks merely to the ownership of a material asset without making any productive contribution. Ricardo in his *Principles* sought to solve the problem through the theory of differential rent, which explained rent by differences in the productivity of labour on different pieces of land. But he denied the existence of absolute rent that arises even on the poorest patch of land. Marx devotes over 300 pages to solving this problem, in the course of which he reformulates the labour theory of value, drawing his fundamental distinction between the values of commodities, the socially necessary labour time required to produce them, and their prices of production, values modified by the equalisation of the rate of profit on different capitals.

Marx then moves to considering Ricardo's more general theory of value and surplus value (as Vitali Vygodski puts it, here 'Marx proceeds in his analysis first from the concrete to the abstract'), but soon returns to the problem of reproduction.[10] He finally broaches the question of expanded reproduction before developing his longest discussion of crises, and then returns to Ricardo and continues the chronology of political economists. But this 'historico-critical' sequence constantly blurs into more substantive discussions (for example, a brilliant excursus on the expansion of production and circulation under capitalism: *CW*32: 414-23) and then is interrupted by a much more extended analysis of the different forms of capital and the kinds of revenue they attract. This is itself interrupted in turn by nearly 100 pages on 'Capital and Profit', which covers some of the same ground as the first three parts of *Capital*, III. Finally we return again to 'Theories of Surplus Value', though the very interesting discussion of the clergyman-economist Richard Jones is punctuated by two important plans of what would become volumes III and I of *Capital* (*CW*33: 346-7). This completed, Marx picks up the thread of his analysis of the capitalist production process, abandoned for 'Theories of Surplus Value', offering a rich and extensive discussion of relative surplus value and the technological revolutions wrought by capital, and the first version of what becomes the 'Results of the Immediate Production Process', though these are shot through with brief notes on early economists such as David Hume and William Petty. Some final reflections on 'primitive accumulation' trail off and the manuscripts come to a halt, appropriately enough, with polemic and arithmetic—a denunciation of Marx's socialist rival Pierre-Joseph

---

10  Vygodski, *The Story of a Great Discovery*, p99.

Proudhon (with a critique of whose monetary theories the *Grundrisse* commences) and detailed calculations of the rate of interest.

The meandering path taken by Marx's thoughts in the *1861-63 Manuscript* is extreme. But, for example, the reader may be puzzled to find Marx in the penultimate chapters of *Capital*, III, struggling with the same problem that started him off into analysing reproduction in the *1861-63 Manuscript* of whether, as Smith and Ricardo affirmed, the value of the total product could be reduced to the sum of revenues (wages, profit and rent), even though Marx concedes that 'the problem posed here was already solved...in Volume 2, Part Three' (*CIII*: 975). Glissades such as this may explain Jon Elster's complaint about Marx's 'inherent lack of intellectual discipline', but they do not excuse it.[11] Marx will still be making waves long after the eddy in the academic pond made by Elster has vanished. His economic manuscripts are, as Dussel puts it, 'the river of ideas where Marx slowly constructs his categories with all its ebbs and flows'.[12] Far from revealing his intellectual weakness, the hesitations, digressions and repetitions display the depth of the analytical effort he undertook.

The delays were not solely a product of Marx's struggle for conceptual clarity. One of his main preoccupations after publishing *Capital*, I, was to ensure that the empirical scope of the later volumes was adequate to the forms in which capitalism was beginning to transform the globe. In *Capital*, I, Britain figures as the '*locus classicus*' of capitalist relations of production (*CI*: 90).[13] But Marx writes to Nikolai Danielson on 13 June 1871: 'I have decided that a complete revision of the manuscript [of *Capital*, II and III] is necessary. Moreover, even now a number of essential **documents** are still outstanding, which will eventually arrive from the **United States**' (*CW*44: 152). Though Marx also expressed his desire to include in his treatment of rent material on Russian agriculture, his focus seems to have become especially on the US. He wrote to Friedrich Adolph Sorge in New York on 4 April 1876 to ask for American book catalogues: 'The point is that I want to see for myself (for the second

11   Jon Elster, *Making Sense of Marx* (Cambridge, 1985), p390.
12   Enrique Dussel, 'The Discovery of the Category of Surplus Value', in Marcello Musto, ed, *Karl Marx's Grundrisse* (London, 2008), p62.
13   This formulation may represent one of Marx's debts to Engels, who wrote in 1845: 'England is the classic soil of this transformation [the Industrial Revolution]...; and England is, therefore, the classic land of its chief product also, the proletariat. Only in England can the proletariat be studied in all its relations and from all sides,' *The Condition of the Working Class in England: From Personal Observations and Authentic Sources* (Moscow, 1973), p45.

volume of *Capital* [by which Marx means both *Capital*, II and III]) what has appeared that might, perhaps, be of use as regards American agriculture and relations of landownership, ditto as regards credit (panic, money, etc, and anything connected therewith)' (*CW*45: 115).

Making his analysis more comprehensive was at least in part a strategy of evasion on Marx's part. On 10 April 1879 he explains to Danielson that he has to wait till the economic crisis then gripping Britain has reached 'maturity' but then admits: 'the bulk of the materials I have received not only from *Russia*, but from the *United States*, etc, make it pleasant for me to have a "pretext" of continuing my studies, instead of winding them up finally for the public' (*CW*45: 355). Certainly Engels was sceptical about Marx's accumulation of data, telling Sorge after his death (29 June 1883): 'Had it not been for the mass of American and Russian material (there are over two cubic metres of books of Russian statistics alone), Volume II would have long since been printed. These detailed studies held him up for years. As always, everything had to be brought up to date and now it has all come to nothing' (*CW*47: 43). Engels wrote to Danielson (13 November 1885) about Marx's letters to the latter:

> I could not read them without a sorrowful smile. Alas, we are so used to these excuses for the non-completion of the work! Whenever the state of his health made it impossible for him to go on with it, this impossibility preyed heavily upon his mind, and he was only too glad if he could only find out some theoretical excuse why the work should not then be completed. All these arguments he has at the time made use of vis-à-vis *de moi* [with me]; they seemed to ease his conscience.' (*CW*47: 348-349; in English in the original)

The personal story behind the writing of *Capital* encompasses more than Marx's efforts to postpone the completion of his work. The intellectual grandeur of his project contrasts with what he himself called 'the *petites misères de la vie domestique et privée* [the petty miseries of domestic and private life]' (*CW*40: 273). Nowhere is this most striking than the terrible letter of 30 June 1862 where Marx, infuriated by Lassalle's insensitivity during a stay with the Marxes at a moment of particular financial distress and social humiliation, rants to Engels about 'the Jewish **nigger** Lassalle' (*CW*41:389).[14] In counterpoint to this outburst are two following letters, in which Marx first (2 August) outlines to Engels the transformation of values into prices of production that he had hit upon

---

14  On the circumstances of this disastrous visit, see Sperber, *Karl Marx*, pp246-248.

in his critique of Rodbertus and Ricardo and then (7 August) lucidly criticises Engels for his pessimism about the North's fortunes in the American Civil War (which was responsible for the Marx family's difficulties because it brought to an end the income he had received for writing for the *New York Tribune*): 'In my view, all this is going to **take another turn**. The North will, at last, wage the war in earnest, have recourse to revolutionary methods and overthrow the supremacy of the **border slave statesmen**. One single **nigger regiment** would have a remarkable effect on Southern nerves' (*CW*41: 400).

Marx's use of the N-word here, when making a strikingly accurate prediction of the increasingly revolutionary course the war would take, is particularly distressing. The word recurs in the manuscripts and correspondence, creating a powerful dissonance both with the logic of Marx's theory (which makes no resort to racial categories) and with his political identification with the oppressed.[15] The latter is expressed, for example, very late in his life in the letters he wrote while convalescing in colonial Algiers. Thus he writes to his daughter Laura on 13 April 1882:

> Some of these Maures [in a café] were dressed pretentiously, even richly, others in, for once I dare call it *blouses*, sometime of white woollen appearance, now in rags and tatters—but in the eyes of a true Musulman such accidents, good or bad luck, do not distinguish Mahomet's children. *Absolute equality in their social intercourse*, not affected; on the contrary, only when demoralised, they become aware of it; as to the hatred against Christians and the hope of an ultimate victory over these infidels, their politicians justly consider this same feeling and practice of absolute equality (not of wealth or position but of personality) a guarantee of keeping up the one, of not giving up the latter. (*CW*46: 242; in English in the original)

Marx's development of his critique of political economy nearly a quarter of a century earlier was inflected by a very specific location. It was the explosion of a global economic and financial crisis that stimulated him to resume the abandoned work on his 'Economics' in the summer of 1857. 'I am working like mad all night and every night collating my economic studies so that I at least get the outlines clear before the *deluge*,' he told Engels that December (*CW*40: 217). But covering the crisis was part of his day job as London correspondent of the *New York Tribune*, a role he took on in the early 1850s. According to Michael Krätke:

---

15   See August Nimtz's comments on Marx's use of the N-word in 'Marx and Engels on the US Civil War', *Historical Materialism*, 19.4 (2011), p182 n 32.

As the *NYT* was rapidly growing, selling eventually nearly 300,000 copies altogether, and becoming the largest newspaper in the English-speaking world, Marx was actually one of the leading and most widely read economic journalists of his time, a renowned expert on all economic and financial matters whose judgement on monetary and financial crises was highly respected. Marx also earned himself a reputation as a leading expert of international politics—he wrote on all the major international conflicts and wars of his time.[16]

Crucial to Marx's ability to perform this role was his location in London, as he put it, 'a convenient vantage point for the observation of bourgeois society' (*Con*, 21). This is to put it mildly. 'If England be the heart of international trade and cosmopolitan finance, and London be the heart of England, the City is the heart of London,' wrote T H S Escott towards the end of Marx's life in 1879.[17] His long exile in London broadly coincided with what Eric Hobsbawm has called 'the Age of Capital'—the period spanning 1848 to 1875 when an integrated world economy increasingly regulated by the rhythms of industrial capitalism took shape.[18] This process made London, in Herbert Feis's words, 'the centre of a financial empire, more international, more extensive in its variety, than even the political empire of which it was the capital'.[19] The great crises that shook the City gripped Marx's attention, at the same time as he closely followed British political life. A reader of his economic manuscripts and journalism cannot but be astonished by the in-depth character of his knowledge of the history and literature of modern Britain (even if it wasn't always deployed effectively, as in his obsessive pursuit of Lord Palmerston as an agent of the Russian Tsar). He also benefitted from Engels' presence in the hub of the industrial revolution in Manchester; it is worth reminding ourselves that the small island where Marx and Engels took refuge after 1848 embraced the mid-19th century counterparts of Wall Street, Washington and the Pearl River Delta.

From his London vantage point Marx could follow 'the one great event of contemporary history, the American Civil War' (*CI*: 366 n 358), and trace its impact on Britain—whose textiles-centred economy was

---

16  Michael Krätke, 'The First World Economic Crisis: Marx as an Economic Journalist', in Musto, ed, *Marx's Grundrisse*, p163. See also on Marx's journalism Sperber, *Karl Marx*, pp294-296.
17  Quoted in David Kynaston, *The City of London*, I (London, 1994), p330.
18  E J Hobsbawm, *The Age of Capital: 1848-1875* (London, 1975).
19  Herbert Feis, *Europe: The World's Banker: 1870-1914* (New Haven, 1930), p5.

severely hit by the shortage of cotton produced by the slave plantations of the South and whose ruling class weighed the option of intervening in the war to halt the rise of a peer competitor.[20] British working class opposition to military intervention in support of the Confederacy was one of the starting points of the International Working Men's Association, or First International (1864-72). Marx proudly told his old comrade Joseph Weydemeyer (who was fighting in the Union Army): 'Its *English* members consist chiefly of the heads of the **Trade-Unions** here, in other words, the real worker-kings of London, the same people who organised that gigantic reception for Garibaldi and who, by that monster meeting in St James's Hall (under [the bourgeois Radical MP John] Bright's chairmanship), prevented Palmerston from declaring *war on the United States*, which he was on the point of doing' (24 November 1864; *CW*42: 44).[21] Marx completed *Capital*, I, at a time when he was playing his most influential political role, leading the International, for example, to champion the Union cause and support Ireland's right to self-determination, in both cases not out of abstract principle but as a means of uniting the working class across the divisions of race, nation, and religion.[22]

Marx's perspective was indeed global. As early as February 1858 he pointed to Britain's structural deficit in the balance of trade:

> Generally speaking, the so-called balance of trade must...always be in favour of the world against England, because the world has yearly to pay England not only for the commodities it purchases from her, but also the interest of the debt it owes her. The really disquieting feature for England...is this, that she is apparently at a loss to find at home a sufficient field of employment for her unwieldy capital; that she must consequently lend on an increasing scale, and similar in this point, to Holland, Venice and Genoa, at the epoch of their decline, forge herself the weapons for her creditors. (*CW*15: 429-430)

---

20  For a recent popular history of the US-British relationship during the Civil War, see Amanda Forman, *World on Fire: An Epic History of Two Nations Divided* (London, 2010).
21  Marx is probably confusing the St James's Hall rally, which took place in March 1863 and was indeed organised by the trade unions, with a rally addressed by Bright, a militant abolitionist and supporter of the North, in Rochdale in December 1861, during the *Trent* affair, when Britain came close to war with the US; see Bill Cash, *John Bright* (London, 2011), ch 5, and for the *Trent* crisis, Foreman, *World on Fire*, chs 7-9.
22  The importance of the Civil War and the Irish struggle for Marx's intellectual development in these years is stressed in Raya Dunayevskaya, *Marxism and Freedom* (London, 1971), ch v, and Kevin Anderson, *Marx at the Margins* (Chicago, 2010), chs 3 and 4.

The most important of these creditors would be the United States, towards which Marx's attention increasingly turned. He told Danielson on 15 November 1878:

> The most interesting field for the economist is now certainly to be found in the United States, and, above all, during the period of 1873 (since the crash in September) until 1878—the period of chronic crisis. Transformations—which to be elaborated did require in England centuries—were here realised in a few years. But the observer must look not to the older States on the Atlantic, but to the newer ones (*Ohio* is a striking example) and the newest (*California* f.i.). (*CW*45: 344)

## The fall guy

Marx's preoccupation with the US was, as we have seen, one reason why the work was never finished. It was Engels who was left to clear up the mess. This was considerable, as he explained to the German socialist leader August Bebel a few months after Marx's death (30 August 1883):

> As soon as I am back [from Eastbourne] I shall get down to Volume 2 in real earnest and that is an enormous task. Alongside parts that have been completely finished are others that are merely sketched out, the whole being a *brouillon* [draft] with the exception of perhaps two chapters. Quotations from sources in no kind of order, piles of them jumbled together, collected simply with a view to future selection. Besides that there is the handwriting which certainly cannot be deciphered by anyone but *me*, and then only with difficulty. You ask why I of all people should not have been told how far the thing had got. It is quite simple; if I had known, I should have pestered him night and day until it was all finished and printed. And Marx knew that better than anyone else. He knew besides that, if the worst came to the worst, as has now happened, the Ms. could be edited by me in the spirit in which he would have done it himself, as indeed he told Tussy [Marx's youngest daughter Eleanor] as much. (*CW*49: 53)

Whether Engels actually succeeded in carrying out this 'enormous task' in Marx's spirit has come into question in recent years. In particular, the publication of the 1863-65 *Manuscript* in *MEGA²* has provoked widespread criticism of Engels's edition of *Capital*, III. This, of course, isn't the first time that Engels has been in trouble. The discovery after the Second World War of the 'humanist' young Marx of the *Economic and Philosophical Manuscripts of 1844* encouraged some to portray Engels as Marx's evil twin, who, particularly after the latter's death, encouraged the construction of a scientist and determinist 'Marxism'. Whatever the real theoretical differences between the two (and we shall touch on some below), this portrayal of Engels is absurd: towards the end of his life he was particularly concerned to correct dogmatic readings of Marx, as his letters of the early 1890s on historical materialism clearly show.[23]

Now, however, Engels is on trial again. Carl-Erich Vollgraf and Jürgen Jucknickel aptly call the *1863-5 Manuscript* 'Marx's biggest construction site'. The accusation against Engels is that he turned a building site into the facsimile of a finished building. Vollgraf and Jucknickel document the very extensive changes that Engels made to Marx's text—substantially increasing the number of chapters, changing their order, incorporating parenthetical comments and footnotes into the text, adding text of his own, cutting and polishing Marx's text, and making a variety of corrections.[24] The effect of this editing, Michael Heinrich complains, is to make Marx's text seem more finished than it actually was:

> The arrangement of a text and the headings used obviously strongly influence the understanding of a text, especially if the text is not finished but in large part sketchy and incomplete. By putting this material together into chapters and inserting headings, this draft character is concealed. But even more important, the readers can no longer tell at what point in the manuscript 'presentation' turns into 'inquiry'. The difference between presentation and inquiry, however, is of central importance for Marx's own methodical understanding. To Marx, 'presentation' does not just mean the more or less skilful assembly of final results. The factual correlation of the conditions presented should be expressed by the correct presentation of the categories, by 'advancing from the abstract to the concrete'. To Marx, the search for an adequate presentation is an essential part of his process of inquiry. But the difference between complete and incomplete presentation is concealed by the

---

23 Unfortunately there seems to be no satisfactory book-length study of Engels's thought, certainly in English: S H Rigby, *Engels and the Formation of Marxism* (Manchester, 1992) is probably the best of a bad bunch. See also the special issue on Engels, *International Socialism*, 2.64 (1994), http://www.marxists.de/theory/engels/.

24 Carl-Erich Vollgraf and Jürgen Jucknickel, 'Marx in Marx's Words? On Engels's Edition of the Main Manuscript of Book 3 of *Capital*', *Journal of Political Economy*, 32:1 (2002), quotation from p40.

structure imposed by Engels. Additionally, Engels tried to strengthen the coherence of the text through omissions and connecting phrases. The readers do not learn that a large part of Marx's manuscript is open and undecided. Engels gives them a possible solution of the problems without letting them know that there is a problem: the solution given by *Engels* appears as a mostly complete elaboration by Marx.[25]

Heinrich is particularly critical of the very extensive editing and rearranging that Engels made of chapter 5 of the manuscript, 'The Division of Profit into Interest and Net Profit (Industrial or Commercial Profit). Interest-Bearing Capital', which he transformed into Part Five of Volume III. This is especially messy, including two long sections entitled 'Confusion' largely consisting of excerpts from evidence given at the parliamentary enquiries into the suspension of the Bank Act 1844 during the panics of 1847 and 1857, accompanied by Marx's comments. Engels found dealing with this part of the manuscript especially difficult, telling Laura Lafargue (4 November 1892): 'The day I finish that section on Banks and Credit, which has been my stumbling block for 4-5 Years...—the day I finish that, there will be some consumption of alcohol—you bet!' (*CW*50: 23; in English in the original)

Engels divided the manuscript into 15 chapters, in the process reordering the material considerably. He also amended the following sentence: 'It lies outside our plan to give an analysis of the credit system and the instruments this creates (credit money, etc),' by inserting the word 'detailed' before 'analysis' (compare *MEGA²*, II/4.2: 469 and *C*III: 525). According to Heinrich:

> for Marx's concept of presentation the central question is whether the inherent laws regulating credit can actually be discussed on the highly abstract level of *Capital*, or whether they are linked to a number of historically specific institutional factors, such as the constitution of the money and banking system, so that there cannot be a general credit theory. In Marx's manuscript this question remains open. Engels chose to present the research material found in Marx's manuscript on the general level, which led to the reproach against Marx that he had unduly generalised specific historic conditions of the credit system in 19th century England.[26]

---

25 Michael Heinrich, 'Engels' Edition of the Third Volume of *Capital* and Marx's Original Manuscript', *Science and Society*, 60:4 (1996-1997), p457.

26 Heinrich, 'Engels' Edition of the Third Volume of *Capital* and Marx's Original Manuscript', pp462-463.

Heinrich's specific criticism about the treatment of credit can only properly be addressed when we consider the problem of Marx's overall construction of *Capital* in the concluding section of this chapter and examine his method in chapters 2 and 3. But his general indictment of Engels is overstated. Engels inherited from Marx the Herculean labour of completing *Capital* at a time when he himself was ageing, struggling with chronic illness, and engaged in an enormous correspondence with a growing international socialist movement. He was also subject to the same din of enquiries about when *Capital*, III, in particular would appear that Marx had suffered for the latest 15 years of his life. In the event, it was published in 1894, nine years after the publication of Volume II, and not long before Engels's own death. Heinrich is right that Engels's editing of chapter 5 of the manuscript makes it seem more finished than it actually was. But if he had excluded this material he would have been attacked also. He was in an impossible situation. Moreover, Vollgraf and Jucknickel are right to point out that 'Engels's editing work did not conceal the fact that the third volume had remained a torso and that the manuscript remained a draft, even in its published version. The many digressions Marx made in his exposition and in his reflections are recognisable as such even without the optical tool of the parentheses which Engels removed'.[27] One doesn't require the immense apparatus of the *MEGA²* to realise, for example, that the chapter Engels gave the title 'Development of the Law's Internal Contradictions' (another of Heinrich's bugbears) is a fragmentary draft.

This doesn't alter the fact that some of Engels's editing is unfortunate. He changed the subtitle of Volume III from '*Gestaltungen des Gesamtprozeßes*' (Figures of the Process as a Whole) into '*Der Gesamtprozeß der kapitalistischen Produktion*' (The Process of Capitalist Production as a Whole). For reasons that should become clear in the next two chapters, I prefer the original subtitle. It is, moreover, important to know that one of the most frequently cited of Marx's remarks on the causes of crises—'The ultimate reason for all real crises always remains the poverty and restricted consumption of the masses, in the face of the drive of capitalist production to develop the productive forces as if only the absolute consumption capacity of society set a limit to them'— appears in a passage from which Engels removed the parentheses (compare CIII: 615 with *MEGA²* II/4.2: 539-540). He also seems to have replaced every occurrence of 'productive capitalist' with 'industrial

---

27  Vollgraf and Jucknickel, 'Marx in Marx's Words?', p67.

capitalist'. This is misleading because it encourages the view that Marx is offering an account of industrial capitalism when he is quite clear that productive capital includes what we would call service sectors (eg transport). Most seriously of all, Engels interpolates into Marx's discussion of the tendency of the rate of profit to fall, in a passage where Marx is suggesting that higher labour productivity may cause the rate of profit to rise thanks to a cheapening of the elements of constant capital, the reassuring pronouncement: 'In actuality, however, the rate of profit will fall in the long run, as we have already seen' (*C*III: 337; translation modified; compare *MEGA²* II/4.1: 319). Here undoubtedly Engels's politico-historic predilections overcome an accurate rendering of Marx's own thinking.[28]

But the biggest weakness of Engels's edition of Volume III has long been well known, namely the famous Supplement and Addendum where he outlines the so-called historical interpretation of the labour theory of value, claiming that it holds true in conditions of simple commodity production, *prior* to the development of capitalism, but *not* where capitalist productions prevails. This involves a complete misunderstanding of Marx's value theory, as we shall see in chapters 3 and 4; it is rejected by virtually every contemporary commentator on *Capital*. Moreover, as John Weeks points out, the account that Engels gives of the transition from feudalism to capitalism is very different from Marx's: 'Engels argued that the development of capitalism could be explained in "purely economic" terms, "without the necessity for recourse in a single instance" to any "political interference". In contrast, Marx devoted the final section of Volume I of *Capital* to the violent methods that accompanied the emergence of capitalism'.[29]

These theoretical differences are important, both because Engels enormously influenced the reception of Marx's work and because they indicate the distinct perspective from which he edited *Capital*. But they should also remind us that Engels needs to be treated as himself a contributor to the critique of political economy. After all, it was he who first broached this critique publicly in his 1844 article 'Outlines of a Critique of Political Economy' and in *The Condition of the Working Class in England* (1845). These texts were important reference points for Marx while working on *Capital*, when he acknowledged (7 July 1864): 'As you know, 1. I'm always late off the mark with everything, and 2. I invariably

---

28  See Geert Reuten, '"*Zirkel vicieux*" or Trend Fall? The Course of the Profit Rate in Marx's *Capital* III', *History of Political Economy*, 36.1 (2004), pp171-172.

29  John Weeks, *Capital, Exploitation and Economic Crisis* (London, 2010), chs 1 and 2 (quotation from p30).

follow in your footsteps' (*CW*41: 546-547). He calls the 'Outlines' 'brilliant' in the 1859 Preface to *A Contribution to the Critique of Political Economy* (*Con*: 21). Marx reread the *Condition* when writing the *1861-63 Manuscript* and wrote to Engels on 18 April 1863: 'So far as the main theses in your book are concerned, by the by, they have been corroborated down to the last detail by developments subsequent to 1844. For I have been comparing the book with the notes I made on the ensuing period' (*CW*41: 468). While writing *Capital*, I, he modestly told Engels (10 February 1866) that the great chapter on 'The Working Day' 'supplements your book (*sketchily*) up to 1865' (*CW*42: 224). It is, moreover, Engels who first formulates the concept of the industrial reserve army of labour, arguing in the *Condition* that 'English manufacture must have, at all times save the brief periods of highest prosperity, an unemployed reserve army of workers, in order to be able to produce the masses of goods required by the market in the liveliest months'.[30] The influence that Engels and his distinct theoretical perspective (which, as we shall see, highlights the role of competition) had on the development of Marx's own critique of political economy would repay separate study. But these differences don't diminish the scale of Engels's accomplishment in completing *Capital* for publication, for all that it may not pass the test of modern scholarly editing. In publishing *Capital*, III, he made available what he told Danielson (23 April 1885) was 'the concluding and crowning part', 'the most astounding thing I have ever read' to later generations (*CW*47: 278).

## The long and winding road

But if *Capital* has a history, it also has a prehistory. One can tentatively identify three phases in Marx's development as an economic thinker. It is worth noting that the periodisation I have adopted cuts across Louis Althusser's famous 'epistemological break' between the young 'humanist Marx' struggling with the influences of Hegel and Feuerbach in the first half of the 1840s and the 'scientific' Marx that emerges in the 'Theses on Feuerbach' and *The German Ideology* at the middle of the same decade.[31] This doesn't necessarily invalidate

---

30  Engels, *Condition of the Working Class*, p124. Gareth Stedman Jones stresses the independent contribution of Engels's early writings in 'Engels and the Genesis of Marxism', *New Left Review*, I/106 (1977); see also Rigby, *Engels and the Formation of Marxism*, chs 2 and 3, and, for a more sceptical take, Hal Draper, *Karl Marx's Theory of Revolution* (4 vols, New York, 1977-90), chs 7 and 8.

31  Louis Althusser, *For Marx* (London, 1970).

Althusser's interpretation, but it underlines the complexity of Marx's development, particularly in relation to Hegel. (Much more about this in chapters 2 and 3.)

## 1 *1844-7: The humanist critic of political economy*

Marx started his intensive study of political economy after his arrival in Paris in the autumn of 1843. As he later explained, having attempted a critique of Hegel's political philosophy, he had reached:

> the conclusion that...legal relations...[and] political forms...originate in the material conditions of life, the totality of which Hegel, following the example of English and French thinkers of the eighteenth century, embraces within the term 'civil society'; that the anatomy of this civil society, however, has to be sought in political economy. (*Con*: 20)[32]

As was his practice throughout his life, Marx took plentiful notes excerpting from and commenting on the works of political economy he was reading. These *Exzerpthefte* merge into the texts with which we most associate the 'Young Marx', namely the 'Notes on Mill' and the *Economic and Philosophical Manuscripts of 1844*.[33] But we find broadly the same problematic in the slightly later draft article on Friedrich List, written in March 1845, just before Marx and Engels started work on the body of writing published posthumously as *The German Ideology*.[34] Here Marx shows an increasingly confident grasp of the categories of political economy that led him to plan a two-volume *Critique of Politics and Political Economy* and even, in a characteristic letter of 1 August 1846 explaining to his publisher why he hadn't delivered this work, a separate *Critique of Economics* (*CW*38: 49).

In these texts Marx uses the findings of the political economists to exemplify the theme of alienated labour and more broadly to show how bourgeois society violates the human essence. For our purposes, in some ways more interesting than the much better known Paris *Manuscripts* are the 'Notes on Mill', excerpts from and comments on James Mill's

---

32  Important studies of Marx's early development include Michael Löwy, *The Theory of Revolution in the Young Marx* (Brill, 2002), Stathis Kouvelakis, *Philosophy and Revolution: From Kant to Marx* (London, 2003), and David Leopold, *The Young Karl Marx* (Cambridge, 2007). My fullest discussion is in *Marxism and Philosophy* (Oxford, 1983), ch 2.

33  See Jürgen Rojahn, 'The Emergence of a Theory: the Importance of Marx's Notebooks Exemplified by Those from 1844', *Rethinking Marxism*, 14.4 (2002).

34  I owe my understanding of the draft on List and its significance to Lucia Pradella, who discusses it in 'New Developmentalism and the Origins of Methodological Nationalism', *Competition and Change*, 18.2 (2014).

*Elements of Political Economy* (1820). Here Marx endorses but elaborates on Mill's conventional definition of money as the medium of exchange:

> the *mediating function* or movement, human, social activity, by means of which the products of labour mutually complement each other, is estranged and becomes the property of a material thing external to man, viz. money. If a man himself alienates this mediating function he remains active only as a lost, dehumanised creature. The *relation* between things, human dealings with them, become the operations of a being above and beyond man. (*EW*: 260)

Money as the autonomised mediator between human activities is an alienated expression of humans' species being, a concept that Marx takes from Ludwig Feuerbach, but gives a new content. According to Marx, human beings find fulfilment through creative activity:

> Hence this *mediator* is the lost, estranged essence of private property, private property *alienated* and external to itself; it is the *alienated mediation* of human production, the *alienated* species-activity of man. All the qualities proper to the generation of this activity are transferred to the mediator. Thus man separated from this mediator becomes poorer as man in proportion as the mediator becomes *richer*. (*EW*: 261)

This is quite typical of Marx's treatment of political economy at this stage. He broadly accepts the descriptions of economic relations and practices that he finds in the works he studies, but offers a different interpretation of their significance. As Allen Oakley puts it about Marx's more extended discussion in the Paris *Manuscripts*:

> When he turned his attention to the elaboration of his own critique of the system that political economy had enabled him to outline, the *distribution* status of labour is taken as an empirical fact of capitalism. Marx's ultimate concern was with the situation of labour in general, *humanistic* terms rather than only in *material* terms—that is, with labour *vis-à-vis* the realisation of human potential, with labour as an essential ontological process.[35]

Or, as Althusser puts it, 'Marx doesn't modify any of the economists' concepts, he simply reads them, by relating them to their hidden essence: the alienation of human labour, and across this alienation, the

---

35   Allen Oakley, *Marx's Critique of Political Economy: Intellectual Sources and Evolution* (2 vols, London, 1984), I, p49. I'm grateful to Colin Barker for drawing my attention to Oakley's important work.

human essence'.[36] But this interpretation isn't just lowered onto the economists' concepts and descriptions, like an external scaffolding. On the contrary, the philosophical anthropology that guides Marx's assessment is itself formulated thanks to his encounter with political economy, which in particular allows him to begin to transcend Feuerbach by reconceiving the relationship between humans and nature. No longer is this relationship defined, as it was by Feuerbach, by sensibility (*Sinnlichkeit*), the passive faculty of receiving sense impressions emitted by an external nature; now it is labour that binds humans to the rest of nature in an active process of mutual transformation. Thus in the *Manuscripts* Marx praises Hegel because 'he adopts the standpoint of modern political economy. He sees labour as the essence, the self-confirming essence, of man' (*EW*: 386). It is this understanding of human beings as inventive social producers that forms the basis of Marx's critique of alienation: the alienation of labour under capital means that workers are denied the possibility of fulfilling the very core of their species being.[37]

But Marx's endorsement of 'the standpoint of modern political economy' is not complete. Remarkably in the light of his later intellectual evolution, he distances himself from the labour theory of value:

> Both on the question of the relations of money to the value of metal and in his demonstration that the cost of production is the sole factor in the determination of value Mill succumbs to the error, made by the entire Ricardo School, of defining an *abstract law* without mentioning the fluctuations or the continual suspension through which it comes into being. If eg it is an *invariable* law that in the last analysis—or rather in the sporadic (accidental) coincidence of supply and demand—the cost of production determines price (value), then it is no less an *invariable law* that these relations do not obtain, ie that value and cost of production do not stand in any necessary relation... The true law of economics is *chance*, and we learned people arbitrarily seize on a few moments and establish them as laws. (*EW*: 259-260)[38]

Meanwhile, the humanist critique of political economy was being developed independently but in parallel by Marx's fellow Feuerbachian

---

36  Louis Althusser, 'Sur Feuerbach', in *Écrits philosophiques et politiques* (François Matheron, ed; 2 vols, Paris, 1994, 1995), II, p213.

37  Two good studies of Marx on alienation are Christopher J Arthur, *Dialectics of Labour* (Oxford, 1986), and Sean Sayers, *Marx and Alienation* (Basingstoke, 2011).

38  See the discussion of Marx's initial rejection of the labour theory of value in Ernest Mandel, *The Formation of the Economic Thought of Karl Marx* (London, 1971), ch 3.

communist Friedrich Engels, soon to become his lifelong collaborator. In 'Outlines of a Critique of Political Economy', published in 1844 and, as we have seen, an important reference point for Marx (who mentions it in the Paris *Manuscripts*), Engels also rejects the labour theory of value in very similar terms: 'Abstract value and its determination by the costs of production are, after all, only abstractions, nonentities' (*CW*3: 425). But, whereas Marx treats private property as an expression of alienated labour, Engels (perhaps thanks to the influence of the followers of Robert Owen he encountered during his first stay in Manchester in 1842-44) relates it to competition:

> in the end everything comes down to competition, so long as private property exists...because private property isolates everyone in his own crude solitariness, and because, nevertheless, everyone has the same interest as his neighbour, one landowner stands antagonistically confronted by another, one capitalist by another, one worker by another. In this discord of identical interests resulting precisely from this identity is consummated the immorality of mankind's condition hitherto; and this consummation is competition. (*CW*3: 431-432)[39]

Informing the young Marx's and Engels's rejection of Ricardian value theory is a hostility to abstraction very different from the stance taken by Marx in his later economic works. In the writings of the early and mid-1840s abstraction is associated to what is limited and partial compared to the concrete existence of what Marx and Engels call in *The German Ideology* 'the real individuals, their activity and the material conditions under which they live,' which can 'be verified in a purely empirical way' (*CW*5: 31). Thus Marx already uses the expression 'abstract labour' in the Paris *Manuscripts*, but merely to characterise the alienation of the worker, who 'lives from one-sided, abstract labour' (*EW*: 288). By contrast, in *Capital* and the drafts preceding it, abstraction is the essential analytical tool to identifying the inner structure of capitalist economic relations. As we shall see in chapter 2, by the time Marx writes the *1861-63 Manuscript* one of his main criticisms of Ricardo has become that he isn't abstract enough.[40]

---

39    See the interesting, if severe, discussion of Engels's early writings in Kouvelakis, *Philosophy and Revolution*, ch 4, and, on Engels's first encounter with Manchester, Hunt, *The Frock-Coated Communist*, ch 3. It should be stressed that competition is also a major thematic preoccupation of the 1844 *Manuscripts*, where, for example, Marx writes: 'The only wheels which political economy sets in motion are *greed* and *the war of the avaricious—competition*' (*EW*: 323).

40    I'm grateful to Rob Jackson for this point.

## 2  1847-1857: *The critical Ricardian*

Marx's stance towards 'the Ricardo School' decisively changes in the second phase of his treatment of political economy, but this is part of a more complex and comprehensive theoretical recasting. *The Poverty of Philosophy* (1847)—Marx's first 'mature, complete and conclusive work' (Georg Lukács)—marks a decisive shift.[41] Devoted to a critique of the French socialist Pierre-Joseph Proudhon's *Philosophie de la misère*, this text is the site of Marx's first explicit formulation of the concept of the relations of production (*Produktionsverhältnisse*). In an excellent discussion of the origins of the basic concepts of historical materialism, Göran Therborn notes: 'The term *"Produktivkräfte"* ("forces of production" or "productive forces") was bequeathed to Marx by the classical economists. In the form of "productive powers", it occurs in Smith and Ricardo, and his excerpts and quotations from them, Marx (from the *Economic and Philosophical Manuscripts* onwards) usually translates it into German as *Produktivkräfte*.' Marx's first formulation of his theory of history in the manuscripts drafted in 1845-7 and posthumously published as *The German Ideology*, treats the development of the productive forces as the cause of transformations in social relations. But, as Therborn points out, in this text, 'the concept that accompanies the forces of production is *Verkehr* or *Verkehrsform*, a much broader term meaning approximately communication, commerce or intercourse'.[42]

As late as his letter of 28 December 1846 to Pavel Annenkov where Marx roughs out the argument of *The Poverty of Philosophy*, he still uses the concept of *Verkehr* where in his later writing we would expect to find that of the relations of production, to refer to the social relations that interact with the productive forces:

> Man never renounces what he has gained, but this does not mean that he never renounces the form of society in which he has acquired certain productive forces. On the contrary. If he is not to be deprived of the results obtained or to forfeit the fruits of civilisation, man is compelled to change all his traditional social forms as soon as the mode of commerce ceases to correspond to the productive forces acquired. Here I use the word *commerce* in its widest sense—as we would say *Verkehr* in German... Thus, the economic forms in which man produces, consumes

---

41  Georg Lukács, *History and Class Consciousness* (London, 1971), p33. It is to be regretted that as shrewd a commentator as Oakley is so dismissive of *The Poverty of Philosophy*, which he says 'delivers little that was of lasting relevance to the evolution of Marx's critique of political economy', *Marx's Critique of Political Economy*, I, pp109-110.

42  Göran Therborn, *Science Class and Society* (London, 1976), pp355, 368.

and exchanges are *transitory and historical*. With the acquisition of new productive faculties man changes his mode of production and with the mode of production he changes all the economic relations which were but the necessary relations of that particular mode of production. (*CW*38: 96-97)

In *The Poverty of Philosophy* Marx maintains the contrast between the productive forces, whose development is cumulative, and 'transitory and historical' social relations, but the latter are given a much more precise specification as the social relations of production, which in turn have definite economic meaning as the relations of effective control over the productive forces.[43] This conceptual shift then allows a reformulation of Marx's critique of political economy: 'Economic categories are only the theoretical expressions, the abstractions of the social relations of production' (*CW*6: 165). The association of production relations and economic categories is a persisting theme in *Capital* and its drafts, as we see in chapters 2 and 3. The introduction of the concept of relations of production serves two crucial functions in *The Poverty of Philosophy*. First, it permits Marx to conceptualise capital as a social relation. For example: 'Machinery is no more an economic category than the bullock that drags the plough. Machinery is merely a productive force. The modern workshop, which depends on the application of machinery, is a social production relation, an economic category' (*CW*6: 183). In a slightly later text, *Wage Labour and Capital* (published in 1849 but based on lectures given in 1847), Marx takes this a step further, specifying the capital relation as one between capital and wage labour:

> *Thus capital presupposes wage labour; wage labour presupposes capital. They reciprocally condition the existence of each other; they reciprocally bring forth each other.*
>
> Does a worker in a cotton factory produce merely cotton textiles? No, he produces capital. He produces values which serve afresh to command his labour and by means of it to create new values. (*CW*9: 214)

The view of the capital relation expressed in this passage (the first paragraph of which is quoted in *Capital*, I: 724 n 21) implies a theory of how value is created, something Marx dismissed in the 'Notes on Mill'. This brings us to the second function of his introduction of the concept of the relations of production: it allows him to historicise and denaturalise classical political economy, but also to use it as a basis of analysis. So

---

43  See G A Cohen's classic treatment: *Karl Marx's Theory of History* (Oxford, 1978), ch III.

in *The Poverty of Philosophy* he famously criticises the 'Metaphysics of Political Economy', writing, for example: 'Economists express the relations of bourgeois production, the division of labour, credit, money, etc, as fixed, immutable, eternal categories' (*CW*6: 162). But his attitude to Ricardo changes. In his 'Critical Notes on the Article "The King of Prussia and Social Reform"' (1844), Marx refers to 'the cynic Ricardo' (*EW*: 406). Now he writes: 'Doubtless, Ricardo's language is as cynical as can be. To put the cost of manufacture of hats and the cost of maintenance of men on the same plane is to turn men into hats. But do not make an outcry at the cynicism of it. The cynicism is in the facts and not in the words which express the facts' (*CW*6: 125). And he goes considerably further:

> Ricardo shows us the real movement of bourgeois production, which constitutes value... Ricardo establishes the truth of his formula by deriving it from all economic relations, and by explaining in this way all phenomena, even those like rent, accumulation of capital and the relation of wages to profits, which at first sight seem to contradict it; it is precisely that which makes his doctrine a scientific system. (*CW*6: 123-124)

This is an especially interesting passage because Marx here praises Ricardo for what, as we shall see in chapter 3, he will criticise him for doing in the *1861-63 Manuscript*, namely trying to establish a deductive connection between value and other economic relations. Marx now explicitly embraces the labour theory of value: 'the determination of value by labour time...is therefore merely the scientific expression of the economic relations of present-day society, as was clearly and precisely demonstrated by Ricardo long before M Proudhon' (*CW*6: 138). And towards the end of *The Poverty of Philosophy* Marx defends Ricardo's theories of rent and wages in some detail. So at this stage in his intellectual development Marx is critical of Ricardo and other political economists for eternising the historically specific and transitory relations of production of bourgeois society, but believes they give an accurate account of the substance of these relations.[44] A particularly

---

44 The 'Draft Article on List' represents an important step towards the theoretical position Marx takes in *The Poverty of Philosophy*. Thus he writes there: 'if Adam Smith is the theoretical starting-point of political economy, then its real point of departure, its real school, is "civil society" (*die bürgerliche Gesellschaft*), of which the different phases of development can be accurately traced in political economy' (*CW*4: 273). Moreover, Marx in this text accepts the labour theory of value, as the following passage makes clear: '"*Labour*" is the living basis of private property, it is private property as the creative source

remarkable example of this is in his 1847 lecture on wages, where he concedes that the political economists are right to criticise trade unions, since any wage increases will by, reducing profits, lead directly or indirectly (via labour-saving innovations) to workers losing their jobs, but insists that this is besides the point:

> If in the associations it really were a matter only of what it appears to be, namely the fixing of wages, if the relationship between labour and capital were eternal, these combinations would be wrecked on the necessity of things. But they are the means of uniting the working class, of preparing for the overthrow of the entire old society with its class contradictions. (*CW*6: 435)[45]

This position—that trade unions are ineffective or worse economically but are valuable as forms of class organisation—is an instable one that was only overcome when Marx criticised in the London Notebooks of 1850-53 (partially published in *MEGA²*) the idea common to Ricardo and Malthus that population pressures prevent real wages from rising above a subsistence minimum; this critique was most fully developed in 'Value, Price, and Profit' (1865). In my view, Marx nevertheless remains in the framework forged in *The Poverty of Philosophy* of critical Ricardianism up to and beyond his resumption of his economic studies in London in the early 1850s. The London Notebooks contain excerpts from and comments on Ricardo's *Principles*, alongside (among other topics) extensive notes on British debates on currency and banking, excerpts from a wide range of political economists, and studies of world history and colonialism. By this period Marx is becoming more critical of Ricardo, as is clear also in his correspondence of the early 1850s, which explores the currency debates and Ricardo's theory of rent (see chapter 2). As a result, Marx's economic analysis developed in ways that threaten to burst out of the Ricardian framework: for example, Lucia Pradella argues that it is in the notes on Ricardo that 'Marx distinguished for the first time the value of wages from the value produced by workers'.[46] But something new happens in 1857.

---

of itself. Private property is nothing but *objectified* labour' (*CW*4: 278).

45 Marx may have been influenced here by Engels, whose first stint working at the family firm of Ermen & Engels in Manchester in 1842-44 had given him much more direct experience of an actual workers' movement: see the very similar assessment of the trade union struggle in *The Condition of the Working Class*, pp250-262.

46 Lucia Pradella, *Globalization and the Critique of Political Economy: New Insights from Marx's Writings* (London, 2014). See ch IV for extensive discussion of the London Notebooks. The passage in question is *MEGA²* IV/8: 413-414. Note also this somewhat

## 3  *1857-83: the artificer of categories*

Beyond any specific theoretical changes, what appears in the *Grundrisse* is a new preoccupation with the construction and ordering of categories. These categories in turn are seen as articulating the structure of capitalist relations of production. Even if prompted by Marx's rereading of Hegel's *Science of Logic*, this shift must be understood in terms of the problems Marx inherited from Ricardo. This will form the subject matter of the next two chapters and, to some extent, of this book as a whole.

It is, however, worth stressing the continuities in Marx's critique of political economy. There is, to begin with, a set of theoretical presuppositions that remain unchanged. The philosophical anthropology that Marx formulated in the Paris *Manuscripts* underlies all his later economic writings. This is most obvious in the account of the labour process in *Capital*, I, chapter 7. This passage, for example, lucidly states the basis of Marx's critique of Feuerbach in *The German Ideology*:

> Labour is, first of all, a process between man and nature, a process by which man, through his own actions, mediates, regulates and controls the metabolism (*Stoffwechsel*) between himself and nature. He confronts the materials of nature as a force of nature. He sets in motion the natural forces which belong to his own body, his arms, legs, head and hands, in order to appropriate the materials of nature in a form adapted to his own needs. Through this movement he acts upon external nature and changes it, and in this way he simultaneously changes his own nature. (*C*I: 283)

*The German Ideology* also includes, as we have already seen, Marx's and Engels's first outline of their theory of history. Not only is this presupposed by the evolving critique of political economy, but, as the example of *The Poverty of Philosophy* shows, the latter provides the occasion for the clarification and reformulation of the basic concepts of historical materialism. Most of the best books on Marx's theory of history draw heavily on remarks he makes in passing in *Capital*. There are also thematic continuities. At least some of the content of Marx's theory of fetishism, according to which social relations among persons take the form of relations between things, is already present in his

---

earlier passage in 'Wage Labour and Capital': 'The worker receives means of subsistence in exchange for his labour, but the capitalist receives in exchange for his means of subsistence labour, the productive activity of the worker, the creative power whereby the worker not only replaces what he consumes but gives to the accumulated labour a greater value than it previously possessed' (*CW*9: 213).

writings of the mid-1840s. Thus in the 'Notes on Mill' he identifies this happening with money:

> In money the unfettered dominion of the estranged thing over man becomes manifest. The rule of the person over the person now becomes the universal rule of the *thing* over the *person*, the product over the producer. Just as the *equivalent*, value, contained the determination of the alienation of private property, so now we see that *money* is the sensuous, corporeal existence of that *alienation*. (EW: 270)

In *Capital*, III, Marx writes in very similar vein about

> that inversion [*Verkehrung*] of subject and object which already occurs in the course of the production process itself. We saw in that case how all the subjective productive forces of labour present themselves as productive forces of capital. On the one hand, value, ie the past labour that dominates living labour, is personified into the capitalist; on the other hand, the worker conversely appears as mere objectified labour power, as a commodity. (*C*III: 136)

There is, as we shall see, a lot more going on in the later passage, but the continuity with the earlier one is also evident. Roman Rosdolsky even comments on the 'Notes on Mill': 'All the elements of the later theory of commodity [fetishism] are present here, even if they appear in philosophical guise'.[47] This can't be exactly right, since, as we have seen, Marx didn't accept the labour theory of value in the earlier text, while the theory is presupposed by the distinction between living and dead labour in the later one (for more on this distinction see chapter 4). Nevertheless, the resonances are indeed striking. Another recurring preoccupation is with Chapter XXVI of Ricardo's *Principles*, 'On Gross and Net Revenue'. Here Ricardo criticises Adam Smith for arguing that a country's wealth is a function of its gross revenue:

> Provided its net real income, its rent and profits be the same, it is of no importance whether the nation consist of ten or of twelve millions of inhabitants, its power of supporting fleets and armies, and all species of unproductive labour, must be in proportion to its net, and not its gross income. If five millions of men could produce as much food and clothing as was necessary for ten millions, food and clothing for the five millions would be the net revenue. Would it be of any advantage to the country, that to produce this same net revenue, seven millions

---

47 Roman Rosdolsky, *The Making of Marx's Capital* (London, 1977), p128.

of men should be required, that is to say, that seven millions should be employed to produce food and clothing sufficient for twelve millions? The food and clothing of five millions would still be the net revenue. The employing a greater number of men would enable us neither to add a man to our army and navy, nor to contribute one guinea more to taxes. (*R*, I: 348)

Ricardo is here targeting the idea, with which his predecessors (David Hume as well as Smith) had struggled, that a state's prosperity (and hence its power) was a function of the size of its population. The passage fascinated Marx. In the 1844 *Manuscripts* it was evidence of political economy's indifference to human beings: 'For Ricardo men are nothing, the product everything' (*EW*: 306). In an article of March 1853 Ricardo is described as regarding '"Net Revenue" as the Moloch to whom entire populations must be sacrificed' (*CW*11: 531). But by the time of the *Economic Manuscript of 1861-63* his attitude towards Ricardo had become more charitable: 'Ricardo expressed these tendencies [towards maximising profitability] consistently and ruthlessly. Hence much howling against him on the part of the philanthropic philistines' (*CW*32: 175). As is made even clearer in *Capital*, III, by the 1860s Marx is now praising Ricardo for what he had earlier criticised him for:

> What other people reproach him for, ie that he is unconcerned with 'human beings' and concentrates exclusively on the development of the productive forces when considering capitalist production—whatever sacrifices of human beings and capital *values* this is bought with—is precisely his significant contribution. The development of the productive forces of social labour is capital's historic mission and justification. (*C*III: 368)

### In what sense is *Capital* unfinished?

So even when there is an apparent continuity of preoccupation in Marx's economic writings, closer attention suggests the discontinuities are more important—not, perhaps, with respect to the basic understanding of human nature and history than he developed in the mid-1840s, but certainly in the theoretical development of his critique of political economy. The same sense of a project constantly undergoing reconstruction is evident when we consider what may seem like a silly question: in what sense is *Capital* unfinished? It seems silly because Marx died before he had published more than the first volume, and Engels finishes *Capital*, III, with a note that the manuscript had broken off at this point. As Althusser rather melodramatically puts it, 'the reader will know how Volume Three ends. A title: *Classes*. Forty lines, then silence'.[48]

But there is a bigger problem, which concerns how precisely Marx conceived *Capital* itself. No sooner had he started on the *Grundrisse* than he started sketching out a plan of the work of which it would be the basis:

> The order obviously has to be (1) the general, abstract determinants which obtain in more or less all forms of society... (2) The categories which make up the inner structure of bourgeois society and on which the fundamental classes rest. Capital, wage labour, landed property. Their interrelation. Town and country. The three great social classes. Exchange between them. Circulation. Credit system (private). (3) Concentration of bourgeois society in the form of the state. Viewed in relation to itself. The 'unproductive' classes. Taxes. State debt. Public credit. The population. The colonies. Emigration. (4) The international relation of production. International division of labour. International exchange. Export and import. Rate of exchange. (5) The world market and crises. (*G*: 108)

A littler later Marx comes up with another version of this plan, where he drops the initial discussion of 'the general, abstract determinants', but considerably elaborates on his projected analysis of capital (in the process showing the influence that Hegel's *Logic* was having on him at this stage):

> < I. (1) General concept of capital.—(2) Particularity of capital: circulating capital, fixed capital. (Capital as the necessaries of life, as raw material, as instrument of labour.) (3) Capital as money. II. (1) *Quantity of capital. Accumulation.* (2) *Capital measured by itself. Profit. Interest. Value of capital:* ie capital as distinct from itself as interest and profit. (3) *The circulation of capitals.* (α) Exchange of capital and capital. Exchange of capital with revenue. Capital and *prices*. (β) *Competition of capitals*. (γ) *Concentration of capitals*. III. Capital as credit. IV. Capital as share capital. V. *Capital as money market*. VI. Capital as source of wealth. The capitalist. After capital, landed property would be dealt with. After that, wage labour. All three presupposed, *the movement of prices*, as circulation now defined in its inner totality. On the other side, the three classes, as production posited

---

48  Althusser, 'The Object of *Capital*', p193. See on the subject of this entire section, the highly informed study by Michael Krätke, '"Hier bricht das Manuskript ab" (Engels). Hat das *Kapital* einen Schluss?', *Beiträge zur Marx-Engels-Forschung. Neue Folge* (2001) and (2002).

in its three basic forms and presuppositions of circulation. *Then the state.* (State and bourgeois society.—Taxes, or the existence of the unproductive classes.—The state debt.—Population.—The state externally: colonies. External trade. Rate of exchange. Money as international coin.—Finally the world market. Encroachment of bourgeois society over the state. Crises. Dissolution of the mode of production and form of society based on exchange value. Real positing of individual labour as social and vice versa.)> (*G*: 264)

A slightly later revision of what Marx will come to think of as the first 'book' on capital shows his concepts settling on a more definitive shape, still Hegelian in form: both capital in general and capital as a totality are organised as the Hegelian triad of universal-particular-singular:

> '*Capital.* I. *Generality*: (1) (a) Emergence of capital out of money. (b) Capital and labour (mediating itself through *alien* labour). (c) The elements of capital, dissected according to their relation to labour (Product. Raw material. Instrument of labour.) (2) *Particularization of capital*: (a) Capital circulant, capital fixe. Turnover of capital. (3) *The singularity of capital*: Capital and profit. Capital and interest. Capital as *value*, distinct from itself as interest and profit. II. *Particularity*: (1) Accumulation of capitals. (2) Competition of capitals. (3) Concentration of capitals (quantitative distinction of capital as at same time qualitative, as measure of its size and influence). III. *Singularity*: (1) Capital as credit. (2) Capital as stock-capital. (3) Capital as money market. (G: 275)

In the three parts of '*Capital.* I. *Generality*' in this plan, we can roughly discern the beginnings of the three volumes of *Capital* devoted respectively to production, circulation, and the unity of production and circulation. Marx outlined a boiled down version of the overall structure roughed out in the *Grundrisse* in a letter to Lassalle of 22 February 1858: 'The whole is divided into 6 books: 1. On Capital (contains a few introductory *Chapters*). 2. On Landed Property. 3. On Wage Labour. 4. On the State. 5. International Trade. 6. World Market' (*CW*50: 270). Marx set out exactly the same structure in the Preface to *A Contribution to the Critique of Political Economy*, published with Lassalle's help the following year. Table 2, drawn up by Oakley, gives a helpful overview of Marx's plan for his critique of political economy at this stage (see also his letter to Engels, 2 April 1858 [*CW*50: 297]). So, when he finally came to write *Capital* between 1863 and 1867, did Marx stick by this 'six-book plan'? If he did, then *Capital* is a mere fragment of a vast and unfinished work—and indeed necessarily unfinished since, as David Harvey puts it, 'Marx would have had to become Methuselah to have completed this gargantuan project'.[49] Dussel argues that Marx 'only *began* his theory and it was *unfinished* upon publication of the first of the three projected parts (which represented only 1/72 of his total project'.[50]

**Table 2**

*Marx's Planned Critique of Political Economy (1858-9)*

> BOOK I: CAPITAL
> Part 1: Capital in general
>> Chapter 1: The commodity
>> Chapter 2: Money
>> Chapter 3: Capital
>>> Section 1: Production process of capital
>>> 1: Transformation of money into capital
>>> 2: Absolute surplus value
>>> 3: Relative surplus value
>>> 4: Original accumulation
>>> 5: Wage labour and capital
>>> 6: Appearance of the law of accumulation in simple circulation
>>> Section 2: Circulation process of capital
>>> Section 3: Capital and profit
> Part 2: Competition of capitals
> Part 3: Credit as capital
> Part 4: Share capital
> BOOK II: LANDED PROPERTY
> BOOK III: WAGE LABOUR
> BOOK IV: THE STATE
> BOOK V: FOREIGN TRADE
> BOOK VI: WORLD MARKET AND CRISES

*Source*: Allen Oakley, *Marx's Critique of Political Economy* (2 vols, London, 1984), I, p159.

Maximilien Rubel goes even further, treating the six-book plan as the realisation of the 'Economics' Marx conceived in the mid-1840s. Indeed, *The German Ideology*, *The Poverty of Philosophy*, and the *Communist Manifesto* 'were, broadly speaking, part of the "Economics"'. According to Rubel, in the first of the plans in the *Grundrisse*:

---

49  David Harvey, *A Companion to Marx's **Capital**, Volume 2* (London, 2013), p384.
50  Dussel, *Towards an Unknown Marx*, p211.

we have the logical and dialectical structure of a plan that was never subjected to further modification except in several points of detail and was
ultimately fixed as a double triad of rubrics with a rigorous and definitive
order. Marx was, consequently, committed both morally and scientifically
to fulfil the established schema; and it was in this spirit that he described
his plan when informing his closest friends of its concretisation.[51]

Rubel contends that the reason why Marx left the six-book plan
unrealised was that the initial book on capital simply proved far too long
for him to complete his project. But Rubel relies on assertion rather than
argument to support this interpretation. Michael Lebowitz, who agrees
that Marx never abandoned the six-book plan, concedes: 'Even the most
sympathetic reader must conclude, however, that Rubel failed to *prove*
his case'.[52] The alternative view is put most powerfully by Rosdolsky, who
argues that Marx found himself in the *1861-63 Manuscript* increasingly
dealing with material—for example, competition and landed property,
that was supposed to be excluded from the analysis of 'capital in general'
to which the manuscript was devoted. Therefore, in 1864-5 he modified
the six-book plan, absorbing the content of the books on landed property and wage labour into, respectively, *Capital*, III, Part 6, on ground
rent, and *Capital*, I, Part 6, on wages. What about the final three books,
on the state, international trade, and the world market? According to
Rosdolsky, 'they were never really "abandoned". That is to say, their subject matter was never fully assimilated into the second structure of the
work but rather held back for the "eventual continuation" itself'.[53]

At issue in these disagreements is in part a question of method. Even
if we leave aside Rubel's claim that Marx's theoretical writings from *The
German Ideology* onwards are all instalments of the 'Economics', there is

---

51  Joseph O'Malley and Keith Algozin, eds, *Rubel on Karl Marx* (Cambridge, 1981), pp127, 207.

52  Michael A Lebowitz, *Beyond **Capital**: Marx's Political Economy of the Working Class* (2nd
    edn; Basingstoke, 2003), p29. Lebowitz by contrast does offer arguments, but these
    represent a substantive critique of the limits of Marx's critique of political economy that I
    touch on in chapter 5 below.

53  Rosdolsky, *The Making of Marx's **Capital***, p23; see generally, ch 2, which summarises the
    debates among early 20th century Marxists about Marx's plans. Michael Heinrich takes a
    broadly similar line to Rosdolsky, though he dates the shift in Marx's plans to 1863-4:
    'Reconstruction or Deconstruction? Methodological Controversies about Value and
    Capital, and New Insights from the Critical Edition', in Bellofiore and Fineschi, eds,
    *Rereading Marx*, pp82-83. Daniel Bensaïd suggests that the 1857 plan represents 'an
    intermediary stage [in the move from the historical to the logical order of presentation]
    where the structural primacy of production remains obscured by the classical analysis of
    the factors of production. Thus the three first books announced relate to Capital, to Land,
    and to Labour. The moments of the total process are still conceived in relation to these
    factors;' *La Discordance des temps* (Paris, 1995), p17.

something problematic about the assumption that the vast cycle of writing spread over nearly 20 years from the *Grundrisse* to the French edition of *Capital*, I, are realisations of a plan formulated in the early pages of the former text. Such an interpretation leaves no space for the creative process in which Marx confronts problems, lets his pen do his thinking for him by working them through on paper, and then reformulates categories and theories. As Regina Roth puts it, 'revision was one of the main characteristics of Marx's working style'.[54] There is no reason why this process of constant self-criticism should have spared Marx's overall conception of the structure of his work any more than it did specific concepts. This doesn't mean that we can assume that Marx abandons the six-book plan, merely that his persisting with it must be demonstrated. (These criticisms apply with equal force to Harvey's use of another passage from the *Grundrisse*, which I discussed in the Introduction.)

Developing an understanding of the theoretical recastings through which Marx's analysis develops is impeded by a tendency to treat the *Grundrisse* as the standard by which his subsequent theoretical development is to be judged. Sometimes this involves treating the later manuscripts, and especially *Capital*, as vulgarisations of the more 'critical' and Hegelian *Grundrisse*, a view especially prevalent in 'etherealist' readings of Marx's value theory.[55] I have more to say about this in later chapters, but let me express now my preference for the approach adopted by Jacques Bidet:

> Unlike other commentators, I do not seek the 'truth' of *Capital* in the earlier versions. I hold that Marx works like an ordinary researcher, never producing a new version except because of the insufficiency of its predecessor with respect to the project he was pursuing, and under no obligation to explain to himself the reasons for the changes to which he proceeds.[56]

Following this path, we can see how, across successive manuscripts, Marx increasingly incorporates into his conceptualisation of 'capital in general' topics that were originally meant to be covered in later books. This is clear in two plans that he wrote in January 1863 as part of the *1861-63 Manuscript*:

---

54 Roth, 'Karl Marx's Original Manuscripts in the Marx-Engels-Gesamtausgabe (MEGA)', p33.
55 For example, Hans-Georg Backhaus, 'On the Dialectics of the Value Form', *Thesis Eleven*, 1 (1980). See also Roberto Fineschi, 'Dialectic of the Commodity and its Exposition: The German Debate of the 1970s—A Personal Survey', in Bellofiore and Fineschi, eds, *Rereading Marx*. Toni Negri offers a strongly anti-Hegelian version of this argument in *Marx beyond Marx* (South Hadley, MA, 1984).
56 Jacques Bidet, *Explication et reconstruction du Capital* (Paris, 2004), p11.

//The third section 'Capital and Profit' to be divided in the following way: 1) Conversion of surplus value into profit. Rate of profit as distinguished from rate of surplus value. 2) Conversion of profit into average profit. Formation of the general rate of profit. Transformation of values into prices of production. 3) Adam Smith's and Ricardo's theories on profits and prices of production. 4) *Rent.* (Illustration of the difference between value and price of production. 5) History of the so-called Ricardian law of rent. 6) Law of the fall of the rate of profit. Adam Smith, Ricardo, Carey. 7) Theories of profit. Query: whether Sismondi and Malthus should also be included in the *Theories of Surplus Value*, 8) Division of profit into industrial profit and interest. Mercantile capital. Money capital. 9) Revenue **and its sources.** The question of the relation between the processes of production and distribution also to be included here. 10) **Reflux** movements of money in the processes of capitalist production as a whole. 11) Vulgar economy. 12) *Conclusion. 'Capital and wage labour'. //*...

//The first section '*Production Process of Capital*' to be divided in the following way: 1) Introduction. Commodity. Money. 2) Transformation of money into capital. 3) *Absolute surplus value.* (a) Labour process and valorization process. (b) Constant capital and variable capital. (c) Absolute surplus value. (d) Struggle for the normal working day. (c) *Simultaneous working days* (number of simultaneously employed labourers). Amount of surplus value and rate of surplus value (magnitude and height?). 4) *Relative surplus value.* (a) Simple cooperation. (b) Division of labour. (c) Machinery, etc. 5) Combination of absolute and relative surplus value. Relation (proportion) between wage labour and surplus value. Formal and real subsumption of labour under capital. Productivity of capital. Productive and unproductive labour. 6) Reconversion of surplus value into capital. Primitive accumulation. Wakefield's theory of colonisation. 7) *Result of the production process.* Either *sub* 6) or *sub* 7) the **change** in the form of the **law of appropriation** can be shown. 8) Theories of surplus value. 9) Theories of productive and unproductive labour.// (*CW*33: 346-347)

These plans correspond relatively closely to, respectively, the draft of *Capital*, III, in the *1863-5 Manuscript* and *Capital*, I, as it finally appeared (plus 'The Results of the Immediate Process of Production', and minus Part 6, 'Wages'). Among the notable changes here is Marx's decision to replace the discussion of the commodity and money in the 1859 *Contribution* (the *1861-63 Manuscript* had been conceived as the continuation of the *Contribution*) with a new treatment. But the inclusion of subsequently abandoned parts on 'Theories of profit' and Theories of surplus value' show that Marx was still following the model of combining substantive exposition with critique of the political economists that we find in the *Contribution*. The plan for 'Capital and Profit' (Section 3 of the 'Chapter' on 'Capital' in the plans of 1857-9) includes treatments of interest and rent that go beyond what Marx had initially envisaged for his analysis of 'capital in general'. This change in all likelihood was a consequence of his grappling with Ricardo's theory of rent in the *1861-63 Manuscript*. As noted above and explored further in chapter 2, this involved a decisive development of Marx's value theory with the formulation of the concept of price of production, which is also now included in 'Capital and Profit'. But this concept itself makes reference to a topic that Marx had initially excluded from the analysis of capital in general, namely competition between capitals, which brings about the equalisation of the rate of profit on which the transformation of values into prices of production depends.

Further evidence that Marx was moving away from the six-book plan is provided by a slightly earlier letter to Ludwig Kugelmann of 28 December 1862:

> I was delighted to see from your letter how warm an interest is taken by you and your friends in my critique of political economy... It is a sequel to Part I [*Contribution to the Critique of Political Economy*], but will appear on its own under the title *Capital*, with *A Contribution to the Critique of Political Economy* as merely the subtitle. In fact, all it comprises is what was to make the third chapter of the first part, namely 'Capital in General'. Hence it includes neither the competition between capitals nor the credit system. What *Englishmen* call '**The Principles of Political Economy**' is contained in this volume. It is the quintessence (together with the first part), and the development of the sequel (with the exception, perhaps, of the relationship between the various forms of state and the various economic structures of society) could easily be pursued by others on the basis thus provided. (*CW*41: 435)[57]

---

57  Rubel cites this letter as evidence that Marx 'reserved for himself the whole of the second triad; in other words, the rubrics on the state, foreign commerce, and the world market!', *Rubel on Karl Marx*, p198. But Marx makes no mention of these topics, apart from his intriguing reference to 'the relationship between the various forms of state and the various economic structures of society'. A little later in the same letter he writes: 'I am going either to write the sequel in German, ie to conclude the presentation of capital, competition and credit, or condense the first two books [the 1859 *Contribution* and a revised version of the *1861-63 Manuscript*] for *English* consumption into one work. I do not think we can count

Marx is certainly here retreating from the idea of completing the six-book plan himself. But the letter is also evidence of how much his ideas about his project were in flux: thus he still envisages *Capital* as a continuation of the *Contribution*, an idea he seems to have abandoned a few weeks later. And he still proposes to exclude competition and credit. This remains his official position in the *1863-5 Manuscript*. Thus he writes at the beginning of what becomes the section on 'Revaluation and Devaluation of Capital; Release and Tying Up of Capital' in *Capital*, III, Chapter 6:

> The phenomena that we study in this § require for their full development the credit system and competition on the world market, which is always the basis of the capitalist mode of production, [and] which in any case they need as their sphere of action. But these—more concrete forms of capitalist production 1) can only be depicted after the general nature of capital is understood and 2) are outside scope of our work and belong to its possible continuation. Nonetheless, the phenomena referred to in the heading of this § can be treated here in general. (*MEGA²* II/4.2: 178)

As Heinrich points out, Engels inserted the word 'comprehensively' before 'depicted' when editing *Capital*, III (*CIII*: 205).[58] But, once again, one appreciates Engels's problem. Marx simultaneously excludes credit and competition from the scope of *Capital*, and then immediately goes on to discuss them; he does this on a much larger scale in his exploration of the 'confusion' surrounding financial markets in Volume III, Part 5. This reflects, it seems to me, an ambivalence about what to cover in *Capital* that is quite systematic. In part this is because of the increasing analytical importance of competition, a subject to which I return in chapter 3. But it is worth noting that the process in which the construction of *Capital* progressively devours content reserved for the later parts of the six-book plan continues into Volume I. Thus the state, international trade and the world market figure heavily in chapter 31, which, under the apparently technical title of 'Genesis of the Industrial Capitalist', gives an astonishingly powerful account of the process of primitive accumulation that includes inter-state wars, the colonial system, credit, banking, taxation, and slavery—all methods relying on 'the power of the state, the concentrated and organised force of society

---

on its having any effect in Germany until it has been given the seal of approval abroad' (*CW*41: 436). This indicates only that that Marx was maintaining the option (but only the option) of completing the first 'book' of the 1858-9 plan.

58  Heinrich, 'Engels's Edition of the Third Volume of *Capital*', pp461-462.

[*die Staatsmacht, die konzentrierte und organisierte Gewalt der Gesellschaft*]' (*CI*: 916, MI: 703). Moreover, in the French edition of *Capital*, I, the treatment of the industrial reserve army and the business cycle in chapter 25 ('The General Law of Capital Accumulation'), section 3, is substantially extended to include material on the world market and colonialism.[59]

Thus, as Oakley puts it, 'the *tendency* was for the scope of *Capital* per se to increase. The ultimate significance of this tendency is unclear.' He elaborates on this judgement thus:

> There are some indications that Marx intended *Capital* to present a self-contained and self-sufficient exposition of his critical theories. The reorganisation of the categories treated relative to his original plans seem [sic] to have been directed towards that end. This is qualified by the suggestion that such self-sufficiency represented an intellectual compromise relative to the ideal of a much larger work such as the Six-Book project. There can be no doubt that *Capital* as it was left by Marx was unfinished. And it is not clear just what the finished work would have included. In this respect, at least, the status of the work as it was eventually published must be assessed with caution. This difficulty is compounded by the lack of any definitive evidence as to how Marx ultimately perceived the work.[60]

This seems a shrewd assessment of the uncertainties surrounding the shape Marx sought to give his critique of political economy, and all the more remarkable because Oakley made it in the early 1980s, before even the full version of the *1861-63 Manuscript* had been published, let alone all the other material that has issued from the *MEGA²* cottage industry. Oakley's overall judgement is that '*Capital is an unfinished climax to an ambiguous critico-theoretical project of uncertain dimensions.* It certainly cannot legitimately be read as a definitive or axiomatic statement of Marx's critical theory'.[61] So once again *Capital* appears like a mirage, shimmering without any definite shape. And once again this seems to go too far.

*Capital* is certainly unfinished, not simply in the literal sense but also because of the uncertainties about Marx's overall plan of his critique of

---

59  See Lucia Pradella, *L'attualità del **Capitale**: Accumulazione e impoverimento nel capitalismo globale* (Padua, 2010), and 'Imperialism and Capitalist Development in Marx's Capital', *Historical Materialism*, 21.2 (2013), and Anderson, *Marx at the Margins*, ch 5.

60  Allen Oakley, *The Making of Marx's Critical Theory: A Bibliographical Analysis* (London, 1983), pp110, 115.

61  Oakley, *The Making of Marx's Critical Theory*, p4.

political economy. And it can't be described as 'a definitive...statement of Marx's critical theory', if only because he never stopped working on it (it's not clear what form an 'axiomatic statement' of the theory would take). But that doesn't explain why we should think that Marx's project is 'ambiguous', which suggests some deep and inherent inconsistency. Marx's theory may be internally contradictory or indeed empirically false, but this needs demonstration, which Oakley doesn't offer. The multiplicity of unfinished manuscripts and Marx's shifting plans might suggest that the resulting theory is indeterminate. But this again needs to be shown. Some of what I have called the 'etherealist' readings of *Capital* with which I will engage in subsequent chapters point in such a direction.

It seems clear that Marx's own protracted labours—from the summer of 1857 till the early 1880s—were a struggle simultaneously for greater theoretical determinacy and deeper empirical scope. He sought to give greater precision to the categories that he formulated and the theories that he used them to state. Of course, in various cases, he left problems unresolved, but the overall theory of the capitalist mode of production that he wrought had taken a definite shape in the course of the 1860s that Marx doesn't seem to have subsequently abandoned (see, for example, his letter to Engels of 30 April 1868: *CW*43: 20-6). Stavros Tombazos puts it well: 'By saying that it [*Capital*] is "complete", we are simply observing that its categories are sufficiently articulated in order to criticise their critiques, more than a century after Marx's death'.[62] The importance that he attributed to *Capital* is indicated by the ever greater material that he incorporated in it—not merely what has preoccupied us in this section, the topics reserved for later sections of the six-book plan, but also the empirical data that would allow him to offer an analysis of the capitalist mode of production as a global system.[63] This achievement was, in multiple senses, incomplete—in large part because of Marx's inability to let go and an accumulation of new empirical material as relentless and unending as that of capital itself. But we shouldn't therefore lose sight amid the manuscripts of its grandeur and of the conceptual architecture that sustains it. Let us then turn to examining this architecture.

62  Stavros Tombazos, *Time in Marx: The Categories of Time in Marx's Capital* (Leiden, 2014), p312.

63  The global nature of the object of Capital is one of the main themes of Pradella, *L'attualità del Capitale*: see esp 'Introduzione' and ch III; see also chapter 7 below.

# 2

# Method, I: Ricardo

## The logic of *Capital*

Hegel casts a long shadow over *Capital*. This is obvious to anyone sampling the *Grundrisse*, a text impregnated with Hegelian terminology. But Hegel's presence in *Capital* itself was obvious to perceptive commentators who lacked the benefit of having read the earlier manuscripts of Marx's critique of political economy. Most famously, while studying Hegel's *Science of Logic* during the First World War, Lenin wrote: '*Aphorism*: it is impossible completely to understand Marx's *Capital*, and especially its first chapter, without having thoroughly studied and understood the *whole* of Hegel's *Logic*. Consequently, half a century later none of the Marxists understood Marx!'[1] From a rather different intellectual and political perspective, Karl Löwith shrewdly noted of Marx in 1941: 'How well-schooled he is in Hegel is shown less by his early writings referring directly to Hegel, which were influenced by Feuerbach, than by *Das Kapital*. The analyses in this work, although far removed from Hegel in content, are unthinkable without the incorporation of Hegel's method of reducing a phenomenon to a notion'.[2]

As both Lenin and Löwith recognise, the critical issue in Marx's relation to Hegel concerns the method the former employs in *Capital*. Lenin expressed this in another famous remark: 'If Marx did not leave behind him a "Logic" (with a capital letter), he did leave the *logic of Capital*'.[3] As we have already noted, Hegel's role as the source of Marx's method in *Capital* is the main theme of the contemporary Marxist school committed to systematic dialectics. A preoccupation with his own method, and

---

1    V I Lenin, *Collected Works* (50 vols, Moscow, 1961), 38: 180. For discussions of Lenin's reading of Hegel, see Louis Althusser, 'Lenin before Hegel', in *Lenin and Philosophy and Other Essays* (London, 1971), Michael Löwy, 'From the "Logic" of Hegel to the Finland Station', in Löwy, *Changing the World* (Atlantic Highlands NJ, 1993), and Stathis Kouvelakis, 'Lenin as Reader of Hegel', in Sebastian Budgen et al, eds, *Lenin Reloaded* (Durham, 2007).
2    Karl Löwith, *From Hegel to Nietzsche* (London, 1965), p92.
3    Lenin, *Collected Works*, 38: 319.

in particular with the proper construction and ordering of categories, certainly runs throughout Marx's economic manuscripts. But fully to understand this method requires us to cast the net wider than Hegel. In a brilliant passage Gramsci brushes aside the conventional account of the three sources of Marxism ('English' political economy, French socialism, and German philosophy): 'One could say in a sense, I think, that the philosophy of praxis equals Hegel plus David Ricardo.' Gramsci's focus is on what he regards as Ricardo's innovation in developing the 'the formal logical principle of the "law of tendency"', but his intuition admits of wider application.[4] Marx forges his own method in dialogue with both Hegel and Ricardo—the latter very explicitly, especially in the *1861-63 Manuscript*, the former usually more tacitly, though we will shortly encounter his more explicit discussions.[5] Across successive drafts, he widens his distance from both as he forges a distinctive and original synthesis of his own.

Though it is hard to separate any of the three partners to this complex intellectual dance, in this chapter I focus on Marx's relationship with Ricardo, in the next on his struggle to use but also to surmount Hegel. The structure of the present chapter is as follows. I start off presenting the problem of Hegel's influence on Marx's conception of his own method. I then argue that Marx's resort to Hegel can only be understood in the context of his problem situation when writing the *Grundrisse* and the *1861-63 Manuscript* in particular, namely to overcome the limitations of Ricardo's value theory. This requires consideration of Ricardo's own historical and theoretical context, which then allows us to understand how Marx sought to transcend Ricardian value theory—in particular by developing the transformation of values into prices of production. This involved him developing a different conception of the relationship between abstract and concrete levels of analysis from what he found in Ricardo. The chapter concludes with Evald Ilyenkov's suggestion that Marx's critique of Ricardo bears analogies to Hegel's critique of Spinoza—a conclusion that sets the scene for the full-on discussion of Hegel in chapter 3.

One of the earliest parts of the *Grundrisse*, the so-called 1857 Introduction, involves a celebrated discussion of method:

---

4   Antonio Gramsci, *Selections from the Prison Notebooks* (London, 1971), pp400, 401. Gramsci's main economic writings appear in English in *Further Selections from the Prison Notebooks* (London, 1995), pp161-277, 428-435. See the excellent discussion in Michael Krätke, 'Antonio Gramsci's Contribution to a Critical Economics', *Historical Materialism*, 19:3 (2011).

5   Interestingly, in November 1850, Marx and Engels bracket Hegel and Ricardo together as representatives of 'unfeeling thinking' with a sense for 'development and struggle' (*CW*10: 530).

It seems to be correct to begin with the real and the concrete, with the real precondition, thus to begin, in economics, with eg the population, which is the foundation and the subject of the entire social act of production. However, on closer examination this proves false. The population is an abstraction if I leave out, for example, the classes of which it is composed. These classes in turn are an empty phrase if I am not familiar with the elements on which they rest. Eg wage labour, capital, etc. These latter in turn presuppose exchange, division of labour, prices, etc. For example, capital is nothing without wage labour, without value, money, price etc. Thus, if I were to begin with the population, this would be a chaotic representation (*Vorstellung*) of the whole, and I would then, by means of further determination, move analytically towards ever more simple concepts (*Begriff*), from the imagined concrete towards ever thinner abstractions until I had arrived at the simplest determinations. From there the journey would have to be retraced until I had finally arrived at the population again, but this time not as the chaotic conception of a whole, but as a rich totality of many determinations and relations. The former is the path historically followed by economics at the time of its origins. The economists of the seventeenth century, eg, always begin with the living whole, with population, nation, state, several states, etc; but they always conclude by discovering through analysis a small number of determinant, abstract, general relations such as division of labour, money, value, etc. As soon as these individual moments had been more or less firmly established and abstracted, there began the economic systems, which ascended from the simple relations, such as labour, division of labour, need, exchange value, to the level of the state, exchange between nations and the world market. The latter is obviously the scientifically correct method. The concrete is concrete because it is the concentration of many determinations, hence unity of the diverse. It appears in the process of thinking, therefore, as a process of concentration, as a result, not as a point of departure, even though it is the point of departure in reality and hence also the point of departure for observation (*Anschauung*) and conception. Along the first path the full conception was evaporated to yield an abstract determination; along the second, the abstract determinations led towards a reproduction of the concrete by way of thought. In this way Hegel fell into the illusion of conceiving the real as the product of thought concentrating itself, probing its own depths, and unfolding itself out of itself, by itself, whereas the method of rising from the abstract to the concrete is only the way in which thought appropriates the concrete, reproduces it as the concrete in the mind. But this is by no means the process by which the concrete itself comes into being. (*G*: 100-101; translation modified)

The meaning of this passage has been much disputed by commentators, but it seems clear enough to me.[6] Marx rejects an inductive movement from concrete particulars to abstract generalisations, preferring instead 'the method of rising from the abstract to the concrete' as 'the scientifically correct method'. It is interesting that he should take such care to differentiate this method from that of Hegel, since 'the progression' in the *Science of Logic* has been described also as one 'from the abstract to the concrete'.[7] According to Mark Meaney, 'the entire [1857] introduction is indebted for its logical structure to the final chapters' of the *Logic*.[8] And Hegel does indeed towards the end of the *Logic* present first analytic cognition, which reduces a given content to concepts, and then synthetic cognition, which seeks to integrate these concepts in a unity. But he also argues that both suffer from the limitation that their content is external to them: this is only overcome in the Absolute Idea, where 'the method has resulted as the *absolutely self-knowing concept* [*Begriff*], as the *concept that has* the absolute, both as subjective and objective, *as its subject matter*, and consequently as the pure correspondence of the concept and reality'. Hegel goes on to elaborate that 'what is to be considered as method here is only the movement of the *concept* itself...; but it now has...the added significance that the *concept is all, and that its movement is the universal absolute activity*, the self-determining and self-realising movement' (*GL*: 737).[9]

Marx's eagerness to dissociate himself from exactly this idea of a self-moving concept is made clear when he goes on, shortly after the passage cited, to say:

to the kind of consciousness—and this is characteristic of the philosophical consciousness—for which conceptual thinking is the real human

---

6    See the detailed interrogations of the 1857 Introduction in Stuart Hall, 'Marx's Notes on Method: A "Reading" of the "1857 Introduction",' *Cultural Studies*, 17:2 (2003), and Derek Sayer, *Marx's Method: Ideology, Science, and Critique in* **Capital** (Hassocks, 1979).

7    George di Giovanni, 'Introduction', to G W F Hegel, *The Science of Logic* (Cambridge, 2010), pxxxv.

8    Mark E Meaney, *Capital as Organic Unity: The Role of Hegel's* **Science of Logic** *in Marx's* **Grundrisse** (Dordrecht, 2002), p170; see generally Meaney, ch 7.

9    '*Begriff*' has usually been rendered as 'notion' by Hegel's English translators; George di Giovanni's new edition of the *Science of Logic* instead translates it as 'concept', which not only makes Hegel's argument easier to understand but also it makes the resonances with Marx's use of the term in *Capital* easier to spot. See the entry 'concept' in Michael Inwood, *A Hegel Dictionary* (Oxford, 1992), pp58-61.

being, and for which the conceptual world as such is thus the only reality, the movement of the categories appears as the real act of production—which only, unfortunately, receives a jolt from the outside—whose product is the world; and—but this is again a tautology—this is correct in so far as the concrete totality is a totality of thoughts, concrete in thought, in fact a product of thinking and comprehending; but not in any way a product of the concept which thinks and generates itself outside or above observation and conception; a product, rather, of the working-up of observation and conception into concepts. The totality as it appears in the head, as a totality of thoughts, is a product of a thinking head, which appropriates the world in the only way it can, a way different from the artistic, religious, practical and mental appropriation of this world. The real subject retains its autonomous existence outside the head just as before; namely as long as the head's conduct is merely speculative, merely theoretical. Hence, in the theoretical method, too, the subject, society, must always be kept in mind as the presupposition. (*G*: 102-3)

So the 'concrete in thought', the result of the process of 'rising from the abstract to the concrete', must be kept distinct from its 'presupposition', 'the real subject', namely 'society'.[10] As soon as he talks about method, Marx seeks to distance himself from Hegel. One might see this as an example of what Harold Bloom calls 'the anxiety of influence'.[11] We can see the same oscillation between tacit reference and explicit rejection in *Capital* itself. Thus, as Jairus Banaji has noted,

the entire process by which the concrete is reproduced in thought as something rationally comprehended is described in places by Marx as the 'dialectical development' of the 'concept' of capital, and all moments within this movement which are derivable as essential determinations, including, of course, the forms of appearance, no matter how illusory they are, count as moments (forms, relations) 'corresponding to their concept'.[12]

Some examples may bring this out: '*M'* thus appears as a sum of values which is internally differentiated, undergoes a functional (conceptual) differentiation, and expresses the capital relation [*So erscheint G' als in sich differenzierte, sich funktionell (begrifflich) in sich selbst*

---

10   See the extensive discussion of this passage by Althusser in 'On the Materialist Dialectic', in *For Marx* (London, 1970).

11   Harold Bloom, *The Anxiety of Influence: A Theory of Poetry* (2nd edn; Oxford, 1997).

12   Jairus Banaji, 'From the Commodity to Capital: Hegel's Dialectic in Marx's *Capital*', in Diane Elson, ed, *Value: The Representation of Labour in Capitalism* (London, 1979), p18.

*unterscheidende, das Kapitalverhältnis ausdrückende Wertsumme]*' (CII: 128). Or again: 'In a general analysis of the present kind, it is assumed that actual conditions correspond to their concept [*dass die wirklichen Verhältnisse ihren Begriff entsprechen]*.' (CIII: 242) 'It is in fact this divorce between the conditions of labour on the one hand and the producers on the other that forms the concept of capital [*die den Begriff des Kapitals bildet]*' (CIII: 354). Correlatively, externalised and fetishised relations such as those in the money markets are described as 'concept-less (*begrifflos*)'—a usage that is not always captured in the English translations of *Capital*. So take this passage from Volume III: 'In *M–M'* we have the concept-less [*begrifflose*] form of capital, the inversion and objectification [*Verkehrung und Versachlichung*] of the relations of production, in its highest power' (CIII: 516; translation modified).

Now, of course, this language is pure Hegel: we have already seen the crowning role of *das Begriff* in the *Logic*, whose third and concluding book, after the Doctrines of Being and Essence, is devoted the Doctrine of the Concept. But how are we to interpret Marx's use of this language? The passage where he talks about the separation of the producers from the conditions of labour 'form[ing] the concept of capital' is particularly striking since this implies the kind of movement between concept and reality that Marx excludes in the 1857 Introduction. In an even more famous text, the 1873 Afterword to the 2nd German edition of *Capital*, where he gives his most exact account of his relationship with Hegel, Marx once again insists on the difference between concept and reality:

> My dialectical method is, in its foundation, not only different from the Hegelian, but exactly opposite to it. For Hegel, the process of thinking, which he even transforms into an independent subject, under the name of 'the Idea', is the creator of the real world, and the real world is only the external appearance of the idea. With me the reverse is true: the ideal is nothing but the material world reflected in the mind of man, and translated into forms of thought... The mystification which the dialectic suffers in Hegel's hands by no means prevents him from being the first to present its general forms of motion in a comprehensive and a conscious manner. With him it is standing on its head. It must be inverted, in order to discover the rational kernel within the mystical shell. (*CI*: 102-3)

The metaphors that Marx uses here to differentiate between the 'rational' and 'mystical' aspects of Hegel's dialectic haven't exactly found favour with commentators, who have also taken issue with the distinction Engels draws in 'Ludwig Feuerbach and the End of Classical German Philosophy' between 'the whole dogmatic content of the Hegelian system' and 'his dialectical method, which dissolves all that is dogmatic' (*CW*26: 361).[13] Engels's formulation in particular implies a distinction between form and content that Hegel is especially concerned to deny. For Hegel, 'the form is the indwelling process of the concrete content itself'.[14] The highest instantiation of this truth is the Absolute Idea itself, where, as we have seen, the distinction between method and external content is supposedly overcome. Marxist philosophers have tended to respond to the difficulty of separating method and system in one of two ways. First, like Althusser in *For Marx* and *Reading Capital*, one can argue that there is a fundamental difference between Hegel's and Marx's dialectic. The difficulty that this approach faces is the presence of Hegelian terminology in the work that Althusser identifies as the pinnacle of Marx's scientific achievement, namely *Capital* itself. Secondly, one can accept that there is a deep theoretical identity between the *Logic* and *Capital*. This is the course taken by the proponents of 'systematic dialectics', most boldly by Chris Arthur: 'Speaking for myself, I believe it is patent that the movement of the *Logic* is indeed that of the self-acting Idea... What we can see, however, is a striking *homology* between the structure of Hegel's *Logic* and Marx's *Capital*, or, at least, a homology given some minor reconstructive work on either or both'.[15] Remarkably, Althusser said something quite similar some 15 years after his initial intervention: 'The process which begins with the abstract to produce the concrete doesn't break with the Hegelian *Denkprozess* [thought process]. One can even say that, formally, this *Denkprozess* of concretization apes from afar the process of Hegel's *Logic*'.[16]

Neither option seems particularly palatable. Hegelian categories and themes plainly figure in *Capital*. But I take seriously Hegel's pronouncement that 'logic is to be understood as the system of pure reason, as the realm of pure thought. *This realm is truth unveiled, truth as it is in and for itself.* It can therefore be said that this content is *the exposition of God as he is in his eternal essence before the creation of nature and of a finite spirit.*' (*GL*, 29)[17] Marx was right to be anxious about Hegel's influence

---

13   See especially Louis Althusser, 'Contradiction and Overdetermination', in *For Marx*.
14   G W F Hegel, *The Phenomenology of Spirit* (Oxford, 1977), §56; p35 (translation modified).
15   Christopher J Arthur, *The New Dialectic and Marx's **Capital*** (Leiden, 2003), p7.
16   Louis Althusser, 'Avant-propos' to Gérard Duménil, *Le concept de loi économique dans 'Le Capital'* (Paris, 1978), p17.
17   See the discussion in Gérard Lebrun, *La patience du Concept: Essai sur le discours hégélien* (Paris, 1972), pp164-166, and more generally, ch III.

on him. The solution, as I argued in my doctoral thesis some 35 years ago, lies in recognising 'the ambiguity of the way in which Marx's categories function in *Capital*. For they both serve to enable Marx to conceptualise various relationships and constitute an obstacle to this conceptualisation'.[18] Remarkably and completely independently, Jacques Bidet (although with far greater erudition and acuity than I had achieved) undertook in the early 1980s

> a study based on a problematic of the '*epistemological support/obstacle*'. I mean by this that, from 1857 on, Marx's project of a theory of the capitalist social system sought expression with the aid of the method and figures of discourse of Hegelian philosophy, and that he found here a certain measure of support and a possibility of deployment, but at the same time an obstacle and cause of stagnation and confusions.[19]

What such an interpretive approach entails should become clearer in what follows. But it needs a point of orientation. In my view, Marx follows 'the method of rising from the abstract to the concrete' in *Capital*. In other words, he starts from highly abstract determinations (the commodity, money and capital) and from them develops (exactly how is a crucial issue discussed in chapter 3) more complex determinations, involving, for example, all the perplexities of entrepreneurial calculations, the money market, and real estate. Marx gives an important overview of this process at the beginning of *Capital*, III:

> In Volume I we investigated the phenomena exhibited by the *process of capitalist production*, taken by itself, ie the immediate [*unmittelbarer*] production process, in which connection all secondary influences external [*fremder*] to this process were left out of account. But this immediate production process does not exhaust the life cycle of capital. In the world as it actually is [*der wirchlichen Welt*], it is supplemented by the *process of circulation*, and this formed our object of investigation in the second volume. Here we showed, particularly in Part Three, where we considered the circulation process as it mediates the social production process, that the capitalist production process, taken as a whole, is a unity of the production and circulation processes. It cannot be the purpose of the present, third volume simply to make general reflections on this unity. Our concern is rather to discover and present the concrete

---

18   Alex Callinicos, 'The Logic of *Capital*' (DPhil Thesis, Oxford University, 1978), pp174-175. I draw on this dissertation at several points in this chapter and the following.

19   Jacques Bidet, *Exploring Marx's **Capital*** (Brill, 2007), p3.

forms which grow out of the *process of capital's movement considered as a whole*. In their actual movement, capitals confront one another in certain concrete forms, and, in relation to these, both the shape capital assumes in the immediate production process and its shape in the process of circulation appear merely as particular moments [*besondere Momente*]. The configurations [*Gestaltungen*] of capital, as developed in this volume, thus approach step by step the form in which they appear on the surface of society, in the action of the different capitals on one another, ie in competition, and in the everyday consciousness of the agents of production themselves. (CIII: 117)

In this context, it's worth saying something about the hares that have been started by the paragraph in the 1873 Afterword that immediately precedes the passage cited above:

Of course the method of presentation must differ in form from that of the inquiry [*Allerdings muß sich die Darstellungsweise formell von der Forschungsweise unterscheiden*]. The latter has to appropriate the material in detail, to analyse its different forms of development and to track down their inner connection [*innres Band*]. Only after this work has been done can the real movement be appropriately presented. If this is done successfully, if the life of the subject matter is now reflected back in the ideas, then it may appear as if we have before us an *a priori* construction. (CI: 102)

This remark underlines that Marx attaches great importance to ensuring that the 'real movement' is 'appropriately presented' through the proper ordering of well formulated categories, even though this carries the danger that this presentation may appear to be 'an *a priori* construction'. But some commentators have been encouraged by this passage to counterpose the method of inquiry to that of presentation, arguing that the former, conceived as an inductive moment from the concrete to the abstract, precedes the latter, the moment of moving from the abstract to the concrete proper. For example, Ernest Mandel writes: 'there is no doubt that Marx considered that the *empirical appropriation of the material* should precede the analytical process of cognition'.[20] Marx's journalism, notebooks and manuscripts, as well as *Capital* itself, reveal his strenuous efforts to record and interpret the empirical data of capitalist development. But it would be a concession to the idea (criticised by Hegel in the first chapter of the *Phenomenology of Spirit*, where he shows that

---

20   Ernest Mandel, *Late Capitalism* (London, 1975), p15.

the most unique case of 'sense-certainty' presupposes universal concepts) that the 'facts' present themselves to observation pre-conceptually, to accept the opposition of 'the *empirical appropriation of the material*' and 'the analytical process of cognition' that Mandel makes here. We see very clearly, notably in the *1861-63 Manuscript*, how the scrutiny of empirical patterns is bound up for Marx with the critique of pre-existing theories.

Ilyenkov puts it very well:

> The data of observation and conception were always interpreted by Marx as the entire mass of the socially accumulated empirical experiences, the entire colossal mass of empirical data available to the theoretician from books, reports, statistical tables, newspapers, and accounts. It stands to reason, however, that all these empirical data are stored in social memory in an abridged form, reduced to abstract expression. They are expressed in speech, in terminology, in figures, tables, and other abstract forms. The specific task of the theoretician who uses all this information about reality does not, of course, consist in lending this abstract expression still more abstract form. On the contrary, his work always begins with a criti-cal analysis and revision of the abstractions of the empirical stage of cognition, with the critical overcoming of these abstractions, attaining progress through a critique of the one-sidedness and subjective character of these abstractions and revealing the illusions contained in them, from the standpoint of reality as a whole, in its concreteness. In this sense (and only in this sense) the transition from the empirical stage of cogni-tion to the rational one also appears as a transition from the abstract to the concrete.[21]

So, as Ilyenkov puts it, 'the method of presentation in *Capital* is nothing but the "corrected" method of its *investigation*'.[22] This supports the argument I set out in chapter 1 against treating how Marx proceeds in *Capital* as simply the actualisation of the method projected near the beginning of the *Grundrisse*. Michael Heinrich is right to argue:

> Many authors see in [the 1857] 'Einleitung' [Introduction] Marx's mature conception of method, but it is rather the 'first' rather than the 'last' word

---

21  E V Ilyenkov, [1960] *The Dialectics of the Abstract and the Concrete of Marx's* **Capital** (Moscow, 1982; translation modified), p148. Ilyenkov's reading is not that far removed from the model of scientific practice offered by Althusser, in which 'Generality I', pre-existing theories and concepts, is transformed into 'Generality III', a new 'concrete-in-thought', by 'Generality II', 'the "theory" that defines the field in which all the problems of the science must necessarily be posed', 'On the Materialist Dialectic', pp184-185.

22  Ilyenkov, *Dialectics of the Abstract and the Concrete of Marx's* **Capital**, p144.

on method. The often quoted 'method of advancing from the abstract to the concrete' is much too vague to describe the complex way in which Marx actually argued in Volume I of *Capital* some ten years later.[23]

The conceptual construction of *Capital* has to be interpreted in the light of Marx's understanding of the problems that he had to resolve as this understanding evolved across successive manuscripts. This is relevant to those readings of Marx that treat his critique of political economy as an actualisation of either Hegel's *Logic* as a whole or some specific part of that *Logic*. Meaney argues that 'the ordering of economic categories in the *Grundrisse* reflects the ordering of the logical categories' in the *Science of Logic*.[24] Now even if that argument were valid—and Meaney's reading of the *Grundrisse* is certainly cogent and interesting— this doesn't explain why Marx turned to Hegel's *Logic* when broaching his critique of political economy, and it doesn't guarantee that later economic manuscripts preserved the Hegelian structure that Meaney discerns in Marx's first attempt at this critique. More generally, to understand why and how, some 50 years after the *Science of Logic* was published, a revolutionary communist used it to analyse the structural logic of the capitalist economic system requires giving some thought to Marx's problem situation. Althusser famously argued: 'there is no such thing as an innocent reading'.[25] I take this to demand that reading a theoretical text involves attending to what Althusser calls the problematic informing a text—not merely the implicit presuppositions of the explicit assertions it makes, but also the constellation of problems that it seeks to address.

## Marx's problem situation

So what was the problem situation that Marx confronted as he embarked on what became the *Grundrisse*? As we have seen, he was prompted to resume his economic studies by the outbreak of a global economic and

---

23 Michael Heinrich, 'Reconstruction or Deconstruction? Methodological Controversies about Value and Capital, and New Insights from the Critical Edition', in Riccardo Bellofiore and Roberto Fineschi, eds, *Rereading Marx: New Perspectives after the Critical Edition* (Basingstoke, 2009), p79.

24 Meaney, *Capital as Organic Unity*, pix. Another study along similar lines to Meaney's (though criticised by him for underestimating the tightness of the relationship between the two works) is Hiroshi Uchida, *Marx's Grundrisse and Hegel's Logic* (Terrell Carver, ed; London, 1988).

25 Louis Althusser, 'From *Capital* to Marx's Philosophy', in Louis Althusser and Étienne Balibar, *Reading Capital* (London, 1970), p14.

financial crisis, which started in the United States and then spread to Britain and the rest of the world economy.[26] We will see in chapter 6 that economic crises had come to occupy a strategic political significance in Marx's thought. But in the *Grundrisse* he begins by looking at money. For some commentators this reflected deep architectonic reasons: thus, according to Meaney, 'Marx begins his exposition of capital in the precise manner that is recommended by Hegel. He begins with capital as it first appears to consciousness. He begins with the immediate content of knowledge, that is, the most simple, and therefore the most abstract determinations of capital'—ie simple circulation.[27] In fact, the very first portion of the manuscript we call the *Grundrisse* is a brilliant fragment written in July 1857 where Marx critically appraises two contemporary bourgeois economists, the American protectionist Henry Carey and the French free-trader Frédéric Bastiat (*G*: 883-893).[28] This text is both an indication of the extent to which Marx's perspective is already a global one and a warning against attributing more coherence to his manuscripts than they actually possess.

Marx had good reasons for initially focusing on money in the *Grundrisse*. One was conjunctural: the crisis started as a financial panic that spread from one centre to another. Another was political: Marx launches the initial 'Chapter on Money' with detailed critical appraisal on the proposals for banking reform recently made by the Proudhonist Alfred Darimon. Although Marx and Engels had withdrawn from the Communist League in the early 1850s, they continued to attach great importance to the ideological struggle against rival socialist currents, chief among which was Proudhon and his followers. Amid a tightly technical discussion of Darimon's argument that crises could be avoided through reforms of the monetary system that ended its reliance on precious metals and credit, Marx states the bigger theoretical and political stakes:

We have here reached the fundamental question, which is no longer related to the point of departure. The general question would be this:

---

26 For the American origins of the crisis, see Charles W Calomiris and Larry Schweikart, 'The Panic of 1857: Origins, Transmission, and Containment', *Journal of Economic History*, 51:4 (1991). The intimate web of economic, financial and geopolitical connections (and antagonisms) binding together the US and Britain for most of the 19th century is well brought out in Alasdair Roberts, *America's First Great Depression: Economic Crisis and Political Disorder after the Panic of 1837* (Ithaca, 2012).

27 Meaney, *Capital as Organic Unity*, p15.

28 In the early 1850s Marx critically discusses Carey, for example, in relation to what would prove to be a crucial issue for the development of his own value theory, Ricardo's theory of rent: see for example the long letter to Adolf Cluss (5 October 1853), *CW*39: 378-384.

Can the existing relations of production and the relations of distribution which correspond to them be revolutionised by a change in the instrument of circulation, in the organisation of circulation? Further question: Can such a transformation of circulation be undertaken without touching the existing relations of production and the social relations which rest on them? If every such transformation of circulation presupposes changes in other conditions of production and social upheavals, there would naturally follow from this the collapse of the doctrine which proposes tricks of circulation as a way of, on the one hand, avoiding the violent character of these social changes, and, on the other, of making these changes appear to be not a presupposition but a gradual result of the transformations in circulation. An error in this fundamental premiss would suffice to prove that a similar misunderstanding has occurred in relation to the inner connections between the relations of production, of distribution and of circulation. (*G*: 122)

The Proudhonists, in other words, have a superficial understanding of capitalism, which leads them to locate its faults in the process of circulation and therefore to argue that these could be overcome gradually by limited monetary reforms. (This is an idea still very much around, for example, in the idea that the solution to financial crises is more regulation.[29]) So at issue in this abstruse discussion of money is the necessity of social revolution. Marx's discussion proceeds along two tracks—a detailed theorisation of money and its functions and broader historico-political reflections on the distinctive form of social dependence that arises when economic relations are regulated by the circulation of commodities and money (represented symbolically as $C$ and $M$ respectively), as they are in bourgeois society. Marx's analysis leads him to broach the relationship between money and capital (it is here that a distinction is first drawn between the formula of simple circulation, $C$-$M$-$C$, and that of capital, initially $M$-$C$-$C$-$M$ [*G*: 200ff]) and to argue in a brilliant passage that anticipates but greatly exceeds in theoretical elaboration his

---

29  George Monbiot offers a contemporary version of Proudhonian monetary reform when he supports the introduction of 'demurrage, or negative interest. This means that it is impossible to invest in money, which is another way of saying that, if it could be universally applied, capitalism comes to an end,' *The Age of Consent: A Manifesto for a New World Order* (London, 2003), pp239-240. David Graeber's vast and stimulating historical and anthropological account, *Debt: The First 5,000 Years* (New York, 2011), is too complex and sprawling to be reduced to a simple theoretical formula, but his presentation of capitalism as based on an 'alliance of warriors and financiers' (p367) that imposes the abstract logic of the market onto the particularities of social practice (in which credit and debt relations were originally embedded) has a Proudhonian ring to it.

famous remark in *Capital*, I, that the 'sphere of circulation' is 'the exclusive realm of Freedom, Equality, Property and Bentham' (*CI*: 280):

> Equality and freedom are thus not only respected in exchange based on exchange values but, also, the exchange of exchange values is the productive, real basis of all *equality* and *freedom*. As pure ideas they are merely the idealised expressions of this basis; as developed in juridical, political, social relations, they are merely this basis to a higher power. (*G*: 245)[30]

This argument serves to undercut the Proudhonists' criticism of capitalism for violating the ideals of freedom and equality. They, like Marx, see these ideals as inherent in the process of commodity exchange, but they fail to recognise, he argues, that this process necessarily involves exploitation. To substantiate this claim, he seeks to derive capital from money (an attempt that I discuss in chapter 3) and makes the decisive move in conceptualising the capital relation by arguing that what the worker exchanges with capital is his labour capacity (*Arbeitsvermögen*) (*G*: 282-3).[31] Proudhon and his followers then largely forgotten (though see, towards the very end of the manuscript, *G*: 804-5), Marx elaborates his analysis of the capitalist mode of production, broadly following the plan he lays out of production, circulation, and their unity (capital and profit) (*G*: 275).

But this first march onto the terrain of *Capital* shouldn't be allowed to obscure the importance of Marx's initial discussion of money (to which he returns towards the end of the *Grundrisse*). Money and credit became a subject of intense debate among British political economists during the first half of the 19th century—indeed Marx writes that 'the [English] economic literature worth mentioning since 1830 principally boils down to writing on currency, credit and crises' (*CIII*: 624).[32] At stake in these debates was an idea that still haunts us, the quantity theory of money.

---

30  Although the passage from this quotation is included in Marx's 'Chapter on Capital', Uchida argues this is a mistake on the part of the editors of the *Grundrisse*: *Marx's Grundrisse and Hegel's Logic*, pp152-153 n 1.

31  In the *Grundrisse* and the *1861-63 Manuscript* Marx uses '*Arbeitsvermögen*' (labour capacity), adopting instead '*Arbeitskraft*' (labour power) only in *Capital*: see *CW*28: p554 n 85, and chapter 5 below.

32  See the excellent summary of the classical economists' debates about money and credit (to which the following discussion is much indebted) in Makoto Itoh and Costas Lapavitsas, *Political Economy of Money and Finance* (London, 1999), ch 1, and the close reading of Marx's journalism in relation particularly to the issues involved by Sergio Bologna (1973), 'Money and Crisis: Marx as Correspondent of the *New York Daily Tribune*, 1856-7', http://www.wildcat-www.de/en/material/cs13bolo.htm. Marx gives his own account of these debates in *Con*: 157-187.

David Hume gave this doctrine its classic formulation in 1754: 'the price of commodities is always proportioned to the plenty of money.' To substantiate this claim he laid one of the main foundation stones of *laissez faire* economics, arguing that rising prices in one country would lead to an outflow of money (and falling prices to an inflow) till equilibrium was reached. Drawing an analogy with the tendency of 'water, wherever it communicates, to find a level', Hume appeals to, not 'a physical attraction in order to explain the necessity of this operation', but 'a moral attraction, arising from the interests and passions of men,' that 'makes it impossible for money to lose its level, and either to rise or sink beyond the proportion of labour and commodities which are in each province' or country.[33]

As its most famous recent exponent, Milton Friedman, makes clear, the quantity theory treats money as an inessential veil over 'real' market transactions: 'Despite the importance of enterprises and money in our actual economy, and despite the numerous and complex problems they raise, the central characteristic of the market technique of achieving coordination is fully displayed in the simple exchange economy that contains neither enterprises nor money'.[34] Such a conception is at least more plausible where money takes the form of a commodity (gold and/or silver) that flows freely between countries in accordance with the fluctuations of supply and demand expressing Hume's 'moral attraction'. But what happens when the link to gold is suspended and the banknotes in circulation are underpinned by government fiat, as was the case in Britain during the period of Restriction occasioned by the wars with Revolutionary France (1797-1819)? Ricardo's first intervention in economic and political debates was as an advocate of a return to gold and (as a Member of Parliament) a critic of the discretion that Restriction gave the Bank of England and bankers in general. He became the main intellectual ornament of the currency school, led by one of Marx's bugbears, Samuel Jones Loyd (later Lord Overstone), who argued that the quantity theory required tight controls over the banks' ability to create credit money. Their political victory was embodied in the Bank Charter Act 1844, which created what would now be called a firewall between the banking and issuing departments of the Bank of England and limited the amount of banknotes it could issue against bullion and securities.[35]

33 David Hume, *Essays Moral, Political, and Literary* (Eugene F Miller, ed; Indianapolis, 1985), pp281, 313.
34 Quoted in Hyman P Minsky, *Stabilizing an Unstable Economy* (New York, 2008), p129.
35 David Kynaston, *The City of London*, I (London, 1994), pp29-30 (Ricardo on Restriction), 126-130 (the Bank Charter Act).

This device in many ways anticipated the unsuccessful attempts by the Thatcher government during the 1980s mechanically to control the money supply as a means of reducing the rate of inflation and reviving British capitalism.

The theoretical arguments and policy recommendations of Ricardo, Loyd, and their supporters were strongly contested by the banking school. Their critique was anticipated by the 18th century mercantilist economist Sir James Steuart:

> The circulation of every country...must ever be *in proportion to the industry of the inhabitants, producing the commodities which come to market...* If the coin of a country, therefore, falls below the *proportion* of the produce of industry *offered for sale*, industry itself will come to a stop; or inventions, such as symbolical money, will be fallen upon to provide an equivalent for it. But if the specie be found above the proportion of the industry, it will have no effect in raising prices, nor will it enter into circulation. It will be hoarded upon in treasures, where it must wait not only the call of a desire in the proprietors to consume, but of the industrious to satisfy this call.[36]

Makoto Itoh and Costas Lapavitsas write: 'Compared to Hume, who put inordinate stress on the functions of means of circulation alone, Steuart offered a considerably richer analysis, discussing money as unit of account, means of debt repayment, and means of payment in international transactions'.[37] The banking school—for example, the pioneering economic historian Thomas Tooke, Henry Thornton, and John Fullarton, took over Steuart's stress on hoarding, an issue that resurfaces in Keynes's concept of liquidity preference, and on what came to be known as the law of reflux—the tendency of credit money to return to its issuer. They also argued that legislation such as the Bank Charter Act could not prevent money markets from generating what Fullarton called 'speculation and over-trading'.[38]

In the portion of the London Notebooks written between March and June 1851 Marx intensively studied the debates between the currency and banking schools in a section entitled 'Bullion. The Perfect Money System'. He also read Steuart before turning to Ricardo. Marx seems to

---

36  Sir James Steuart, *An Inquiry into the Principles of Political Oeconomy* (2 vols, London, 1767), I, p402. I have taken the liberty of modernising Steuart's spelling and punctuation.
37  Itoh and Lapavitsas, *Political Economy of Money and Finance*, p11.
38  John Fullarton, *On the Regulation of Currencies* (London, 1844), p154. Marx gives this book the most attention in his extracts on 'Bullion. The Perfect Money System', in the London Notebooks: *MEGA²* IV/8: 95-113.

have developed a soft spot for Steuart, whom he liked for his historical realism. Thus at the beginning of the 1857 Introduction he praises Steuart for avoiding the abstract individualism of Smith and Ricardo 'because as an aristocrat and in antithesis to the eighteenth century, he had in some respects a more historical footing' (*G*: 84). References to a passage marked in the London Notebooks where Steuart bluntly expresses the brutal logic of primitive accumulation, declaring that 'the revolution must then mark the purging of the lands of superfluous mouths, and forcing these to quit the mother earth, in order to retire to towns and villages, where they may usefully swell the number of free hands and apply to industry', reappear in Marx's later manuscripts (*MEGA²* IV/8: 323; *G*: 276; *C*III: 921).[39] One of the main results of these studies was that Marx took over the critique of the quantity theory of money developed by Steuart and the banking school.[40]

His account of the multiple functions of money (as measure of value, means of circulation, standard of price, means of payment), and the law of monetary circulation that he presents in the 1859 *Contribution* and in *Capital*, according to which 'the quantity of the circulating medium is determined by the sum of the prices of the commodities in circulation and the average velocity of the circulation of money', are heavily indebted to these economists' arguments (*CI*: 219).[41] Indeed, Marx's definition of money as the universal equivalent (which I discuss in chapter 4) seems to derive, in formulation at any rate, from Steuart's description of 'the precious metals' as 'an universal equivalent for every thing'.[42] These theoretical arguments informed the analyses that Marx put forward in his journalism. Thus he published a critique of the Bank Charter Act as early as September 1853 and accurately predicted at the height of the financial panic in November 1857 that, since the act's restriction on the Bank of England's ability to create credit money exacerbated crises, it would have to be suspended, just as it had been during the crisis of 1847

---

39  Steuart, *An Inquiry into the Principles of Political Oeconomy*, I, p153. Steuart refers here to 'the revolutions of the last centuries' arising from 'the dissolution of the feudal form of government' and the formation of 'a perfectly new system of political oeconomy' (p150).

40  Lucia Pradella, *Globalization and the Critique of Political Economy: New Insights from Marx's Writings* (London, 2014), ch 4.

41  See Itoh and Lapavitas, *Political Economy of Money and Finance*, ch 2, and the detailed examination in Pichit Likitkijsomboon, 'Marx's Anti-Quantity Theory of Money: A Critical Evaluation', in Fred Moseley, ed, *Marx's Theory of Money: Modern Appraisals* (Basingstoke, 2005).

42  Steuart, *An Inquiry into the Principles of Political Oeconomy*, I, p327, quoted in *G*: 226-227. But see, for Marx's tendency to treat money in the *Grundrisse* as a mere symbol of value, Roman Rosdolsky, *The Making of Marx's Capital*, pp113-114.

(*CW* 12: 295-300; 15: 379-84). (We will return to Marx's theory of money and banking when discussing crises in chapter 6.)

But there is then a tension between Marx's critical endorsement of the banking school and his reliance on Ricardo's version of the labour theory of value. From *The Poverty of Philosophy* onwards Marx insists on Ricardo's scientific superiority over the other political economists. Thus he writes in the *1861-63 Manuscript* that, after the fertile inconsistencies of Smith:

> at last Ricardo steps in and calls to science: Halt! The basis, the starting-point for the physiology of the bourgeois system—for the understanding of its internal organic coherence and life process—is the determination of *value by labour-time*. Ricardo starts with this and forces science to get out of the rut, to render an account of the extent to which the other categories—the relations of production and commerce—evolved and described by it, correspond to or contradict this basis, this starting-point; to elucidate how far a science which in fact only reflects and reproduces the manifest forms of the process, and therefore also how far these manifestations themselves, correspond to the basis on which the inner coherence, the actual physiology of bourgeois society rests or the basis which forms its starting-point; and in general, to examine how matters stand with the contradiction between the apparent and the actual movement of the system. This then is Ricardo's great historical significance for science. (*CW*31: 391)

Reading Ricardo's *Principles* made the same impression on Thomas de Quincey in 1819, stirring him from his opium-induced dreams:

> Had this profound work been really written in England during the nineteenth century?... Could it be that an Englishman, and he not in academic bowers but oppressed by mercantile and senatorial cares, had accomplished what all the universities of Europe and a century of thought, had failed to advance even by one hair's breadth? All other writers had been crushed and overlaid by an enormous weight of facts and documents; Mr Ricardo had deduced, *a priori*, from the understanding itself, laws which first gave a ray of light into the unwieldy chaos of materials, and had constructed what had been but a collection of tentative discussions into a science of regular proportions, now first standing on an eternal basis.[43]

---

43  Thomas de Quincey, *Confessions of an English Opium Eater and Other Writings* (Oxford, 2013), p65.

But, as Marx had already shown at some length in the 1859 *Contribution*, Ricardo was a hopeless guide to 'the other categories' insofar as they concerned money, credit and crises. This was a very dangerous position for Marx to find himself in, since it seemed to support the argument of Ricardo's critics that the labour theory of value was a metaphysical doctrine, as de Quincey puts it, 'deduced, *a priori*, from the understanding itself', of no empirical relevance. Marx doesn't directly confront this problem in the *Grundrisse*, where he approaches Ricardo largely in the context of his developing analysis of the capital relation. Thus he criticises Ricardo along with other economists because 'they do not conceive capital in its *specific character as form*, as a *relation of production* reflected into itself, but think only about its material substance, raw material etc' (*G*: 309). Marx's fullest engagement with Ricardo is, as we have already seen, in the *1861-63 Manuscript*. Properly to understand this—and therefore Marx's resort to Hegel—we have to consider more directly the tensions in Ricardo's value theory.

**The impasse of Ricardian value theory**[44]

Marx's positive assessment of Ricardo stemmed from the latter's clear and rigorous statement of the labour theory of value: *'the value of a commodity, or the quantity of any other commodity for which it will exchange, depends on the relative quantity of labour which is necessary for its production, and not on the greater or less compensation which is paid for that labour.'* (*R*: I, 11) Having, however, introduced this assertion at the very beginning of Chapter One of his *Principles*, Ricardo goes on to add a significant exception. This arises from that fact that, depending on the variations of the physical conditions of production in different sectors, industries will be more capital-intensive or more labour-intensive.[45] If there is a rise in average wages, the general rate of profit will fall. This will affect capital- and labour-intensive industries alike. But since wages

---

44  This section draws heavily on my doctoral thesis, 'The Logic of *Capital*', and on a preliminary draft, 'Ricardo, Marx and Classical Political Economy' (1975), much of which was not included in the final thesis. Like all students of Ricardo, I'm greatly indebted to Piero Sraffa's superb edition of his *Works and Correspondence*, and to his Introduction to volume I.

45  Ricardo in fact distinguishes between two cases, one in which the ratio of fixed to circulating capital in different industries varies and the other in which the durability of capital varies from sector to sector, but he writes: 'According as capital is rapidly perishable, and requires to be reproduced, or is of slow consumption, it is classed under the heads of fixed and circulating capital' (*R*: I, 31). This implies that the first case reduces to the second.

represent a lower proportion of costs in capital-intensive industries, their costs will not rise as rapidly as those in labour-intensive industries, and therefore the prices of goods produced in the former will *fall* relative to those of goods produced in the latter (*R*: I, 33-35). Ricardo's general statement of his value theory makes relative prices—the amount commodities exchange for each other—depend on the labour necessary for their production. But in this case the relative prices of commodities change without there being a change in the relative amounts of labour time required to produce them.

This argument relies on two assumptions. First, 'there can be no rise in the value of labour without a fall in profits' (*R*: I, 35); wages and profits are thus inversely related. Second, implicit in the argument is the existence of the general rate of profit. In other words, Ricardo assumes that capital flows between different branches of production under the impetus of rises or falls in the rate of profit until returns on capital in different sectors are equalised across the economy. It is this that prevents capital-intensive firms from successfully resisting the fall in the relative prices of their goods (*R*: I, 41-42).[46] The same assumptions are to be found also in Chapter Two of the *Principles*, where, with their assistance and two other key items in Ricardo's repertoire—the law of diminishing returns in agriculture and the theory of wages, he develops the theory of differential rent.

A number of commentators have isolated the theoretical core of the *Principles* in its first seven chapters, where Ricardo deals with value, rent, natural and market prices, wages, profits, and foreign trade. But the chapters on wages and profits (V and VI respectively) are, as Marx puts it, 'not only taken for granted, but fully developed in the first two chapters "On Value" and "On Rent"' (*CW*31: 394). However, Ricardo's exception to the labour theory of value proved to be the symptom of a contradiction inherent in this set of theoretical principles consisting the kernel of his system. Ricardo explicitly admitted that the case of wage rises in different production conditions represented a limitation of his value theory. He wrote in the first edition of the *Principles* (1817):

> It appears that the accumulation of capital, by occasioning different proportions of fixed and circulating capitals to be employed in different

---

46  Indeed, Marx comments, 'one can see that in this first chapter not only are *commodities* assumed to exist—and when considering value as such, nothing further is required—but also wages, capital, profit, and even…the general rate of profit, the various forms of capital as they arise from the process of circulation, and also the difference between "**natural and market-price**"' (*CW*31: 393).

trades, and by giving differing degrees of durability to such fixed capital, introduces a considerable modification to the rule, which is of universal application in the early stages of society. (*R*: I, 66)

This concession was seized on by Ricardo's opponents. His friend and critic Thomas Malthus wrote to him (24 February 1818):

> For myself, I own, I am quite satisfied with your own concessions; and if as you yourself acknowledge, taxation, foreign materials, and the different quantities of fixed and circulating capitals employed all prevent the exchangeable value of commodities from being determined by the labour they cost in production, I should say that your theory was only true *ceteris paribus*, which might be said of the cost of materials. (*R*: VII, 253)

And Robert Torrens writes in an article attacking the labour theory of value:

> But, as equal capitals seldom possess precisely equal degrees of durability, this [Ricardo's modification of the labour theory of value], instead of limiting what he calls the general principle, subverts it altogether, and proves, that the relative worth of all things is determined, not by the quantities of labour required to procure them, but by the universally operating law of competition, which equalises the profits of stocks and, consequently, renders the results obtained from the employment of equal capitals of equal value in exchange.[47]

Both Malthus and Torrens were pointing to the fact that the labour theory of value and the assumption of a general rate of profit are *prima facie* inconsistent. If commodities exchange according to the labour required to produce them, then the rate of profit will vary from industry to industry depending on wage rates and production conditions. If, on the other hand, what Torrens calls 'the universally operating law of competition' is admitted, and capitals are assumed to flow between different sectors until a general rate of profit equalising returns is formed, then commodities cannot exchange according to the labour necessary for their production.

The problem for Ricardo was that he required *both* principles to construct his theory. He wrote to James Mill (28 December 1818) commenting on Torrens's article:

---

47  Robert Torrens, 'Structures concerning Mr Ricardo's Doctrine respecting Exchangeable Value', *Edinburgh Magazine and Literary Miscellany*, III, October 1818, p336.

He makes it appear that Smith says that after capital accumulates and industrious people are set to work the quantity of wealth is not the only circumstance that determines the value of commodities and that I oppose this opinion. Now I want to shew that I do not oppose this opinion in the manner he represents me to do so, but Adam Smith thought, that as in the earlier stages of society, all the produce of labour belonged to the labourer, and as after stock was accumulated, a part went to profits, that accumulation, necessarily without regard to the different degrees of durability of capital, or any other circumstance whatever, *raised* the prices or exchangeable value of commodities, and consequently that their value was no longer regulated by the quantity of labour necessary to their production. In opposition to him, I maintain that this is not because of this division into profits and wages,—it is not because capital accumulates, that exchangeable value varies, but it is in all stages of society, owing only to two causes: one the more or less quantity of labour required, the other the greater or less durability of capital:—and that the former is never superseded by the latter, but is only modified by it. (*R*: VII: 377)

Ricardo's development of the labour theory of value arose from his dissatisfaction with the theory of value outlined by Smith in *The Wealth of Nations* and accepted by the other major economists of the day, including Malthus and Torrens.[48] For Smith, it is only 'in that early and rude state of society which precedes both the accumulation of capital and the appropriation of land' that commodities exchanged according to 'the quantities of labour necessary for acquiring different objects'. He argues that, assuming the accumulation of capital, ie assuming that the means of production are owned, not by the direct producers, but by capitalists employing wage labourers, 'when the price of any commodity is neither more nor less than what is sufficient to pay the rent of the land, the wages of the labour, and the profits of the stock employed in raising, preparing, and bringing it to market, according to their natural rates, the commodity is then sold for what may be called its natural price,' around which market prices fluctuate.[49] It follows that if one of these

---

48  See the brilliant overview of Smith's, Ricardo's and Marx's differing approaches to value theory in Dimitris Milonakis and Ben Fine, *From Political Economy to Economics* (London, 2009), ch 4, and, on Smith and Ricardo, I I Rubin, *A History of Economic Thought* (London, 1979), chs 27 and 28.

49  Adam Smith, *An Inquiry into the Nature and Causes of the Wealth of Nations* (2 vols, Oxford, 1976), I vi, I viii; I pp65, 72. Smith equivocates over whether he actually means quantities of labour performed or rather the amount of labour that a commodity could *command* thanks to its price measured by wages. (Malthus adopts the latter solution.) In the *1861-63 Manuscript* Marx analyses in detail the tensions and ambiguities in Smith's

'component parts' of the exchange value of a commodity rises, its price will also rise.

Ricardo's opposition to this theory was stimulated by the intense controversies among British economists and policy makers at the end of the wars with France.[50] After his first intervention over the bullion controversy, he crossed swords with Malthus (initially in their private correspondence) over whether or not the Corn Laws restricting the import of grain should be repealed. Both were responding to an economic conjuncture in which a steep rise in the price of corn had been accompanied by the improvement and extension of cultivation, high government spending and a decline in Britain's profitability relative to that of other countries. The high cost of living and the slump that followed Napoleon's final defeat in 1815 led to increasing tensions between the politically dominant aristocracy, the new industrial bourgeoisie, and an emerging workers' movement. In 1812 Luddism spread from Nottingham to the West Riding, to Lancashire and to Cheshire. According to Élie Halévy, 'in the summer of 1812 there were no fewer than 12,000 troops in the disturbed counties, a greater force than Wellington had under his command in the Peninsula.' During the passage of the Corn Laws in 1815 parliament was besieged by the London crowd. In 1815, after Waterloo, there were 155 newly constructed barracks and 100,000 troops on garrison in the United Kingdom.[51]

---

value theory: *CW*30: 376-411.

50  See, for example, G S L Tucker, *Progress and Profits in British Economic Thought 1650-1850* (Cambridge, 1960), ch VIII.

51  Élie Halévy, *A History of the English People in 1815* (London, 1912), pp68, 280-283. This situation hardly supports Marx's contention in his Afterword to the Second German Edition of *Capital*, I, that British 'classical political economy belongs to a period in which the class struggle was as yet undeveloped,' and that its decline followed as 'the class struggle took on more and more explicit and threatening forms' after 1830. He contradicts himself, saying that 'the class struggle between capital and labour...broke out openly after the passing of the Corn Laws' (*CI*: 96, 97). Ricardo was writing at a time of political and social polarisation, and the internal tensions in his theoretical discourse certainly contributed to its rapid abandonment, well before 1830, even by his own followers. Marx further undermines his own claim by writing in the *1861-63 Manuscript* that 'the real science of political economy ends' with Richard Jones, whose main works appeared after 1830, and whom Marx praises for historicising capitalist economic relations: 'What distinguishes Jones from the other economists (except perhaps Sismondi) is that he emphasises that the essential feature of capital is its socially determined form, and that he reduces the whole difference between the capitalist and other modes of production to this distinct form,' so that 'the capitalist mode of production is regarded as a determinate historical category and no longer as an eternal natural relation of production' (*CW*33: 345, 341, 344). Unlike the case of the detested Malthus, Marx even finds occasion to praise Jones's status as an Anglican clergyman: 'The ministers of the English Church seem to think more than their continental brethren' (*CW*33: 344).

Ricardo and Malthus alike reacted with horror to the Peterloo massacre of August 1819, which represented the peak of post-war working class insurgency. Both sought to find the economic causes of these discontents. For Malthus the problem was one of overproduction and a shortage of 'effectual demand', which could only be overcome with the assistance of 'unproductive consumers', especially the landowners and the state. Marx, who loathed Malthus, said of him: '—being a staunch **member** of the **Established Church** of England—he was a professional sycophant of the landed aristocracy, whose rents, sinecures, squandering, heartlessness etc he justified *economically*' (*CW*31: 345). Ricardo by contrast, though himself a stock-jobber in the City, took the side of the alliance of workers and manufacturers opposed to the Corn Laws, declaring: 'The interest of the landlord is always opposed to the interest of every other class in the community' (*R*: VI, 21).

For Ricardo, both rising prices and falling profitability were a consequence of declining productivity in agriculture that reflected the law of diminishing returns, according to which increasing a given factor of production will, other things being equal, lead to a fall in the additional output gained. The only way of remedying this situation would be to bring down the price of corn by improving the productivity of agriculture or by importing cheaper grain. In his *Essay on the Influence of a Low Price of Corn on the Profits of Stock* (1815) Ricardo seeks to give his argument theoretical foundations. He argues that a general wage increase will lead, not to a rise in the level of absolute prices (as was implied by Smith's value theory), but to a fall in the average rate of profit. He therefore postulates an inverse relationship between wages and profits. The theory of differential rent also developed in the *Essay* enables him to reject the proposition that rent is a component of a commodity's natural price: rent is conceived there as a residue after income has been apportioned to wages and profits.

We can now see why the 'modification' of the labour theory of value Ricardo presented in Chapter One of the *Principles* was so important. It showed that an increase in the general level of wages could lead to a *fall* in some relative prices (ie those of goods produced in capital-intensive industries). Nevertheless, the labour theory of value and Ricardo's theory of profits are closely connected. If an inverse relation between wages and profits is postulated, then the value of a commodity cannot be conceived as their sum, as it was by Smith. Some principle of value determination independent of wages and profits is necessary. In the Essay Ricardo relies on the assumption that in agriculture corn is both input and output.[52] As he started working on the *Principles*, he sought to develop a more general value theory, writing to James Mill (30 December 1815): 'I know I shall soon be stopped by the word price... Before readers can understand the proof I mean to give [that improvements in agriculture have no other effect than that of raising the rate of profit], they must understand the theory of currency and of price' (*R*: VI, 348-349). The labour theory of value fitted the bill, serving to give expression to Ricardo's theory of profits.

The centrality of this relationship was closely connected to his conception of political economy. He wrote to Malthus (9 October 1820): 'Political Economy you think is an enquiry into the nature and causes of wealth—I think it should rather be called an enquiry into the laws which determine the division of the produce of industry among the classes who concur in its formation' (*R*: VIII, 278). The inverse relationship between wages and profits was the theoretical determination of what Ricardo saw as the antagonistic relations of distribution between the classes: the workers' gain was the capitalists' loss, and vice versa. As Marx puts it, 'Ricardo exposes and describes the economic antagonism of classes—as shown by the intrinsic relations—and...consequently political economy perceives, discovers the root of the historical struggle and development' (*CW*31: 392). The labour theory of value, by defining the social product independently of the relations of distribution, allowed Ricardo to give theoretical expression to this class antagonism.

Ricardo's value theory and his theory of profits were therefore imbricated with each other. At the same time, however, the coexistence within his discourse of the labour theory of value and the assumption of Torrens's 'universally operating law of competition, which equalises the profits of stock', introduced an incoherence into the system. This incoherence made itself felt even within Ricardo's lifetime in the efforts of his followers, most notably J R McCulloch and James Mill, to rescue his value theory by reinterpreting it in such a way as to make it irrefutable, primarily by defining profits as a form of wages. Mill, for example, argues that, since:

> capital is allowed to be correctly described under the title hoarded labour...profits are simply remuneration for labour. They may, indeed, without doing any violence to language, hardly even by a metaphor, be

---

52  Piero Sraffa, 'Introduction', to *The Works and Correspondence of David Ricardo* (11 vols, Cambridge, 1951-52), I, xxxi.

dominated wages: the wages of that labour which applied, not immediately by the hand, but mediately, by the instruments which the hand has produced.[53]

McCulloch went further in correspondence with Ricardo, suggesting that profits were the wages of machines and natural processes! (5 December 1819, *R*: VIII, 138) Publicly he followed Mill: 'The profits of capital are only another name for the *wages of accumulated labour*'.[54] Smith had already rejected a version of this idea, arguing that 'in the price of commodities...the profits of stock constitute a component part altogether different from the wages of labour, and regulated by quite different principles'.[55] Ricardo was careful to distance himself from these 'conventionalist stratagems' (as Karl Popper would call them) designed to protect the theory through redefinition, while holding fast to his value theory. Not long before his sudden fatal illness and death in September 1823 he told Malthus (3 August 1823): 'As far as I have been able to reflect on M Culloch [sic] and Mill's suggestion I am not satisfied with it' (*R*: IX, 323). In the third edition of the *Principles* (1821) he wrote of his 'modification' of the labour theory of value: 'The reader, however, should remark that this cause of the variation of commodities is comparatively slight in its effects... Not so with the other great cause of the variation, in the value of commodities, namely, the increase or diminution in the quantity of labour necessary to produce them' (*R*: I, 36).

This is not to say that Ricardo did not feel that the theory involved major difficulties. He wrote to McCulloch (13 June 1820):

I sometimes think that if I were to write the chapter on value again, I should acknowledge that the relative value of commodities was regulated by two causes instead of by one, namely by the relative quantity of the commodities required to produce the commodities in question, and by the rate of profit for the time that the capital remained dormant, and until the commodities were brought to market. Perhaps I should find the difficulties nearly as great in this view of the subject as in that which I have adopted. (*R*: VIII, 194)

These difficulties may help to explain why the Ricardian school stagnated and gradually disintegrated after Marx's death. Marx called the 1820s 'metaphysically speaking the most important period in the

53   James Mill, *Elements of Political Economy*, in *Selected Economic Writings* (Donald Winch, ed; Edinburgh, 1966), pp261, 262-263.
54   J R McCulloch, *The Principles of Political Economy* (Edinburgh, 1825), p291.
55   Smith, *Wealth of Nations*, I vi; I, p67.

history of English political economy' (*CW*32: 298). On the one hand, the precursors of the marginalist revolution of the 1870s that is the source of the contemporary neoclassical orthodoxy (for example, Samuel Bailey) mounted a series of powerful attacks on the labour theory of value; on the other, the so-called Ricardian socialists (most prominently Thomas Hodgskin) used the theory to champion the interests of the workers' movement, arguing that, if capital was indeed merely accumulated labour, as James Mill and McCulloch argued, why shouldn't the workers receive the full value of their product? John Stuart Mill, schooled by his father James and Jeremy Bentham to be Ricardo's heir, completed the euthanasia of his value theory by adopting the theory developed by Nassau Senior (and the object of much scorn on Marx's part in *Capital*, I), according to which profits are the reward of the capitalist's abstinence from consumption. As Joseph Schumpeter puts it, Mill 'places Ricardo's thought as it were on a soft bed, in order to let it die quietly'.[56] By 1844 de Quincey, one of Ricardo's most loyal followers, could lament: 'Political economy does not advance. Since the revolution effected in that science by Ricardo, (1817), upon the whole it has been stationary'.[57]

The source of the impasse lay in the internal construction of Ricardo's discourse. The labour theory of value provided an indispensable component of this discourse by providing a principle of value determination independent of wages and profits, which were treated as inversely related. But Ricardo at the same time treated his value theory as simply a quantitative empirical proposition whose validity is a matter of contingent fact. Hence, given certain other assumptions, above all the proposition that equal capitals will receive equal profits, the generality and validity of the theory are limited by the existence of differing production conditions. Thus the labour theory of value is both necessary in order to make Ricardo's system coherent and at the same time limited by other assumptions of that very system.

Underlying Ricardo's treatment of his value theory as a contingent proposition is an essentially empiricist notion of the economic process. The workings of the economy are treated as readily accessible to observation. Therefore, the propositions produced through the scientific knowledge of the economy will be ones summarising these observations—propositions of an equivalent epistemological status, all equally refutable and contingent. The only exception will be self-evident premises that serve as the

---

56   Joseph Schumpeter, *Economic Doctrine and Method* (London, 1954), p37.
57   Thomas de Quincey, *The Logic of Political Economy* (Edinburgh, 1844), p iii.

ordering principles of economic science.[58] As we have seen, among the propositions selected for this role is the assumption that a general rate of profit exists. But this assertion is in fact far from self-evident. Marx shows it to presuppose the separation of the direct producers from the means of production, the existence of a capitalist class controlling these means, the creation of surplus value, its transformation into profit, and the competition of capitals necessary for the equalisation of profits. The existence of the general rate of profit is thus specific to a determinate social order, namely capitalism. The structure, however, of what Marx calls the 'theoretical part' of the *Principles* (the first six chapters) is such as to make it clear that Ricardo presupposes the existence of a general rate of profit as a basic premiss of his argument (*CW*31: 393). In this way, the existence of the capitalist mode of production is inscribed within Ricardo's discourse as *natural*.

From this perspective, Marx found Smith superior to Ricardo:

It is Adam Smith's great merit that it is just in the chapters of Book I (chapters VI, VII, VIII [of the *Wealth of Nations*]) where he passes from simple commodity exchange and its law of value to exchange between objectified and living labour, to exchange between capital and wage-labour, to the consideration of profit and rent in general—in short, to the origin of surplus-value—that he feels some flaw has emerged. He senses that somehow—whatever the cause may be, and he does not grasp what it is—in the actual result the law is suspended: more labour is exchanged for less labour (from the labourer's standpoint), less labour is exchanged for more labour (from the capitalist's standpoint). His merit is that he emphasises—and it obviously perplexes him—that with the *accumulation of capital* and the *appearance of property in land*—that is, when the conditions of labour assume an independent existence over against labour itself—something new occurs, apparently (and actually, in the result) the law of value changes into its opposite. It is his theoretical strength that he feels and stresses this contradiction, just as it is his theoretical weakness that the contradiction shakes his confidence in the general law, even for simple commodity exchange; that he does not perceive how this contradiction arises, through labour capacity itself becoming a commodity, and that in the case of this specific commodity its use-value—which therefore

---

58  Such a conception of economic science is developed by the Ricardian J E Cairnes: *The Character and Logical Method of Political Economy* (London, 1875). But it is also embraced by leading advocates of neoclassical orthodoxy: for example, Lionel Robbins, *An Essay on the Nature and Significance of Economic Science* (London, 1933).

has nothing to do with its exchange-value—is precisely the energy which creates exchange-value. Ricardo is ahead of Adam Smith in that these apparent contradictions—in their result real contradictions—do not confuse him. But he is behind Adam Smith in that he does not even suspect that this presents a problem, and therefore the *specific* development which the law of value undergoes with the formation of capital does not for a moment puzzle him or even attract his attention. (*CW*30: 393-394)

In Ricardo's case the treatment of the general rate of profit as a self-evident fact requiring no explanation introduced an element of incoherence into his discourse that led to the disintegration of his school. The inconsistency of this premiss with the labour theory of value could lead to two courses of action. Since, as a matter of fact, returns on capital *do* tend to be equalised, then, either the labour theory of value should be abandoned, or the apparent inconsistency of the two principles should be removed by a theory that seeks to explain the existence of the general rate of profit starting from the labour theory of value. Neoclassical economics took the first course, Marx the second.[59]

## Ricardo, Hegel and Spinoza

Towards the end of the lengthy excursus on 'Theories of Surplus Value' in the *1861-63 Manuscript*, Marx summed up his view of the causes of the disintegration of Ricardianism:

> The first difficulty in the Ricardian system was **the exchange of capital and labour—so as to be corresponding to the *'law of value'*.**
> The second difficulty was that *capitals of equal magnitude*, no matter what their organic composition, yield *equal profits* or the ***general rate of profit***. (*CW*32: 361)

As Marx acknowledged, these problems were identified by Ricardo's critics. Bailey, for example, highlighted the first problem, namely that in treating wages as the price of labour and simultaneously making labour the source of value, Ricardo found himself caught in a contradiction: 'If this principle [the labour theory of value] is rigidly adhered to, it follows, that the value of labour depends on the quantity of labour producing it—which is evidently absurd. By a dexterous turn, therefore, Mr Ricardo makes the value of labour depend on the quantity of labour

---

59   The sorry tale of the transformation of economics as a result of the marginalist revolution is told in Milonakis and Fine, *From Political Economy to Economics*.

required to produce wages'.[60] Marx in the *Grundrisse* discovers the solution to this problem when he argues that what the worker sells to the capitalist is not labour, but labour capacity, whose value, determined like that of all other commodities by the socially necessary labour time required to produce it (or, in this case, to reproduce the worker in which the labour capacity is embodied), is represented by the wage. As he puts it in the *1861-63 Manuscript*:

> Instead of *labour*, Ricardo should have discussed labour *capacity*. But, had he done so, capital would also have been revealed as the material condition of labour, confronting the labourer as power that has acquired an independent existence. And capital would at once have been revealed as a *definite social relationship*. Ricardo thus only distinguishes capital as **'accumulated labour'** from **'immediate labour'**. And it is something purely physical, only an element in the **labour process**, from which the relation between the worker and capital, **wages and profits**, could never be developed. (*CW*32: 36-7)

So in this case as well it is Ricardo's naturalising of the capital relation that underlies the theoretical contradiction. But it is the problem of the general rate of profit that dominates Marx's discussion of Ricardo in the *1861-63 Manuscript*. As we saw in chapter 1, Marx comes at the problem from the angle of the theory of rent, and more particularly in his critique of Rodbertus. Here he argues that competition, in equalising returns across sectors, transfers surplus value from capitals with a lower than average organic composition (the ratio of capital invested in means of production to capital invested in labour power) to those with a higher than average organic composition. As result, commodities exchange, not at their values (= the socially necessary labour time required to produce them), but at what he initially calls their average prices, later in the *1861-63 Manuscript* cost prices, and in *Capital* prices of production:[61]

> the capitalists strive (and this striving is competition) to divide among themselves the quantity of unpaid labour—or the products of this quantity of labour—which they squeeze out of the working class, not according to the surplus-labour produced directly by a *particular* capital,

---

60   Samuel Bailey, *A Critical Dissertation on the Nature, Measures and Causes of Value* (London, 1825), p51.
61   On the multiple meanings Marx gives the term 'cost price' in the *1861-63 Manuscript*, see Enrique Dussel, *Towards an Unknown Marx: A Commentary on the **Manuscripts of 1861-63*** (London, 2001), p250 n 4.

but corresponding *firstly* to the relative portion of the aggregate capital which a particular capital represents and *secondly* according to the amount of surplus-labour produced by the aggregate capital. The capitalists, like hostile brothers, divide among themselves the loot of other people's labour which they have appropriated so that on an average one receives the same amount of unpaid labour as another.

Competition achieves this equalisation by regulating average prices. These average prices themselves, however, are either above or below the value of the commodity so that no commodity yields a higher rate of profit than any other. It is therefore wrong to say that competition among capitals brings about a general rate of profit by equalising the prices of commodities to their values. On the contrary it does so *by converting the values of the commodities into average prices, in which a part of surplus value is transferred from one commodity to another*, etc. The *value* of a commodity equals the quantity of paid and unpaid labour *contained in it*. The *average price* of a commodity = the quantity of paid labour it *contains* (objectified or living) + an average quota of unpaid labour. The latter does not depend on *whether this amount* was contained in the commodity itself or on whether more or less of it was embodied in the value of the commodity. (*CW*31: 264)[62]

So it is here that Marx is prompted to develop his famous (or notorious) transformation of values into prices of production. He is prompted to make this move, which Dussel calls 'a central moment of the *Manuscripts of 1861-63*, perhaps the most important creative moment', to overcome Ricardo's denial of the existence of absolute rent—ie rent that arises simply from the ownership of land, unlike differential rent, which is a consequence of differences in levels of productivity.[63] Acknowledging absolute rent appeared to Ricardo to be inconsistent with the labour theory of value. Marx's solution, developed first in the *1861-63 Manuscript* and restated in *Capital*, III, Part 6, is to argue that absolute rent is possible so long as one assumes that the organic composition of capital and labour productivity are lower and hence the rate of profit higher in agriculture than in other sectors. If capital were fully mobile, it would flow into agriculture until prices in the sector fell to a level that would secure investors the average profit, transferring surplus value to other sectors. But the institution of private property in land prevents this happening;

---

62  Marx in fact anticipates this solution, arguing that competition leads to capitals sharing surplus value in proportion to their size, in a passage in the *Grundrisse* that isn't developed further in this manuscript: *G*: 435-436.

63  Dussel, *Towards an Unknown Marx*, p103.

agricultural products are therefore sold at their values rather than their prices of production, and the landowners appropriate the difference as (absolute) rent:

> It is quite simply the *private ownership* of land, mines, water, etc by certain people, which enables them to snatch, intercept and seize the *excess surplus-value over and above profit* (average profit, the rate of profit determined by the general rate of profit) contained in the commodities of these particular spheres of production, these particular fields of capital investment, and so to prevent it from entering into the general process by which the general rate of profit is formed. (*CW*31: 271)[64]

It is in the course of this critique of Ricardo that Marx begins to reflect systematically on his method. Thus he interpolates during a discussion of Rodbertus:

> //Adam Smith, as we saw above, first correctly interprets value and the relation existing between profit, wages, etc, as component parts of this value, and then he proceeds the other way round, regards the prices of wages, profit and rent as antecedent factors and seeks to determine them independently, in order then to compose the *price of the commodity* out of them. The meaning of this change of approach is that first he grasps the problem in its *inner relationships*, and then in the *reverse form, as it appears in competition*. These two concepts of his run counter to one another in his work, naively, without his being aware of the contradiction. Ricardo, on the other hand, consciously *abstracts* from the form of competition, from the appearance of competition, in order to comprehend the *laws as such*. On the one hand he must be reproached for not going far enough, for not carrying his abstraction to completion, for instance, when he analyses the *value* of the commodity, he at once allows himself to be influenced by consideration of all kinds of concrete conditions. On the other hand one must reproach him for regarding the phenomenal form as *immediate and direct* proof or exposition of the general laws, and for failing to *interpret* it. In regard to the first, his abstraction is too incomplete; in regard to the second, it is formal abstraction which in itself is wrong.// (*CW*31: 338)

The first criticism is a point Marx repeatedly makes against Ricardo: far from being, as he is commonly represented, the author of an abstract and deductive theory that takes no account of concrete circumstances,

---

64  On Marx's theory of rent, see Ben Fine and Alfredo Saad-Filho, *Marx's 'Capital'* (5th edn; London, 2010), ch 13, and David Harvey, *The Limits to Capital* (Oxford, 1982), ch 11.

Ricardo fails sufficiently to differentiate the abstract from the concrete. Thus Marx goes on to reproach him for failing to 'consider *surplus value* separately and independently from its particular forms—profit (interest) and rent' (*CW*32: 9). But, as the following passage makes clear, Ricardo's failure to bring 'his abstraction to completion' leads to the problems that bedevil his value theory:

> Some of the observations that occur in Ricardo's writing should have led him to the distinction between surplus value and profit. Because he fails to make this distinction, he appears in some passages to descend to the vulgar view—as has already been indicated in the analysis of **Ch. I** '*On Value*'—the view that profit is a mere addition over and above the value of the commodity; for instance when he speaks of the determination of profit on capital in which the fixed capital predominates, etc. This was the source of much nonsense among his successors. This vulgar view is bound to arise, if the proposition (which in practice is correct) that on the average, *capitals of equal size yield equal profits* or that profit depends on the size of the capital employed, is not connected by a series of intermediary links with the general laws of value etc: in short, if profit and surplus-value are treated as identical, which is only correct for the aggregate capital. Accordingly Ricardo has no means for determining a *general rate of profit*. (*CW*32: 60-61)

Ricardo's failure to develop the relationship between abstract and concrete through 'a series of intermediate links' is the essence of the second criticism:

> He presupposes *a general rate of profit* or an *average profit of equal magnitude* for different capital investments of equal magnitude, or for different spheres of production in which capitals of equal size are employed—or, which is the same thing, profit in proportion to the *size* of the capital employed in the various spheres of production. Instead of *postulating* this *general rate of profit*, Ricardo should rather have examined in how far its *existence* is in fact consistent with the determination of value by labour-time, and he would have found that instead of being consistent with it, *prima facie*, it *contradicts* it, and that its existence would therefore have to be explained through a number of intermediary stages, a procedure which is very different from merely including it under the law of value. (*CW*31: 401)

By the time Marx wrote this comment he had, thanks to his development of the transformation from values to prices of production, a much clearer idea of what this explanation 'through a number of intermediary stages' involved. *Capital* offers the fullest picture of this process. In *Capital*, I, Marx analyses the immediate process of production. This involves in particular presenting the forms of extraction of surplus value within this process and the accumulation of capital. Among the important concepts introduced at this stage is that of the organic composition of capital (to repeat, the ratio between constant and variable capital, invested respectively in means of production and labour power). But at this stage of the analysis Marx does not distinguish between the aggregate social capital and individual capitals (with one very important exception that we will consider in chapter 3). One of the major shifts that takes place in *Capital*, III, is that, having presented the process of circulation in the preceding volume, Marx introduces the effects of the differences both among individual capitals and between different kinds of capital (productive, commercial, interest-bearing).

In Part 1, he introduces the concept of the rate of profit. While the rate of surplus value—the ratio of surplus value to variable capital—measures the degree of exploitation of the worker, the rate of profit is the ratio between surplus value and the total capital (constant as well as variable) advanced. Then in Part 2 he shows how competition among capitals leads to the formation of a general rate of profit equalising returns across sectors and hence the transformation of values into prices of production. This involves, in Chapter 10, a detailed discussion of the process through which competition leads, via the fluctuation of market prices in response to shifts in supply and demand, to the formation in individual sectors of market values, which represent the norm of socially necessary labour time for individual kinds of product. The relationship between these two processes is established in the following passage: 'What competition brings about, first of all in one sphere, is the establishment of a uniform market value and market price out of the various individual values of commodities. But it is only the competition of capitals in *different* spheres that brings forth the production price that equalises the rates of profit between those spheres' (*C*III: 281).[65]

---

65    Compare an earlier version of this passage in the *1861–63 Manuscript*, which shows that Marx had not then formulated the concept of market value: *CW*31: 356. *Capital*, III, Part 2 is called 'The Transformation of Profit into Average Profit'. See Dussel on the decisive importance of Marx's formulation of the concept of average profit in the *1861–63 Manuscript: Towards an Unknown Marx*, pp83ff. Figure 4.1, 'Some categorial mediations between surplus value and profit' (Dussel, p46), conveys the complexity of the constellation of concepts that Marx develops.

The transformation of values into prices of production thus allows Marx to avoid Ricardo's errors.[66] In *Capital*, I, he formulates his theory of value and surplus value, abstracting from the 'concrete conditions' that interfere with Ricardo's argument in Chapter I of the *Principles*. Then, in the course of *Capital*, II, and the first two parts of Capital, III, Marx develops the 'series of intermediate links' that allow him to explain the formation of a general rate of profit and hence how commodities, though regulated by the **'rule of value'**, do not exchange at their values (*CW*32: 361). There is much more to be said about what this method of proceeding through 'intermediary links' involves, and I return to this in chapter 3. But for the moment I want to focus on its bearing on Hegel's influence on *Capital*. Fred Moseley has developed one of the most important recent interpretations of Marx's method, based on the idea that 'there are two main stages (or levels of abstraction) in Marx's theory in *Capital*. The first stage has to do with the *production of surplus value* and the *determination of the total surplus value*, and the second stage has to do with the *distribution of surplus-value* and the *division of the pre-determined total surplus value into individual parts* (equal rates of profit, commercial profit, interest, and rent).' *Capital*, I, is concerned with the production of surplus value and the bulk of *Capital*, III, with its distribution through the formation of a general rate of profit and the fragmentation of the surplus value created in production into revenues—commercial profit, interest, profit of enterprise, rent—appropriated by different fractions of the capitalist class. But Moseley further argues that the relationship between these two levels is best understood through the connection that Hegel draws in *The Science of Logic* between the categories of universal, particular and singular.[67]

---

66   Out of incompetence and a concern for my own sanity, I abstain in this book from the debate about the 'transformation problem'. Impressive recent contributions include Alfredo Saad-Filho, *The Value of Marx* (London, 2002), Andrew Kliman, *Reclaiming Marx's 'Capital'* (Lanham MD, 2007), and Fred Moseley's review of the latter in *Historical Materialism*, 18.4 (2010). Moseley offers a comprehensive treatment of the subject in *Money and Totality: Marx's Logical Method and the End of the 'Transformation Problem'* (forthcoming).

67   Fred Moseley, 'The Universal and the Particulars in Hegel's *Logic* and Marx's *Capital*', in Moseley and Tony Smith, eds, *Marx's Capital and Hegel's Logic* (Leiden, 2014). Moseley's overall interpretation of *Capital* has been developed in a number of articles, for example, 'Hostile Brothers: Marx's Theory of the Distribution of Surplus Value in Volume III of *Capital*', in Martha Campbell and Geert Reuten, eds, *The Culmination of Capital* (Basingstoke, 2002). There are other aspects of this interpretation that I touch on in the next chapter. Hiroshi Uchida also argues that Marx's theory of capital must be understood through Hegel's dialectic of universality, particularity, and singularity: *Marx's Grundrisse and Hegel's Logic*.

Moseley's distinction between the two levels of abstraction in *Capital* is a persuasive one (though, as we have seen, these two levels in fact involve a succession of different determinations). And he points to passages such as the following (which we encountered in chapter 1) in the *Grundrisse*:

> Capital. I. *Generality*: (1) (a) Emergence of capital out of money. (b) Capital and labour (mediating itself through alien labour). (c) The elements of capital, dissected according to their relation to labour (Product. Raw material. Instrument of labour.) (2) *Particularization of capital*: (a) Capital circulant, capital fixe. Turnover of capital. (3) *The singularity of capital*: Capital and profit. Capital and interest. Capital as value, distinct from itself as interest and profit. II. *Particularity*: (1) Accumulation of capitals. (2) Competition of capitals. (3) Concentration of capitals (quantitative distinction of capital as at same time qualitative, as measure of its size and influence). III. *Singularity*: (1) Capital as credit. (2) Capital as stock-capital. (3) Capital as money market. (*G*: 275)

But fully to establish the depth of Marx's adoption of Hegel's categories, we need to consider the categories themselves. One theme of the *Science of Logic* that is central to Hegel's system as a whole is the critique of the concept of universal inherited from traditional Aristotelian logic. The old logic distinguished sharply between a universal concept and its particular instances. The relationship between universal and particular was an external one: the universal provided a principle for classifying the particulars, but remained an empty form imposed on the reality (the particulars) it sought to classify. Such a universal was abstract for Hegel in the sense that it lacked the concrete content of mediation provided by the particulars and their relationships:

> what makes this universality an abstraction is that the mediation is only a *condition*, or is not *posited in it*. Because it is not *posited*, the unity of the abstraction has the form of immediacy, and the content has the form of indifference to its universality, for the content is nothing but this totality which is the universality of absolute negativity. (*GL*: 537)

Thus separated from each other, particular and universal represent an obstacle to knowledge: the classification of particulars in the absence of any attempt to articulate their internal structure does not deepen our comprehension of reality. But this is not the only mode of relation between universal and particular. Hegel advances as the resolution of the contradiction between universal and particular the concept of the singular, or the concrete universal, in which the universal is the *unifica-tion* of the particulars:

> the turning back of this side [the particular] into the universal is two-fold, *either* by virtue of an *abstraction* that lets the particular fall away and climbs into a higher and the highest *genus*, or by virtue of the *sin-gularity* to which the universality in the determinateness descends. —Here is where the false start is made that makes abstraction stray away from the way of the concept, abandoning the truth. Its higher and highest universal to which it rises is only a surface that becomes progressively more void of content; the singularity which it scorns is the depth in which the concept grasps itself and where it is posited as concept. (*GL:* 546)

This critique of abstract universality has its echoes in the 1857 Introduction, where Marx rejects the sort of abstraction in which, because it starts from the concrete, and ascends in exactly the way Hegel describes, 'the full conception was evaporated to yield an abstract deter-mination'. And Marx's notion of 'the scientifically correct method', ie 'the method of rising from the abstract to concrete', recalls Hegel's con-ception of the concrete universal, which 'is not a mere sum of features common to several things, confronted by a particular which enjoys an existence of its own. It is, on the contrary, self-particularising or self-specifying, and with undimmed clearness finds itself at home in its antithesis'.[68] The 'totality which is the universality of absolute negativity' is the universal as synthesis of particulars. As such it is subjectivity as the return of self out of other, the universal that retains its identity when mediated in particularity: 'The concrete is the universal which makes itself particular, and in this making itself particular and finite yet remains eternally at home with itself'.[69]

Perhaps the best way into considering further how this conception of universality throws further light on the nature of Marx's method is pro-vided by the very interesting interpretation offered by Ilyenkov. He suggests that the differences between Marx and Ricardo are best under-stood in the light of Hegel's critique of Spinoza.[70] Hegel's differences with Spinoza derived from the very thesis that he took over from him— *omnis determinatio negatio est* (all determination is negation). Spinoza deduced from this doctrine that all finite existence involves negation the

---

68  *Hegel's Logic* (Oxford, 1975), §163; p227.
69  G W F Hegel, *Lectures on the History of Philosophy* (3 vols, London, 1963), II, p381.
70  Ilyenkov, *Dialectics of the Abstract and the Concrete of Marx's* **Capital**, ch 3.

conclusion that all finite beings are modifications of the self-sufficient substance that is God. The result, according to Hegel, is that the world is effaced. Spinoza's system is, Hegel insists, not (as the common accusation held) Atheism, but 'Acosmism': the various determinations of reality (conceived by Spinoza primarily as the attributes of thought and extension and a variety of more concrete modes) are resolved into Substance.[71]

For Spinoza, universal and particular are distinct; therefore their unity, Hegel claims, consists in the abolition of the particular. To have formed the concept of concrete universality would have involved conceiving negation as 'absolute determinateness, or negativity, which is absolute form; in this way of looking at it negation is the negation of the negation, and therefore true affirmation'.[72] To appreciate the significance of this criticism we need to bear in mind the structure that Hegel attributes to the dialectical process whose basic forms are unfolded in the *Logic*. The starting point of both the dialectic as a whole (the first category of the *Logic*, being), and of each stage of the dialectic, is an original, simple unity. Because this unity is simple and hence without distinction it is unconscious. Consciousness presupposes differentiation. This is brought out most sharply at the start of the *Logic*, where being, the absolute beginning of all philosophy, lacks any sort of determination at all. This absence of determination means that being passes into nothing, which is equally an absolute lack of differentiation. Being as such is unknowable, ineffable. But to give the original starting point the determinateness that it lacks and that it requires in order to be known is also to limit and deny it. *Omnis determinatio negatio est*, Hegel follows Spinoza in affirming: that is, to determine a thing is to establish its limits, to state what it is *not*. Thus negativity is introduced—the second stage of the dialectic, and the moment that Hegel describes as the properly dialectical stage, first negation. The original unity is broken up; a thing finds identity by means of its relation to its other, to what it is not. It is estranged from itself.

The third moment of the dialectic is what Hegel describes as its speculative moment—second negation, or *the negation of the negation*. Here the entity that has passed over into its other as a result of first negation discovers that its other is identical with itself and thus returns out

---

71  Hegel, *Lectures on the History of Philosophy*, III, pp280-282. Hegel's interpretation of Spinoza is of course highly controversial. For a Marxist critique, see Pierre Macherey, *Hegel ou Spinoza* (Paris, 1977). Gilles Deleuze provides an influential alternative reading in *Spinoza et le problème d'expression* (Paris, 1968).

72  Hegel, *Lectures on the History of Philosophy*, III, p286.

of its other to itself. This is the movement of subjectivity. Subjectivity presupposes first negation, the differentiation of its original unity, but if it remains at this stage consciousness is estranged from the reality of which it is part, for it acquires its identity by means of its relation to what it is not, to the other. It finds itself, transcending this self-estrangement by recognising it for what it is—*self-estrangement*. Thus by recognising the other as itself, by finding itself *in its other*, subjectivity establishes itself.[73]

Hegel famously puts forward the slogan: 'Everything turns of grasping the True, not as *Substance*, but equally as *Subject*'.[74] It is through the process just described that substance is transformed into subject. The original unconscious unity of substance is broken up through first negation, and then re-established at a different level. The unity that is restored is different from that with which we started because it has gone through the process of self-estrangement and achieved conscious comprehension of the process as a whole through the recognition of the other as itself. This solution operates at all levels of the dialectic. Logic is the original unity of the Absolute Idea that, divided and self-estranged in the externality of Nature, finds a subjective, self-conscious unity at the level of Absolute Spirit in the self-comprehension of the total process in speculative philosophy. God passes from an unquestioning unconscious unity with his creation through the agony of separation to the conscious realisation of the unity between creator and created in the Christian congregation. Social man passes out of the natural and organic unity of the family to the estrangement of an atomised civil society only to find reconciliation between substantial and subjective in the state.[75]

In the absence of negation of the negation, subjectivity falls outside substance and we have the position that, according to Hegel, we find in Spinoza, where:

---

73  Fredric Jameson is one of a number of commentators who are dismissive of what he calls 'the tripartite formula': *The Hegel Variations: On the **Phenomenology of Spirit*** (London, 2010), p19. In support he cites a passage where Hegel argues that, because it is also 'the *restoration* of the *original immediacy*', the negation of the negation 'can also be counted as fourth, and instead of a triplicity, the abstract form may also be taken to be a *quadruplicity*'. But Hegel goes on to reaffirm his commitment to the triple form taken by the dialectic. He acknowledges that formalistic treatment of triplicity, for example in traditional logic and Kantian philosophy, 'has rendered that form tedious and has given it a bad name. Yet the insipidity of this use cannot rob it of its inner worth, and the fact that the shape of reason was discovered, albeit without conceptual comprehension at first, is always to be highly valued.' *GL*: 746-747.

74  Hegel, *Phenomenology of Spirit*, §17; p10.

75  See Charles Taylor's patient and lucid exploration of Hegel's system in *Hegel* (Cambridge, 1977).

cognition is an external reflection that fails to comprehend what appears a finite—that is, the determinateness of the attribute and the mode, and in general itself as well—by not deriving them from substance; it behaves like an external understanding, taking up the determinations as *given* and *reducing* them to the absolute but not taking their beginning from it. (*GL*: 472)

The expulsion of particularity, mediation, subjectivity, and the negation of the negation from substance is reflected, Hegel claims, in Spinoza's geometrical method, which reproduces the deductive system of the classical model of science common to both the so-called rationalists and empiricists of the 17th and 18th centuries: 'Absolute substance, attribute and mode, Spinoza allows to follow one another as definitions, he adopts them as ready-made, without the attributes being developed from the substance, or the modes from the attributes'.[76] Hegel's injunction to comprehend substance as subject is directed against Spinoza (and his own mentor Schelling, whom he tends to class with Spinoza).[77] Advance beyond Spinoza, Hegel argues in a key passage in the *Phenomonology* whose full meaning will become clearer in the following chapter, involves understanding that:

the living Substance is being which is in truth *Subject*, or, what is the same, is in truth actual only in so far as it is the movement of positing itself, or is the mediation of its self-othering with itself. This Substance is, as Subject, pure, *simple negativity*, and it is for this very reason the bifurcation of the simple; it is the doubling which sets up opposition, and then again the negation of this indifferent diversity and of its antithesis. Only this *self-restoring* sameness, or this reflection in otherness within itself—not an *original* or *immediate* unity as such—is the True. It is the process of its own becoming, the circle that presupposes its end as its goal, having its end also as its goal, having its end also as its beginning; and only by being worked out to its end, is it actual.[78]

Ilyenkov argues that, like Spinoza, Ricardo treats reality as 'modifications of one and the same universal substance', value. And value is conceived by Ricardo as an abstract universal, as what is generic to its

76  Hegel, *Lectures on the History of Philosophy*, III, p269.
77  On the significance of Spinoza to the development of German classical idealism, see Dieter Henrich, *Between Kant and Hegel: Lectures on German Idealism* (Cambridge MA, 2003), Part II.
78  Hegel, *Phenomenology of Spirit*, §18; p10.

particular forms. These forms are thus external to value; the necessity of their existence as forms of value is not proved, but is the arbitrary result of an empirical induction. Ilyenkov concludes:

> All the merits of Ricardo's method of inquiry are closely connected with the point of view of substance, that is, with the conception of the object as a single whole coherent in all its manifestations. Contrariwise, all the defects and vices of his mode of unfolding his theory are rooted in complete failure to understand this whole as a historically formed one.[79]

Ilyenkov somewhat muddies the water by linking his argument to a version of the historical interpretation of Marx's value theory.[80] But this should not be allowed to obscure the real insight that Ilyenkov's comparison between Ricardo and Spinoza offers. For the latter, Hegel claims, differentiation, because it is negation, is external to substance. For Hegel, differentiation is inherent in the concept. In other words, the difference between Spinoza and Hegel lies in the absence in the former's work of the concept of negation of negation or of *internal contradiction*. So Marx is indeed right that Ricardo fails to treat capitalism as the result of a historical process. But he had already diagnosed Ricardo's naturalisation of capitalism in *The Poverty of Philosophy*. The problem that he identifies in the *1861-63 Manuscript* is that none of the classical political economists, even Ricardo, are able to treat their object as an internally differentiated and contradictory structure.

We can adapt Hegel's criticism of Spinoza's method to apply to Ricardo: 'Value, general rate of profit and price, Ricardo allows to follow one another as definitions, he adopts them as ready-made, without the general rate of profit being developed from value, or price from the general rate of profit.' This criticism is identical with the one that, as we have seen, Marx made of Ricardo: 'Instead of *postulating* this *general rate of profit*, Ricardo should rather have examined in how far its *existence* is in fact consistent with the determination of value by labour-time, and he would have found that instead of being consistent with it, *prima facie*, it

79  Ilyenkov, *Dialectics of the Abstract and the Concrete*, pp183, 194.
80  Thus Ilyenkov argues that 'Marx formed scientific definitions of "value in general", "value as such", on the basis of concrete consideration of direct exchange of one commodity for another involving no money...precisely that kind of value which proves to be elementary, primordial both logically and historically,' *Dialectics of Abstract and Concrete*, pp79-80. Apart from the fact, as Marx emphasises in his 'Notes on Wagner', he starts in *Capital*, not from 'value in general', but with the commodity ($CW24$: 544), his analysis of the value form in Volume I, Chapter 1, does not stop short at the elementary and relative forms, which indeed posit exchange without money, but concludes with the money form and price (the expression of values in money). More on all this in chapter 4.

*contradicts* it, and that its existence would therefore have to be explained through a number of intermediary stages.'

Ilyenkov sums up the difference in a particular daring formulation that invokes Hegel's slogan of transforming substance into subject in the Preface to the *Phenomenology*:

> The essence of the Marxian upheaval in political economy may be expressed in philosophical terms in the following manner: in Marx's theory, *not only the substance* of value, labour, was understood (Ricardo also attained this understanding), but, for the first time, value was simultaneously understood *as the subject* of the entire development, that is, as a reality developing through its inner contradictions into a whole system of economic forms. Ricardo failed to understand this latter point.[81]

So how far is Marx tributary to Hegel?

---

81   Ilyenkov, *Dialectics of the Abstract and Concrete*, p278.

3

# Method, II: Hegel

## The Hegel problem

Hegel offers Marx the resource of a different conception of science from the classical one on which both Ricardo and his successors rely. In his system knowledge no longer takes the form of a deductive system whose premises are typically justified by the claim they derive from some direct encounter between thought and reality. Hegel offers an explicit critique of what is now called the covering-law conception of explanation, where a phenomenon is explained by having its description deduced from a universal law and the statement of a set of initial conditions. Here explanation proceeds through the subsumption of phenomena under principles:

> Now, here, according to the conception of the non-speculative sciences, it is placed in this dilemma: the principle is either an unproved hypothesis or demands a proof which in turn implies the principle. The proof that is demanded of this principle itself presupposes something else, such as the logical laws of proof; these laws are, however, themselves propositions such as required to be proved; and so it goes on to infinitude, if an absolute hypothesis to which another can be posed is not made... But these forms of proposition, of consecutive proof, etc, do not apply to what is speculative...as though the proposition before us here, and the proof were something separate from it there; for in this case the proof comes with the proposition. The concept is a self-movement, and not, as a proposition, a desire to rest; nor is it true that the proof brings forward another ground and middle term and is another movement; for it has this movement in itself.[1]

---

1   G W F Hegel, *Lectures on the History of Philosophy* (3 vols, London, 1963), II, pp368-369 (translation modified). The classic discussion of the covering law model is Carl G. Hempel, *Aspects of Scientific Explanation* (New York, 1965). In economics, Milton Friedman offered a way out of Hegel's dilemma by arguing that the premises of economic theories must be conceived as fictions from which fruitful empirical consequences can nevertheless be derived: see *Essays in Positive Economics* (Chicago, 1964). Interestingly

The idea that 'the proof comes with the proposition' is an interesting anticipation of Imre Lakatos's idea of 'proof-generated concepts': 'Conjectures and concepts both have to pass through the purgatory of proofs and refutations. *Naïve conjectures and naïve concepts are superseded by improved conjectures (theorems) and concepts (proof-generated or theoretical concepts) growing out of the method of proofs and refutations'.*[2] The idea that the process of proving a theory can generate new concepts is radically inconsistent with the classical model of science. On the latter conception, the basic concepts of a science are formulated through the process of analysis that precedes the deduction of the science from the basic axioms incorporating these concepts. To assert that the deduction itself could generate new concepts would violate the principle of logic that deductive inference cannot increase content. As we shall see more fully in the following section, Marx's discourse in *Capital* is one where 'the proof comes with the proposition'. The successive transformations through which this discourse unfolds involve the introduction of new concepts, where the assertions incorporating them, and adding new content to the analysis, are not simply deduced from those with which it starts.

So Marx's debt to Hegel lies much deeper that the terminological overlap evident to readers especially of the *Grundrisse*. But the relationship is a problematic one. Hegel's breach with the classical model of science is possible because of the new conception of subjectivity that he develops. For Hegel, subjectivity is not the external guarantee of the validity of the science's axioms. Subjectivity is the result of a process, and this process is at the same time the conceptual cognition of reality. The system of science is the process whereby the essential structures of subjectivity are constituted. This interpenetration of the concepts of science and of subjectivity transforms them both. In this chapter I first

---

Marx criticises Ricardo for using unrealistic assumptions in what might now be called his models: 'The *presuppositions* in the illustrations must not be self-contradictory. They must therefore be formulated in such a way as to be real presuppositions, *real* hypotheses, and not assumed absurdities or hypothetical realities and impossibilities' (*CW*31: 121). This contradicts the claim made by Leszek Nowak in his interesting study of Marx's method in *Capital* that 'Marx introduces some assumptions of which he knows *a priori* to be false in empirical reality' and then subsequently drops 'these counterfactual assumptions': *The Structure of Idealisation: Towards a Systematic Interpretation of the Marxian Idea of Science* (Dordrecht, 1980), p21. The more abstract levels of determination in *Capital* govern the more concrete levels.

2    Imre Lakatos, *Proofs and Refutations* (Cambridge, 1976), p91. This text is a superb demolition of the classical conception of science on its home ground—mathematics. It is interesting that Lakatos should go on to argue that 'Hegel and Popper represent the only fallibilist traditions in modern philosophy,' p139, n 1.

consider how Marx draws, somewhat eclectically, on the categories through which Hegel develops this unification of science and subjectivity, but also how across successive manuscripts he increasingly reworks his own concepts so as to reduce his dependence on the Hegelian dialectic. I then consider in detail how Marx moves from the abstract to the concrete, by progressively introducing new determinations that, as we have just noted, add new content to the theory; one important resulting shift is the rising profile of competition in the later drafts. Finally, I discuss how the structure of externalisation that Marx traces through the three volumes of *Capital* provides the context in which to understand his mature conceptualisations of ideology (as fetishism) and of science.

The goal of Hegel's system is to overcome the distinction between subject and object in Absolute Spirit. But this distinction is to be overcome through the self-development of an articulated system of concepts. In other words, Hegel rejects the notion that knowledge is dependent on the subject's *immediate* access to the real; here he differs not only with other proponents of absolute idealism like Schelling, but rejects a basic tenet of classical empiricism, where knowledge derives from sense-experience. Mediation—relation to other—is a necessary moment in the Absolute's progression to self-knowledge. Thus the speculative aim of Hegel's system—the identity of subject and object in Absolute Spirit— can only be achieved discursively, ie as a structured system of concepts. He commences the *Science of Logic* by rejecting the

> separation, presupposed once and for all in ordinary consciousness, of the *content* and its *form*, or of *truth* and *certainty*. Presupposed *from the start* is that the material of knowledge is present in and for itself as a ready-made world outside thinking; that thinking is by itself empty, that it comes to this material as a form from outside, fills itself with it, and only then gains a content, thereby becoming real knowledge. (*GL*: 24)

Hegel rejects this separation of form and content because for him the categories of Logic, which provide the structure of all the sciences, are not a set of concepts that we construct in order to know a reality external to thought. Their movement provides the process whereby the form generates content, ie whereby thought constitutes reality. Such a move is open to Hegel because the structure of his dialectic is one in which the concept is forced to pass beyond the primal unity of Being and to externalise itself in the mediations of Essence, where, to account for the appearances, an underlying substratum must be postulated. This is the moment of first negation in the *Logic*. It is thus that form acquires content for 'the *necessity* of the connectedness and the *immanent emergence* of distinctions must be found in the treatment of the fact itself, for it falls within the concept's own progressive determination' (*GL*: 34).

But the connection between the concept and its manifestation in Essence (and Nature) is an external one. The relations constituting the categories of Essence link entities that preserve their independence even in their unity. The Doctrine of Essence:

> includes all the categories of metaphysic and of the sciences in general. They are products of reflective understanding, which, while it assumes the differences to possess a footing of their own, and at the same time also expresses their relativity, still combines the two statements, side by side, or one after another, by an 'also', without bringing these thoughts or unifying them in the concept.[3]

Spinoza's philosophy remains, for Hegel, trapped at the level of the understanding, as opposed to reason, the truly speculative dimension of thought. The inner connection of the concept into which the mediations of Essence pass does not only overcome the independence that persisted between the terms of these mediations; it also abolishes the related distinction between the understanding and the reality on which it reflects. The concept forms a spiritual unity, the third term of the dialectic, the negation of the negation, in which the subject and object are united. Thus the unity of the concept, whose realisation is the Absolute Idea, is subjectivity, the return to self out of other: 'In this turning point of the method, the course of cognition returns at the same time into itself. This negativity is as self-sublating contradiction, the *restoration* of the *first immediacy*, of simple universality; for the other of the other, the negative of the negative, is immediately the *positive*, the *identical*, the *universal*' (*GL*: 746).

But, as we have already seen, the unity of the Absolute Idea is not the simple restoration of the primal unity of Being. Subjectivity is the identity of self in the other, but it is also return *out* of other: if the recollection of its passage into otherness were effaced, it would cease to be subjectivity:

> In the absolute method, the concept *maintains* itself in its otherness, the universal in its particularisation, in judgement and reality; at each stage of further determination, the universal elevates the whole mass of its

---

3   *Hegel's Logic* (Oxford, 1975), §114; p166 (translation modified).

preceding content, not only not losing anything in its dialectical advance, or leaving it behind, but, on the contrary, carrying with itself all that it has gained, inwardly enriched and compressed. (*GL*: 750)

The content of the Absolute Idea is, however, in no way distinct from its form, and this form is the dialectical method, the structure of the process whereby Being has become the Absolute Idea, which 'is not an extraneous form, but the soul and notion of the content'.[4] The consequence of evolving the content out of the form and then resuming it back into the Idea is that the Idea is nothing other than the process by which it is arrived at:

> Seeing that there is in it no transition, or presupposition, and in general no specific character other than what is fluid or transparent, the Absolute Idea is for itself the pure form of the concept, which contemplates its contents as its own self. It is its own content, in so far as it ideally distinguishes itself from itself, and one of the two things distinguished is a self identity in which however is contained the totality of the form as the system of terms describing its content. This content is the system of Logic. *All that is at this stage left for the Idea is the Method of this content—the specific consciousness of the value and currency of the 'moments'.*[5]

This dialectical method describes a circle: 'By nature of the method just indicated, the science presents itself as a *circle* that winds around itself, where the mediation winds the end back to the beginning which is the simple ground' (*GL*: 751). Subjectivity consists in the circular structure of the dialectic and the circular structure results from the peculiar aim assigned to science, the transformation of substance into subject. The process whereby the subject constitutes itself is identical with the scientific comprehension of reality, and with reality itself. Subjectivity consists in the teleological structure of both thought and reality.

All this underlines very strongly that it is impossible to separate Hegel's method and his system in the way that Engels advocated. But it also highlights the difficulty that Marx faces in inheriting from Hegel the thesis that knowledge is a process of internal differentiation, or, more precisely, a process driven by its immanent contradictions. For Hegel conceptualises this process using the concept of the negation of the negation. Not simply is this concept central to Hegel's account of the

---

4  *Hegel's Logic*, §243; p296.
5  *Hegel's Logic*, §237; p292 (translation modified); italics added.

structure of subjectivity, but he sees the contradictions that develop in finite things as serving to resume them into the spiritual unity of the Absolute. The negation of the negation overcomes the finitude of material reality. Hegel berates 'the ordinary tenderness for things, the overriding worry of which is that they do not contradict themselves' (*GL*: 367). The 'principle: "All things are in themselves contradictory"' serves to enthrone absolute idealism: 'the truth is that the absolute is just because the finite is the immanently self-contradictory opposite, because it *is not*' (*GL*: 381, 385). In a famous passage Hegel pronounces: 'The claim that the *finite is an idealisation* defines *idealism*. The idealism of philosophy consists in nothing else than the recognition that the finite is not truly an existent... A philosophy that attributes to finite existence, as such, true, ultimate, absolute being, does not deserve the name of philosophy' (*GL*: 124).

There is, particularly among contemporary philosophers, much discussion about the exact meaning of such remarks of Hegel's. In his introduction to his new translation of the *Science of Logic*, George di Giovanni distinguishes between two broad approaches. The first, and more traditional, asserts that 'the Logic makes an ontological commitment and to that extent advances a dogma'; according to the second, 'the Logic still operates within the framework of Kant's and Fichte's idealism and to that extent never abandons the realism of discursive thought'.[6] The latter, as di Giovanni describes it, 'hermeneutic' approach embraces a variety of positions, including that of Slavoj Žižek, who attacks 'the absurd image of Hegel as the "absolute idealist", who "pretended to know everything", to posses Absolute Knowledge, to read the mind of God, to deduce the whole of reality from the self-movement of (his) Mind'. Here is one of his many elaborations of this 'deflated' view of Hegel:

> The standard talk about the Hegelian Spirit which alienates itself to itself, and then recognises itself in its otherness, and thus reappropriates its content, is deeply misleading: the Self to which Spirit returns is produced in the very movement of this return, or, that to which the process of return is returning is produced by the very process of returning. In a subjective process, there is no 'absolute subject', no permanent central agent playing with itself the game of alienation and disalienation, losing or dispersing itself and then reappropriating its alienated content; after a substantial totality is dispersed, it is another agent—previously its

---

6 George Di Giovanni, 'Introduction', to G W F Hegel, *The Science of Logic* (Cambridge, 2010), pplv-lvi.

subordinated moment—which retotalises it. It is this shifting of the centre of the process from one moment to another which distinguishes a dialectical process from the circular movement of alienation and its overcoming. It is because of this shift that the 'return to itself' coincides with accomplished alienation (when a subject retotalises itself). In this precise sense, substance returns to itself as subject, and this transubstantiate is what substantial life cannot accomplish.[7]

The extracts that I have perhaps too plentifully cited above from Hegel indicate that Žižek is engaging in what Freud called 'wild analysis'. Shortly after the passage just quoted he complains about Hegel's 'many misnomers'; the general thrust of Žižek's interpretation of Hegel is to save him from himself by reworking his conception of subjectivity with the help of Žižek's own version of Lacanian psychoanalysis.[8] What is valid in his argument is that Hegel's conception of subjectivity is *structural*. The absolute isn't a substance, and certainly is nothing like a personal God; it is, as we have seen, identical with the process of its own becoming. But the references to the idea of Hegel pretending (or being misread as pretending) to 'know the mind of God' are a ridiculous caricature of the position of those who take the ontological reading of the *Logic* seriously. Di Giovanni engages in a similar *canard*. Thus he writes of one exponent of this interpretation, J M E McTaggart:

> It transpires...that, despite all protestations that the Logic must be read as *logic*, McTaggart has in fact invested it from the beginning with pre-Kantian, Spinozist overtones. While taking the Logic to lay out the blueprint of a universe of meaning that makes the discovery of an actual cosmos possible, he assumes that it thereby also lays out the blueprint of that cosmos. It is from the start an exercise in cosmogony.[9]

7   Slavoj Žižek, *Less Than Nothing* (London, 2012), p239, pp234-235. More conventional examples of the 'hermeneutic' approach include Robert Pippin, *Modernism as a Philosophical Problem* (Oxford, 1991), and Terry Pinkard, *Hegel's Phenomenology* (Cambridge, 1994). Fredric Jameson shrewdly observes: 'this rescue operation, which makes Hegel respectable and allows him re-entry into the fraternity of professional philosophers, has a consequence which elementary dialectics might have predicted in advance, namely...the slippage of the non-philosophical (or "sociological") chapters [of the *Phenomenology of Spirit*] into the impressionistic flabbiness of a generalising "culture critique",' *The Hegel Variations: On the **Phenomenology of Spirit*** (London, 2010), pp10-11. Gérard Lebrun's impressive study, *La patience du Concept: Essai sur le discours hégélien* (Paris, 1972), underlines how hard it is to assimilate Hegel to either the dogmatic or the hermeneutic readings.
8   Žižek, *Less Than Nothing*, p235.
9   Di Giovanni, 'Introduction', plvii. See J M E McTaggart, *A Commentary on Hegel's Logic* (New York, 1964).

Di Giovanni goes on to refer to 'McTaggart's Absolute Idea from which, allegedly, every minute detail of reality can in principle be deduced'.[10] Whether or not this is a fair reading of McTaggart, it certainly isn't Hegel's version of the Absolute: he famously, and scornfully, demolished 'Herr Krug [who] once challenged the Philosophy of Nature to perform the feat of deducing *only* his pen'. Thus Hegel argues that in Nature, as the sphere where the Idea is alienated, 'contingency and determination from without has its right, and this contingency is at its greatest in the realm of concrete individual forms... This is the *impotence of Nature*, that it preserves the determinations of the Concept only *abstractly*, and leaves their detailed specification to external determination.' But we should note that this conception of Nature implies its inferiority relative to thought: 'Thus Nature has also been spoken as the *self-degradation of the Idea*, in that the Idea, in this form of externality, is in a disparity with its own self'.[11] So, in affirming Nature as the realm of contingency, Hegel is asserting, and not qualifying his absolute idealism.

There is an obvious sense in which Hegel's project is a continuation of those developed by Kant and Fichte. Like them, he is concerned to develop a philosophical theory of the constitution of subjectivity.[12] But everything turns on what is meant by the word 'constitution' here. Kant's transcendental argument in the *Critique of Pure Reason* is concerned to establish the conditions of possible experience, in the process deducing a set of categories through which the sense-impressions given to the mind are organised as the causally governed objective world of appearances presented to a unitary, enduring subject. But this kind of constitution is for Hegel the paradigmatic case of the separation of form and content against which he so continuously polemicises. The implication of this polemic is that the categories of his *Logic* are the essential forms of being—not so that everything can be deduced from them (apart from anything else, Hegel regards deductive logic as a relatively flawed form of reasoning), but in order to grasp their role in the process of constitution of (absolute) subjectivity. Moreover, as I have relentlessly

---

10  Di Giovanni, 'Introduction', plviii.

11  *Hegel's Philosophy of Nature* (Oxford, 1970), § 250, pp22-23, and p23*; § 248; p17.
    Di Giovanni cites the idea of the 'impotence of Nature' against McTaggart, without seeing that it cuts across his own preferred interpretation, according to which 'Nature is for Hegel, just as it was for Schelling', 'the "pre-self" of the "self", not just the "other-than-self" of Fichte.' 'Introduction', pplvii, lix.

12  See Dieter Henrich, *Between Kant and Hegel: Lectures on German Idealism* (Cambridge MA, 2003).

emphasised, the Hegelian subject is nothing other than the teleological structure of the dialectical process, that is, the absolute method that is posited at the end of the *Science of Logic*.[13]

Where does this leave Marx? We can begin to answer this by considering more closely the points at which he resorts to Hegelian categories systematically. One of the latest is the 2nd edition Chapter 1 of *Capital*, I, where in seeking to articulate his theory of the commodity, Marx uses Hegel's dialectic of quantity/quality/measure to structure the first three sections. These categories come from the Doctrine of Being, which is best understood as an immanent critique of the treatment of knowledge as a mere register of the immediate aspects of things and of their quantitative and mutually indifferent relations. One can see why this would be attractive to Marx when struggling with critics of Ricardo such as Samuel Bailey who seek to reduce value to a purely quantitative relationship.[14] But more useful for understanding the development of Marx's method is another case, namely his formulation in the *Grundrisse* of the distinction between 'capital in general' and 'many capitals'.

Marx presents his conception of capital in general here:

> *Capital in general*, as distinct from the particular capitals, does indeed appear (1) *only as an abstraction*; not an arbitrary abstraction, but an abstraction which grasps the specific characteristics which distinguish capital from all other forms of wealth—or modes in which (social) production develops. These are the aspects common to every capital as such, or which make every specific sum of values into capital. And the distinctions within this abstraction are likewise abstract particularities which characterise every kind of capital, in that it is their position (*Position*) or negation (*Negation*) (eg fixed capital or circulating capital); (2) however, capital in general, as *distinct* from the particular real capitals, is itself a *real* existence. This is recognised by ordinary economics, even if it is not *understood*, and forms a very important moment of its doctrine of equilibrations etc. For example, capital in this *general form*, although belonging to individual capitalists, in its *elemental form* as capital, forms the capital which accumulates in the banks or is distributed through

---

13   See the very close interrogation of Hegel on these issues in Michael Rosen, *Hegel's Dialectic and its Criticism* (Cambridge, 1982), and Louis Althusser's suggestive lecture, 'Marx's Relation to Hegel', in *Politics and History: Montesquieu, Rousseau, Hegel and Marx* (London, 1972), an extract from a longer posthumously published text, (1967) 'La Querelle de l'humanisme', in *Écrits philosophiques et politiques* (François Matheron, ed; 2 vols, Paris, 1994, 1995), II, pp447-456.

14   See the extensive discussion of these issues in Alex Callinicos, 'The Logic of *Capital*' (DPhil Thesis, Oxford University, 1978), ch III, and also chapter 4 below.

them, and, as Ricardo says, so admirably distributes itself in accordance with the needs of production. (*G*: 449)

Capital in general itself includes, as we saw in the preceding chapter, three moments—production, circulation, and their unity. But 'the three processes of which capital forms the unity are external; they are separate in time and space. As such, the transition from one into the other, ie their unity as regards the individual capitalists, is accidental. Despite their *inner unity*, they exist *independently* alongside one another, each as the presupposition of the other' (*G*: 403). Thus in the case of the devaluation of capital, a capitalist is unable to sell his product, or only at prices lower than their value. The externalisation of the inner unity of capital provides the basis for the transition from capital in general to many capitals:

> (... Conceptually, *competition* is nothing other than the inner *nature of capital*, its essential character, appearing in and realised as the reciprocal interaction of many capitals with one another, the inner tendency as external necessity.) (Capital exists and can only exist as many capitals, and its self-determination therefore appears as their reciprocal interaction with one another.) (*G*: 414)

The *Grundrisse* contains many other passages like this, where the distinction between capital in general and many capitals is mapped onto the opposition of inner and outer (for example, *G*: 443-444, 520, 552, 651, 657). Now this opposition derives directly from the category of inner and outer in *The Science of Logic*. This comes in the Doctrine of Essence, which, as McTaggart puts it, 'consists in the assertion of the duplicity of reality—its possession of an internal and external nature, capable of distinction from each other, but not indifferent to each other'.[15] So, unlike in the Doctrine of Being, the determinations of Essence are not mutually indifferent; their relationship to each other is now posited:

> Outer and inner are determinateness so posited that each, as a determination, not only presupposes the other and passes over into it as its truth, but, in being this truth of the other, remains *posited as determinateness* and points to the totality of both.—The *inner* is thus the completion of essence according to form. For in being determined as inner, essence implies that it is deficient and that it is only with reference to its other, the outer; but this other is not just being, or even concrete existence, but

---

15    McTaggart, *Commentary on Hegel's Logic*, p88.

*is* the reference to essence or the inner. What we have here is not just the reference of the two to each other, but the determining element of absolute form, namely that each term is immediately its opposite, and each is a common reference to a *third*, or rather *to their unity*. (*GL*: 461)

The point about the inner is that it remains inner. The unity of which it is constituted is not manifested as unity. Thus the inner unity corresponds to an apparently unrelated external reality. As Charles Taylor puts it:

> There is a link of equivalence between the state where reality is purely inner, in the sense of hidden, and reality is purely outer, in the sense of external to itself, not inwardly related to any links of necessity. The more that the essence is hidden (inner), the more reality is purely externally related outer. That is what Hegel calls the immediate unity of outer and inner.[16]

We can see now how this corresponds to Marx's argument in the *Grundrisse*. Because there is no direct social connection between the producers in the capitalist mode of production, the relationships that must exist if this mode is to be reproduced become operative by means of competition: 'competition is nothing more than the way in which the many capitals force the inherent determinants of capital upon one another and upon themselves' (*G*: 651). Hegelian categories not only serve to conceptualise the relation of capital in general and many capitals; they also provide the transition from one to other:

> Since value forms the foundation of capital, and since it therefore necessarily exists only through exchange for *counter-value*, it thus necessarily repels itself from itself. A *universal capital*, one without alien capitals confronting it, with which it exchanges—and from the present standpoint, nothing confronts it but wage labourers or itself—is therefore a non-thing. The reciprocal repulsion between capitals is already contained in capital as realised exchange value. (*G*: 421n)

The economic content of this statement is clear enough: the labour theory of value presupposes a situation where the means of production are controlled by autonomous but mutually interdependent producers. Therefore, in the circulation process, where the capitalist seeks to realise the value of his product, he is confronted by other, competing capitalists—'many capitals'. But Marx conceptualises this by resorting

---

16   Charles Taylor, *Hegel* (Cambridge, 1977), p278.

to another Hegelian category, repulsion and attraction. This time it comes from the Doctrine of Being, where we are still dealing with surface relationships, rather than the articulated structure of Essence. With many capitals, we have entered the sphere of competition—the sphere that, Marx consistently argues in successive manuscripts, if we take as our starting point, leaves us the captive of the superficial, the appearances rather than the inner structure of the relations of production (see below). In the sphere of Being, the negativity of finite reality can only be posited as a limit—that is, as what distinguishes something from its other. We are in a world of subsistent things whose distinctness consists in the limits separating them. This means that their necessary unity (necessary because relation to other is the mode by which Being differentiates itself) arises from their interaction. The one gives rise to the many and the latter's unity consists in their mutual repulsion and attraction. Similarly, for Marx, the unity of capital consists in the interaction of competing 'many capitals'.

But the employment of their categories is far from unproblematic. For Hegel the external is concept-less (*begrifflos*) in two related senses. First, the external is unconceptualised—the inner connections that form its essence have not been articulated and therefore reality appears unrelated. This could perhaps be called the epistemological sense of externality. Externality, however, is also the externalisation of the concept—the point at which it passes over into reality, thereby becoming self-estranged (as in Nature). This, if you like, is the ontological sense of externality. Of course, for Hegel the two senses are not really separable. The inner connections that once articulated reveal the structure of externality are simultaneously the means by which the concept resumes reality back into its now self-conscious spiritual unity. But it is important to keep the two separate from Marx's point of view, as he makes clear in the 1857 Introduction and the Afterword to the Second German Edition of *Capital*, I.

Marx himself, however, does not always make the distinction. Sometimes it seems as if the realm of many capitals, of competition, is the realisation of the concept of capital in general elaborated previously: 'Competition merely *expresses* as real, posits as an external necessity, that which lies within the nature of capital' (*G*: 651). We see a similar ambiguity in the highly Hegelian expression Marx often resorts to in the *Grundrisse* of 'positing the presupposition' (*setzen die Voraußetzung*). One of Hegel's preoccupations is with the self-justification of Logic as an 'absolute science' dependent on no presuppositions. Hence he starts the *Science of Logic* with being as a pure, abstract, undifferentiated and unmediated unity, but from which all the categories can be developed thanks to the activity of 'determinate negation', which operates thanks to the flaw inherent in every concept. This process is the self-development of the content because it is driven by internal contradiction, but it involves the progressive positing of the various determinations that are required to provide the abstract starting point with both concrete content and rational support. Not only is this a process of internal differentiation; through the positing of the presuppositions the starting point becomes rationally grounded. The circular movement of the dialectic reflects this process through which being simultaneously generates its concrete content and achieves its retrospective justification:

> In this advance the beginning thus loses the one-sidedness that it has when determined as something immediate and abstract; it becomes mediated, and the line of scientific forward movement consequently turns into a *circle*.—It also follows that what constitutes the beginning, because it is something still undeveloped and empty of content, is not yet truly known at that beginning, and that only science, and science fully developed, is the completed cognition of it, replete with content and finally truly grounded. (*GL*: 49)[17]

Hegel's conception of positing has the same ambiguity as that of externality. The term 'posit' [*setzen*] plays an important role in the philosophical writing of Hegel's slightly older contemporary Fichte, who developed a theory of absolute subjectivity in which the self posits both itself and its other. Dieter Henrich writes:

> '*Setzen*' has a richness of connotations, and Fichte constantly plays with them. For instance,...[t]o posit implies to constitute something, to establish it originally as a state that comes into being by way of the establishment of its constitution... Another association with *setzen* is the word 'law' (*Gesetz*); and still another is 'investiture' (*Einsetzung*), in the sense of a ruler or prelate being 'invested'.[18]

Michael Inwood identifies the key ambiguity in Hegel's own usage: 'To say that something is *gesetzt* [posited] has two implications, either of which may be dominant in a given context. (1) What is

---

17   The circular movement through which the presupposition is posited in Hegel and Marx is discussed in Hiroshi Uchida, *Marx's Grundrisse and Hegel's Logic* (Terrell Carver, ed; London, 1988), chs 1 and 3.

18   Henrich, *Between Kant and Hegel*, p233.

*gesetzt* is explicit or set out rather than implicit or in itself... (2) What is *gesetzt* is produced by or dependent on something else... Such positing can be either physical or conceptual'.[19] So to posit a presupposition may be more than to state the dependence between two concepts: it may be really to produce the referent of the posited concept. Patrick Murray rightly notes that Marx does not follow Hegel in imagining a presupposition-less science:

> Marx does not leave the circle of Hegelian systematic dialectics unbroken; he objects to the 'presuppositionlessness' of Hegelian systematic dialectics and insists that science has premises, which he and Engels sketched in *The German Ideology*. These premises are given by nature and are not themselves subject to being incorporated as 'results' of some more cosmic systematic dialectic, reappear in *Capital* and testify to Marx's explicit and frequently reaffirmed divergence from strictly Hegelian systematic dialectics (at least as he, questionably, understood Hegel).[20]

One could indeed go further and argue that Marx's theory presupposes, not just nature, but all the relations and mechanisms it posits as existing independently as the real 'premises' of his theory. But he does not therefore abandon the Hegelian usage of positing the presupposition, notably in this important passage in the *Grundrisse*:

> The conditions and presuppositions of the *becoming*, of the *arising*, of capital presuppose precisely that it is not yet in being but merely in *becoming*; they therefore disappear as real capital arises, capital which itself, on the basis of its own reality, posits the conditions for its realisation... These presuppositions, which originally appeared as conditions of its becoming—and hence could not spring from its *action as capital*—now appear as results of its own realisation, reality, as *posited by it—not as conditions of its arising, but as results of its presence*. It no longer proceeds from presuppositions in order to become, but rather it is itself presupposed, and proceeds from itself to create the conditions of its maintenance and growth. (*G*: 459-60)

The substantive point that Marx is making is developed considerably further in *Capital*, I, Parts 7 and 8, on the accumulation of capital. In the *Grundrisse* it allows him to copper-bottom the claim he has already made

---

19   Michael Inwood, *A Hegel Dictionary* (Oxford, 1992), p224.
20   Patrick Murray, 'Marx's "Truly Social" Labour Theory of Value: Part I,' *Historical Materialism*, 7 (2000), p38.

in the 1857 Introduction that the categories must be studied according to the role they play in the functioning of the capitalist mode of production rather than their historical genesis: 'In order to develop the laws of bourgeois economy, therefore, it is not necessary to write the *real history of the relations of production*. But the correct observation and deduction of these laws, as having themselves become in history, always leads to primary equations—like the empirical numbers eg in natural science—which point towards a past lying behind this system' (G: 460-461). These reflections precede the *Formen*, Marx's discussion of precapitalist forms of production.[21]

But there remains this idea that 'capital creates its own presuppositions'. Here is how Marx restates the idea, without the Hegelian terminology, in *Capital*, I:

> It is not enough that the conditions of labour are concentrated at one pole of society in the shape of capital, while at the other pole are grouped masses of men who have nothing to sell but their labour power. Nor is it enough that they are compelled to sell themselves voluntarily. The advance of capitalist production develops a working class which by education, tradition and habit looks upon the requirements of that mode of production as self-evident natural laws. The organisation of the capitalist process of production, once it is fully developed, breaks down all resistance. The constant generation of a relative surplus population keeps the law of supply and demand of labour, and therefore wages, within narrow limits which correspond to capital's valorisation requirements. The silent compulsion [*stumme Zwang*] of economic relations sets the seal on the domination of the capitalist over the worker. Direct extra-economic force [*Außerökonomische, unmittelbare Gewalt*] is still of course used, but only in exceptional cases. In the ordinary run of things, the worker can be left to the 'natural laws of production', ie it is possible to rely on his dependence on capital, which springs from the conditions of production themselves, and is guaranteed in perpetuity by them. It is otherwise during the historic genesis of capitalist production. The rising bourgeoisie needs the power of the state, and uses it to 'regulate' wages, ie to force them into the limits suitable for making a profit, to lengthen the working day, and to keep the worker himself at his normal level of dependence. This is an essential aspect of so-called primitive accumulation. (*CI*: 899-900)

---

21 Eric Hobsbawm's introduction to Karl Marx, *Precapitalist Economic Formations* (London, 1964), is still of great value in understanding the *Formen*.

The thought then is that the normal functioning of capitalist economic relations tends to generate the conditions of their reproduction. The *Grundrisse* version alarmed Edward Thompson, who sees in the idea of capital positing its presuppositions 'an organicist structuralism... (ultimately an Idea of capital unfolding itself)' from which 'many activities and relations (of power, of consciousness, sexual, cultural, normative)' are excluded.[22] In the last passage cited Marx invokes both economic mechanisms—the reserve army of labour—and a broader process of socialisation ('education, tradition and habit') to explain why the 'silent compulsion of economic relations' replaces direct coercion in subordinating labour to capital. Much more would need to be said, particularly about the latter, for this argument to be persuasive and capable of addressing Thompson's objection, but it certainly doesn't depend in any way on 'an Idea of capital unfolding itself'.[23] Even the *Grundrisse* passage has the felicitous comparison of the relics of the historical formation of capitalism with the empirical constants in the physical sciences, which cuts across any suggestion that the positing of the presuppositions is a movement from concept to reality. The presence of historical remnants is a sign of the recalcitrance of the material. But the assimilation of the conceptual and the real built into Hegel's conception of positing the presupposition is a potential source of confusion.[24]

Marx from time to time signals his concern about the misleading effects of an overreliance on Hegelian categories. For example, he writes in the *Urtext* of the 1859 *Contribution*, using another of Hegel's favourite terms, *voraussetzen*, to preposit or presuppose:

---

22 E P Thompson, *The Poverty of Theory and Other Essays* (London, 1978), p254.

23 The idea of capital positing its presuppositions has been taken up in the postcolonial critique of Marxism: see Dipesh Chakrabarty, *Provincializing Europe: Postcolonial Thought and Historical Difference* (Princeton, 2000), ch 2. Vivek Chibber offers a generally persuasive rebuttal in *Postcolonial Theory and the Spectre of Capital* (London, 2013), though he fails to address the distinctive role of imperialist violence and racism in colonial (and postcolonial) contexts.

24 Marx's commitment to the Hegelian vocabulary of positing is nevertheless persistent, as is shown by this interesting passage in a discussion of the circuit of money capital ($M \ldots M'$) in a manuscript he started in 1877: '$M'$ exists as a capital relation; $M$ no longer appears as mere money, but is expressly postulated [*gesetzt*] as money capital, expressed as value that has valorised itself, ie thus also possesses the property of valorising itself, of breeding more value than it itself has. $M$ is posited [*gesetzt*] as capital by its relation to another part of $M'$ as something posited by itself, as to the effect of which it has been the cause, as to the consequence of it is the ground. $M'$ thus appears as a sum of values which is internally differentiated, undergoes a functional (conceptual) differentiation, and expresses the capital relation [*So erscheint G' als in sich differenzierte, sich funktionell (begrifflich) in sich selbst unterscheidende, das Kapitalverhältnis ausdrückende Wertsumme*]' (*CII*: 128).

---

It is made quite definite at this point that the dialectical form of presentation is right only when it knows its own limits. The examination of the simple circulation shows us the general concept of capital, because within the bourgeois mode of production the simple circulation itself exists only as preposited by capital and as prepositing it. The exposition of the general concept of capital does not make it an incarnation of some eternal idea, but shows how in actual reality, merely as a necessary form, it has yet to flow into the labour creating exchange value, into production resting on exchange value. (*CW*29: 505)

This passage is particularly interesting because it comes in a text that in some ways shows Marx at his most Hegelian, seeking to deduce capital from money (a move criticised in the next section). The worries expressed in passages like this do not lead him ever to abandon Hegelian categories. Consider, for example, the following criticism of the political economists in *Capital*, II, edited from late manuscripts: 'one confuses the economic determination of form [*die ökonomische Formbestimmtheit*] which arises from the circulation of value with an objective property; as if objects which in themselves are not capital at all but rather become so only under definite social conditions could *in themselves* and in their very nature be capital in some definite form, fixed or circulating' (*M*II: 164; translation modified).[25] As Isaac Rubin points out, the Hegelian concept of *Formbestimmtheit* is consistently used by Marx to designate what is distinctive to his conception of the economic: the forms and functions constitutive of a specific set of production relations.[26] Thus in the *1861-63 Manuscript* he refers explicitly to 'the form determination [*Formbestimmtheit*], the definite social relation of production' (*CW*30: 117; translation modified). Or again, when criticising Ricardo's confused treatment of fixed and circulating capital, he comments: 'What is at issue here is not a set of definitions [*Definitionen*] under which things are to be subsumed. It is rather definite functions [*bestimmte Funktionen*] that are expressed in definite categories [*bestimmte Kategorien*]' (*C*II: 303; translation modified).

Nevertheless, the overall structure of Marx's argument shifts away from the Hegelian forms that he originally adopted. Thus in the preceding chapter we encountered Fred Moseley's interpretation of *Capital*

---

25 The Penguin version of this passage (*C*II: 241) omits a phrase; neither translation captures the meaning of *Formbestimmtheit*.

26 I I Rubin, *Essays on Marx's Theory of Value* (Detroit, 1972), p37.

through the lens of the Hegelian categories of universality/particularity/singularity. As we saw there, this interpretation draws attention to the role that the *Logic* plays in helping Marx to develop his critique of Ricardo, and in this respect it is valuable. But it has limits. The passage from the *Grundrisse* where Marx most explicitly invokes the categories of universal/particularity/singularity includes under singularity '(1) Capital as credit. (2) Capital as stock-capital. (3) Capital as money market' (*G*: 275). But *Capital*, III, does not conclude in this way. Instead, finance and credit are covered in Part 5, which is followed by Part 6 on rent and Part 7 on the different forms of class incomes. As Jacques Bidet puts it:

> Contrary, therefore, to what Marx foresaw in his initial plans, these categories of universal/particular/singular ceased to organise the exposition and prescribe a hierarchical order between the various moments. There is no genuine universal relation, but a dominant and global one. Particularity is omnipresent, but it is diverse, cannot be united as particularity, and is thus not theoretically pertinent. Singularity dissolves into a range of different relations.[27]

Moseley himself in effect concedes the point when he writes: 'In Hegel's singularity, a particular form is the perfect embodiment of the true nature of the universal; whereas for Marx, credit capital is the opposite of the true nature of capital—it is the *most fetishised* form of capital, which makes it appear as if interest comes from capital itself, without any relation to labour and the production process'.[28] In other words, Marx in *Capital* does not conceive the financial markets as the concrete universal in Hegel's terms. In the case of interest-bearing capital, the normal formula of capital, $M–C–M'$, is reduced to $M–M'$: capital appears to expand without investing in means of production and in the labour power that alone creates new value by using these means to produce commodities: 'In interest bearing capital, the capital relationship reaches its most externalised [*äußerlichte*] and fetishised form. Here we have $M–M'$, money that produces more money, self-valorising value, without the process that mediates the two extremes' (*C*III: 515; translation modified). Marx elaborates in a passage we have already encountered: 'The fetish character of capital and the representation of this capital fetish is now complete. In $M–M'$

27  Jacques Bidet, *Exploring Marx's Capital* (Leiden, 2007), pp182-183.
28  Fred Moseley, 'The Universal and the Particulars in Hegel's *Logic* and Marx's *Capital*', in Moseley and Tony Smith, eds, *Marx's Capital and Hegel's Logic* (Leiden, 2014).

we have the concept-less [*begrifflose*] form of capital, the inversion and objectification [*Verkehrung und Versachlichung*] of the relations of production, in its highest power' (*C*III: 516).

So, unlike Hegel's concrete universal, which 'with undimmed clearness finds itself at home in its antithesis', the financial markets are characterised in *Capital* by the absence of the concept. This indicates the fundamental structural difference between Hegel's *Logic* and Marx's *Capital*. The movement of the *Science of Logic* is one of internalisation. The inner connection that forms the ground of reality is developed out of the externalisation of Being in Essence. This internal connection is progressively articulated as the spiritual unity of the concept in the third book of the *Logic*. It is through the concept's retrospective comprehension of this process as its own self-formation (*Erinnerung*) that this internalisation is effected. Thus Hegel writes: 'the restoration of their [form and matter's] original identity is the inner recollection [*Erinnerung*] of their exteriorisation' (*GL*: 393). The same path is taken by the *Phenomenology*, which concludes in Absolute Spirit's retrospective survey of the different forms of consciousness (or Spirits) through which it is constituted. The final paragraph declares: 'The *goal*, Absolute Knowing, or Spirit that knows itself as Spirit, has for its path the recollection [*Erinnerung*] of the Spirits as they are in themselves and as they accomplish the organisation of their realm.' Hegel goes on to say that the historical unfolding of these different forms of consciousness and their philosophically 'comprehended organisation' in the *Phenomenology*, 'comprehended history, form alike the inwardising and the Calvary of absolute spirit [*die begriffne Geschichte, bilden die Erinnerung und die Schädelstätte des absoluten Geistes*]'.[29]

By contrast, the structure of *Capital* is that of a process of progressive *externalisation*. This is a theme to which Marx constantly returns in *Capital*, III. Thus towards the end of the book he reflects on the distorting effects of circulation and competition:

> In Volume 2, of course, we had to present this sphere of circulation only in relation to the determinations of form [*Formbestimmungen*] it produces, to demonstrate the further development of the form of capital that takes place in it. In actuality [*Wirklichkeit*], however, this sphere is the sphere of competition, which is subject to accident in each individual case; ie where the inner law that prevails through the accidents and governs them is visible only when these accidents are

---

29  G W F Hegel, *The Phenomenology of Spirit* (Oxford, 1977), § 808; p493.

combined in large numbers, so that it remains invisible and incomprehensible to the individual agents of production themselves. Further, however, the actual [*wirkliche*] production process, as the unity of the immediate [*unmittelbaren*] production process and the process of circulation, produces new configurations [*Gestalten*] in which the threads of the inner connection get more and more lost [*mehr und mehr die Ader des innern Zusammenhangs verlorengeht*], the relations of production becoming independent of one another and the components of value ossifying into independent forms. (CIII: 966-967; translation modified)

The disappearance of 'the threads of the inner connection' is a function of the ways in which the surplus value created in production is transformed and fragmented thanks, crucially, to competition. Thus the presentation of the rate of profit—the ratio of surplus value to the total capital advanced—in *Capital*, III, Part 1, represents a first step in this process of externalisation:

In surplus value the relationship between capital and labour is laid bare. In the relationship between capital and profit, ie between capital and surplus value as it appears on the one hand as an excess over the cost price of the commodity realised in the circulation process and on the other hand as an excess determined more precisely by its relationship to the total capital, *capital appears as a relationship to itself,* a relationship in which it is distinguished as an original sum of value, from a new value that it posits. It appears to consciousness as if capital creates this new value in the course of its movement through the production and circulation processes. But how this happens is now mystified, and appears to derive from hidden qualities that are inherent in capital itself.

The further we trace out the valorisation process of capital, the more is the capital relationship mystified and the less are the secrets of its internal organisation laid bare. (CIII: 139)

This process of externalisation is crucially a consequence of the new forms that arise through the circulation process:

In the circulation process, as we have already shown, the production of surplus value, and of value in general, assumes new characteristics. Capital runs through the cycle of its transformations, and finally it steps as it were from its inner organic life into its external relations [*aus seinem innern organischen Leben in auswärtige Lebensverhältnisse*], relations where it is not capital and labour that confront one another, but on the one hand capital and capital, and on the other individuals as simple buyers and sellers once again. (CIII: 135)[30]

The transformation of values into prices of production—presented in Part 2, and crucial, as we have seen, in Marx's ability to advance beyond Ricardo—represents a further step in this process; now capitals appropriate surplus value in proportion to their size, and the actual extraction of surplus value in production is further concealed: 'the price of production is already a completely externalised and *prima facie* concept-less form [*ganz veräusserlichte und prima facie begrifflose Form*] of commodity value, and is therefore in the consciousness of the vulgar capitalist and consequently also in that of the vulgar economist' (CIII: 300; translation modified). And externalisation continues with the fragmentation of surplus value into industrial and commercial profit, rent, and interest. The trinity formula—according to which these forms of revenue correspond to the productive contribution of different 'factors of production'—is the ideological apex of this process. Marx discusses it at the beginning of the concluding Part 7 of *Capital*, III, 'The Revenues and Their Sources':

> Capital-profit (or better still capital-interest), land-ground rent, labour-wages, this economic trinity as the connection between the components of value and wealth in general and its sources, completes the mystification

---

30  This passage clearly contradicts the interpretation offered by Stavros Tombazos, according to which *Capital* must be understood in the light of Hegel's distinction in Book 3 of the *Science of Logic* between mechanism, chemism, and teleology: 'The categories of Volume I obey a linear and abstract temporality, homogeneous, a time that is supposed to be calculable, measurable. We call the latter "the time of production". The determinations of Volume II fit into a cyclical temporality. The various categories of "the time of circulation" concern the turnover of value. Finally, Volume III is the volume of capital's "organic time", the unity of the time of production and the time of circulation,' *Time in Marx: The Categories of Time in Marx's Capital* (Leiden, 2014), p3. In the passage cited in the text Marx does talk about capital's 'organic life', but he identifies it with the 'inner' value relations of *Capital*, I, where the capital/wage labour relation is analysed, while *Capital*, III, deals with the 'external relations' in which we are confronted with competition between capitals and market interactions among individuals. Moreover, the contrast Tombazos draws between the linear temporality of Volume I and the cyclical temporality of Volume II is over-stated: already in Part 7 of *Capital*, I, Marx presents the reproduction of capital as a periodic process and discusses the business cycle (see chapter 6 below). Tombazos's reading of Marx, to which I return in chapter 5, and which (despite the disagreement expressed here and below) contains many valuable insights, plainly influenced Daniel Bensaïd's interpretation of *Capital*: see especially *Marx for Our Times: Adventures and Misadventures of a Critique* (London, 2002), ch 7.

of the capitalist mode of production, the reification [*Verdinglichung*] of social relations, and the immediate coalescence of the material relations of production with their historical and social determination [*geschichtlich-sozialen Bestimmtheit*]: the bewitched, inverted and topsy-turvy world haunted by Monsieur le Capital and Madame la Terre, who are at the same time social characters and mere things [*die verzauberte, verkehrte und auf den kopf gestellte Welt, wo Monsieur le Capital und Madame la Terre als soziale Charaktere und zugleich unmittelbar als blosse Dinge ihren Spuk treiben*]. (CIII: 968-9; MIII: 830; translation modified)[31]

It is in this light that we must understand Marx's own preferred subtitle for *Capital*, III, '*Gestaltungen des Gesamtprozeßes*' (Figures of the Process as a Whole). The volume is devoted to analysing the specific configurations taken by the externalised forms of capital relations of production. Of course, *Capital*, III, is unfinished. But we know how Marx intended it to end. He wrote to Engels on 30 April 1868: 'Finally, since those 3 items (wages, rent, profit (interest)) constitute the sources of income of the 3 classes of landowners, capitalists and wage labourers, we have the *class struggle*, as the conclusion in which the movement and disintegration of the whole shit resolves itself' (*CW*43: 26). So rather than closing in on the unity of the concept, *Capital* opens out onto the class struggle.

One of the weaknesses of many 'Hegelian' interpretations of *Capital* is that they ignore the fact that Hegel was himself, like Marx after him, an attentive reader of political economy and that he developed a complex analysis of civil society as the sphere in which the infinitely expanding subjective desires of modern individuals can be realised but which leads to a destabilising polarisation of wealth and poverty. Hegel's logic is thereby disjoined from his social philosophy.[32] He argues in his *Philosophy of Right*: 'The inner dialectic of society drives

---

31  See the detailed discussion of *Capital*, III, Part 7, in Michael Krätke, '"Hier bricht das Manuskript ab." (Engels) Hat das *Kapital* einen Schluss?', II, *Beiträge zur Marx-Engels-Forschung. Neue Folge* (2002). The fetishistic character of the forms of revenue is also one of the main themes of Marx's earlier discussion, '*Revenue and Its Sources*', in the *1861-63 Manuscript* (*CW*32: 449-541).

32  So Tombazos, in the middle of an ultra-Hegelian interpretation of *Capital*, makes the astonishingly misleading pronouncement that, for Hegel, 'civil society, when examined on its own, is ethically inferior' to the family: *Time in Marx*, p138. For much more satisfying discussions of Hegel's social philosophy, see Lucia Pradella, 'Hegel, Imperialism, and Universal History', *Science & Society* 78 (2014), Allen W Wood, *Hegel's Ethical Thought* (Cambridge, 1990), ch 14, Domenico Losurdo, *Hegel and the Freedom of the Moderns* (Durham NC, 2004), and Zizek, *Less Than Nothing*, pp416-53.

it—or in the first instance *this specific society*—to go beyond its own confines and look for consumers, and hence the means it requires for subsistence, in other nations which lack those means of which it has a surplus or which generally lag behind it in creativity, etc.' This process leads to the development of international trade, with all its 'fluidity, danger, and destruction', and to the establishment of colonies for the surplus population of civil society. 'Through their representations and reflections, human beings expand their desires, which do not form a closed circle like animal instinct, and extend them to false infinity. But on the other hand, deprivation and want are likewise boundless, and this confused situation can be restored to harmony only through the forcible intervention of the state.' Thus, while Hegel sees modern societies as liable to inherent economic and social contradictions that went unrecognised by Smith and Ricardo, he argues that the state (which is 'objective spirit' so that 'it is only through being a member of the state that the individual [*Individuum*] himself has objectivity, truth, and ethical life') represents a moment of reconciliation in which these antagonisms can at least be contained.[33] Quite unlike Marx's critique of political economy, Hegel's dialectic of civil society concludes in the 'harmony' established by the state.

Given this fundamental difference of structure from the *Logic* and the *Philosophy of Right*, Marx's resort to Hegelian categories is best seen as a philosophical cannibalisation. His critique of political economy is not simply directed at the theories of the political economists; it implies also a critique of the concept of science presupposed by these theories. Only Hegel offered a critique of this concept of science and the epistemology it involved. Marx then extracted categories from the *Logic* to set them to work, but in a fairly pragmatic way. This is true even in the manuscript most deeply indebted to Hegel, the *Grundrisse*, where, in order to conceptualise the relation between capital in general and many capitals, Marx draws on categories from the Doctrines of Being (repulsion and attraction) and of Essence (inner and outer). And as he revises and reformulates his concepts across successive manuscripts his distance from the *Logic* grows. Thus the dialectic of universality/particularity/singularity undoubtedly helped Marx think through the difference between his method and Ricardo's. But, as we have seen, by the time he reaches the *1863-5 Manuscript*, it no longer functions as a blueprint.

---

33  G W F Hegel, *Elements of the Philosophy of Right* (Cambridge, 1991), §243, pp267-268; §247, p268; §185, p223; §258, p276.

## Rising from the abstract to the concrete

The formula of 'rising from the abstract to the concrete' as the 'scientifically correct method' put forward by Marx in the 1857 Introduction functions there as a slogan, although one with tremendous resonances thanks to its source in the *Science of Logic*. I have already said that it does in fact accurately summarise how Marx, in the light of the extended methodological discussions in the *1861-63 Manuscript*, actually proceeds in *Capital*. But what does this involve more precisely?

The method of *Capital* is effectively that of the progressive introduction of increasingly complex determinations. (Commentators sometimes distinguish between the oppositions abstract/concrete and simple/complex. I'm dubious that this can be made out successfully.) Gérard Duménil calls this process 'dosed abstraction...a concretisation constructed element by element', and Fred Moseley 'the *sequential determination* of the key variables'.[34] Thus Marx starts in *Capital*, I, Part 1, with the commodity and money before introducing in Part 2 the more complex category of capital. This process continues across successive volumes, culminating in Marx's exploration of the configurations of externalisation in *Capital*, III. The earlier and more abstract concepts serve to explain the later and more concrete ones. This is very clear in the overall structure of *Capital*: the formation of value and surplus value and the accumulation of capital in the immediate process of production (Volume I) has explanatory priority over the circulation of capital (Volume II) and the unity of production and circulation (Volume III). Moreover, the concrete figures studied in *Capital*, III, are mystified only if considered in their own terms, which means from the perspective of competition. Take, for example, the following discussion of the rate of profit:

> Surplus value and the rate of surplus value are, relative to this, the invisible essence to be investigated [*das Unsichtbare und das zu erforschende Wesentliche*], whereas the rate of profit and hence the form of surplus value as profit are visible surface phenomena [*der Oberfläche der Escheiningen zeigen*].

As far as the individual capitalist is concerned, it is evident enough

---

34 Gérard Duménil, *Le Concept de loi économique dans 'Le Capital'* (Paris, 1978), p89; Fred Moseley, *Money and Totality: A Macro-Monetary Interpretation of Marx's Logic in Capital and the Transformation Problem* (forthcoming). Despite the disagreements expressed above, I find Moseley's approach the most satisfactory to resolving issues such as the transformation problem.

that the only thing that interests him is the ratio of the surplus value, the excess value which he receives from selling his commodities, to the total capital advanced for the production of these commodities, whereas not only do the specific ratios of this excess value to the particular components of his capital, and its inner connections [*innerer Zusammenhang*] with them, not interest him, but it is actually in his interest to disguise these particular ratios and inner connections.

Even though the excess value of the commodity over its cost price arises in the immediate process of production, it is only in the circulation process that it is realised, and it appears all the more readily to derive from the circulation process in as much in actuality, the world of competition, ie on the actual market, [*in der Wirklichkeit, innerhalb der Konkurrenz, auf dem wirchlichen Markt*] it depends on market conditions [*Marktverhältnissen*] whether or not this excess is realised and to what extent. (*C*III: 134; translation modified)

One very important point that emerges here is that the mystification involved in the rate of profit is functional from the perspective of the individual capitalist. This theme—that the externalised forms of appearance of the capital relation are real and necessary—recurs in *Capital*, III, and I return to it in the next section. Of more immediate relevance here is that surplus value is the 'invisible essence' relative to which the 'visible surface phenomena' can be explained. So notice that Marx in a passage cited a little earlier says that price of production is '*prima facie* concept-less': in other words, once situated within Marx's value theory such externalised forms acquire their concept—that is, they can be explained. The significance of Marx of the distinction between value and price of production is that it permits an advance in the understanding of how the law of value governs concrete market phenomena.

Explanation on this method thus means something like being placed correctly in the system of concepts that together form the theory of the capitalist mode of production. It is worth underlining here that the distinction between abstract and concrete (and indeed between all the different determinations) is one between *concepts*. To return to a contrast drawn in the preceding section, Marx's concept of externality is epistemological, not ontological. The relationship between the different determinations is not one between the concept and its realisation, but between different levels of a system of concepts. In this sense the relations arrived at in *Capital*, III, Part 7—the trinity formula, etc—are no longer external. In *Capital* they have been woven into a wider set of conceptual connections that demonstrates their necessity. Their externality consists in their isolation and definition as the object of political economy by the vulgar economists who rejected Ricardo's value theory. The distinction between inner and external connections refers to the *places* of the concepts concerned within Marx's theory. This conceptual grasp of the *Gesamtprozeß* is not the same as Hegelian *Erinnerung*, for here there is a bifurcation between the conceptual and the real, not their fusion.

The same is true of abstract and concrete more generally. These aren't properties that somehow inhere in concepts. Let's take as paradigmatic examples of abstract and concrete the concepts of value and price of production. In what sense is one abstract and the other concrete? Certainly the concept of value isn't *vaguer* than that of price of production. It is a determinate concept involving a fairly clear specification of what value is and what it means for a commodity to sell at its value. Nor is the relation of value and price of production one of genus and species; the extension of the two concepts is the same, the difference lying in the fact that in the case of the price of production surplus value is apportioned to capitals on the basis of the general rate of profit rather than of the rate of profit on their own capital.[35] Nor is the relation one between thought and reality such that the abstract (value) provides a theoretical model of the concrete reality (price of production). Price of production is (to use the vocabulary of the 1857 Introduction) a 'concrete in thought', defined in terms of the theoretical discourse of *Capital* rather than some reference to the reality beyond the theory. Abstract and concrete are a matter of the places concepts occupy within this discourse. As Bidet puts it, 'the abstract/concrete relationship is to be understood as something within the totality of thought that the theory provides: it is an ordering relationship within the theoretical'.[36]

If the movement from abstract to concrete is thus something that unfolds within thought, how does Marx's theoretical discourse acquire factual content? Hegel's solution, namely that this very movement unfolds the content implicit in the categories themselves by means of determinate negation, is ruled out since it is dependent on the teleology that is the vehicle of Hegel's absolute idealism. Equally, however, Marx's

---

35  From Part 4 of *Capital*, III, onwards Marx deals with specific configurations (eg commercial and money capital, landed property) that aren't common to capital as a whole, but this differentiation does not characterise the abstract/concrete relationship in general.

36  Bidet, *Exploring Marx's Capital*, p174.

method is inconsistent with the classical conception of science, where a theory is conceived as a deductive system whose content is implicit in its premisses and is then made explicit through the subsumption of particulars under the covering laws included in the premisses. It follows that the process of 'dosed abstraction' involves at each stage the introduction of new content that has not presented earlier in the process. To be more precise, by the time that Marx writes the manuscripts that have come down to us as *Capital*, he has rejected the idea, common to both Hegel and the classical conception of science, that the content of a science is implicit in its starting point.

This way of proceeding is something that Marx achieves rather than using from the start. The methodological shift is clearest in Marx's discussion of the relationship between money and capital. In both the *Grundrisse* and the *Urtext* of the 1859 *Contribution* he seeks to derive capital from money. In both texts (the *Urtext* takes over quite a lot of material from the *Grundrisse*) Marx's analysis of the different forms and functions of money concludes with:

> money as *universal material representative of wealth* emerges from circulation, and is as such itself *a product of circulation*, both of exchange at a higher potentiality, and a *particular* form of exchange…; it stands independent of circulation, but this independence is only its own process. It derives from it just as it returns to it again… In this character it is just as much its precondition as its result. Its independence is not the end of all relatedness to circulation, but rather a *negative* relation to it. This comes from its independence as a result of $M-C-C-M$. (G: 216-217)

So here money takes the autonomous form of self-expanding value, expressed in an early version of the general formula for capital, $M-C-M'$. Marx develops this thought most fully in the concluding section 6 of chapter 2 ('Money') in the *Urtext*, 'Transition to Capital'. The following passage sums up his argument:

> As a form of universal wealth, as exchange value become independent, money is incapable of any other movement but the quantitative one: to expand itself. By concept it is the essence of all the use values; but its quantitative limits, as the limits of what is always merely a definite magnitude of value, a definite sum of gold and silver, is in contradiction with its quality. That is why rooted in its nature is a constant drive to go beyond its own limits… So, fixed as wealth, as the universal form of wealth, as value that counts as value, money is a constant drive to go

beyond its quantitative limits; an endless process. Its own viability consists exclusively in this; it preserves itself as self-important value [*für sich geltender Wert*] distinct from use value only when it *continually multiplies itself* by means of the process of exchange itself. The active value is only a surplus-value-positing value. (*CW*29: 495, 496)

The thought then is that money can only sustain its role as the universal representative of wealth if it assumes the form of capital and therefore seeks constantly to expand quantitatively through the extraction of surplus-value—a process that, as Marx goes on to argue in both texts, requires the purchase and exploitation of labour power:

Money [as capital] is now *objectified labour*, irrespective of whether it possesses the form of money or of a particular commodity. None of the reified modes of being of labour confronts capital, but each of them appears as a possible mode of its existence which it can assume through a simple change of form, passage from the form of money into the form of commodity. The only opposite of *reified* labour is *unreified* labour, and the opposite of *objectified* labour, *subjective* labour. Or, the opposite of past labour, which exists in space, is living labour, which exists in time. As the presently existing unreified (and so also not yet objectified) labour, it can be present only as the *power*, potentiality, ability, as the *labour capacity* of the living subject. The opposite of capital as the independent, firmly self-sufficient objectified labour is living labour capacity itself, and so the only exchange by means of which money can become capital is the exchange between the possessor of capital and the possessor of the living labour capacity, ie the worker. (*CW*29: 502)

It's worth noting that this argument really has the form of a hypothetical inference: *if* money is to function as the universal representative of wealth, *then* it must take the form of self-expansion of value (which itself requires the appropriation of the worker's living labour). In other words, the deduction is a conditional one rather than the kind of immanent conceptual drive that is supposed to prompt us from one determination to another in Hegel's *Logic*. In any case this argument disappears in the 1859 *Contribution* and only figures very briefly in the *1861-63 Manuscript*, which Marx intended as a continuation of the chapters on the commodity and money in the former book. The manuscript starts with the general formula of capital during a discussion of which he throws in the highly Hegelian remark that 'the more the quantity of exchange-value or money is increased the more it corresponds to its concept' (*CW*30: 19).

But Part 2 of *Capital*, I, 'The Transformation of Money into Capital', contains not a hint of this kind of conceptual derivation. Marx analyses the general formula of capital, $M-C-M'$, and goes on critically to examine mainstream explanations of the self-expansion of capital, and in particular the idea of profit on alienation, arguing that this can only hold in specific cases where commodities are sold above their value, but not in general. This analysis leads him to conclude: 'The transformation of money into capital has to be developed on the basis of the immanent laws of the exchange of commodities in such a way that the starting point is the exchange of equivalents,' even though the capitalist emerges from the circuit with more money than he originally invested. 'These are the conditions of the problem. *Hic Rhodus, hic salta!*' (*C*I: 268-9)[37] The solution comes in the existence of 'a commodity whose use value possesses the peculiar property of being a source of value, whose actual consumption is therefore itself an objectification (*Vergegenständlichung*) of labour. The possessor of money does find such a special commodity on the market: the capacity for labour (*Arbeitsvermögen*), in other words labour power (*Arbeitskraft*)' (*C*I: 269).

What is noteworthy about this version of the movement from money to capital is that Marx simply introduces first $M-C-M'$ and then the purchase and sale of labour power successively as new determinations without any attempt to deduce them from the preceding determinations. Bidet puts it like this: 'the procedure followed is no longer a dialectic of forms, nor a logical deduction, but a specific mode of progression that, by recourse to the "ordinary experience" contained in the "formula" $M-C-M'$, and the critique based on the categorial results of Part One, is able to provide the means of presenting the new determinations, those of the capitalist relations of production'.[38] There is in fact a problem with how Bidet puts it here that is best brought out by considering Heinrich's assertion that 'an intrinsic necessary relationship between money and capital must be revealed.' He criticises Marx's abandonment of the deduction of capital from money in *Capital*, I: 'With this omission, Marx abetted the interpretations...

---

37  The Latin tag means: 'Here is Rhodes! Leap over it here!'—a challenge in *Aesop's Fables* to a boaster who claimed to have jumped over the island of Rhodes.

38  Bidet, *Exploring Marx's Capital*, p168. See also the important critique of Marx's early attempts to derive capital from money in John Mepham, 'From the *Grundrisse* to *Capital*', in Mepham and David-Hillel Ruben, eds, *Issues in Marxist Philosophy* (3 vols, Brighton, 1979), I.

that contrast a market economy and capital as separate things'.[39] This opens the door to 'something like a "socialist market economy"'.[40]

Heinrich may have in mind Bidet's work, which particularly subsequent to his study of *Capital* has developed the argument that Part 1 of *Capital*, I, 'Commodities and Money', presents a general theory of a market economy of which capitalism is merely one possible realisation.[41] But this is an interpretation that demonstrably contradicts Marx's own view that the object of *Capital* is the capitalist mode of production. Thus he explicitly rejects Torrens's view, discussed in Chapter 2, that the law of value only obtains prior to the accumulation of capital, writing:

> the product wholly assumes the form of a commodity only—as a result of the fact that the entire product has to be transformed into exchange-value and that also all the ingredients necessary for its production enter it as commodities—in other words it wholly becomes a commodity only with the development and on the basis of capitalist production. (*CW*32: 265)

The italicised sentence in the following passage is one of many where Marx makes it clear that Part 1 of *Capital*, I, is as much about capitalism as the rest of the three volumes:

> the *prerequisite*, the *starting-point*, of the formation of capital and of capitalist production is the development of the product into a commodity, commodity circulation and consequently money circulation within certain limits, and consequently trade developed to a certain degree. It is as such a prerequisite that we treat the commodity, since we proceed from it as the simplest element in capitalist production. On the other hand, the product, the result of capitalist production, is the commodity. What appears as its element is later revealed to be its own product. *Only on the basis of capitalist production does the commodity become the general form of the product and the more this production develops, the more do the products in the form of commodities enter into the process as ingredients.* (*CW*32: 300-301; italics added in final sentence.)

---

39  Michael Heinrich, *An Introduction to the Three Volumes of Karl Marx's* **Capital** (New York, 2012), pp84, 231 n 20.

40  Michael Heinrich, 'Reconstruction or Deconstruction? Methodological Controversies about Value and Capital, and New Insights from the Critical Edition', in Riccardo Bellofiore and Roberto Fineschi, eds, *Rereading Marx: New Perspectives after the Critical Edition* (Basingstoke, 2009), p80 n 8.

41  See Jacques Bidet, *Théorie de la modernité* (Paris, 1990), and *Théorie générale* (Paris, 1999), criticised in Alex Callinicos, *The Resources of Critique* (Cambridge, 2006), ch 1.

So the pattern of economic relations that Marx analyses in Part 1 of *Capital*, I, prevails only where the capitalist mode of production is dominant. Moreover, all the categories of *Capital* have as their object the capitalist mode of production. They do so as a totality: let's recall that in the 1857 Introduction Marx calls the concrete as 'a rich totality of many determinations and relations', 'the concentration of many determinations, hence unity of the diverse' (*G*: 100, 101). The implication is that it is a mistake to isolate specific categories and relate them to referents abstracted from the real totality. The categories refer to the capitalist mode *collectively*. This is as true of those presented in Volume I, Part 1, as it is, say, of those through which Marx analyses financial markets in Volume III, Part 5. Whether or not the later categories are in some way implicit in their predecessors is irrelevant, since all have same referent. Therefore Heinrich is mistaken when he argues that Marx's abandonment of the attempt to derive capital from money prevents him from ruling out market socialism. There is, with respect to Marx's method, nothing special about the transition from money to capital. Each step in his analysis involves the presentation of a new determination that introduces further content and thereby contributes to an understanding of the capitalist mode of production as a totality.

Althusser puts it very well:

> Far from proceeding by the *auto-production* of concepts, Marx's thought proceeds rather by the *position* of concepts, inaugurating the exploration (analysis) of the theoretical space opened and closed by this position, then by the position of a new concept, enlarging the theoretical field, and so on, up to the constitution of theoretical fields of an extreme complexity.[42]

If Marx doesn't proceed by deduction, either conventional or Hegelian, how are the specific determinations connected? Is the move from one to the next merely arbitrary?[43] The answer is that the presentation of each determination poses a problem that is resolved by the next. Ilyenkov treats the move from money to capital as exemplary of this approach:

---

42  Louis Althusser, 'Avant-propos' to Duménil, *Le concept de loi économique dans 'Le Capital'*, pp17-18. Althusser is here summarising Duménil's account of Marx's method, but by counterposing 'internal' conceptual determinations (value) and 'external' material determinations (use value) Duménil both misrepresents Marx's mature view of the relationship between value and use value (see chapter 4 below) and fails to capture the way in which new content is continually incorporated into the analysis as Marx's presentation of his categories proceeds.

43  This question was posed to me by my much missed friend and comrade Chris Harman.

The axiomatic and unquestionable principle of Hegelian dialectics is that the entire system of categories must be developed from the immanent contradictions of the basic concept. If the development of commodity-money circulation into capitalistic commodity circulation had been presented by an orthodox follower of Hegelian logic, he would have had to prove, in the spirit of this logic, that the immanent contradictions of the commodity sphere generate by themselves all the conditions under which value becomes spontaneously growing value.

Marx adopts the reverse procedure: he shows that commodity-money, however long it may go on within itself, cannot increase the overall value of commodities being exchanged, it cannot create by its movement any conditions under which money put into circulation would necessarily fetch new money.

At this decisive point in the analysis, thought goes back again *to the empirics* of the capitalistic commodity market. It is *in the empirics* that the economic reality is found which transforms the movement of the commodity-money market into production and accumulation of surplus-value. Labour power is the only commodity which, at one and the same time, is included in the sphere of application of the law of value and, without any violation of this law, makes surplus-value, which directly contradicts the law of value, both possible and necessary.[44]

Fredric Jameson offers a more generalised account of Marx's procedure:

One of the ways of reading *Capital*—that is, of grasping the place of its individual analyses and propositions in the construction of the whole—lies in seeing it as a series of riddles, of mysteries and paradoxes, to which at the proper moment the solution is supplied. Unsurprisingly, this solution will be a dialectical one; it will not dissipate the strangeness of the initial paradox or antinomy by way of a dry and rational unmasking, but preserve the strangeness of the problem within the new strangeness of the dialectical solution. The elaboration of these riddles is of unequal length; they overlap, they find their dénouements at unpredictable moments, in which from time to time the identity of some of the riddles with each other is unexpectedly revealed.[45]

---

44  E V Ilyenkov, *The Dialectics of the Abstract and the Concrete of Marx's Capital* (Moscow, 1982), pp275-276.
45  Fredric Jameson, *Representing Capital* (London, 2011), p14.

## Competition, appearance and science

This way of thinking about *Capital*, as a chain of problems, the solution to each of which drives us on to the next, has the great merit of capturing the intensive creative process involved in writing it, the constant construction and reconstruction of categories through which Marx developed, refined, and reworked his analysis. The chain pushes through the successive parts of the *1863-5 Manuscript* and of *Capital*, I, pointing beyond them to the books that Marx originally planned but was forced to abandon and on to the efforts of later Marxists to develop his critique of political economy. One consequence of this process is that oppositions that were important at one stage of the project become less important later on. Thus take the distinction between capital in general and many capitals, as we have seen, so important in the *Grundrisse*. Roman Rosdolsky argues that the contrast continues to organise *Capital*: 'whereas the first two volumes of *Capital* do not fundamentally go beyond the analysis of "capital in general", the third volume is the place where competition, credit and share capital are introduced, in the originally envisaged order, even if not quite as extensively as Marx had intended at the outset'.[46] Moseley also argues that:

> he maintained these two basic levels of abstraction in his final manuscripts after 1863. Marx clearly did not abandon the distinction between the production and the distribution of surplus value in his theory, nor did he abandon the key quantitative premiss of the prior determination of the total surplus value. Therefore he did not abandon the corresponding levels of abstraction of capital in general and competition. The subjects added to Volume III in the January 1863 outline are all related to the distribution of surplus value, which still belongs to the level of abstraction of competition.[47]

The broad contrast that Moseley draws between the production of surplus value in Volume I and its distribution (and fragmentation) in Volume III seems to me correct. But it is hard to sustain the idea that competition is restricted to *Capital*, III. For one thing, Marx in a passage in the *1863-5 Manuscript* that we discussed in chapter 1 denies that this volume is concerned with credit and competition: 'these—more

---

46  Roman Rosdolsky, *The Making of Marx's* **Capital** (London, 1977), pp40-41. I followed this interpretation in 'The Logic of *Capital*', and *The Revolutionary Ideas of Karl Marx* (London, 1983).

47  Fred Moseley, 'The Development of Marx's Theory of the Distribution of Surplus-Value in the 1861-63 Manuscripts', in Bellofiore and Fineschi, eds, *Rereading Marx*, p145.

concrete forms of capitalist production 1) can only be depicted after the general nature of capital is understood and 2) are outside scope of our work and belong to its possible continuation. Nonetheless, the phenomena referred to in the heading of this § can be treated here in general' (*MEGA²* II/4.2: 178). For another, competition nevertheless plays an explanatory role at a crucial stage in the analysis in *Capital*, I. One of the most critical distinctions Marx draws in this volume is that between absolute and relative surplus value. These two ways of raising the rate of surplus value involve, respectively, lengthening the working day and reducing the share taken by replacing the value of labour power in the working day. The latter method, because it involves the technological transformation of the production process required to increase the productivity of labour, constitutes the real subsumption of labour under capital, as opposed to the merely formal subsumption where direct producers using unchanged technology become wage labourers employed by capital (*CI*: 1023-5; *CW*34: 428-9).

But how exactly does higher productivity increase the rate of surplus value? In *Capital*, I, Chapter 12, 'The Concept of Relative Surplus Value', Marx offers what seems like two stories, the official and the unofficial. The official version focuses on the effect of raising productivity in consumption goods industries, which reduces the value of labour power and therefore (assuming that money wages fall accordingly) raises the rate of surplus value. But Marx then offers a strange disclaimer:

> The general and necessary tendencies of capital must be distinguished from their forms of appearance.
>
> While it is not our intention here to consider the way in which the immanent laws of capitalist production manifest themselves in the external movement of individual capitals, assert themselves as coercive laws of competition, and therefore enter into the consciousness of the individual capitalist as the motives which drive him forward, this much is clear: a scientific analysis of competition is possible only if we grasp the inner nature of capital, just as the apparent motions of the heavenly bodies are intelligible only to someone who is acquainted with their real motion, which is not perceptible to the senses. Nevertheless, for the understanding of the production of relative surplus value, and merely on the basis of the results already achieved, we may add the following remarks. (*CI*: 433)

Marx then proceeds to show how an individual capital in any sector may, through technical innovation, reduce its costs of production below the average for that sector. This means that the individual value of its commodities are reduced below what Marx calls here their social value, but which he names as the market value in *Capital*, III. In other words, in every sector competition establishes a norm of average efficiency that constitutes the socially necessary labour time required to produce a given type of commodity, represented by its market value. The innovating capital, if it sells its products at this market value, will reap a surplus profit over and above the prevailing average. Marx argues that it will in fact, in order to attract a sufficient market, charge a price lower than that equivalent to the market value but higher than the individual value, and thus still secure a surplus profit. The value of labour power falls as a proportion of the total value created, and hence the rate of surplus value for the individual capital rises. But this advantage is only temporary since other capitals may copy the innovation and reduce their own costs. Once this happens on a sufficiently large scale the sectoral norm of efficiency changes and the market value falls, eliminating the innovator's surplus profit but reflecting a higher level of labour productivity and technological development. Marx's summing up again implicitly disavows the significance of this unofficial story:

> The law of determination of value by labour-time makes itself felt to the individual capitalist who applies the new method of production by compelling him to sell his goods under their social value; the same law, acting as a coercive law of competition, forces his competitors to adopt the new method. The general rate of surplus value is therefore ultimately affected by the whole process only when the increase in the productivity of labour has seized upon those branches of production and cheapened those commodities that contribute towards the necessary means of subsistence, and are therefore elements of the value of labour power. (CI: 436)[48]

---

48 Interestingly, in the 'Immediate Results of the Process of Production', the abandoned 'Sixth Chapter' of *Capital*, I, Marx when introducing relative surplus value presents it through this case: CI: 1023-4. There is some resemblance between Marx's theory of differential profit and Joseph Schumpeter's conception of entrepreneurial profit, which arises when innovation causes a fall in the entrepreneur's costs: *The Theory of Capitalist Development* (New Brunswick, 1983), ch 4. But Schumpeter, following neoclassical orthodoxy, holds that at equilibrium 'production must flow on essentially profitless' (p31); accordingly, profit only arises in the disequilibrium situation generated by innovation, and disappears once the innovation has been imitated, eliminating the entrepreneur's advantage: 'entrepreneurial profit...and also the entrepreneurial function as such, perish in the vortex of the competition which streams after them' (p134). For Marx, however, surplus value is generated at equilibrium; the theory of differential profit explains only the temporary *increases* in the rate of surplus value gained by innovating capitals.

These qualifications indicate Marx's discomfort about giving competition an explanatory role so early in his analysis. As Bidet observes:

> Marx's awkwardness is clear: he tries to resist the necessity forced upon him of dealing here with competition, but despite his denials and references to a later moment, he ends up well and truly engaged in a full exposition of the principles of competition within the branch... The thesis of the chapter [12], which is that of the whole of Part Four, can be summed up in one phrase: there is in capitalism a *historical tendency* to relative surplus value, in other words to a relative decline in the value of labour power resulting from an increase in productivity in the branches producing wage goods, because there is a *constant tension* among capitalists in *all* branches, arising from the fact that none of them has any future unless they succeed in raising their productivity as rapidly as their competitors. To put it another way, the competitive relationship between capitalists, far from being a subsequent category whose natural place would be Volume Three, is involved right from the start in explaining the global movement of capital, the production of surplus value.[49]

As Alfredo Saad-Filho also notes, Marx in fact deals with two types of competition.[50] In *Capital*, III, he is concerned with inter-branch competition—in particular, the flow of capital between different sectors in response to fluctuations in profitability that leads to the formation of the general rate of profit. It is this form of competition that Dussel emphasises when discussing Marx's crucial confrontation with the problem of rent in the *1861-63 Manuscript*: '"Competition" is the movement of the totality of capital within which prices are *levelled, equalised* (*ausgleichen* means to level, make equal), and so an "average level (*Durchschnittsniveau*)" is produced in all branches of production'.[51]

---

49  Bidet, *Exploring Marx's Capital*, p145. Bidet also claims: 'this couple "extra surplus value/relative surplus value" that occupies an absolutely central place in the theory was only recognised by Marx at a very late stage. It does not yet appear either in the *Grundrisse*, nor in the *1861-3 Manuscripts*' (p142). But there is a very clear discussion in the *1861-63 Manuscript*: see CW30: 238-240. And as early as 'Wage Labour and Capital' (1849), Marx observes that innovation allows the innovating capitalist to undercut his rivals: CW9: 223-224.

50  Alfredo Saad-Filho, *The Value of Marx* (London, 2002), pp40-41.

51  Enrique Dussel, *Towards an Unknown Marx: A Commentary on the Manuscripts of 1861-63* (London, 2001), p84. But, despite the importance of the transformation of values into prices of production to Marx's discussion of rent, in the portion of the *1861-63 Manuscript* devoted to 'Capital and Profit' (forerunner of *Capital*, III), he excludes discussion of 'the difference between the real prices—even the normal prices of the commodities—and their values. The more detailed [XVI-994] investigation of this point belongs to the chapter on *competition*' (CW33: 101). This seems another symptom of

But Marx also deals with *intra*-branch competition, which is initially a differentiating force, when an innovating capital lowers its costs below the sectoral average, thereby allowing it to undercut its rivals and secure a surplus-profit. But this is also the process through which a new norm of average efficiency represented by market value is established, so differentiation serves ultimately (through the reactions of other capitals in the sector) a force of equalisation, but at a more advanced productive level. Hence the importance of Marx's most systematic discussion of market value in *Capital*, III, Chapter 10 (see chapter 4).

According to Bidet:

> what really breaks down in the process of elaboration of *Capital*, beyond the articulation of 'capital in general' and 'multiple capitals', is the very idea of 'many', which disappears because it divides into two kinds of multiplicity corresponding to two kinds of competition, within the branch and between branches...with each of these having its own proper moment of introduction: one in Volume One, Part Four, the other in Volume Three, Part Two [on the formation of the general rate of profit]. In short, the specific logic of the specific object that is capital does not call for the relegation of competition to Volume Three, but rather a more complex distribution of this 'determination'.[52]

So, rather than stick to the organising principle of capital in general/many capitals, what Marx does in his later manuscripts is to widen the scope of capital in general. He is uneasy about this, in all probability for two reasons. First, he is determined to maintain the analytical priority of production over circulation, and bringing competition into the analysis of the process of production might seem to compromise this priority. Secondly, as we saw in chapter 1, he is, as it were, systematically uncertain about how legitimate it is for him to cover material intended for later books in *Capital*. The following formulation late in *Capital*, III, is seen by some commentators as expressing the compromise Marx eventually hits on to justify broaching the subject of competition: 'the actual movement of competition lies outside our plan, and we are only out to present the internal organisation of the capitalist mode of production, its ideal average, as it were' (*C*III: 970).[53] But whatever ambivalence Marx continues to feel about this shouldn't be allowed to obscure how

---

Marx's uneasiness about how to deal with competition.

52  Bidet, *Exploring Marx's Capital*, p151.
53  For example, Michael Heinrich, 'Capital in General and the Structure of Marx's *Capital*', *Capital & Class*, 13:2 (1989), and Dussel, *Towards an Unknown Marx*, p254 n 4.

the movement from abstract to concrete ceases to be a set of global oppositions and becomes a much more differentiated process in which the introduction of new determinations continuously refines the analysis. Within this procedure, production retains its general priority over circulation, even though the unity of production and circulation is previewed in *Capital*, I, Chapter 12. The effect is to pull how Marx conceptualises competition away from the idea common in the *Grundrisse* of it realising the inner nature of capital to a very different stress on the dependence of the general tendencies of capital accumulation on competition, a thought also present in the *Grundrisse*, as this passage cited earlier in this chapter indicates: 'competition is nothing more than the way in which the many capitals force the inherent determinants of capital upon one another and upon themselves.' As Riccardo Bellofiore puts it, 'the originality of Marx's position, if it is "translated" into the later terminology, is not only in his macro-social foundation of microeconomics, but also in his careful analysis of the micro-competitive mechanism realising the systemic tendency, that is, in his *circular* journey from "macro" to "micro", and from "micro" to "micro".'[54]

It should be noted that Marx discusses competition elsewhere in *Capital*, I, in Section 2 of Chapter 25, 'The General Law of Capitalist Accumulation'. Here he analyses how the accumulation of capital leads to a rise in the organic composition of capital (the ratio of constant to variable capital) and also to the concentration and centralisation of capital. The latter process involves respectively the growth in the size of individual capitals (concentration) and the absorption of smaller by larger capitals (centralisation). The concentration of capital is a relatively slow process, and

> the increase of each functioning capital is thwarted by the formation of new capitals and the subdivision of old. Accumulation, therefore, presents itself on the one hand as increasing concentration of the means of production, and of the command over labour; and on the other hand as repulsion of many individual capitals from one another.
>
> This fragmentation of the total social capital into many individual capitals, or the repulsion of the fractions from each other, is counteracted by their attraction... It is concentration of capitals already formed,

54  Riccardo Bellofiore, 'Marx and the Macro-monetary Foundations of Microeconomics', in Bellofiore and Nicola Taylor, eds, *The Constitution of Capital: Essays on Volume I of Marx's Capital* (Basingstoke, 2004), p201. Marx's uneasiness about competition in *Capital* may in part reflect a reaction against the central role he and (more strongly) Engels attributed to competition in their early humanist critique of political economy (see chapter 1).

destruction of their individual independence, expropriation of capitalist by capitalist, transformation of many small into few large capitals.
(CI: 776-7)

As early as *The Poverty of Philosophy* Marx writes: 'Monopoly produces competition, competition produces monopoly' (*CW*6: 195). But
here in *Capital*, I, the differences and relations between attraction
(=concentration), repulsion (=fragmentation), and centralisation are
better explained than, for example, in the *1861-63 Manuscript*. In the
French edition of *Capital*, I, Marx adds a much more detailed discussion
of the centralisation of capital, which he plainly regards a much more
transformative force than mere concentration ('which grows directly out
of accumulation, or rather is identical with it': CI: 776). Centralisation
demands organisational changes with the development of the joint stock
company and allows large-scale investments such as those in the rail-
ways. But it in turn is dependent on 'a development of the two most
powerful levers of centralisation—competition and credit' (CI: 778-
779). So here again we see Marx broaching topics that he had previously
excluded from the scope of *Capital*. His reason is once again their role in
accounting for the fundamental tendencies of capital accumulation:

> And while in this way [eg the development of railway companies] cen-
> tralisation intensifies and accelerates the effects of accumulation, it
> simultaneously extends and speeds up those revolutions in the technical
> composition of capital which raise its constant portion at the expense of
> its variable portion, thus diminishing the relative demand for labour.
> (CI: 780)[55]

Marx's shift towards giving competition a place in *Capital*, I, is related
to another interesting feature of his discussion of relative surplus value,
namely that it invokes the interests and intentions of individual actors.
The innovating capitalist adopts a new technology with the aim of secur-
ing a surplus profit; that technology is generalised through the reactions
of other capitalists. In *Capital*, III, Part 3, Marx invokes the same mechanism to explain why capitalists make innovations that, by raising the
organic composition of capital, bring down the rate of profit:

> No capitalist voluntarily applies a new method of production, no matter
> how much more productive it may be or how much it might raise the rate

---

55    I'm grateful to Lucia Pradella for drawing my attention to the importance of competition
      in Marx's discussion of the tendency towards the concentration and centralisation of
      capital in Volume I.

of surplus value, if it reduces the rate of profit. But every new method of production of this kind makes commodities cheaper. At first, therefore, he can sell them above their price of production, perhaps above their value. He pockets the difference between their costs of production and the market price of the other commodities, which are produced at higher production costs. This is possible because the average socially necessary labour time required to produce these latter commodities is greater than the labour time required with the new method of production. His production procedure is ahead of the social average. But competition makes the new procedure universal and subjects it to the general law. A fall in the profit rate then ensues—firstly perhaps in this sphere of production, and subsequently equalised with the others—a fall that is completely independent of the capitalists' will. (CIII: 373-374; see the almost identical passage in the *1861-63 Manuscript*: *CW*33: 147-148)

This form of reasoning provides an answer to the criticism made by Thompson that Marx tends to portray capital as a self-reproducing hypostasis, as well as to rational choice theorists such as Jon Elster who argue that *Capital* lacks 'micro-foundations' referring to the interests and intentions of individual actors. As a methodological individualist Elster seeks to reduce social structures to the unintended effects of individual actions.[56] But the kind of analysis that Marx offers in his discussion of relative surplus value serves to integrate economic structures and individual agency without reducing either to the other. Bidet once again puts it very well:

> The reference to the tendencies of the system and the interests of the ruling class would be purely metaphysical if they were not linked to the question of the interests of the 'individuals' who compose the system, and the compulsions that weigh on them as individuals—individual capitals 'personified', as Marx says, by their holders. Capitalism possesses no general tendency unless this is connected with what moves individuals, with the structure of interests and compulsions that the competitive relationship defines. This is the object of the theory of extra surplus value, which defines what constitutes the main dynamic of the capitalist structure, that through which it has a tendency, ie relative surplus value. This determination is just as 'inner', 'essential' and 'primary' as the general class articulation that makes

---

56   See especially Jon Elster, *Making Sense of Marx* (Cambridge, 1985) and, for an alternative perspective, Alex Callinicos, *Making History: Agency, Structure and Change in Social Theory* (2nd edn; Leiden, 2004).

146

the bourgeoisie bearer of a project and common interest, thus of a general 'tendency'.[57]

But of course the 'main dynamic of the capitalist structure' is not visible to individual actors. Discussing the effects of competition on the behaviour of prices, Marx makes a point that he repeats regularly in *Capital*, especially Volume III:

> All these phenomena *seem* to contradict both the determination of value by labour time and the nature of surplus value as consisting of unpaid surplus labour. *In competition, therefore, everything appears upside down* [*verkehrt*]. The finished configuration [*Gestalt*] of economic relations, as these are visible on the surface, in their actual [*realen*] existence, and therefore also in the notions with which the bearers and agents [*Träger und Agenten*] of these relations seek to gain an understanding of them, is very different from the configuration of their inner core [*Kerngestalt*], which is essential but concealed, and the concept corresponding to it. It is in fact the very reverse and antithesis of this. (*C*III: 310)

But the configurations encountered in competition are simultaneously inverted and functional. They have, in other words, a certain reality rather than being purely illusory. This is signalled at the very start of *Capital*, I, when, in presenting commodity fetishism, Marx writes:

> Objects of utility become commodities only because they are the products of the labour of private individuals who work independently of each other. The sum total of the labour of these private individuals forms the aggregate labour of society. Since the producers do not come into social contact until they exchange the products of their labour, the special social characteristics of their private labours appear only within this exchange. In other words, the labour of the private individual manifests itself as an element of the total labour of society only through the relations which the act of exchange establishes between the products, and, through their mediation, between the producers. To the producers, therefore, *the social relations between their private labours appear as what they are*, ie they do not appear as direct social relations between persons in their work, but rather as material (*dinglich*) relations between persons and social relations between things. (*C*I: 165-166; italics added)

---

57  Bidet, *Exploring Marx's Capital*, p152. See Tony Smith, *The Logic of Marx's 'Capital'* (Albany, 1990), p229 n 30, for a very similar argument.

In other words, the value relations governing the producers of commodities appear misleadingly as 'the socio-natural properties [*gesellschaftliche Natureigenschaften*] of these things' (CI: 165) because these producers really are governed by the exchange of their products on the market.[58] Appearances are misleading, but also real. Hegel's distinction between *Schein*—sometimes translated as 'illusory being', but 'shine' in the latest English edition of the *Science of Logic*—and *Erscheinung* (appearance or phenomenon) is relevant here. According to Inwood, '*Schein* is correlative to *Wesen* ("essence"): essence shows or appears (*scheint*), but itself remains hidden behind a veil of *Schein*.' By contrast:

> (1) *Erscheinung* is also the appearance of an essence, but the essence fully discloses itself in *Erscheinung* and keeps nothing hidden... (2) An *Erscheinung* is, like *Schein*, transient and dependent, but what it depends on and succumbs to is not, immediately at least, an essence but another *Erscheinung*. Hence *Erscheinung*, in contrast to *Schein*, is a diverse, interdependent and fluctuating whole or world. (3) *Erscheinung* contrasts primarily not with 'essence' but 'concept' or 'actuality' (as what fully embodies the concept), and is contingent and fleeting rather than necessary, rational, and stable:[59]

'Essence must appear' (*GL*: 418). As Inwood puts it, for Hegel, 'the essence or nature of anything essentially manifests itself. It is only an essence in virtue of its manifestation, and the manifestation is as essential as the essence'.[60] So, even if individual appearances are 'contingent and fleeting', their existence itself is not. Marx's own treatment of how capitalist relations appear draws on both the Hegelian categories *Schein* and *Erscheinung*. *Schein*: the 'inner connection', Marx says in numerous passages, is invisible, concealed, etc, behind the appearances. *Erscheinung*: the different externalised configurations—profit, interest, rent, etc—are related to each other, forming an 'inverted world'. And

---

58  Valuable studies of Marx's theory of commodity fetishism include Jacques Rancière, 'Le Conception de critique et de critique de l'économique politique des "Manuscrits de 1844" au "Capital",' in Louis Althusser et al, *Lire le Capital* (Paris, 1973), Norman Geras, 'Essence and Appearance: Aspects of Fetishism in Marx's *Capital*', *New Left Review*, I/65 (1971), John Mepham, 'The Theory of Ideology in *Capital*', in Mepham and David Hillel-Ruben, eds, *Issues in Marxist Philosophy* (3 vols, Brighton, 1979), I, Ali Rattansi, ed, *Ideology, Method and Marx* (London, 1989), and Stuart Hall, 'The Problem of Ideology—Marxism without Guarantees', in Betty Matthews, ed, *Marx: A Hundred Years On* (London, 1983).

59  Inwood, *A Hegel Dictionary*, p39. I put into lower case terms that Inwood capitalised for purposes of cross-reference.

60  G W F Hegel, *Introductory Lectures on Aesthetics* (Michael Inwood, ed; London, 1993), pxxi.

what they are contrasted to involves a fusion of essence and concept, as in the passage cited a little earlier: 'The finished configuration of economic relations...is very different from the configuration of *their inner core, which is essential but concealed, and the concept corresponding to it*'.[61]

As forms of appearance (*Erscheinungsformen*) of capitalist production relations, derivative categories such as interest and rent are systematically misleading about the real nature of these relations: what above all disappears is the origins of the various forms of revenue in the extraction of surplus value in the immediate process of production. But Marx goes to great trouble to show that these forms are not therefore arbitrary or illusory. Near the end of *Capital*, III, in Chapter 50: 'The Illusion Created by Competition [*Der Schein der Konkurrenz*]', he presents five distinct mechanisms that lead working capitalists to treat the new value created by living labour as 'autonomous and mutually independent forms of revenue, namely wages, profit and ground rent' (*C*III: 1007). The following passage gives a sense of his argument:

> The value determination as such interests and affects the individual capitalist, and capital in any particular sphere of production, only in so far as the diminished or increased amount of labour that is required with the rise or fall in the productivity of the labour producing the commodities in question enables him in the one case to make an extra profit at the existing market prices, while in the other case it compels him to increase the price of his commodities, since more wages, more constant capital, and hence more interest, falls to the share of each unit product or individual commodity. This interests him only in so far as it raises or lowers his own production costs for the commodity, ie only in so far as it places him in an exceptional position.
>
> Wages, interest and rent, on the other hand, appear to him as governing limits not only to the price at which he can realise the portion of the profit that accrues to him as a functioning capitalist, the profit of enterprise, but also the price at which he has to sell the commodity, if continuing reproduction is to be possible. It is a matter of complete indifference to him whether he realises the value and surplus value contained in the commodity on its sale or not, as long as he extracts from the price the customary profit of enterprise, or greater profit, above the cost price as individually given for him by wages, interest and rent. Apart from the constant capital component, therefore, wages, interest

---

61  Bidet distinguishes four different meanings Marx gives to *Erscheinung: Exploring Marx's Capital*, pp188-189.

and rent appear to him as the limiting elements to commodity price, and hence as creative and determining elements. (*C*III: 1013)

For the purposes of his daily calculations and decisions, the capitalist doesn't need to know about value and surplus value. Categories such as wages, profit, rent and interest serve simultaneously as ideological representations and as means of orienting his practical activities. Though, as Marx's denunciation of the trinity formula indicates, they represent the apogee of fetishism, they at the same time have a social reality. This fascinating passage captures the duality:

> In this quite alienated form [*ganz entfremdeten Form*] of profit, and in the same measure as the form of profit hides its inner core, capital more and more acquires a material shape [*sachliche Gestalt*], is transformed more and more from a relationship into a thing, but a thing which embodies, which has absorbed, the social relationship, a thing which has acquired a fictitious life and autonomy [*Selbständigkeit*] in relationship to itself, a sensuous-supersensous [*sinnlich-übersinnliches*] entity; in this form of *capital and profit* it appears superficially as a ready-made presupposition. It is the form of its actuality, or rather its actual form of existence [*die Form seiner Wirklichkeit oder vielmehr seine wirkliche Existenzform*]. And it is the form in which it lives in the consciousness of its bearers [*Träger*], the capitalists, and is reflected in their representations [*Vorstellungen*].' (*CW*32: 484; translation modified)

I have substantially changed the original, to be frank rather poor translation, partly in order to bring out that Marx associates 'the quite alienated form of profit' with the Hegelian category of actuality (*Wirklichkeit*). For Hegel, 'actuality is the *unity of essence and concrete existence*; in it, *shapeless* essence and *unstable* appearance...have their truth.' (*GL*: 465) So, in being actual, profit and the other forms of revenue partake of the essential relations of the capitalist mode of production at the same time as (mis)representing them. Bidet puts it well: 'It is as function rather than illusion that ideology is strictly deduced as a categorial ensemble implied in a function defined by the structure, that of the capitalist acting in the competitive relationship'.[62] Thus, as Jameson notes, Marx's critique of fetishism:

> locates the ideological, not in opinions or errors, worldviews or conceptual systems, but in the very process by which daily life is systematically

---

62  Bidet, *Exploring Marx's Capital*, p200 and see generally, ch 8.

reorganised on all its levels (the body and the senses, the mind, time, space, work process, and leisure) by that total quasi-programming process that is rationalisation, commodification, instrumentalisation, and the like...this is somehow a process without a subject.[63]

The movement of externalisation that *Capital* traces is therefore not that from reality to illusion; Marx seeks rather to reconstruct the inner logic of a reality that encourages individual actors to accept representations that obscure this logic. As Stuart Hall puts it, 'the ideological categories in use...*position us* in relation to the account of the process as depicted in the discourse' they help to articulate and thereby lead us to accept a partial and one-sided explanation of the whole.[64] This is why starting from these representations is a scientific catastrophe: 'Vulgar political economy does nothing more than express in doctrinaire fashion this consciousness [ie that of the individual capitalist], which, in respect of its motives and notions, remains in thrall to the appearance of the capitalist mode of production' (*CW*32: 486). The merit of the 'critical economists', and chief among them Ricardo, is that they seek 'to grasp the inner connection in contrast to the multiplicity of outward forms', though, as we have seen, 'classical economy is not interested in elaborating how the various forms come into being, but seeks to reduce them to their unity by means of analysis, because it starts from them as given premises' (*CW*32: 498, 499, 500). Marx's own method is designed to overcome the defects of both approaches.

It should be clear from the foregoing that Rosa Luxemburg was quite mistaken when she asserted in her critique of the reproduction schemes in *Capital*, II, Part 3 that the 'analysis of individual capitals...is given in *Capital*, Volume I'.[65] Jairus Banaji has repeated the same error more recently: '*Capital*, Volume 1 comprises the analysis of the enterprise (of capitalist production) as an *isolated entity*, as individual capital'.[66] In general, *Capital* concerns itself with aggregate social capital. The distinction between aggregate social capital and individual capitals is not posited in *Capital*, I, with the exception, as we have seen, of the analysis of relative surplus value in Chapter 12, about which Marx feels decidedly

---

63   Fredric Jameson, *Valences of the Dialectic* (London, 2009), p331.
64   Hall, 'The Problem of Ideology', p76.
65   Rosa Luxemburg, *The Accumulation of Capital* (London, 1971), p349, criticised by N I Bukharin, 'Imperialism and the Accumulation of Capital', in Luxemburg and Bukharin, *Imperialism and the Accumulation of Capital* (London, 1972), p239.
66   Jairus Banaji, *Theory as History: Essays on Modes of Production and Exploitation* (Leiden, 2010), p60.

uneasy. The individual capitalist figures, as Marx makes amply clear, only as the personification of social capital (see chapter 5). So, when individual capitalists and workers confront each other in *Capital*, I, it is as cases of social types, to exemplify the relationship 'between collective capital, ie the class of the capitalists, and collective labour, ie the working class' (*C*I: 344), and on the basis that 'each individual capital forms only a fraction of the total social capital' (*C*II: 427).

It is only in *Capital*, II, Part 1, on the basis of his analysis of the circuits of money, productive, and commodity capital that Marx is able to posit the distinction between individual capitals and aggregate social capital. He does so in the course of discussing the circuit of commodity capital ($C'$—$M'$—$C$... $P$... $C''$, or $C'$... $C'$):

> $C'$... $C'$... presupposes $C (= L + mp)$ as other commodities in the hands of others, commodities which are drawn into the circuit and changed into productive capital by way of the opening process of circulation. Then, as a result of productive capital's function, $C'$ once again becomes the closing form of the circuit.
>
> But precisely because the circuit $C'$... $C'$ presupposes in its description the existence of another industrial capital in the form $C (= L + mp)$ ..., it itself demands to be considered not only as the *general* form of the circuit, ie as a social form in which every industrial capital can be considered (except in the case of its first investment), hence not only as a form of motion common to all individual capitals, but at the same time as the form of motion of the sum of individual capitals, ie of the total social capital of the capitalist class, a movement in which the movement of any individual industrial capital appears as a partial one, intertwined with the others and conditioned by them. (*C*II: 176-7; here '$P$' stands for production, '$L$' for labour power, and '$mp$' for means of production.)

Only now that the interrelationship of individual capitals has been posited can the reproduction of the aggregate social capital be analysed, as Marx proceeds to do in *Capital*, II, Part 3, where he explains:

> What we were dealing with in both Parts One and Two, however, was always no more than an individual capital, the movement of an autonomous part of the social capital.
>
> However, the circuits of individual capital are interlinked, they presuppose one another and condition one another, and it is precisely by being interlinked in this way that they constitute the movement of the total social capital [*gesellschaftlichen Gesamtkapitals*]... What we have

now to consider is the circulation of the individual capitals as components of the total social capital, ie the circulation process of this total social capital. Taken in its entirety, this circulation process is a form of the reproduction process. (CII: 429-430)

Marx's analysis of the reproduction process in fact continues to treat individual capitals as tokens of general types, though these are now the two main departments of social production (I, means of production, and II, means of consumption). It is only in *Capital*, III, Part 2, when presenting the formation of the general rate of profit through flows between sectors where the organic composition of capital varies, that he explicitly posits the *differences* between capitals. Aggregate social capital remains the object of Marx's enquiry, but now he is providing himself with the conceptual tools needed to analyse its fractioning (as surplus value is broken up into industrial and commercial profit, interest, rent, etc) and its individualisation as competing units of capital.

Through this continuous process of 'dosed abstraction' Marx constantly integrates more empirical material into his analysis. Both Dussel and Ilyenkov emphasise this aspect to his moves from one determination to another. And it is evident from even the briefest scan of *Capital* the extent to which it is based on the most intensive (and indeed unending) process of empirical study. But the incorporation of empirical material into specific determinations should be seen primarily as the way in which Marx adds fresh content to his analysis. It does not represent any kind of direct empirical corroboration of individual propositions. As I have already emphasised, *Capital* confronts its real object, the capitalist mode of production, as a totality. Marx himself makes this point in the celebrated letter to Kugelmann of 11 July 1868 where he comments on a review of *Capital*, I, in *Literarisches Centralblatt für Deutschland*:

the man is making the greatest concession possible by admitting that, if value means anything at all, then my conclusions must be conceded. The unfortunate fellow does not see that, even if there were no chapter on 'value' at all in my book, the analysis I give of the real relations would contain the proof and demonstration of the real value relation. The chatter about the need to prove the concept of value arises only from complete ignorance both of the subject under discussion and of the method of science. Every child knows that any nation that stopped working, not for a year, but let us say, just for a few weeks, would perish. And every child knows, too, that the amounts of products corresponding to the differing amounts of needs demand differing and quantitatively determined amounts of society's aggregate labour. It is **self-evident** that this *necessity* of the *distribution* of social labour in specific proportions is certainly not abolished by the *specific form* of social production; it can only change its *form of manifestation*. Natural laws cannot be abolished at all. The only thing that can change, under historically differing conditions, is the *form* in which those laws assert themselves. And the form in which this proportional distribution of labour asserts itself in a state of society in which the interconnection of social labour expresses itself as the *private exchange* of the individual products of labour, is precisely the *exchange value* of these products.

Where science comes in is to show *how* the law of value asserts itself. So, if one wanted to 'explain' from the outset all phenomena that apparently contradict the law, one would have to provide the science *before* the science. It is precisely Ricardo's mistake that in his first chapter, on value, all sorts of categories that still have to be arrived at are assumed as given, in order to prove their harmony with the law of value... The vulgar economist thinks he has made a great discovery when, faced with the disclosure of the intrinsic interconnection, he insists that things look different in appearance. In fact, he prides himself in his clinging to appearances and believing them to be the ultimate. Why then have science at all? (*CW*43: 68-69)

Marx is saying a number of things here. First, he is presenting the law of value—that commodities exchange in proportion to the socially necessary labour time required to produce them—as the specific form taken under capitalism of a transhistorical law requiring that labour be allocated to different branches of production to meet social needs.[67] Secondly, he is reaffirming the critique developed at length in the *1861-63 Manuscript* of Ricardo's abstract and deductive method and,

---

67  Compare this interesting passage, inserted in the *1861-63 Manuscript* into a passage transcribed from the *Grundrisse* (*G*: 454-461, *CW*34: 231-238): '//*Natural laws of production*! Here, it is true, it is a matter of the *natural laws of bourgeois production*, hence of the laws within which production occurs at a *particular historical stage* and under *particular historical conditions of production*. If there were no such laws, the *system of bourgeois production* would be altogether incomprehensible. What is involved here, therefore, is the presentation of *the nature* of this particular mode of production, hence its *natural laws*. But just as it is itself *historical*, so are its *nature* and the *laws of that nature*. The natural laws of the Asiatic, the ancient, or the feudal mode of production were essentially different. On the other hand, it is entirely certain that human production possesses definite *laws* or *relations* which remain the same in all forms of production. These identical characteristics are quite simple and can be summarised in a small number of commonplace phrases//' (*CW*34: 236). Duménil offers the most extended (though problematic) study of Marx's concept of law: *Le concept de loi économique dans le Capital*.

correlatively, of the vulgar economists' insistence of sticking to the systematically misleading appearances. And finally he is offering a conception of science where validation does not arrive from establishing the truth of the premises (which is presumably what the reviewer was asking for when he demand a proof of the labour theory of value at the start of *Capital*). To do so would be to 'provide the science *before* the science'. One hears the echoes here of Hegel's critique of the classical deductive conception of science and insistence that 'the proof comes with the proposition'. But Hegel can only be of limited help here because it is solely the self-movement of the concept through its different determinations that establishes the truth of the science. Marx too believes that 'the True is the whole',[68] but here truth is secured by the success of the theory in capturing the real object: 'the analysis I give of the real relations would contain the proof and demonstration of the real value relation.'

Marx offers no elaboration of what this might involve, but there is an interesting passage in a letter to Engels of 9 August 1862 where he explains the results of his critique of Rodbertus and Ricardo on rent:

> I. All I have to prove *theoretically* is the *possibility* of absolute rent, without infringing the law of value. This is the point round which the *theoretical controversy* has revolved from the time of the Physiocrats until the present day...
>
> II. As regards the *existence* of absolute rent, this would be a question that would require *statistical* solution in any country. But the importance of a purely theoretical solution may be gauged from the fact that for 35 years statisticians and practical men generally have been maintaining the existence of absolute rent, while the (Ricardian) theoreticians have been seeking to explain it away by the dint of very forced and theoretically feeble abstractions. Hitherto, I have invariably found that, in all such **quarrels**, the theoreticians have always been in the wrong. (*CW*41: 403)

So here we have Marx, pupil of Hegel and critic of empiricism, siding with 'statisticians and practical men' against the 'theoreticians'. Implicit here is a conception of corroboration very similar to that offered by Elie Zahar to Lakatos's philosophy of science. Lakatos followed his teacher Karl Popper in arguing that scientific theories involve empirically falsifiable hypotheses. But he criticised Popper's tendency to compare isolated

---

68   Hegel, *Phenomenology of Spirit*, §20; p11.

hypothesis and empirical evidence. What are tested, he contended, are scientific research programmes, articulated systems of theories whose implicit structure (or 'heuristic') allowed the generation of new hypotheses. A research programme is empirically progressive if it predicts a 'novel fact' and if this prediction is corroborated. Zahar added the nuance that *'a fact will be considered as novel with respect to a given hypothesis if it did not belong to the problem situation which governed the hypothesis'.*[69] Now this isn't exactly the situation that confronted Marx, inasmuch as it was a recognised empirical phenomenon, absolute rent, that represented an anomaly for Ricardian value theory. But he was able to overcome this anomaly by reformulating the labour theory of value in a way that, through the analysis of relative surplus value discussed above, integrated a range of empirical phenomena ignored by the Ricardians. How well it captured the whole process of capitalist development will, I hope, become clearer in the following chapters.

It is, however, worth stressing Marx's empirical focus against suggestions such as the following by Daniel Bensaïd: 'Under the influence of "English" science, he thought within the constraints of a strange object—capital—an understanding of which required another causality, different laws, another temporality—in short, a different mode of scientificity. "German science" marks the spot'.[70] Bensaïd is right about the very complex form of conceptualisation required by *Capital*'s 'strange object', and he has written very well about the distinctive conception of historical temporality developed by Marx and later figures such as Walter Benjamin.[71] But the implication of his invocations of 'German science' is that Marx drew on early 19th century *Naturphilosophie*. Tracking back the reference Bensaïd makes causes this impression to dissolve. Marx is at his most playful when he writes to Engels on 20 February 1866:

> You will understand, **my dear fellow**, that in a work such as mine, there are bound to be many **shortcomings** in the detail. But the *composition*, the structure, is a triumph of German science [*deutsche Wissenschaft*], which an individual German may confess to, since it is **in no way his**

69 Elie Zahar, 'Why Did Einstein's Programme Supersede Lorentz's?', *British Journal of the Philosophy of Science*, 24 (1973), p103; see also Imre Lakatos, *Philosophical Papers* (2 vols, Cambridge, 1978).
70 Bensaïd, *Marx for Our Times*, p206.
71 See Alex Callinicos, 'Daniel Bensaïd and the Broken Time of Politics', *International Socialism*, 2.135 (2012). For studies of time in *Capital*, see Tombazos, *Time in Marx*, and Massimiliano Tomba, *Marx's Temporalities* (Brill, 2013).

merit but rather belongs to the nation. Which is all the more gratifying, as it is otherwise the **silliest nation** under the sun!

Schönbein proved (by experiment) that any flame burning in the air converts a certain quantity of the nitrogen in the air into ammonium nitrate, that every process of decomposition gives rise to both nitric acid and ammonia, that the mere evaporation of water is the means causing the formation of both plant nutrients.

Finally, Liebig's 'jubilation' at this discovery:

'The combustion of a pound of coal or wood restores to the air not merely the elements needed to reproduce this pound of wood or, under certain conditions, coal, but the process of combustion *in itself*' (note the Hegelian category) 'transforms a certain quantity of nitrogen in the air into a nutrient indispensable for the production of bread and meat'.

**Feel proud of the Germans. It is our duty to emancipate this 'deep' people.** (*CW*42: 232; translation modified)

Marx shows here his continuing commitment to Hegelian categories, as he does indeed in *Capital* itself, when he cites the 'molecular theory of modern chemistry' as an illustration of 'the law discovered by Hegel, in his *Logic*, that at a certain point merely quantitative differences pass over by a dialectical inversion into qualitative distinctions' (*CI*: 423).[72] The examples he cites of 'German science', however, come from no Romantic weird science (Bensaïd suggests the structure of *Capital* is modelled on that of Hegel's *Philosophy of Nature*) but from particular instances of the empirical and mathematical physical sciences of Marx's day. He is best understood as seeking to forge a distinctive conception of scientificity that can integrate the empirical data of the statisticians and the formal quantifications of the political economists with the conceptual articulation, involving the progressive introduction of ever more concrete categories, required to grasp the complex totality that is the capitalist mode of production.

To conclude: the story I have told here is of how Marx, in forging his own method, draws on Hegel but progressively moves away from him. This idea, of a certain methodological Hegelianism, is open to the criticism that it relies on precisely the kind of separation of form and content that Hegel denounces.[73] This is a tricky subject, because Hegel's own account of the integration of form and content is inseparable from his

---

72  See my discussion of the dialectic(s) of nature in *Resources of Critique*, ch 6.

73  This criticism was, for example, made by Jairus Banaji in a panel at the *Historical Materialism* conference in London, November 2012.

conception of the dialectical method as the self-development of the Absolute Idea.[74] The ideal of integrating form and content nevertheless seems to me necessary for Marxist thinking that is both dialectical and materialist. It is in this way that thought can capture the contours of its object in their full depth, achieving what Marx calls in his early *Critique of Hegel's Doctrine of the State* 'the discovery of the particular logic of the particular object' (*EW*: 159). He affirms this ideal in a sardonic comment to Engels (1 February 1858) on Lassalle's plan 'to expound political economy in the manner of Hegel. He will discover to his cost that it is one thing for a critique to take a science to the point at which it admits of a dialectical presentation, and quite another to apply an abstract, ready-made system of logic to vague presentiments of just such a system' (*CW*39: 261). *Capital* as I interpret it can only be condemned for failing this ideal if the form remains Hegelian. In other words, if Marx simply took over the categories of the *Science of Logic* and applied them to capitalist economic relations that would amount to a separation of form and content.[75] But this is just what Marx doesn't do. As I have shown, even in the *Grundrisse* he cannibalises Hegelian oppositions for his own purposes. By the time we get to *Capital*, he has thoroughly reworked his categories into a distinctive conceptual system that is his own. The aim of this endless adjusting and polishing is to develop a set of categories that can conceptually grasp capitalist economic relations. In other words, what Marx is trying to achieve is just the alignment of form and content that dialectical thought seeks. So let's consider some of the contours of this alignment.

---

74  See Rosen, *Hegel's Dialectic and Its Criticism*, esp ch 2.

75  I criticise in chapter 5 the idea, put forward by, among others, Chris Arthur and Moishe Postone, that Hegel's Idea somehow corresponds to capital, and that therefore Hegelian form is fitted to capitalist content.

# 4

# Value

## Where to begin?

In a late text, the 'Notes on Wagner' completed after January 1881, Marx is adamant that he does 'not proceed from "concepts", hence neither from the "concept of value"... What I proceed from is the simplest social form in which the product of labour presents itself in contemporary society, and this is the "*commodity*"' (*CW*24: 544). Whereas Ricardo's *Principles* begins with a chapter 'On Value', the first chapter of *Capital*, I, is devoted to 'The Commodity', the 'economic cell form' of 'bourgeois society', the 'elementary form' of wealth where 'the capitalist mode of production prevails' (*CI*: 90, 125). As Daniel Bensaïd wittily puts it, 'Spinoza begins with God. Marx with the commodity'.[1] This way of commencing is indicative of the method defended by Marx in the letter to Kugelmann that we discussed in the last chapter: the task is not to prove the labour theory of value at the start, but to show how the law of value governs all the complex configurations through which capitalist economic relations are formed and reproduced. But it also symbolises the shift that Marx makes in how to conceptualise value: no longer is it treated as a quasi-natural substance inhering in commodities, but instead it becomes the web of relationships articulating capitalism into a totality. The main aim of this chapter is not to expound Marx's value theory—there are a number of good modern introductions—but rather to clarify two issues—Marx's celebrated and problematic initial presentation of his value theory in *Capital*, Volume I, Chapter 1, and subsequent debates about the form of value.[2]

Marx admits: 'Beginnings are always difficult in all sciences.' (*CI*: 89) This is certainly true of *Capital*, I. Like many of his readers, Marx

---

1    Daniel Bensaïd, *La Discordance des temps* (Paris, 1995), p21.
2    See especially Joseph Choonara, *Unravelling Capitalism: A Guide to Marxist Political Economy* (London, 2009), Ben Fine and Alfredo Saad-Filho, *Marx's 'Capital'* (5th edn; London, 2010), and Duncan Foley, *Understanding Capital: Marx's Economic Theory* (Cambridge MA, 1986).

struggled with the opening chapter. In response to Engels's complaints about the obscurity of Chapter 1 in proof ('Sheet 2 in particular has the marks of your carbuncles rather firmly stamped upon it', Engels told Marx on 10 June 1867: *CW*42: 381), he added an appendix, 'The Value Form'. In the second edition (1872) Marx extensively revised Chapter 1, dividing it into four sections, the third of which was a rewritten version of the appendix. Further revisions were made in the French edition, where, Marx told Nikolai Danielson (15 November 1878), 'I was also sometimes obliged—principally in the first chapter—to *"aplatir"* [flatten] the matter in its French version' (*CW*45: 343). Even by Marx's standards this is a particularly strenuous process of revision. How deep do the problems lie?

Responding to later complaints by Engels about the proofs of what would become Part 4 on relative surplus value, Marx offers him an overview of what he regards as his main intellectual achievements (24 August 1867):

> The best points in my book are: 1. (this is fundamental to all understanding of the **facts**) *the two-fold character of labour* according to whether it is expressed in use-value or exchange-value, which is brought out in the very *First* Chapter; 2. the treatment of *surplus-value regardless of its particular* forms as profit, interest, ground rent, etc. This will be made clear in the second volume [= *Capital*, II and III] especially. The treatment of the particular forms in classical political economy, where they are for ever being jumbled up together with the general form, is an *olla potrida* [hotchpotch]. (*CW*43: 407-408)

The second point we have already encountered in the two preceding chapters: it is crucial both to Marx's critique of Ricardo and to his presentation in *Capital*, III, of the distribution of surplus value and the accompanying process of externalisation of capitalist economic relations. But the first is also crucial to the double movement through which Marx transcends Ricardo by, on the one hand, introducing a far more articulated set of categories designed to present the 'intermediate links' between the law of value and its externalised configurations, and, on the other, developing a more abstract starting point for value theory. This starting point is the distinction between abstract social labour and concrete useful labour:

> On the one hand, all labour is an expenditure of human labour power in the physiological sense, and it is in this quality of being equal, or

abstract, human labour that it forms the value of commodities. On the other hand, all labour is an expenditure of human labour power in a particular form and with a definite aim, and it is in this quality of being definite useful labour that it produces use values. (*CI*: 137)

Abstract and concrete labour thus correspond respectively to value and use value. Note here the reference to *value*, and not exchange value. In the course of Chapter 1 Marx complicates the traditional distinction drawn by Adam Smith between 'the utility of some particular object, and…the power of purchasing other goods which the possession of that object conveys. The one may be called "value in use"; the other, "value in exchange".'[3] Exchange value, as Ricardo emphasises in Chapter I of his *Principles*, corresponds to the relative price of a commodity. Marx takes over this conception of exchange value at the opening of Chapter 1: 'Exchange value appears first of all as the quantitative relation, the proportion, in which use values of one kind exchanges for use values of another kind' (*CI*: 126). But then he distinguishes exchange value from and subordinates it to value, understood as the socially necessary labour-time required to produce a commodity. He writes midway through his discussion of the form of value in Chapter 1, Section 3:

> the value of a commodity is independently expressed through its expression (*Darstellung*) as 'exchange value'. When, at the beginning of this chapter, we said in the customary manner that a commodity is both a use value and an exchange value, this was, strictly speaking, wrong. A commodity is a use value or object of utility, and a 'value'. It appears as the twofold thing it really is as soon as its value possesses its own particular form of manifestation, which is distinct from its natural form. This form of manifestation is exchange value, and the commodity never has this form when looked at in isolation, but only when it is in a value relation or an exchange relation with a second commodity of a different kind. (*CI*: 152)

Differentiating value from both exchange value and use value points Marx's analysis in two directions. In one we have the exchange relations between commodities as forms of appearance (*Erscheinungsformen*) of their values, culminating in the differentiation of money as a distinct commodity that acts as the universal equivalent in which the values of all other commodities are expressed. This is part of what is addressed in

---

3   Adam Smith, *An Inquiry into the Nature and Causes of the Wealth of Nations* (2 vols; Oxford, 1976), I, ch iv; I, p44.

the problematic of the form of value (discussed below), but it also constitutes the basis of Marx's theory of money, which informs the unfolding analysis across all three volumes of *Capital*. In the other direction, the distinction between abstract labour/value and concrete labour/use value organises the entire discourse of *Capital*, I. This is expressed most crucially in the conception, put forward in Chapter 7, of the immediate process of capitalist production as 'the unity of the labour process and the process of valorisation [*Verwertungsprozeß*]', where the elements of the unity refer respectively to the role of concrete useful labour in making use values and to that of abstract social labour in creating value and surplus value (*CI*: 304). The distinction functions at more detailed points: for example in Chapter 8, concrete labour by using up means of production transfers their value to its products, while abstract labour creates the new value that is divided between capitalist and worker. This whole development modifies earlier positions Marx had taken. Thus he writes in the 1859 *Contribution*: 'Use value as such, since it is independent of the determinate economic form, lies outside the sphere of investigation of political economy. It belongs in this sphere only when it is itself a determinate form' (*Con*: 28). By contrast use value and the concrete labour that produces it play an integral role in the discourse of *Capital*.[4]

In these ways Marx's development of the distinction between abstract and concrete labour plays fits in with his overall approach to method discussed in chapters 2 and 3. But what are we to make of the famous first section of *Capital*, I, Chapter 1, where he moves from exchange value and use value to abstract and concrete labour? It is here that he argues that where two commodities are treated as equivalent, 'both are equal to a third thing, which in itself is neither the one nor the

---

4   Roman Rosdolsky lists the following cases where use value plays an explanatory role in *Capital*: the money commodity, the exchange between capital and labour, fixed and circulating capital, ground rent, raw materials, and the reproduction schemes: *The Making of Marx's Capital* (London, 1977), pp83-88. Marx's exclusion of use value from political economy in the 1859 *Contribution* is odd because it is directly contradicted in the *Grundrisse*, to which the later text is heavily indebted: 'the distinction between use value and exchange value belongs within economics itself, and...use value does not lie dead as a simple presupposition, which is what Ricardo makes it do' (G: 320). Gérard Duménil's massive and impressive study of *Capital* is premised on the exclusion of use value from political economy, while he conceives Marx's value theory as the exposition of internal, conceptual relations: *Le concept de loi économique dans 'Le Capital'* (Paris, 1978). As Bidet puts it, 'Duménil's reading transforms the theory of *Capital* into pure formalism on the side of the theory of value, interpreted in strictly tautological terms, and into pure empiricism on the side of use value, presented as mere contingency,' *Exploring Marx's Capital* (Leiden, 2007), p149.

other. Each of them, so far as it is exchange value, must therefore be reducible to this third thing' (CI: 127). Marx proceeds by elimination. Use values are necessarily qualitatively different from one another; this heterogeneity is inherent in use value, since it consists in nothing more than the ability to meet some particular human need, and this rules out both use value and the concrete labour that produces it from acting as the 'third thing' that makes commodities commensurable. By elimination Marx identifies the abstract social labour expended on products as what renders them equivalent: 'Let us now look at the residue of the products of labour. There is nothing left of them in each case but the same ghostly objectivity [*gespenstige Gegenständlichkeit*]; they are merely congealed quantities of homogeneous human labour, ie of human labour expended without regard to the form of its expenditure' (CI: 128; translation modified).

It has to be said that if interpreted as the 'proof' of the labour theory of value, as it was, for example, by the leading marginalist theorist Eugen von Böhm-Bawerk, this argument hasn't gone down well.[5] What Marx's method of elimination seeks to do here is to find an abstract property common to commodities that would render them commensurable. But why hit on abstract labour? Why not, as the marginalists did, home in on utility—in other words, not the concrete quality of a particular use value but the property they all share of fulfilling desire (or, in more contemporary terms, satisfying preferences)? The effect of adopting this alternative property is, as Maurice Dobb puts it, to shift the focus of economic analysis from 'relations of production' to 'the relations of commodities to the psychology of consumers'.[6] The most effective way of parrying this rebuttal is offered by Marx's overall approach of developing a set of determinations that progressively capture the complexity of capitalist relations by articulating them into a totality. To be fair, this is a difficult point to get over at the start of a demanding scientific treatise, but Marx seems almost to glory in the misunderstandings to which the way he precedes gives rise. Replying to yet another objection by Engels to

---

5   Paul Sweezy, ed, *Karl Marx and the Close of His System* by Eugen von Böhm-Bawerk and *Böhm-Bawerk's Criticism of Marx* by Rudolph Hilferding (London, 1975). See also the critique of the labour theory of value in Anthony Cutler et al, *Marx's 'Capital' and Capitalism Today* (2 vols, London, 1977, 1978), I, Part 1, and my response, 'Marx's *'Capital'* and *Capitalism Today*—A Critique', *International Socialism*, 2.2 (1978).

6   Maurice Dobb, *Political Economy and Capitalism* (London, 1937), p21. As Dobb demonstrates, the tendency of neoclassical economics has been progressively to formalise this psychology: see Dobb, ch V, and Maurice Godelier, *Rationality and Irrationality in Economics* (London, 1972).

the proofs of *Capital*, I, he explains (27 June 1867) that the problem will be solved in Volume III:

> Here it will be shown how the philistines' and vulgar economists' *manner of conceiving things* arises, namely, because the only thing that is ever reflected in their minds is the immediate *form of appearance* of relations, and not their *inner connection*. Incidentally, if the latter were the case, we would surely have no need of *science* at all.
>
> Now if I wished to *refute* all such objections in *advance*, I should spoil the whole dialectical method of exposition. On the contrary, the good thing about this method is that it is constantly *setting traps* for those fellows which will provoke them into an untimely display of their idiocy. (*CW*43: 390)

Not only vulgar economists have fallen into Marx's traps. Chapter 1 in its different versions remains a difficult and unsatisfactory text; this is the justification for Althusser's advice to skip Part 1, 'Commodities and Money', when first reading *Capital*, I, and return to it only after finishing the rest of the book.[7] Widely denounced as a sign of Althusser's distaste for the Hegelianisms in Chapter 1, this recommendation has the merit of common sense; Marx himself advised one correspondent to start with Part 8 on primitive accumulation (letter to Mrs Wollman, 19 March 1877: *CW*45: 211-212). But struggle with Chapter 1 we must. One source of the difficulty is the *sotto voce* argument that Marx pursues throughout the chapter. Isaak Rubin was the first to notice this:

> If in the *Critique* Marx passed imperceptibly from exchange value to value, in *Capital* he seems, on the contrary, to remain on a given point, as if foreseeing objections from his opponents. After the statement which is common to both books, Marx points out: 'exchange-value appears to be something accidental and purely relative, and consequently an intrinsic value, ie, an exchange-value that is inseparably connected with, inherent in it, seems a contradiction in terms. Let us consider the matter a little more closely.' (*CI*: 126)
>
> One can see that here Marx had in mind an opponent who wanted to show that nothing exists except relative exchange values, that the concept of value is thoroughly superfluous in political economy. Who was the opponent alluded to by Marx?[8]

---

7   Louis Althusser, 'Avertissement aux lecteurs du livre I du Capital', *Le Capital, Livre I* (2 vols, Paris, 1985), I, pp18-25.

8   I I Rubin, *Essays on Marx's Theory of Value* (Detroit, 1972), pp107-108. I have altered the quotation and reference to *Capital* to the Penguin translation.

The answer is the Sheffield merchant and radical pamphleteer Samuel Bailey, critic of Ricardo and pioneer of the subjective theory of value that came to dominate mainstream economics thanks to the marginalist revolution.[9] Rubin suggests that Marx's 'third thing' argument disposes of Bailey, but this seems too quick. He remains a ghostly presence throughout Chapter 1, and is honoured by having the concluding footnote devoted to him: 'If the followers of Ricardo answer Bailey somewhat rudely, but by no means convincingly, this is because they are unable to find in Ricardo's own works any elucidation of the inner connection [*inneren Zusammenhang*] between value and the form of value, or exchange value' (*CI*: 177 n 38). So Bailey tops and tails Chapter 1. As the much more extended discussion of him in the *1861-63 Manuscript* makes clear, Marx regarded Bailey as a worthy opponent who scores some points against the Ricardians. To appreciate this we have to return to Ricardo.

In 'Absolute Value and Exchangeable Value', a very late text that he was working on in the weeks before his death in September 1823, Ricardo makes explicit a distinction implicit in the *Principles*, between the exchangeable value, by which he means what he calls a commodity's 'proportional value', or its relative price, that is 'the power which a commodity has of commanding any given quantity of another commodity', and its 'absolute value', the regulator of relative price, largely a function of the quantity of labour required to produce a commodity. Changes in relative price do not provide an adequate indicator of absolute value: 'Anything having value is a good measure of the comparative value of all other commodities at the same time and place, but will be of no use in indicating the variations in their absolute value at distant times and in distant places' (*R*, IV: 398, 396). The problem that Ricardo struggles with unsuccessfully is that, in his view, no measure capable of accurately indicating changes in absolute value can be constructed because no commodity's value is immune from the effects of changes in the distribution of the net product between wages and profits, effects that, as we saw in chapter 2, vary according to the organic composition of capital in different branches of production.

---

9   On Bailey, see T A B Corley, 'Bailey, Samuel (*bap.* 1791, d. 1870)', *Oxford Dictionary of National Biography* (Oxford, 2004), http://www.oxforddnb.com/view/article/1056, J A Schumpeter, *History of Economic Analysis* (London, 1954), pp486-487, 599, and Robert M Rauner, *Samuel Bailey and the Classical Theory of Value* (Oxford, 1961). In what follows I draw on my discussion of Marx and Bailey in 'The Logic of *Capital*' (DPhil thesis, Oxford University, 1978), ch III, though this has been superseded by James Furner's outstanding treatment, 'Marx's Critique of Samuel Bailey', *Historical Materialism*, 12:2 (2004). See also Enrique Dussel, *Towards an Unknown Marx* (London, 2001), p128.

Bailey offers a subjective interpretation of value that is directly targeted at Ricardo's concept of absolute (or intrinsic) value: 'Value, in its ultimate sense, appears to mean the esteem in which any object is held. It denotes, strictly speaking, an effect produced on the mind.' This conception justifies the reduction of value to relative price: 'It is impossible to designate, or express the value of a commodity, except by a quantity of some other commodity.' From this Bailey concluded that the very idea of trying to construct a measure of value presupposing a causal relation between changes in the productivity of labour and changes in relative price is misconceived:

> Value is a relation between contemporary commodities, because such only admit of being exchanged for one another; and if we compare the value of a commodity at one time with its value at another, it is only a comparison of the relation in which it stood at these different times to some other commodity. It is not a comparison of some intrinsic, independent quality at one time, with the same quality at another period; but a comparison of ratios, or a comparison of the relative quantities in which commodities exchanged for one another at two different times.[10]

Bailey contends that 'the only use of a measure of value, in the sense of a medium of comparison, is between commodities existing at the same time.' Understood in this sense, the measure of value is a non-problem, or rather a problem that is continually solved in practice by the market: 'The requisite condition in the process [of measuring value] is, that the commodities should be reduced to a common denominator, which may be done at all times with equal facility; or rather it is ready done for our hands, since it is the prices of commodities which are recorded, or their relations to value in money'.[11] Remarkably, Marx agrees with Bailey about this in the *1861-63 Manuscript*:

> His book has only one positive merit—that he was the first to give a more accurate definition of the *measure of value*, that is, in fact, of one of the functions of money, or money in a particular, determinate form. In order to measure the *value* of commodities—to establish an *external* measure of value—it is not necessary that the value of the commodity in

---

10   Samuel Bailey, *A Critical Dissertation on the Nature, Measures and Causes of Value* (London, 1825), pp1, 26, 72-73. This book is a reply to Thomas de Quincey, 'Dialogues of Three Templars on Political Economy', *London Magazine*, vol 9, April-May 1824, a particularly effective statement of the differences between Ricardo's value theory and the mainstream approach represented by Smith and Malthus.

11   Bailey, *Critical Dissertation on the Nature, Measures and Causes of Value*, pp117, 112.

terms of which the other commodities are measured, should be invariable… If, for example, the value of money changes, it changes to an equal degree in relation to all other commodities. Their relative values are therefore expressed in it just as correctly as if the value of money had remained unchanged. The problem of finding an 'invariable measure of value' is thereby eliminated. (*CW*32: 320)

But although Bailey is right that the measure of value is a non-problem, it 'conceals a much more profound and important question':

for commodities to express their exchange-value independently in money, in a third commodity, the exclusive commodity, the *values of commodities* must already be presupposed. Now the point is merely to compare them quantitatively. A *homogeneity* which makes them the same—makes them values—which as values makes them qualitatively equal, is already presupposed in order that their value and their differences in value can be represented in this way. (*CW*32: 320, 321)

Hence:

The problem of an 'invariable measure of value' was in fact simply a spurious name for the quest for the concept, the nature, *of value* itself, the definition of which could not be another value, and consequently could not be subject to variations as value. This was *labour time, social labour*, as it presents itself specifically in commodity production. A quantity of labour has no value, is not a commodity, but is that which transforms commodities into values, it is their *common substance*; as manifestations of it commodities are *qualitatively equal* and only *quantitatively different*. They [appear] as expressions of definite quantities of social labour time. (*CW*32: 322)

Ricardo commits this confusion because, as Marx repeatedly complains, 'he is concerned only with the *magnitude of value*' (*CW*32: 318). What eludes both Ricardo and Bailey in different ways is more than the reduction of exchange value to 'an identical social substance, human labour' (*CI*: 138). The theory of value in Marx's hands addresses a new problem whose nature is suggested in his comment (written largely in English) on a passage where Bailey stresses the relative character of value by comparing it to the concept of distance, which only makes sense as a relation between two objects:

**If a thing is distant from another, the distance is in fact a relation between the one thing and the other; but at the same time, the**

distance is something different from this relation between the two things. It is a dimension of space, it is some length which may as well express the distance of two other things besides those compared. But this is not all. If we speak of the distance as a relation between two things, we presuppose something 'intrinsic', some 'property' of the things themselves, which enables them to be distant from each other. What is the distance between the syllable A and a table? The question would be nonsensical. In speaking of the distance of two things, we speak of their difference in space. Thus we suppose both of them to be contained in space, to be points of space. Thus we equalise them as being both existences of space, and only after having them equalised *sub specie spatii* we distinguish them as different points of space. To belong to space is their unity.

But what is this **unity of objects exchanged against each other?** This exchange is not a relation which exists between them as natural things. It is likewise not a relation which they bear as natural things to human needs, for it is not **the degree of their utility that determines the quantities in which they exchange.** What is therefore their identity, which enables them **to be exchanged in a certain measure for one another?** As what **do they become *exchangeable*?** (*CW*32: 330)

In other words, what makes it possible for the products of labour to take the form of commodities, ie, of use values that are exchanged in proportions expressed by their relative prices? The problem is no longer that of measuring changes in relative prices over time. This question, which so preoccupied Ricardo, is now embedded in a theory whose starting point is to explain why, as *Capital*, I, begins by announcing, 'the wealth of societies in which the capitalist mode of production prevails appears as an "immense collection of commodities"' (*CI*: 125). Marx goes on to deliver a killer punch against Bailey:

> In this context Ricardo is not a fictionist but Bailey is a fetishist in that he conceives value...as a *relation of objects to one another*, while *it is only a representation in objects, an objective expression, of a relation between men, a social relation, the relationship of men to their reciprocal productive activity.* (*CW*32: 334; second italics added)

Here we have the key to Marx's famous complaint against classical political economy:

> Even its best representatives, Adam Smith and Ricardo, treat the form of value as something of indifference, something external to the nature of

the commodity itself. The explanation for this is not simply that their attention is entirely absorbed by the analysis of the magnitude of value. It lies deeper. The value form of the product of labour is the most abstract, but also the most universal form of the bourgeois mode of production; by that fact it stamps the bourgeois mode of production as a particular kind of social production of a historical and transitory character. (*CI*: 174 n 34)

What neither the Ricardians nor their subjectivist critics get is the sheer weirdness of value relations, a thought expressed in this striking passage from Marx's revisions to the first edition of *Capital*, I, which didn't end up in the second:

> The reduction of the products of labour to their *existence as value* [*Werthsein*], is accomplished by abstracting from their use value. Or it is fixed as value objectivity [*Werthgegenständlichkeit*], by ignoring all physical properties that make it a certain thing, and therefore also a certain useful thing (use-value). What remains is a fantastic objectivity [*phantastische Gegenständlichkeit*]—objectivity of abstract human labour, objective form of abstract human labour, ie human labour, not in the liquid state but in a congealed state, not in the form of movement but in the form of rest. (*MEGA²* II/6: 32)

The weirdness lies in the way in which commodities come attached with 'a supra-natural property [*übernatürliche Eigenschaft*], their value, which is something purely social [*rein Gesellschaftliches*]' (*CI*: 149). Marx even at one point calls value objectivity imaginary: 'When we speak of the commodity as a materialisation of labour—in the sense of its exchange-value—this itself is only an imaginary [*eingebildete*], that is to say, a purely social mode of existence of the commodity which has nothing to do with its corporeal reality; it is conceived as a definite quantity of social labour or of money' (*CW*31: 26-27). Ghostly, fantastic, imaginary, supra-natural—these different adjectives are all intended to convey that condensed in the value of commodities, appearing as a property of objects exchanged on the market, is a nexus of social relations. This is what the form of value is about.

### Value form and money

There is, however, an ambiguity in what Marx means by the value form. After all, in *Capital*, I, Chapter 1, Section 3, 'The Value Form, or Exchange Value', he analyses four kinds of relationship among commodities, starting from the simple form of a binary exchange of two products and culminating in the differentiation of a universal equivalent, the money commodity, 'in which all the products of labour are presented as mere congealed quantities of undifferentiated human labour' (*C*I: 160). Rubin, who has come to be seen as the founder of a distinctive interpretation of Marx known as value form theory, however, does not see this analysis as central to the problem of value form. 'By form of value we do not mean those various forms which value assumes in the course of its development (for example, elementary form, expanded form, and so on), but value conceived from the standpoint of its social forms, ie, value as form'.[12] Rubin points to a passage in the first edition of *Capital*, I:

> The *form* in which the commodities *count* to one another as values—as coagulations of human labour—is consequently their *social form*. *Social form* of the commodity and *value form* or form of *exchangeability* are thus one and the same thing. If the natural form of a commodity is at the same time its value-form, then the commodity possesses the form of *immediate exchangeability* with other commodities and consequently an *immediately social form*.[13]

So the form of value consists in a commodity's 'form of exchangeability'. This in turn requires an account of the conditions of possibility of commodities' exchangeability—to use the terms of Marx's critique of Bailey, to identify the shared space within which we can measure commodities' distance from one another. This account requires reference to the relations of production. Like Marx, Rubin relates economic forms and production relations: 'the basic notions or categories of political economy express the basic *social-economic forms* which characterise various types of production relations among people and which are held together by the things through which these relations among people are established'.[14]

What, then, is it about capitalist relations of production that imprints on commodities the form of exchangeability? The capitalist mode is, as the opening sentence of *Capital*, I, proclaims, a system of generalised commodity production. It is, in other words, a system of autonomous but specialised and interdependent producers whose reproduction depends on selling their products on the market to each other. It is

---

12   Rubin, *Essays on Marx's Theory of Value*, p68 n 1. See also the discussion of the value form in Jacques Bidet, *Exploring Marx's Capital*, ch 9.

13   Karl Marx, 'The Commodity, Chapter 1 of *Capital*, Volume I (1st Edition)', in Albert Dragstedt, ed, *Value: Studies by Karl Marx* (London, 1976), pp28-29. See Rubin, *Essays on Marx's Theory of Value*, p115.

14   Rubin, *Essays on Marx's Theory of Value*, p31.

through the competitive interaction of the units of production on the market that the social character of the labour performed within them is established. Marx brings this out in a long passage in the appendix on 'The Value Form' in the first edition of *Capital*, I, where he is discussing the equivalent form, the basis of the transformation of a specific commodity into money:

> *Products of labour* would not become commodities, were they not products of separate *private labours* carried on independently of one another. The *social interconnection* of these private labours exists materially, insofar as they *are members of a naturally evolved social division of labour* and hence, through their products, satisfy wants of *different kinds*, in the totality (*Gesamtheit*) of which the similarly *naturally evolved system of social wants* (*naturwüchsiges System der gesellschaftlichen Bedürfnisse*) consists. This *material* social interconnection of private labours carried on independently of one another is however only *mediated* and hence is realised only through the *exchange* of their products. The product of private labour hence *only* has *social form* insofar as it has *value-form* and hence the *form of exchangeability* with other products of labour. It has *immediately social form* insofar as its own bodily or natural form is *at the same time* the form of its exchangeability with other commodities or *counts as value-form for another commodity* (*anderer Ware*). However... this only takes place for a product of labour when, through the *value relation of other commodities to it*, it is in *equivalent-form* or, with respect to other commodities, plays the *role of equivalent*.
>
> The *equivalent* has *immediately social form* insofar as it has the form of *immediate exchangeability* with *another commodity*, and it has this form of immediate exchangeability insofar as it *counts* for another commodity as the *body of value*, hence *as equal* (*als Gleiches*). Therefore the definite useful labour contained in it also counts *as labour in immediately social form*, ie as labour which possesses the form of equality with the labour contained in *another* commodity... Thus...because the *definite concrete labour* contained *in the equivalent counts as the definite form of realisation* or *form of appearance of abstract human labour*, it possesses the *form of equality* with *other* labour, and hence, *although it is private labour*, like all other labour which produces commodities, it is nevertheless *labour in immediately social form*. Precisely because of this it is represented in a product that is *immediately exchangeable* with the other commodities.[15]

15  Karl Marx, 'The Value Form', Appendix to *Capital*, Volume I (1st Edition), *Capital & Class*, 4 (Spring 1978), pp140-141.

So it is the necessity of commodity producers to go onto the market and exchange their products in order to reproduce themselves that leads to the transformation of concrete useful labours into units of abstract social labour. The equalisation of labours that Marx describes in this passage is a real process. As he puts it in the 1859 *Contribution*: 'This reduction [of concrete to abstract labour] appears to be an abstraction, but it is an abstraction which is made every day in the social process of production' (*Con*: 30).[16] Moreover, he affirms a few pages later, the reduction involves exchange as well as production:

> the different kinds of individual labour represented in these particular use-values, in fact, become labour in general, and in this way social labour, only by actually being exchanged for one another in quantities which are proportional to the labour-time contained in them. Social labour-time exists in these commodities in a latent state, so to speak, and becomes evident only in the course of their exchange. The point of departure is not the labour of individuals considered as social labour, but on the contrary the particular kinds of labour of private individuals, ie, labour which proves that it is universal social labour only by the supersession of its original character in the exchange process. Universal social labour is consequently not a ready-made prerequisite but an emerging result. Thus a new difficulty arises: on the one hand, commodities must enter the exchange process as materialised universal labour-time, on the other hand, the labour-time of individuals becomes materialised universal labour-time only as the result of the exchange process. (*Con*: 45)

Marx reaffirms the same point some 15 years later in the French edition of *Capital*, I, where he writes: 'it is exchange alone that achieves this reduction by setting the most diverse products together on a footing of equality'.[17] I'll return to the difficulty Marx identifies here, which is at

---

16 This is a passage where Marx comes close to the usage popular among contemporary Marxists that value is 'real abstraction [*Realabstraktion*]'. This usage seems to originate in the writing of Alfred Sohn-Rethel: for a discussion that criticises Sohn-Rethel for arguing that labour becomes abstract solely in exchange, see Anselm Jappe, 'Sohn-Rethel and the Origin of "Real Abstraction": A Critique of Production or a Critique of Circulation?', *Historical Materialism*, 21.1 (2013).

17 Marx, *Le Capital*, I, p102. Passages like this contradict the argument put by some value form theorists that Marx progressively dumbs down his value theory across successive manuscripts, retreating to a substantialist version of the labour theory of value closer to Ricardo. Although the French edition in particular does in some respects simplify the exposition in Part 1, Marx doesn't retreat from his emphasis on the value form—for example, adding in the 2nd German edition the long footnote quoted towards the end of the previous section criticising classical political economy for neglecting the value form.

the heart of debates on value form theory. I want first to focus on what seem to me at once the central strength and weakness of Rubin's approach. Rubin argues forcefully and successfully against the misleading impression created by Marx's unfortunate reference in the second edition of *Capital*, I, to abstract labour as 'expenditure of human labour power in the physiological sense':

> In Marx's theory of value, the transformation of concrete into abstract labour is not a theoretical act of abstracting for the purpose of finding a general unit of measurement. This transformation is a real social event. The theoretical expression of this social event, namely the *social equalisation* of different forms of labour and not their *physiological equality*, is the category of abstract labour.[18]

Rubin's conceptualisation of abstract labour as the result of a process of social equalisation dovetails with an interpretation of the law of value, very much in line with Marx's own account in the letter to Kugelmann discussed in the last chapter, as the mechanism through which social labour is distributed between different units and branches of production in response to changes in market prices:

> The increase of productivity of labour changes the quantity of abstract labour necessary for production. It causes a change in the value of the product of labour. A change in the value of products in turn affects the distribution of social labour among the various branches of production. *Productivity of labour–abstract labour–value–distribution of social labour*: this is the schema of a commodity economy in which value plays the role

---

18    Rubin, *Essays on Marx's Theory of Value*, p144. Strangely, there is no reference to abstract labour in physiological terms in Marx's draft revisions of *Capital*, I, even though he wrote three versions of the concluding paragraph of (what became in the second edition) Section 1, where the distinction between abstract and concrete labour is presented: Karl Marx, 'Ergänzungen und Veränderungen zum ersten Band des *Kapitals*', *MEGA²* II/6: 5. Rubin notes that in the French edition of *Capital*, I, Marx precedes the offending sentence with one that he had in the first German edition but omitted from the second: 'there are not, strictly speaking, two kinds of labour in the commodity, however the same labour is opposed to itself depending on whether it is related to the use value of the commodity, as to its product, or to the value of the commodity, as to its objective expression,' Marx, *Le Capital*, I, pp69-70. See Rubin, *Essays on Marx's Theory of Value*, pp146-147 n 20. Patrick Murray argues that a proper understanding of Marx's value theory involves breaking down the concept of abstract labour into no less than three concepts—labour in general, abstract physiological labour, and 'practically abstract labour'—and recognising that it is only the third that creates value: 'Marx's "Truly Social" Labour Theory of Value', *Historical Materialism*, 6 and 7 (2000). The main merit of this argument is that it draws attention to the real processes of equalisation discussed in the final section of this chapter, though Murray understands these much more broadly.

of regulator, establishing equilibrium in the distribution of social labour among the various branches of the national economy (accompanied by constant deviations and disturbances). *The law of value is the law of equilibrium of the commodity economy.*[19]

But, as the last sentence makes clear, the bulk of Rubin's analysis is developed with respect to simple commodity production, that is, to an economy where the units of production produce for the market but where labour power is not a commodity because the direct producers (artisan or peasant households) control the means of production. It is only towards the end of his book that he focuses specifically on capitalist economic relations, arguing with respect of the transformation of values into prices of production: 'In the capitalist society, *the distribution of labour is regulated by the distribution of capital*'.[20] This is an elegant formulation, but can the two processes—the allocation of labour to different units and sectors in response to price fluctuations and the movement of capital between branches of production—be treated as separable in this fashion? Marx, as we saw in the preceding chapter, thought not.

John Weeks has provided a powerful argument that the law of value only becomes operative where the capitalist mode of production prevails:

> Consider first the case of individual producers that own their means of production. For simplicity, we assume that the inputs used in production are produced within a self-contained labour process without exchange. A credible example might be a subsistence farmer selling a portion of his product. In this case, only the final product of the labour process is a commodity. The means of production, both equipment and current inputs, are produced by each producer and do not directly face the discipline of competition. There is no social mechanism for bringing about a normal expenditure of labour time for the means of production. In such a case, the limited function of competition is to impose a uniform selling price in a market place. Price is a 'merely formal moment for the exchange of use values'.
>
> This hypothetical situation is not commodity production. Exchange does not appear until the end of the process, when all aspects of the labour process have been determined independently of exchange. Because the means of production are not exchanged, the producer faces no direct necessity to expend any specific amount of labour time on them.[21]

19  Rubin, *Essays on Marx's Theory of Value*, pp66-67.
20  Rubin, *Essays on Marx's Theory of Value*, p226.
21  John Weeks, *Capital, Exploitation and Economic Crisis* (London, 2010), p15.

In effect, what Weeks is saying is that in conditions of simple commodity production what Robert Brenner calls market dependence does not obtain. Brenner explains this concept as follows:

> unless they are devoid of their full means of subsistence (…not necessarily of production) and the ability to secure their subsistence by force from the direct producers, economic producers will not be *required* to buy inputs on the market. Unless they are required to buy necessary inputs on the market, they will not be obliged to sell on the market in order to survive. Unless they are required to sell on the market in order to survive, they will not be subject to the competitive constraint, their very survival depending on their producing competitively. Unless, finally, they are subject to the competitive constraint, they can be expected to maximise their profits by seeking the gains from trade, so they cannot be counted on to specialise, accumulate, innovate, and move from line to line in response to demand.[22]

One might indeed argue that the law of value only obtains where direct producers are market dependent in the sense developed by Brenner. Market dependence in turn, Weeks argues, only exists where the means of production are themselves commodities, which itself presupposes the separation of the direct producers from the means of production and therefore the prevalence of capitalist economic relations:

> Value can only act as a regulator of price once the entire product, all inputs, are monetised; until this occurs, the product is not a commodity in its entirety and all the concrete labour time expended on it need not be replaced by money. This, in turn, occurs only with the development of capitalist production… 'Value' regulates price only under capitalist relations and can be used as a tool of analysis only in capitalist society.[23]

Another way of putting it might be to say that capitalist relations of production involve two separations. The first is that between the producers, who interact as autonomous, specialised and interdependent units of production through the exchange of their products on the market. The second separation is that between the direct producers and the owners of the means of production, which implies the transformation of labour

---

22  Robert Brenner, 'Property and Progress: Where Adam Smith Went Wrong', in Chris Wickham, ed, *Marxist History-Writing for the Twenty-First Century* (Oxford, 2007), pp60-61. We will return to Brenner's requirement that producers lack access to the means of subsistence rather than the means of production in the next chapter.

23  Weeks, *Capital, Exploitation and Economic Crisis*, p19. See also Alfredo Saad-Filho's critique of value form theory in *The Value of Marx* (London, 2002), pp26-29.

power into a commodity. Although Marx presents these two separations at different points of his analysis in *Capital*—respectively in Part 1
and Part 2 of Volume I, they are in fact interdependent. In other words,
the transformation of labour power into a commodity is only possible in
a system of generalised commodity production; thus only in these circumstances are means of consumption available on the market for
workers to purchase with their wages. Correlatively, it is only where the
means of production are themselves commodities—which presupposes
their separation from the direct producers—that the units of production are fully market dependent and so subject to the law of value.
Hence, to modify Rubin's remark cited earlier, where the law of value
obtains, 'the distribution of labour is regulated by the distribution of
capital.' Or, as Alfredo Saad-Filho puts it, 'there is a relation of mutual
implication between capitalism as the mode of social production, wage
labour as the form of social labour, and the commodity as the typical
form of the output'.[24]

Rubin's preoccupation with simple commodity production may
help to explain why (unlike some later value form theorists) he doesn't
have much to say about money.[25] In this context, it is a mistake on his
part to dismiss the significance of Marx's discussion of the value form
in *Capital*, I, Chapter 1, Section 3. Marx's references to the form of
exchangeability in the first edition focus heavily on the role of a commodity that acts as the equivalent in which the values of other
commodities is expressed. Money emerges as a commodity that takes
on this function in a general and permanent fashion. This is the concrete form in which commodities are rendered commensurable (though
only, Marx takes care to emphasise, because they are all values in the
first place). And at the end of Section 3 in the second edition, Marx,
thanks to the introduction of money as the universal equivalent, presents the exchange ratios of commodities (which reflect the abstract
labour they embody) as (money) prices: 'The simple expression of the
relative value of a single commodity, such as linen, in a commodity
which is already functioning as the money commodity, such as gold, is
the price form.' (*C*I: 163)[26]

So price, 'the monetary expression of value', has already been presented in the very first chapter of *Capital* (*CW*34: 72). It is therefore

---

24  Saad-Filho, *The Value of Marx*, p41.
25  I am grateful to Fred Moseley for emphasising this point in correspondence.
26  See the excellent discussion of Chapter 1, section 3, in Harry Cleaver, *Reading Capital
Politically* (Brighton, 1979), ch V.

bizarre that a leading contemporary value-form theorist, Michael Heinrich, should argue that 'it was Marx himself who used a non-monetary theory when discussing the transformation of values into prices of production'.[27] Values have already been converted into money prices (and are indeed constantly illustrated by examples using pounds or thalers) long before Marx comes to the transformation of values into prices of production in *Capital*, III, Part 2. Elsewhere Heinrich correctly states that 'Marx's value theory is rather a *monetary theory of value*: without the value form, commodities cannot be related to one another as values,

---

27   Michael Heinrich, 'Reconstruction or Deconstruction? Methodological Controversies about Value and Capital, and New Insights from the Critical Edition', in Riccardo Bellofiore and Roberto Fineschi, eds, *Rereading Marx: New Perspectives after the Critical Edition* (Basingstoke, 2009), p92. Heinrich is supported in this claim by John Milios, Dimitris Dimoulis, and George Economakis in their interesting and erudite study, *Marx and the Classics: An Essay on Value, Crises and the Capitalist Mode of Production* (Aldershot, 2002). They argue that Marx broke with classical political economy in the late 1850s, but subsequently backslid: 'Marx retreats to the *empiricism* of the Ricardian theory' (p119) in treating the relationship between value and price of production as a quantitative one, and thereby forgetting that 'value and price are not commensurate. They are concepts existing on different analytical planes, categories between which there is an unbridgeable semantic gulf' (p127). They claim Marx commits this error particularly when trying to transform values into prices of production and in his theory of absolute rent (chs 5 and 6). As we saw in chapter 2, these two theoretical problems are closely related in the development of Marx's *critique* of Ricardo, so if Milios, Dimoulis and Economakis are right, the rot goes much deeper than they suggest. They insist, rightly, that Marx puts forward a monetary theory of value, but this is a commonplace in contemporary Marxist value theory, as I note below. Indeed, it is often the basis of what is called a 'single system' approach to the transformation problem, which treats values and prices of production as monetary and (hence) commensurable quantities that interact with each other. Milios, Dimoulis and Economakis regard this as a category mistake, but they seem to me to confuse what single-system theorists regard as an implication of ascribing to Marx a monetary theory of value with the distortion of this theory made by neo-Ricardian critics, starting with Ladislaw von Bortkiewicz in 1907, in assuming the transformation problem must be solved through the construction of a set of simultaneous equations: see, for example, 'Value and Price in the Marxian System', *International Economic Papers*, 2 (1952), and, in criticism, Alex Callinicos, 'Assault on Marx's Theory of Value', *International Socialism*, 1.90 (1976), http://www.marxists.org/history/etol/writers/callinicos/1976/07/value.htm. Some of the most interesting responses to the neo-Ricardian critique have sought to integrate time into the transformation: for example, Anwar Shaikh, 'Marx's Theory of Value and the Transformation Problem', in Jesse Schwartz, ed, *The Subtle Anatomy of Capitalism* (Santa Monica, 1977), Guglielmo Carchedi, *Frontiers of Political Economy* (London, 1991), ch 3, Andrew Kliman, *Reclaiming Marx's 'Capital'* (Lanham MD, 2007), and Fred Moseley, *Money and Totality: A Macro-Monetary Interpretation of Marx's Logic in Capital and the Transformation Problem* (forthcoming). Kliman and Moseley offer different versions of a single-system approach. To dismiss such an approach, Milios, Dimoulis and Economakis must explain why the method of progressively introducing ever more concrete determinations in principle rules out treating these determinations as interacting and expressing the structure of these interactions mathematically, which Marx plainly by his practice believed to be both possible and legitimate.

an only with the money form does an adequate form of value exist'.[28] In this latter view, Heinrich is in line with other contemporary commentators, for example, Fred Moseley, who puts forward what he calls 'a "macro-monetary" interpretation of Marx's theory': Volume I is primarily about the determination of the total increment of money ($\Delta M$), or total surplus value, produced in the capitalist economy as a whole. In other words, Volume I presents mainly a *macroeconomic* theory, and the main macroeconomic variable determined is the total money profit for the economy as a whole'.[29]

Heinrich may have been led into this strange aberration in part because he disagrees with Marx's attempt to show that capitalism requires, not merely money, but a money commodity:

> Marx could not imagine a capitalist money system existing without a money commodity, but the existence of such a commodity is in no way a necessary consequence of his analysis of the commodity and money. Within the framework of the analysis of the commodity form, he developed the form determinations of the general equivalent, and the analysis of the exchange process yields the result that commodity owners do in fact have to relate their commodities to a general equivalent. But that the general equivalent must be a specific commodity was not proved by Marx, merely assumed. That which serves as a general equivalent (whether an actual physical commodity or merely paper money) cannot be determined at the level of simple commodity circulation... Only when the capitalist credit system is taken into consideration...does it become clear that the existence of a money commodity is merely a historically transitory state of affairs, but does not correspond to 'the capitalist mode of production, in its ideal average' that Marx sought to analyse.[30]

This is dubious as an interpretation of Section 3, 'The Value Form', where Marx seeks to trace how in the exchange process a specific *commodity* (not paper or credit) takes on the role of universal equivalent. But of course he may be wrong. Since the Nixon administration broke the link between the dollar and gold in August 1971 many Marxist

28 Michael Heinrich, *An Introduction to the Three Volumes of Karl Marx's **Capital*** (New York, 2012), pp63-64.
29 Fred Moseley, 'Money and Totality: Marx's Logic in Volume I of *Capital*', in Riccardo Bellofiore and Nicola Taylor, eds, *The Constitution of Capital: Essays on Volume I of Marx's Capital* (Basingstoke, 2004), p147. Despite other differences with Moseley, Riccardo Bellofiore shares this overall interpretation of *Capital*: 'Marx and the Macro-monetary Foundations of Microeconomics', in Bellofiore and Taylor, eds, *The Constitution of Capital*.
30 Heinrich, *Introduction to Capital*, p70.

political economists have reached the conclusion that Marx confused the necessity of money with the specific, 'historically transitory' form it took as a commodity.[31] But Dimitris Milonakis and Ben Fine offer a different perspective:

> Marx's theory of money is in part based upon the notion that commodity money is displaced by symbols of money and hence, indirectly, symbols of value—though ratification of such symbols ultimately requires intervention by the state. Paradoxically, it is precisely this displacement in its most modern form, in which the functions of commodity money or gold are more or less confined to the reserves of central banks, which leads many to reject Marx's monetary theory—if they have genuinely considered it. How can a theory of commodity money, based on value theory, be of relevance when commodity money is no longer in use. [sic] In riposte, it can be argued that Marx's monetary theory implies the displacement of commodity money. How this occurs needs to be explored in its theoretical and empirical context, beyond the mere symbolic circulation of values as commodities to incorporate the symbolic, at times, fictitious circulation of surplus value. But this is to anticipate Marx's analysis of finance, though it does root consideration of the currently evolving financial system within the bounds of the production system on which it depends for its profitability, however, much it might wish otherwise. Thus...Marx's theory of money and finance is a neat combination of logical and historical/empirical analysis—examining how (surplus) value relations are expressed through money as a logical, practical and contingent process.[32]

31 This is, for example, the majority view in the essays in Fred Moseley, ed, *Marx's Theory of Money: Modern Interpretations* (London, 2005).

32 Dimitris Milonakis and Ben Fine, *From Political Economy to Economics* (London, 2009), p63. See also Suzanne de Brunhoff, *Marx on Money* (New York, 1976), Alain Lipietz, *The Enchanted World: Inflation, Credit and the World Crisis* (London, 1985), Weeks, *Capital, Exploitation and Economic Crisis*, chs 5-7, Saad-Filho, *The Value of Marx*, ch 8, and Costas Lapavitsas, *Profiting without Producing: How Finance Exploits Us All* (London, 2013), ch 4. While Milonakis and Fine offer a good summary of the strengths of Marx's theory of money, I am wary of the idea of paper money as a symbol. Chris Arthur puts it nicely: 'This money form does not *represent* the "presupposed" value of commodities; rather, it *presents* it to them as their universal moment. Money is not a re-presentation of something given in commodities, but the only way of making value *present* (ie, being there [*Dasein*] concretely, rather than as some unreal abstraction); it is the actuality of value... In circulation inconvertible paper does not "stand for" gold, it "stands in for" gold... It is a mistake, then, to think inconvertible paper is a *representation* of "real money", which therefore necessarily is an inadequate substitute for the real thing. It is in fact money insofar as it presents adequately value for itself; this it does not by being a *representative* commodity value, or by being a *representation of* value, but by playing the role of *presence*

If Milonakis and Fine are right, Marx's conception of commodity money needs to be related to his broader theory of money, which itself is crucial to how he analyses financial markets and economic crises. We return to these matters in chapter 6. The deeper problem with Heinrich's version of value form theory is that, in seeking rightly to underline the extent to which Marx breaks with Ricardo's substantialist value theory, he renders the critique of political economy ethereal. Take his discussion of the role of exchange in validating the value of commodities:

> it is exchange, that consummates the abstraction that underlies abstract labour (independent of whether the people engaged in exchange are aware of this abstraction). But then *abstract* labour cannot be measured in terms of hours of labour: every hour of labour measured by a clock is an hour of a particular *concrete* act of labour, expended by a particular individual, regardless of whether the product is exchanged. Abstract labour, on the other hand, cannot be 'expended' at all. Abstract social labour is a *relation of social validation* (*Geltungsverhältnis*) that is consti-tuted in exchange. In exchange the concrete acts of expended labour *count* as a particular quantum of value-constituting abstract labour, or are *valid* as a specific quantum of abstract labour, and therefore as an element of the total labour of society.[33]

But this interpretation directly contradicts Marx's repeated assertion that abstract labour constitutes an expenditure of labour power. Take this late example from the 'Notes on Wagner':

> this duality of the commodity there presents itself [as] the dual *character* of the *labour* whose product it is: of *useful* labour, ie the concrete modes of the labours which create use-values, and of abstract *labour*, of *labour as expenditure of labour power*, regardless of the 'useful' way in which it is expended (on which the presentation of the production process later depends). (*CW* 24: 546)

Jacques Bidet has pointed to the importance of the concept of the expenditure of labour power, which only appears in Marx's economic manuscripts after the *Grundrisse*, and which has an implicit reference to class relations of domination: '"Socially necessary" time can only be that of a "socially regulated" expenditure. And that returns us to the principle of social regulation of expenditure in any society, in other words, to class

---

of value. It *stands in for* gold functionally, rather than being a representation of gold, *standing for* it,' 'Value and Money', in Moseley, ed, *Marx's Theory of Money*, pp114, 115.
33   Heinrich, *Introduction to Capital*, pp50-51.

relations. For the question of expenditure immediately evokes that of the social compulsion to expenditure.' Hence: 'Value, as quantity, is also, by being the quantity of an expenditure of socially regulated labour power, a social relationship in a specific sense that includes the political dimension'.[34] But what Heinrich is in effect denying is the very idea of value 'as quantity'. That Marx conceives his theory as an empirical and quantitative theory and value itself as having a quantitative dimension is clear from the plethora of calculations and numerical examples that sometimes overwhelm the reader of his manuscripts. As Bidet notes, 'an explicit intent runs through *Capital* from start to finish, that of constituting a science in the modern sense of the term, constructing a homogeneous space in which magnitudes are considered and calculation is possible'.[35]

## Production and exchange

One of the many respects in which Rubin is superior to contemporary value form theorists is in his insistence that 'abstract labour, just as the value which it creates, does not only have a qualitative but also a quantitative side':

> The equality of two amounts of abstract labour signifies their equality as parts of total social labour—an equality which is only established in the process of social equalisation of labour by means of the equalisation of the products of labour. Thus we assert that in a commodity economy, the *social* equality of two labour expenditures or their equality in the form of *abstract* labour is established through the process of exchange. But this does not prevent us from ascertaining a series of quantitative properties which distinguish labour in terms of its material-technical and its physiological aspects, and which causally influence the quantitative determination of abstract labour before the act of exchange and independent of it. The most important of these properties are: 1) the *length of labour expenditure*, or the quantity of *working time*; 2) the *intensity* of labour; 3) the *qualification* of labour; and 4) the *quantity of products* produced in a unit of time.[36]

---

34  Bidet, *Exploring Marx's Capital*, pp43-44, 45.
35  Bidet, *Exploring Marx's Capital*, p11.
36  Rubin, *Essays in Marx's Theory of Value*, pp154, 155-156. Another bugbear of value theory that I abstain from is the so-called reduction problem (ie how skilled labour is reduced to simple labour). See Bidet's outstanding discussion: *Exploring Marx's Capital*, ch 2, and also an interesting formal treatment of these problems: Ulrich Krause, *Money and Abstract Labour* (London, 1982).

Rubin, like Heinrich, argues that 'the *social* equality of two labour expenditures or their equality in the form of *abstract* labour is established through the process of exchange.' As we have seen, Marx in the 1859 *Contribution* describes this as a 'difficulty', presumably because it seems to contradict the main thesis of the labour theory of value that value is created in production. Can both propositions be squared?

Let us first note that Rubin is mistaken to imply that the social equalisation of labour occurs *solely* in exchange. Because he treats the law of value as governing primarily a simple commodity economy, he fails to see how the domination of capitalist economist relations enables social equalisation of labour *within production*. As Lucia Pradella puts it, 'with the industrial revolution, the reduction of individual to abstract labour achieves an *adequate technical basis*: the activity of the worker is emptied of content and becomes purely mechanical and formal, while manual and intellectual functions are split up'.[37] Saad-Filho has analysed the 'normalisation' of labour in production thanks to intra-branch competition and capitalist control of the production process.[38]

This correction of Rubin's version of value theory does not, however, remove the problem of the contribution made by exchange to the social equalisation of labour. To answer this question we have to consider more closely how Marx defines value. At the beginning of *Capital*, I, he writes:

> Socially necessary labour time is the labour time required to produce any use value under the conditions of production normal for a given society and with the average degree of skill and intensity of labour prevalent in that society... What exclusively determines the magnitude of the value of any article is therefore the amount of labour socially necessary, or the labour time socially necessary for its production. (*C*I: 129)

Marx doesn't explore further here what is meant by 'the conditions of production normal for a given society', assuming in *Capital*, I, that socially necessary labour time is determined by the average conditions of production prevailing in the sector in question. He only drops this assumption in *Capital*, III. Bidet puts it like this:

> one of the most surprising paradoxes of the plan of *Capital* is that this famous 'law of value' is officially presented only in Volume Three, more precisely in Part Two, Chapter 10, at the point at which Marx undertakes

---

37  Lucia Pradella, *L'attualità del **Capitale**: Accumulazione e impoverimento nel capitalismo globale* (Padua, 2010), p55. See also Raya Dunayevskaya, *Marxism and Freedom: From 1776 until Today* (London, 1971), pp103-106.

38  Saad-Filho, *The Value of Marx*, pp55-62.

to provide an explanation of the transformation of value into price of production, an explanation in terms of causes that are nothing else than the properties that capital possesses from the fact that it is based on a market structure, in other words on the law of value and the law of *competition* that is inherent in it.[39]

*Capital*, III, Chapter 10, is entitled: 'The Equalisation of the General Rate of Profit through Competition. Market Prices and Market Values. Surplus Profit'. So it is partly a continuation of the analysis to which Chapter 9 is devoted of the formation of a general rate of profit thanks to the movement of capital between different branches of production. But the importance of the chapter lies in its discussion of how *intra*-branch competition sets the market values of commodities. Marx first presents the category here:

> The assumption that commodities from different spheres of production are sold at their values naturally means no more than that this value is the centre of gravity around which price turns and at which its constant rise and fall is balanced out. Besides this, however, there is always a *market value* (of which more later), as distinct from the individual value of particular commodities produced by the different producers. The individual value of some of these commodities will stand below the market value (ie less labour time has been required for their production than the market value expresses), the value of others above it. Market value is to be viewed on the one hand as the average value of the commodities produced in a particular sphere, and on the other hand as the individual value of commodities produced under average conditions in the sphere in question, and forming the great mass of the commodities. Only in extraordinary situations do commodities produced under the worst conditions, or alternatively the most advantageous ones, govern the market value, which forms in turn the centre around which market prices fluctuate—these being the same for all commodities of the same species. If the supply of commodities at the average value satisfies the customary demand, the commodities whose individual value stands below the market price will realise an extra surplus value or surplus profit, while those whose individual value stands above the market price will be unable to realise a part of the surplus value they contain. (CIII: 279)

The reference to 'more later' on market value, followed immediately by the presentation of the concept, underlines the roughness of Marx's

---

39   Bidet, *Exploring Marx's Capital*, p141.

discussion, not just here but throughout *Capital*, II and III. But this doesn't alter its importance. To some extent it recapitulates the theory of differential profit Marx develops in *Capital*, I, Chapter 12, where he shows how the extraction of relative surplus value can arise through individual capitals making an innovation that reduces their costs of production below the average for the sector and thereby reaping a surplus profit (see chapter 3 above). At that stage Marx refers to the difference between a commodity's individual and social value; now the latter is rebaptised market value. The shift in terminology probably indicates that Marx has explicitly introduced competition in *Capital*, III, Part 2, whereas, as we saw, he is uneasy about the role that it plays in *Capital*, I. He might well have been better off to have included the analysis of market value in Volume I (though, as we shall see below, after the capital relation has itself been posited), and thereby have strengthened the presentation of the law of value there. But, for whatever reason (perhaps the vestigial influence of the older capital in general/many capitals scheme), he doesn't do this.

But what is most significant here is that Marx refers here to the 'customary demand'. Contrary to the claim made both by critics and by some Marxists (for example, David Harvey), Marx does not simply ignore the role of supply and demand in his value theory. On the contrary, *Capital*, III, Chapter 10, involves his most developed analysis of the topic. One way of thinking about the presentation of supply and demand here is as a complication of the concept of socially necessary labour time. Now this is to be considered not merely with respect to the conditions of production and the qualities of labour but also to the level of social need for a given product. But how is social need registered where capitalist production relations prevail? Given that production is jointly controlled by competing capitals, this can only be through the distribution of effective demand among different goods and services.

Marx is careful to underline that supply and demand are dependent variables:

> Let us note here...that the 'social need' which governs the principle of demand is basically conditioned by the relationship of the different classes and their respective economic positions: in the first place, therefore, particularly by the proportion between the total surplus value and wages, and, secondly, by the proportion between the various parts into which the surplus value itself is divided (profit, interest, ground rent, taxes, etc). Here again we can see how absolutely nothing can be

explained by the relationship of demand and supply, before explaining the basis on which this functions. (*C*III: 282)

This explains why a presentation of the law of value cannot start with supply and demand, since the latter is determined by the class relations of capitalist society expressed in the rate and distribution of surplus value. But demand plays a necessary explanatory role in determining the market value of a particular type of product:

> To say that a commodity has use value is simply to assert that it satisfies some kind of social need. As long as we were dealing only with an individual commodity, we could take the need for this specific commodity as already given, without having to go into any further detail into the quantitative extent of the need which had to be satisfied. The quantity was already implied by its price. But this quantity is a factor of fundamental importance as soon as we have on the one hand the product of a whole branch of social production and on the other the social need. It now becomes necessary to consider the volume of the social need, ie its quantity. (*C*III: 286)

Despite some equivocations elsewhere in the chapter, the following passage seems to represent Marx's settled view of the role of demand in setting market value:

> There is no necessary connection, however, but simply a fortuitous one, between on the one hand the total quantity of social labour that is spent on a social article, ie the aliquot part of its total labour power which society spends on the production of this article, and therefore the proportion that the production of this article assumes in the total production, and on the other hand the proportion in which the society demands satisfaction of the need appeased by that particular article. Even if an individual article, or a definite quantity of one kind of commodity, may contain simply the social labour required to produce it, and so far as this aspect is concerned the market value of this commodity represents no more than the necessary labour, yet, if the commodity in question is produced on a scale that exceeds the social need at the time, a part of the society's labour time is wasted, and the mass of commodities in question then represents on the market a much smaller quantity of social labour than it contains... These commodities must therefore be got rid of for less than their market value and a portion may even be completely unsaleable. (The converse is the case if the amount of social labour spent on a particular kind of commodity is too small for the

specific social need which the product is to satisfy.) But if the volume of social labour spent on the production of a certain article corresponds in scale to the social need to be satisfied, so that the amount produced corresponds to the customary measure of reproduction, given an unchanged demand, then the commodity will be sold at its market value. The exchange or sale of commodities at their value is the rational, natural law of the equilibrium between them [*das Rationelle, das natürliche Gesetz ihres Gleichgewichts*]; this is the basis on which divergences have to be explained, and not the converse, ie the law of equilibrium should not be derived from contemplating the divergences. (*CIII: 291*)

As Marx makes clear elsewhere, what is at work here is the law of value, allocating social labour among different branches of production in proportion to the social need for different use values:

if in the case of an individual commodity this use value depends on its satisfying in and of itself a social need, in the case of the mass social product it depends on its adequacy to the quantitatively specific social need for each particular kind of product and therefore on the proportionate division of labour between these various spheres of production in accordance with these social needs, which are quantitatively circumscribed. (*CIII: 774*)

The process of competition establishes for each product the conditions of production necessary to satisfy a stable level of demand (given the class determined relations of distribution) for that product. It is through the correspondence thereby achieved between these conditions of production (let's call them for the sake of simplicity the average conditions) and what Marx calls the 'customary demand' that 'the *social* equality of two labour expenditures...is established through the process of exchange'. Where this correspondence holds, commodities of this type sell at their market value. As Rubin puts it, 'Market-value corresponds to the theoretically defined state of equilibrium among the different branches of production. If commodities are sold according to market values, then the state of equilibrium is maintained, ie, the production of a given branch does not expand or contract at the expense of other branches'.[40] In this situation, some of the labour performed producing

---

40 Rubin, *Essays on Marx's Theory of Value*, p178. See Rubin, ch 16, and Carchedi, *Frontiers of Political Economy*, ch 3, for good discussions of market value. Carchedi argues: 'It is clear that here Marx uses the term "average" not in the sense of "mean" but in the sense of "mode" or "modal group", that is, as the value around which, or the class in which, the values of commodities [in a specific sector] tend to be more heavily concentrated.'

commodities in less efficient conditions is wasted; it fails to receive social validation. By contrast, labour performed producing commodities in more efficient conditions creates more value than the same amount of labour performed in average conditions, which is reflected in the surplus profit reaped by more efficient producers. These cases differ from those where market prices fall below market value because in the latter conditions more commodities are produced than are required to meet the 'customary demand'. As Saad-Filho puts it, 'excess supply does not imply that a commodity has lost part of its use value, that the unsold items have lost their entire use value, or that the value of each commodity has shrunk, as if value were determined by price rather than the converse'.[41]

Of course, the level of 'customary demand' may change—for a variety of reasons: the level and/or distribution of income may alter, labour productivity may rise or fall, the array of types of product may be recalibrated thanks to innovation, and so on. As a result, the equilibrium state between production conditions and level of demand will change. Moreover, the associated fluctuations in market prices leading to the establishment of a new market value will be difficult for economic actors to distinguish from the fluctuations where price diverges from market value. But this is a necessary feature of a system of generalised commodity production regulated by the competitive interaction of autonomous but interdependent capitals, where there is only an accidental connection 'between on the one hand the total quantity of social labour that is spent on a social article...and on the other hand the proportion in which the society demands satisfaction of the need appeased by that particular article'. As Marx says of equilibrium elsewhere in *Capital*, 'on the basis of the spontaneous pattern [*naturwüchsigen Gestaltung*] of this production, this balance is itself an accident.' (*C*II: 571)[42]

---

Carchedi, p57. Compare CIII: 283-284, where Marx argues that where commodities produced under worse and better conditions cancel each other out, average conditions determine market value; where the quantity of commodities produced under worse conditions 'forms a relatively significant quantity, both vis-à-vis the average mass and vis-à-vis the opposite conditions' (284), their individual value determines market value; where these conditions apply with respect to commodities produced under better conditions, their individual values determine market value. These differences are important to Marx's theory of rent, which tends to rely on the assumption that in agriculture market value is determined by the worst conditions of production: for example, CIII: 797.

41  Saad-Filho, *The Value of Marx*, pp67-68.

42  In an interesting discussion, Stavros Tombazos argues that Marx offers two contradictory definitions of socially necessary labour time—a 'technological definition. Social labour time depends on the productive power of labour that is its mathematical opposite,' and a second where 'the useful character of the time spent for the production of a commodity asserts itself solely when the commodity is sold,' which cannot be reconciled since 'there is

This interpretation of Marx's value theory underlines that value must be understood relationally. Saad-Filho argues:

> The equalisation of labour and the determination of values and prices are the outcomes of a real process in three stages: first, individual labours are normalised across those producing the same kind of commodity; second, they are synchronised across those who have produced the same kind of commodity in the past or with distinct technologies; and, third, they are homogenised across the other types of labour as the commodity is equalised with ideal money.[43]

Synchronisation corresponds to what Marx analyses as the formation of a single market value:

> The equivalence between labours producing the same commodities at different points in time or with distinct technologies is due to the fact that value is a social relation established by, and reproduced through, capitalist production; rather than a substance historically embodied in the commodities by concrete labour... The social reality of value implies that *only living labour creates value*.[44]

Homogenisation—the assignment of prices to commodities that equalise concrete labours in the dimension of money—underlines that capitalist production is regulated through the competitive interaction of capitals on the market. Capitalist control of the expenditure of labour power is oriented to producing commodities whose price will realise at least the average profit, if not a surplus profit. Value thereby governs production in the shape of prices as units of what Marx calls 'ideal money, or a measure of value' (*CI*: 204). Production is thus oriented to exchange, in a unity that determines the nature of abstract labour. As Riccardo Bellofiore puts it:

---

no immediate relation between these two times. The former is a function of the productive power of labour, whereas the latter is a function of the balance of forces between the social classes,' *Time in Marx: The Categories of Time in Marx's* **Capital** (Leiden, 2014), pp34, 35. Tombazos goes on to argue that 'the so-called "disequilibria of supply and demand" are in reality a mere "tension within value". This tension is at the origin of the movement of capital, of the constant redistribution of labour time in the various productive sectors. Capitalist crises are the method employed by value in order to overcome its internal tension when the latter becomes unbearable' (pp54-55). Though expressed differently, the substance of this analysis seems no different from that given in the text, particularly since Tombazos notes: 'The economic disequilibrium is permanent, but the tendency towards equilibrium, which is manifested with iron necessity, is equally important.' (p55)

43 Saad-Filho, *The Value of Marx*, p54.
44 Saad-Filho, *The Value of Marx*, p62.

The socially necessary labour time (SNLT) constituting value is not just a 'technical' average, because the sociality of private labours and so the *same magnitude to be measured, is eventually fixed in market exchange.* Thus, SNLT is known *only ex-post.*

The key point is the 'unity' of production and circulation, so that abstract labour is both something *presupposed* to, and something fully *actualised* within, final exchange. Commodities are exchanged with money because—Marx says—they are *already* commensurable. As values, commodities count as objectified abstract human labour, and they count as objectified abstract human labour *because they are ex ante ideal money*, and because money is a commodity *produced by labour*. As such, as objectified abstract human labour, values are the *preconditions* of the equalisation going on in exchange. But abstract labour, Marx adds, is achieved *only* in *actual* exchange, when commodities as ideal money turn into real money.[45]

In moving beyond Ricardo's substantialist conception of value, Marx's value theory strikes a delicate balance, neither reducing value to embodied labour nor dissolving it into exchange. The result is an understanding of value that seeks to conceptualise the social relations involved in the two separations constitutive of the capitalist mode of mode of production—that is, the competitive interaction of capitals and the antagonistic relationship between capital and wage labour in the process of production. Unfortunately quite a lot of contemporary Marxist discourse seeks to harden this tissue of relationships into the properties of a collective subject, either capital or labour. In the next chapter I critically discuss the issues involved.

45  Riccardo Bellofiore, 'A Ghost Turning into a Vampire: The Concept of Capital and Living Labour', in Bellofiore and Fineschi, eds, *Rereading Marx*, p185. It is important to stress that homogenisation in the sense of which it is understood here neither abolishes the heterogeneity of different kinds of useful labour nor is inconsistent with the existence of diverse social identities: see the arguments for both these conclusions in Vivek Chibber, *Postcolonial Theory and the Spectre of Capital* (London, 2013), ch 6.

# 5

# Labour

## Living labour and capital

*Capital* is in some very obvious sense *about* labour. For Marx, abstract labour is the substance of value, hence living labour is the source of new value, and the surplus value appropriated from this new value represents surplus labour performed by wage workers. But contemporary discussion of *Capital* frequently marginalises wage labour. In this chapter I critically assess some versions of this marginalisation. The first of these is offered by Enrique Dussel's absolutisation of living labour, which renders invisible the relationality of capital. Then I discuss some of the ways in which the constitutive role of wage labour in the capital relation tends to be displaced in Marxist writing today. Finally, I scrutinise the influential idea that Marx conceives capital as a subject analogous to Hegel's Absolute Idea and the corollary drawn by Moishe Postone that the analysis of *Capital* does not require us to see the working class as the collective agent of their own and humankind's emancipation.

Dussel offers this gloss on Marx's famous letter to Engels of 24 August 1867 (discussed at the beginning of the last chapter):

> I personally believe that Marx thought his greatest discovery was the category of surplus value or the distinction between abstract and concrete labour, but both discoveries depend on the following (which I affirm was the most important of all, and of which Marx himself perhaps was not fully aware): the difference between *living* labour, substance 'of' value 'without' value, and *objectified* labour, 'with' value.[1]

Dussel is commenting here on the following passage from the *1861-63 Manuscript*:

> So far we have not spoken of the *value of labour* but only of the *value of labour capacity*, since a direct exchange of more labour for less would

---

1  Enrique Dussel, *Towards an Unknown Marx: A Commentary on the* **Manuscripts** *of 1861-63* (London, 2001), p172.

contradict the law of commodity exchange, and the form, whether the labour is active or objective, is entirely irrelevant, and the more irrelevant in that the value of a definite quantity of *objectified* labour is measured not by the quantity of labour *objectified* in it but by the average quantity of *living labour* required to reproduce the same commodity. On the other hand, the concept of the commodity in and for itself excludes labour as process—ie the *value* of the commodity—: labour as process, *in actu*, is the substance and measure of value, not value. Only as *objectified* labour is it value. Therefore, in considering capital in general—where the presupposition is that commodities are exchanged at their *value*—labour can only function as *labour capacity*, which is itself an *objective* form of labour.

In the production process, however, this mediation disappears. If we disregard the formal process of the exchange between capital and labour and consider what really occurs in the production process, and appears as the result of the production process, a certain quantity of living labour is exchanged for a smaller quantity of objective labour, and at the end of the process a certain quantity of objectified labour is exchanged for a smaller quantity of objectified labour. (*CW*34: 71)

The distinction between living labour—the labour performed during each circuit of industrial capital that creates new value—and dead (or objectified) labour—the labour performed in preceding circuits and represented by the value of the commodities used to make the new product and consumed by the workers—is indeed fundamental to Marx's analysis. Thus in *Capital*, I, he focuses on the dead labour expressed in the value of the means of production that is transferred to new commodities when living labour uses them up in making this product, writing: 'Capital is dead labour which, vampire-like, lives only by sucking living labour, and lives the more, the more labour it sucks' (*C*I: 342; see generally *C*I, Ch 8). But Dussel extends this indisputable feature of Marx's discourse into a much more ambitious argument: 'The truth of Marx's analysis rests on and departs from the "real reality (*wirkliche Wirklichkeit*)" of the Other, different from capital, the living labour as actuality, as creator of value or source of all human wealth in general, not only capitalist'.[2] That living labour is different from and opposed to capital is fundamental to Marx's argument (though, of course, in *Capital* and the 'Critique of the Gotha Programme' [1875], he explicitly rejects the idea that labour is the 'source of all human wealth').[3] Dussel, how-

2   Dussel, *Towards an Unknown Marx*, pp8-9.
3   'Labour is *not the source* of all wealth. *Nature* is just as much the source of use values (and

ever, goes further: 'The "exteriority" of living labour with respect to the "totality" of capital is the *conditio sine qua non* [necessary condition] for the total comprehension of Marx's discourse'.[4]

Dussel cites in support of this interpretation a striking passage that, having first been written in the *Grundrisse*, Marx repeats in modified form in the *1861–63 Manuscript*:

> *The separation of property from labour* appears as a necessary law of the exchange between capital and labour. As *not-capital, not-objectified labour* labour capacity appears: 1) *Negatively*. Not-raw material, not-instrument of labour, not-product, not-means of subsistence, not-money: *labour* separated from all the means of labour and life, from the whole of its objectivity, as a mere possibility. This complete denudation, this *possibility of labour* devoid of all objectivity. Labour capacity as *absolute poverty*, ie the complete exclusion of objective wealth. The objectivity possessed by labour capacity is only the bodily existence of the worker himself, his own objectivity.
>
> 2) *Positively*. *Not-objectified labour*, the unobjective, subjective existence of labour itself. Labour not as object but as activity, as living source of value. In contrast to capital, which is the reality of general wealth, it is the general possibility of the same, asserting itself in action. As *object*, on the one hand, labour is *absolute poverty*; as subject and activity, [on the other,] it is the general possibility of wealth. This is labour, such as it is *presupposed* by capital as antithesis, as the objective existence of capital, and such as for its part it in turn presupposes capital. (*CW*30: 170-171; compare *G*: 295-296)

Dussel argues :

> Can it be said that the '*living labour*', as reality and category is the same as 'wage labour' or labour already subsumed within the totality of capital? As subsumed, it is an *internal* determination of capital. But while it has not yet been totalised, living labour is *reality* (the most absolute reality for Marx), and the measure of all derealisation in the totality of capital, it is exterior. To this metaphysical position (beyond the being or the ontological reflection) of the labourer as *corporeality* (poor, bodily existence of the nude body), as person, as not-being of capital, we have called it 'exteriority',

---

it is surely of such that material wealth consists!) as labour, which itself is only the manifestation of a force of nature, human labour power' (*CW*24: 81).

4   Dussel, *Towards an Unknown Marx*, p8. Chris Arthur gives his qualified support to this approach: see 'Review of Enrique Dussel's *Towards an Unknown Marx*', *Historical Materialism*, 11:2 (2003).

the alterity of the Other than capital. To be 'Other' than the *totality* of capital is still to be in the exteriority [sic]. From the exterior alterity, on the other hand, is where the theoretical critique of Marx begins.[5]

The philosophical language used here reminds us that Dussel is not simply an outstanding student of *Capital* and its drafts, but a leading liberation theologian.[6] The theme of the worker as suffering body has been taken up by other contemporary commentators. For example, Massimiliano Tomba writes: 'The injustice of which *Capital* speaks is the injustice inflicted on the body by the domination of dead labour over living labour. It is injustice against the body'.[7] David McNally proposes that at the end of *Capital*, I, Part 2, there commences 'a journey from the sphere of form—value form to be precise—to the domain of bodies and their labours'.[8] This last statement is most definitely wrong. Marx refers to 'the specificity of the value form, and consequently of the commodity form together with its further developments, the money form, the capital form, etc' (*CI*: 174 n 34). The capital form is presented in Part 2, but steadily acquires new determinations—constant and variable capital, absolute and relative surplus value, accumulation—throughout the rest of *Capital*, I. Marx's attention for much of this volume is indeed directed at workers' labours, sufferings and struggles, but these actions and passions are examined within the conceptual framework provided by the successive form determinations that Marx constantly introduces. He might moreover think that highlighting workers' bodies mirrors rather than criticises the separation of manual and intellectual labour that he sees communism transcending.

Dussel is quite right to insist on the importance of the role that living labour plays within Marx's analytical framework. Marx does sometimes refer to living labour in a strikingly vitalist way, as the dynamising force animating the capitalist process. For example, early in the *Grundrisse*, as he is building the categories of his value theory: 'Labour is the living,

---

5    Dussel, *Towards an Unknown Marx*, p8.

6    See, for example, Dussel, *Towards an Unknown Marx*, pp240-245, Appendix 2: 'Exteriority in Marx's Thought'.

7    Massimiliano Tomba, *Marx's Temporalities* (Leiden, 2013), p117. It is an oddity of Tomba's interpretation that he boldly describes *Capital* as being about injustice when Marx notoriously denied this, describing the fact that labour power can create more value that it possesses as 'a piece of good luck for the buyer, but by no means an injustice towards the seller' (*CI*: 301). The relationship between Marx's concept of exploitation and the idea of justice has been a matter of much debate, in my view successfully *aufgehoben* by Norman Geras: 'The Controversy about Marx and Justice', *New Left Review*, I/150 (1985). To ignore this in the way that Tomba does seem problematic.

8    David McNally, *Monsters of the Market* (Leiden, 2011), p134.

form-giving fire; it is the transitoriness of things, their temporality, as their formation by living time' (*G*: 180). A decade later in *Capital*, I, he writes of the means of production, inert and deteriorating so long as they are not used in the process of production:

> Living labour must seize on these things, awaken them from the dead, change them from merely possible into real and effective use values. Bathed in the fire of labour, appropriated as part of its organism, and infused with vital energy for the functions appropriate to their concept and to their vocation in the process, they are indeed consumed, but to some purpose, as elements in the formation of new use values. (*CI*: 289-290)[9]

From a more analytical angle, Jacques Bidet argues that, 'by the tiny distance that consists in considering labour first of all outside the wage relation, Marx opened a non-Ricardian space'.[10] Crucially, this move allows him to conceptualise the wage relation as one constituted by exploitation, in which capital directs the expenditure of labour power in order to extract surplus value. But distinguishing between labour and wage-labour doesn't justify treating living labour as a transhistorical, indeed absolute and primitive category, as Dussel does, for example, here: 'In the "development of the concept of living labour" (and thus of capital) the first step is to depart from living labour itself as the absolute simple, first (and hence "non-constructible", "subject of conceptualisation", but not definable *a priori*) category'.[11] This hypostatisation of living labour seems to reflect Dussel's own philosophical preoccupations; it has absolutely no warrant from Marx's writings, where living (or non-objectified) labour is presented in opposition to dead (or objectified) labour, corresponding in value terms to variable capital (invested in labour power) and constant capital (invested in means of production). In other words, it belongs to the set of determinations through which the capital relation is constituted.[12]

---

9   But the following passage may be intended as a corrective to these more vitalist formulations: 'What Lucretius says is self-evident: "*nil posse creari de nihilo*", out of nothing, nothing can be created. "Creation of value" is the transposition of labour-power into labour. Labour power itself is, above all else, the means of nature transposed into a human organism' (*CI*: p323 n 2).
10   Jacques Bidet, *Exploring Marx's* ***Capital*** (Leiden, 2007), p308.
11   Dussel, *Towards an Unknown Marx*, p196.
12   See, for example, this early passage from the *Grundrisse*, which brings out the interdependence of living and dead labour: 'The only thing distinct from *objectified* labour is *non-objectified* labour, labour which is still objectifying itself, *labour* as subjectivity. Or, *objectified* labour, ie labour which is present in space, can also be opposed, as *past labour*, to labour which is *present in time*. If it is to be present in time, alive, then it

As to the broader theme of exteriority, for labour to be other than capital is not the same as being outside the capital *relation*. This is indicated in the passage cited by Dussel, where Marx, having summarised the duality of labour capacity as both negative (absolute poverty) and positive (living labour), concludes: 'This is labour, such as it is *presupposed* by capital as antithesis, as the objective existence of capital, and such as for its part it in turn presupposes capital.' Labour capacity and capital thus mutually presuppose one another. These formulations recall a famous passage from *Wage Labour and Capital* that Marx quotes in *Capital*, I: '*Thus capital presupposes wage labour; wage labour presupposes capital. They reciprocally condition the existence of each other; they reciprocally bring forth each other*' (*CW*9: 214; *C*I: 724 n. 21). The self-expansion of capital can only become an autonomous process when it succeeds in separating the direct producers from the means of production, a historical transition that is constantly reproduced through the process of exploitation; for its part, labour capacity is not merely a poor, bare, forked animal outside capital, but a historical result that presupposes capital's continually renewed success in denying it direct access to the means of production. It is a necessary consequence of this relationship that labour capacity takes the form of wage labour and its value that of the value or price of labour. A couple of paragraphs after the passage from the *1861-63 Manuscript* cited first in this section, Marx writes:

> In this form, *the value*, price *of* labour is a specific expression, which directly contradicts the concept of value. But this contradiction exists. It is mediated through a series of intermediate elements, which we have developed. In reality the relation appears unmediated, and therefore the wage appears as the value or price of a definite quantity of living labour. (*CW*34: 72)

Dussel tries to find support for the idea of the exteriority of living labour to capital by distinguishing labour capacity (*Arbeitsvermögen*) from labour-power (*Arbeitskraft*):

> Once alienated, subsumed, intra-totalised in capital, labour 'capacity' or 'possibility' passes to its act, to its 'actuality', to its effective use. The *potency* becomes *act*. Only at this moment, 'capacity' becomes 'power', from labour capacity now it is '*labour power*'. This new and distinct

---

can be present only as the *living subject*, in which it exists as capacity, as possibility; hence as *worker*. The only *use value*, therefore, which can form the opposite pole to capital is *labour (to be exact, value-creating, productive labour)*' (*G*: 271-272).

category means then the passage to the effective actualisation of labour as such: the effectively productive power, but not before.[13]

It is strange, and a bit distressing to find such a brilliant and learned commentator on Marx making such a fanciful assertion. Marx uses 'labour capacity' from his discovery of the concept in the *Grundrisse* till the *1863-5 Manuscript*, replacing it in *Capital*, I, with 'labour power'. In the *1861-63 Manuscript* he writes of the worker, 'the sole commodity he has to offer, to sell, is precisely his living labour capacity, present in his own living corporeity. (*Capacity* is here absolutely not to be conceived as *fortuna*, **fortune**, but as potency, δυναμις.)' (*CW*30: 37) But Marx's presentation of labour power in *Capital*, I, makes it clear he sees no difference between the two expressions and provides no support for the claim that one is more associated with potency or possibility than the other:

> the capacity for labour (*Arbeitsvermögen*), in other words labour power (*Arbeitskraft*).
>
> We mean by labour power, or labour capacity, the aggregate of those mental and physical capabilities existing in the physical form, the living personality, of a human being, capabilities which he sets in motion whenever he produces a use value of any kind. (*CI*: 270)

## Marginalising wage labour

Dussel's dubious attempt to extract living labour from the form determinations constituting the capital relation and to counterpose it to them is an example of a widespread trend by contemporary critical thought to downgrade or marginalise wage labour. Michael Lebowitz is an exception to this tendency, since he argues that Marx failed sufficiently to recognise the significance of his own stress on the social relativity of needs and therefore did not conceptualise the autonomy of wage labour as a force co-equal to capital. Consequently he didn't stick to his insight in the *Economic and Philosophical Manuscripts of 1844* that:

> there was not one subject—but two. Whatever the shortcomings of his early conceptions, capitalism for him was clearly characterised by two sides and their relations. The relations of capitalism contained within them the relations of capitalism as capital, the same relations as wage labour, and the mutual relations of these two to one another.[14]

---

13  Dussel, *Towards an Unknown Marx*, p12.
14  Michael Lebowitz, *Beyond **Capital**: Marx's Political Economy of the Working Class* (2nd

Bidet offers in my view a much more satisfactory discussion of Marx's analysis of the value and price of labour power in *Capital* that shows how the class struggle is built into these concepts:

> The specificity of the value/price relationship applied to labour power translates into the following 'curious effect': the price movement, in the sense denoted by *Zwischenbewegung* ['subsidiary movements': cf. *C*I: 658-659], rebounds on that of value. In effect, the brake that the workers' resistance brings to the mechanical alignment of the price of labour power to its decreasing value can be analysed as an element that modifies the value and the movement itself, by favouring a growth in the mass of working-class means of subsistence. It stamps on a *value* that productivity tends to decrease a principle of growth, at least in so far as this resistance determines lasting effects; a new 'standard of living'. And this rebound on the magnitude of value is also a rebound for its concept.[15]

It is, however, more common to play down the importance of wage labour in *Capital*. Often this is justified by reference to David Harvey's development of the concept of accumulation by dispossession—'accumulation based on predation, fraud, and violence', whose function is 'to release a set of assets (including labour power) at very low (and in some instances zero) cost'—as not, as is commonly attributed to Marx, merely a key element of the 'primitive' or 'original' accumulation that brings into existence the presuppositions of the capital relation, but a chronic feature of capitalism throughout its history. In his original presentation of the concept, Harvey was careful to insist that 'the two aspects of expanded reproduction [the accumulation of capital based on the exploitation of wage labour] and accumulation by dispossession are organically linked, dialectically intertwined'.[16] More recently, however, Harvey has been less cautious:

---

edn; Basingstoke, 2003), p77.

15  Bidet, *Exploring Marx's Capital*, p87; see generally Bidet, ch 4, and, for a similar argument, Maurice Dobb, *Political Economy and Capitalism* (London, 1937), pp209-210. See Alex Callinicos, *The Resources of Critique* (Cambridge, 2006), ch 4, for a critique of Toni Negri, who moves from a two-subject conception of the capital relation (capital and labour) in *Marx Beyond Marx* (1979) to a one-subject (the multitude) conception in *Empire* (2000).

16  David Harvey, *The New Imperialism* (Oxford, 2003), pp144, 149, 176. See the warning against the overextension of the concept of accumulation by dispossession in Sam Ashman and Alex Callinicos, 'Capital Accumulation and the State System: Assessing David Harvey's *The New Imperialism*', *Historical Materialism*, 14:4 (2006). For an example of the contemporary tendency to give priority to primitive accumulation, see Massimo de Angelis, 'Separating the Doing and the Deed: Capitalism and the Continuous Character of Enclosures', *Historical Materialism*, 12:2 (2004).

Yet there are commonalities as well as complementarities between the two processes [Harvey doesn't specify but presumably he means 'normal' accumulation based on the exploitation of wage labour and accumulation by dispossession], as Luxemburg correctly, in my view, suggests by pointing to the 'organic relation' between them. The extraction of surplus value is, after all, a specific form of accumulation by dispossession, since it is nothing more or less than the alienation, appropriation and dispossession of the labourer's capacity to produce value in the labour process.[17]

This is, in my view, a disastrous move. As Harvey acknowledges elsewhere, Marx's analysis in *Capital*, I, systematically assumes that commodities exchange at their values.[18] Marx was surrounded by radical thinkers (for example, Proudhon and his followers) who treated exploitation as a consequence of capitalists' illegitimate manipulation of the laws of the market. His presentation of the capital relation is intended to show that exploitation is a 'normal' feature of a system of generalised commodity production where labour power has been transformed into a commodity. As we have already seen in chapter 3, Marx therefore treats what Harvey calls extended reproduction as sharply distinct from primitive accumulation, even if we accept that the latter continues in various forms into the present:

> The organisation of the capitalist process of production, once it is fully developed, breaks down all resistance. The constant generation of a relative surplus population keeps the law of supply and demand of labour, and therefore wages, within narrow limits which correspond to capital's valorisation requirements. The silent compulsion of economic relations sets the seal on the domination of the capitalist over the worker. Direct extra-economic force is still of course used, but only in exceptional cases. (*CI*: 899)

By subsuming the extraction of surplus value under accumulation by dispossession Harvey risks regressing to a pre-Marxian position where modern exploitation is a consequence of 'predation, fraud, and violence'. Admittedly, this is a common view on the contemporary radical left, led by Michael Hardt and Tony Negri, who argue: 'Capital accumulation today is increasingly external to the production process, such that exploitation takes the form of *expropriation of the common*.' Accordingly they conclude that 'the exploitation of labour-power and the accumulation of surplus-value should be understood in terms of not profit but *capitalist*

---

17   David Harvey, *A Companion to Marx's **Capital*** (London, 2010), p311.
18   As above, pp244-245, discussing *CI*: 710.

*rent*'.[19] Compare this to how Marx conceptualises capital as constituted in its conflictual relationship with wage labour:

> Capital is productive of value only as a *relation*, in so far as it is a coercive force on wage-labour, compelling it to perform surplus-labour, or spurring on the productive power of labour to produce relative surplus value. In both cases it only produces value as the power of labour's own objective conditions over labour when these are alienated from labour; only as one of the forms of wage labour itself, as a condition of wage labour. (*CW*30: 399)

In treating capital as an external force, Hardt and Negri transform it into a super-subject battening on the commons. The relentless plunder of resources is undoubtedly an important aspect of contemporary neo-liberal globalisation, but repressing the relationality of capital blocks any understanding of the distinctive forms of capital accumulation today, and in particular the gigantic extension of the capital relation in the past generation represented by the expansion of industrial capitalisms in East Asia producing for the world market. It also fails to grasp the *interdependence* of capital and wage labour, which is expressed in the exploitation of workers, but also in their collective capacity to disrupt, paralyse, and take control of the production process.

Harvey is also representative of contemporary left wing thinking in a strange slide that he performs when discussing Marx's distinction between the formal and real subsumption of labour under capital. He writes:

> Under what was called the putting-out system, merchant capitalists would take materials to labourers in their cottages and return to collect the worked up product at a later date. The labourers would not be supervised, and the labour process would be left up to the cottagers (it often entailed family labour and dovetailed with subsistence agricultural practices). But the cottagers depended on the merchant capitalists for their monetary incomes and did not own the product they worked up. This is what Marx means by formal subsumption. When labourers are brought into the factory for a wage, then both they and the labour process are under the direct supervision of the capitalist. This is real subsumption. So the formal is out there, dependent, while the real is inside the factory under the supervision of the capitalist.[20]

---

19  Michael Hardt and Toni Negri, *Commonwealth* (Cambridge MA, 2009), pp137, 141. Slavoj Žižek adopts a similar approach, for example in *First as Tragedy, Then as Farce* (London, 2009), pp138-148.
20  Harvey, *Companion to Marx's Capital*, p174. For another example of this kind of

So, according to Harvey, it is only with the real subsumption of labour under capital that the direct producers become wage workers employed by capitalists. This is an astonishing misinterpretation of Marx. Marx develops the distinction between formal and real subsumption first in the *1861-63 Manuscript* and *1863-5 Manuscript* (notably in the so-called 'Sixth Chapter' of *Capital*, I, 'Results of the Immediate Process of Production'), which he treats as broadly corresponding to the distinction between absolute surplus value (where the rate of exploitation is increased by lengthening the working day) and relative surplus value (which relies instead on increases in labour productivity). But both forms of subsumption presuppose wage labour, as this passage where the distinction is first fully developed in the *1861-63 Manuscript* makes clear:

> The subsumption is formal, in so far as the individual worker, instead of working as an independent commodity owner, now works as a labour capacity belonging to the capitalist, and therefore under his command and supervision; also works no longer for himself but for the capitalist; the means of labour, moreover, no longer appear as means to the realisation of his labour: his labour appears instead as the means of valorisation—ie absorption of labour—for the means of labour. This distinction is formal in so far as it can exist without causing the slightest alteration of any kind in the mode of production or the social relations within which production takes place. (*CW*30: 262)

But in the case of real subsumption:

> the capitalist mode of production has already seized upon the substance of labour and transformed it. The subsumption of the worker under capital is no longer merely *formal*: the fact that he works for someone else, under alien command and alien supervision. Nor is the situation any longer merely as it was in the case of simple cooperation, where the worker cooperates with many others, performing *the same* work with them at the same time, while his work as such remains unchanged and a merely temporary connection is created, a contiguity, which by the nature of things may easily be dissolved and which in most cases of simple cooperation takes place only for specific, limited periods, to satisfy exceptional requirements, as with harvesting, road-building, etc. Nor is it like manufacture in its simplest form, where the main thing is

treatment of formal subsumption see Neil Davidson, *How Revolutionary Were the Bourgeois Revolutions?* (Chicago, 2012), p576.

the simultaneous exploitation of many workers and a saving on fixed capital, etc, and where the worker only formally becomes a part of a whole, whose head is the capitalist, but in which he is not further affected—as a producer—by the fact that many other workers are doing the same thing alongside him, also making boots, etc. With the transformation of his labour capacity into what is merely a function of part of the complete mechanism, the whole of which forms the workshop, he has altogether ceased to be the producer of a commodity. He is only the producer of a one-sided operation, which in general produces something solely in connection with the whole of the mechanism that forms the workshop. He is thus a living constituent of the workshop, and has himself become an accessory to capital through the manner of his work, since his skill can only be exercised in a workshop, only as a link in a mechanism which confronts him as the presence of capital. Originally he had to sell to the capitalist, instead of the commodity, the labour that produced the commodity, because he was not in possession of the objective conditions for the realisation of his labour capacity. Now he has to sell it because his labour capacity only continues to be labour capacity in so far as it is sold to capital. Thus he is now subsumed under capitalist production, has now fallen under the control of capital, no longer just because he lacks the means of labour, but because of his very labour capacity, the nature and manner of his labour; now capital has in its hands no longer just the objective conditions, but the social conditions of subjective labour, the conditions under which his labour continues to be labour at all. (*CW*30: 279-280)

So the real subsumption of labour under capital does not involve, as Harvey asserts, bringing the direct producers 'into the factory for a wage', putting both them 'and the labour process...under the direct supervision of the capitalist'. This has already happened when labour is formally subsumed under capital. By contrast, 'with the real subsumption of labour under capital a complete revolution takes place in the mode of production itself, in the productivity of labour, and in the relation—within production—between the capitalist and the worker, as also in the social relation between them' (*CW*34: 107-108). In a pioneering study of the origins of the factory, Stephen Marglin argues, fully in line with how Marx conceptualises formal and real subsumption, that:

the agglomeration of workers into factories was a natural outgrowth of the putting-out system (a result, if you will, of its internal contradictions) whose success had little or nothing to do with the technological superiority of large-scale machinery. The key to the success of the factory, as well as its inspiration, was the substitution of capitalists' for workers' control of the production process; discipline and supervision could and did reduce costs *without* being technologically superior.[21]

This doesn't mean that Marx ignored cases where labour is subsumed under capital without being transformed into wage labour. Thus he refers to:

> forms in which the capital-relation does not yet exist formally, i.e. under which labour is already exploited by capital before the latter has developed into the form of productive capital and labour itself has taken on the form of wage labour. Such forms are to be found in social formations which precede the bourgeois mode of production; on the other hand they constantly reproduce themselves within the latter and are in part reproduced by the latter itself. (*CW*34: 117)

Marx gives the example of an Indian peasant who mortgages his cotton crop to a usurer. He is sometimes accused of being indifferent, or even hostile to the condition of peasants.[22] But he was full of praise for the mid-19th century economist Richard Jones for showing 'what has been lacking in all English economists since Sir James Steuart, namely, a sense of the *historical* differences in modes of production' (*CW*33: 320). One of Jones's main themes is the historical specificity of the capital/wage labourer relationship, still a comparative rarity in a world where most producers were still peasants.[23] When discussing the genesis of capitalist rent in *Capital*, III, Marx has quite an extensive discussion of small-scale peasant proprietors; it is in the course of this that he makes his famous statement that 'large landed property' under capitalism 'produces conditions that provoke an irreparable rift in the interdependent process of social metabolism, a metabolism prescribed by the natural laws of life itself [*einen unheilbaren Riß hervorrufen in dem Zusammenhang des gesellschaftlichen und durch die Naturgesetze des Lebens vorgeschriebnen Stoffwechsels*]' (CIII: 949).

---

21 Stephen A Marglin, 'What Do Bosses Do? The Origins and Functions of Hierarchy in Capitalist Production', *Review of Radical Political Economics*, vol 6, no 2 (1974), p84.

22 For example, George Monbiot's very lazy reading of the *Communist Manifesto*: *The Age of Consent: A Manifesto for a New World Order* (London, 2003), pp26-30. See the extensive discussion of Marx on the peasantry in Hal Draper, *Karl Marx's Theory of Revolution*, II (New York, 1978), chs 12-14.

23 See Richard Jones, *Literary Remains, consisting of Lectures and Tracts on Political Economy* (ed William Whewell; London, 1859), and Marx's discussion of his work in *CW*33: 320-371.

One question posed by the transitional forms considered by Marx is what counts as the subsumption of labour under capital. It is raised in the work of one leading contemporary Marxist historian, Jairus Banaji. He has strongly criticised attempts to treat free wage labour as a necessary and sufficient condition for the existence of capitalist relations of production, which he associates especially with the school of Political Marxists who claim inspiration from Robert Brenner's work. According to Banaji:

> *historically*, capital accumulation has been characterised by considerable flexibility in the structuring of production and in the forms of labour and organisation of labour used in producing surplus-value. The liberal conception of capitalism which sees the sole basis of accumulation in the individual wage-earner conceived as a free labourer obliterates a great deal of capitalist history, erasing the contribution of both enslaved and collective (family) units of labour-power.
>
> To take this further, it would surely represent an advance in Marxist theory to think of capitalism working through a *multiplicity* of forms of exploitation *based on* wage-labour. In other words, instead of seeing wage-labour as *one* form of exploitation among many, alongside share-cropping, labour tenancy, and various kinds of bonded labour, these specific individual forms of exploitation may just be ways in which paid labour is recruited, exploited, and controlled by employers. The argument is not that *all* sharecroppers, labour-tenants, and bonded labourers are wage-workers, but that these 'forms' may reflect the subsumption of labour into [sic] capital in ways where the 'sale' of labour-power for wages is mediated and possibly disguised in more complex arrangements.[24]

Banaji bases this argument not merely on his historical research but on an influential discussion of modes of production he first published in 1977. His key thesis is 'forms of exploitation derive their specific historical "social forms" and "functions" from the relations of production which they mediate or which are embodied in them'. On this basis he distinguishes between wage labour as a 'simple category', 'common to several epochs of production', and as 'a "concrete" category', ie 'as *abstract, value-producing* labour, hence as labour which already posits the elements of capitalist production'.[25] But Banaji has greatly reinforced the power of this

---

24  Jairus Banaji, *Theory as History: Essays on Modes of Production and Exploitation* (Leiden, 2010), p145. I criticise Political Marxism at length in *Imperialism and Global Political Economy* (Cambridge, 2009), chs 2 and 3.

25  Banaji, *Theory as History*, pp198 n 56, 54, 55, taken from 'Modes of Production in a Materialist Conception of History', first published in *Capital & Class*, 3 (1977).

theoretical argument by demonstrating the extensive existence of wage labour in precapitalist societies, for example, the eastern Mediterranean in late antiquity.[26] He is right to insist that forms of exploitation have to be understood in relations to their role in sustaining the tendencies (what Marx calls the laws of motion) of a specific mode of production. But, if wage labour pre-exists capitalism, under what conditions does it become *'abstract, value-producing labour'* sustaining the laws of motion of capitalism? The same could be asked of forms of non-wage labour that are, as both Banaji and Marx agree, subsumed under capital.[27] The only answer that Banaji has, as far as I know, given to this question is that labour subsumed under capital takes the form of living labour.[28] I'm not sure that this is right: what gives labour the power to create value is its transformation (through the processes of normalisation, synchronisation and homogenisation discussed by Saad-Filho, as we saw in chapter 4) into abstract social labour; the opposition between dead and living labour presupposes this transformation. But even if we accept Banaji's formulation, this simply shifts the question backwards, since, as we have seen, living labour is one of the set of determinations that Marx argues constitutes the capital relation. The problem is under what conditions we can affirm that these determinations exist.

One answer is provided by Robert Brenner's concept of market dependence, which we touched on in the preceding chapter. He argues that 'capitalist social property relations' have 'two defining elements':

> Economic agents must be separated from the means of subsistence. Though they may possess means of production—tools and skills—the individual economic agents cannot possess their full means of subsistence, ie all that is necessary to allow them to directly product what they need to survive. What this usually means is that, at a minimum, they must be deprived of ownership of land, or at least of land that, when combined with their labour and tools, could provide them with everything they need to survive.[29]

---

26  See, for example, Banaji, *Theory as History*, chs 4 and 7, and, for the extensive role of wage labour in Egyptian estates supplying the expanding late Roman market economy made possible by Constantine's early 4th century money reform, Banaji, *Agrarian Change in Late Antiquity: Gold, Labour, and Aristocratic Dominance* (rev edn; Oxford, 2007), ch 7.

27  See Banaji, *Theory as History*, ch 10, another early essay where Banaji discusses peasants in the Deccan in the early 19th century.

28  During Marxism 2012, an event organised by the Socialist Workers Party, London, July 2012.

29  Robert Brenner, 'Property and Progress: Where Adam Smith Went Wrong', in Chris Wickham, ed, *Marxist History-Writing for the Twenty-First Century* (Oxford, 2007), p60. G A Cohen also argues that it is the denial of access to the means of subsistence that is

This condition, together with a second requiring that economic agents lack the means of coercion to extract surplus labour from direct producers, ensures that they can only reproduce themselves by producing as efficiently as possible for the market. By making the first condition separation from the means of subsistence, rather than from the means of production, Brenner casts subsumption under capital more broadly than Marx's concepts of formal and real subsumption do, since (as we have seen) these both presuppose wage labour. This is historically important because of the case, studied by Brenner, of the development of capitalism in the northern Netherlands, where ecological change in the late Middle Ages forced peasants into market dependence that promoted economic specialisation and higher productivity.[30] When Marx discusses the economic content of wage labour, as he does in the following passage where he is contrasting it to slavery, he too highlights how the worker's market dependence makes labour more productive and versatile, allowing it to meet a wider range of needs:

> In the case of the slave the *minimum wage* appears as a constant magnitude, independent of his own labour. In the case of the free worker, the *value of his labour capacity*, and the *average wage* corresponding to it, does not present itself as confined within this predestined limit, independent of his own labour and determined by his purely physical needs. The *average* for the *class* is more or less *constant* here, as is the value of all commodities; but it does not exist in this immediate reality for the *individual* worker, whose wage may stand either above or below this minimum. The *price of labour* sometimes falls below *the value of labour capacity*, and sometimes rises above it. Furthermore, there is room for manoeuvre (**within narrow limits**) for the worker's *individuality*, as a result of which there are differences in wages, partly between *different branches of labour*, and partly in *the same* branch of labour, according to the industriousness, skill, strength, etc, of the worker, and indeed these differences are in part determined by the measure of his own personal performance. Thus the level of the wage appears to vary according to the worker's own labour and its individual quality. This is particularly strongly developed where a *piece wage* is paid. Although the latter...does not change in any way the general relation between capital and labour, surplus labour and necessary labour, it nevertheless expresses the

---

necessary for labour to be subsumed under capital: *Karl Marx's Theory of History* (Oxford, 1978), pp70-73.

30  Robert Brenner, 'The Low Countries in the Transition to Capitalism', in P Hoppenbrouwers and J L Zanden, eds, *Peasants into Farmers* (Brepols, 2001).

relation for each individual worker differently, according to the measure of his own personal performance. Great strength or special skills may increase the *purchase value* of the slave as a person, but this is of no concern to the slave himself. It is different with the free worker, who is himself the proprietor of *his labour capacity*.

The higher value of this labour capacity must be paid to the worker himself, and it is expressed in a higher wage. Great differences in wages are therefore found, according to whether the specific kind of labour requires a more highly developed labour capacity, necessitating greater production costs, or not, and this on the one hand opens up an area of free movement for individual differences, while on the other hand it provides a spur to the development of the individual's own labour capacity. Certain as it is that the mass of labour must consist of more or less **unskilled labour**, and therefore that the mass of wages must be determined by the *value of simple labour capacity*, it remains possible for isolated individuals to make their way upwards into higher spheres of labour by particular energy, talent, etc, just as there remains the abstract possibility that this or that worker could himself become a capitalist and an **exploiter** of alien labour. The slave belongs to a particular **master**; it is true that the worker must sell himself to capital, but not to a particular capitalist, and thus he has a choice, within a particular sphere, as to who he sells himself to, and can change **masters**. All these differences in the relation make the activity of the free worker more intensive, more continuous, more agile, and more dexterous than that of the slave, quite apart from the fact that they fit the worker himself to undertake historical actions of an entirely different nature. The slave receives the means of subsistence necessary for his maintenance in a *natural form*, which is as fixed in kind as in extent—in *use values*. The free worker receives them in the form of *money*, of *exchange value*, of the abstract social form of wealth...*abstract wealth, exchange value*, and not a specific traditionally and locally limited use value, still remains for the worker the purpose and result of his labour. It is the worker himself who turns the money into whatever use values he wants, buys the commodities he wants with it, and as *an owner of money*, as a buyer of commodities, he stands in exactly the same relation to the sellers of commodities as any other buyer. The conditions of his existence—and also the limited extent of the value of the money he has acquired—naturally compel him to spend it on a rather restricted range of means of subsistence. Nevertheless, some degree of variation is possible here, such as eg newspapers, which form part of the necessary means of subsistence of the English urban worker.

He can save something, form a hoard. He can also waste his wages on spirits, etc. But in acting this way he acts as a free agent, he must pay his own way; he is himself responsible for the way in which **he spends his wages**. *He learns to master himself, in contrast to the slave*, who needs a master... Since the purpose of labour is for the wage labourer wages alone, money, a definite quantity of exchange value, in which any specific characteristics of use value have been extinguished, he is completely indifferent to the *content* of his labour, and therefore to the specific character of his activity... Hence in so far as the division of labour has not made his labour capacity entirely one-sided, the free worker is *in principle* receptive to, and ready for, any variation in his labour capacity and his working activity which promises better wages... In North America, where the development of wage labour has least of all been affected by reminiscences of the old guild system, etc, this *variability*, this complete indifference to the specific content of labour, this ability to transfer from one branch to another, is shown particularly strongly. Hence the contrast between this *variability* and the uniform, traditional character of *slave labour*, which does not vary according to the requirements of production, but rather the reverse, requiring that production should itself be adapted to the mode of labour introduced originally and handed down by tradition, is emphasised by all United States writers as the grand characteristic of the free wage labour of the North as against the slave labour of the South. (See *Cairnes*.)[31] The constant creation of new kinds of labour, this continuous variation—which results in a multiplicity of use values and therefore is also a real development of exchange value—this continuing division of labour in *the whole of the society*—first becomes possible with the capitalist mode of production. It begins with the free handicraft guild system, where it does not meet with a barrier in the ossification of each particular branch of the craft itself. (*CW*34: 436-438, largely recapitulating *CW*34: 100-102; *C*I: 1031-1034)

What Marx is describing here are the modes of economic action facilitated by wage labour that are necessary to support the transformation of concrete into abstract labour, and it is this transformation that '*abstract, value-producing* labour' presupposes. One might interpret him

---

31  Marx here refers to the celebrated critique of the American South by the Ricardian J E Cairnes, [1862] *The Slave Power, Its Character, Career, and Probable Designs* (Columbia SC, 2003). Two outstanding recent Marxist studies of American slavery partially overlap with and partially differ from Marx's analysis here: Charlie Post, *The American Road to Capitalism* (Leiden, 2011), chs 3 and 5, and Robin Blackburn, *The American Crucible: Slavery, Emancipation and Human Rights* (London, 2011).

as saying that the wage form provides the framework in which market dependence becomes effective. The test then of when labour is subsumed under capital is the extent to which the direct producer is subjected to economic compulsions to specialise in producing efficiently for the market and thereby intensively to develop the productive forces. Marx, for the reasons spelled out at length in this passage, believes that this will normally take the form of a capitalist employing wage workers who are themselves subject to a similar compulsion through the wage form itself.[32] Thus he considers the case of the Indian cotton producer a very limited form of subsumption under capital that is unlikely to lead to the productivity increases and technological transformations characteristic of the capital relation:

> The usurer functions as a capitalist in so far as the valorisation of his capital occurs *directly* through the appropriation of alien labour, but in a form which makes the actual producer into his debtor, instead of making him a seller of his labour to the capitalist. This form heightens the exploitation of the producer, drives it to its uttermost limits, without in any way, with the introduction of capitalist production—even if at first with the merely formal subsumption of labour under capital—introducing the resulting heightened productivity of labour and the transition to the specifically capitalist mode of production. It is rather a form which makes labour sterile, places it under the most unfavourable economic conditions, and combines together capitalist exploitation without a capitalist mode of production, and the mode of production of independent small-scale property in the instruments of labour without the advantages this mode of production offers for less developed conditions. Here in fact the means of production have ceased to belong to the producer, but they are *nominally* subsumed to him, and the mode of production remains in the same relations of small independent enterprise, only the relations are *in ruins*. (*CW* 34: 118-119)

John Weeks's discussion of simple commodity production cited in the previous chapter underlines the limitations of any form of market dependence where the means of production have not been transformed into commodities and appropriated by capital. Without this transformation, which greatly facilitates the mobility of capital and its ability to create or restructure branches of production, the real conditions of abstract social labour that Marx highlights in his discussion of wage

---

32  See Cohen, *Karl Marx's Theory of History*, ch VII, for an argument in many respects analogous to Marx's, though avoiding reliance on the labour theory of value.

labour cannot be sustained. There may well be cases of market dependence other than wage labour that have the economic content that Marx associates with this form: Brenner's discussion of the late mediaeval/early modern northern Netherlands offers one example, Charlie Post's studies of the role of Northern and Western small farmers in the development of capitalism in the United States another.[33] Being open to these cases seems particularly important given the transformations that agrarian economic relations have been undergoing in contemporary capitalism.[34] But this does not alter the fact that Marx believes the properties of labour that he associates with formal and still more with real subsumption, and which are required for the technological transformations wrought where capitalist production prevails, are only fully present when capital confronts wage labour.

Marcel van der Linden has recently offered an alternative approach to conceptualising labour in modernity:

> Every carrier of labour power whose labour power is sold (or hired out) to another person under economic (or non-economic) compulsion belongs to the class of subaltern workers, regardless of whether the carrier of labour power is him- or herself selling or hiring it out and regardless of whether the carrier him- or herself owns means of production.

As van der Linden points out, the resulting class of 'subaltern workers' is 'a variegated group, including chattel slaves, sharecroppers, small artisans and wage earners'. His main argument for this broader conception (echoing Hardt and Negri he calls it 'this "multitude"') is that the boundaries between these different categories of direct producer are blurred and therefore hard to draw.[35] This is of course true: indeed, it is quite hard to demarcate between things in the physical as well as the social world in general. We still construct concepts that cut up the world along what often seem to be unreasonably sharp lines. The reason why we do this is because it serves our purposes in different ways. What disappear in van der Linden's portmanteau concept of 'subaltern workers' are precisely the differences in economic form determinations on which Marx insists so strongly. Nor is this simply a matter of formalism for its own sake. Marx's approach allows us to isolate those cases where surplus labour is extracted from direct producers as a result of economic

---

33    For the latter case, see Post, *The American Road to Capitalism*.

34    See Henry Bernstein, 'Agriculture, Class, and Capitalism', *International Socialism*, 2.138 (2013).

35    Marcel van der Linden, *Workers of the World* (Leiden, 2008), pp33, 32; see generally ch 2.

compulsion rather than physical coercion. By doing so he connects the subsumption of labour under capital with the intensive development of the productive forces that he holds to be characteristic of the capitalist mode of production. All the other categories of labour listed by van der Linden and more besides may cluster around this central case (which Marx rightly or wrongly associates with the wage form), but those who disagree with him need to address the connection he posits. None of this means that Banaji and van der Linden are wrong to point to a broader spectrum of producers subordinated to capital than simply wage workers. Successful struggles against exploitation may often depend on mobilising broad layers of those subjects of capital, particularly in the Global South. But effective political strategy cannot lose sight of the differences in actors' position in production relations that may lead in particular situations to divergences in interest.[36]

## The pseudo-subjectivity of capital

One way of eliding the relationality of capital is to abstract labour from its relationship with capital, and thereby to transform capital into an external force. Another is to focus on capital itself, treating it as an autonomous subject.[37] Perhaps the leading commentator to express this view is Chris Arthur, for whom 'the key advance of value form theory is the insight that the value form develops to the point at which, with self-valorising value, it is constituted as a *self-relation*, and takes over the world of production and consumption given to it.' The accusation against contemporary value-form theorists of etherealism is presumably one that Arthur would embrace, since he conceives 'Value as Nothing', 'a sheer void, an immediacy unrelated to anything outside itself', a spectre that seeks to capture living labour and turn it to its own ends:

> Self-valorising value posits itself in comprehending within self-production, through negating *dialectically* (ie preserving the material side within it)

---

36  For a much earlier version of the argument made in this section, see Alex Callinicos, 'Wage Labour and State Capitalism', *International Socialism*, 2.12 (1981), http://www.marxists.org/history/etol/writers/callinicos/1981/xx/wagelab-statecap.html.

37  I must acknowledge here the influence on my understanding of the subjectivity of capital of Robert Jackson, who recently completed a PhD thesis under my supervision called 'The Problem of Subjectivity in Marxism' (King's College London, 2013). I also benefited from presenting a paper based on this section at the International Conference on Heritages of Karl Marx's *Capital* and Contemporary Thought, Centre for Contemporary Marxism Abroad, Fudan University, Shanghai (November 2013). I am grateful for the helpful comments of the participants.

the realm of the real labour of production. So far from labour embodying itself in commodities and thereby constituting them as values, the value form embodies itself in production, subordinates its purposes to value creation, and realises itself in the product, posited as nothing but its own othering, when it successfully gains control of the labour process.[38]

Riccardo Bellofiore, another exponent of the thesis articulated by Arthur that there is a homology between capital and Hegel's Absolute Idea, has pointed out that it was anticipated by Lucio Colletti:

> The commodity and, even more so of course, capital and the State, represent *processes of hypostatisation in reality*. Now, our thesis is that, given realities of this nature, it is impossible to understand them fully unless one grasps the structure of the processes of hypostatisation of Hegel's *Logic*. In other words, Marx's critique of Hegel's dialectic and his analysis of capital hold together. Failing to understand the former it is also impossible to understand the latter.[39]

There are, in fact, other antecedents. Thus Theodor Adorno, without subscribing to the idea of capital as subject, argues that Hegel's dialectic in some sense mirrors the reduction of the qualitative to units of abstract labour and the dominance of commodity fetishism under capitalism: 'Even in the theory of the conceptual mediation of all being, Hegel envisaged something decisive in real terms... The act of exchange implies the reduction of the products to be exchanged to their equivalents, to something abstract'.[40] Moishe Postone, a contemporary theorist working in the Frankfurt School tradition that Adorno helped to found, has in his impressive study of the *Grundrisse* and *Capital* criticised Georg Lukács for conceiving the proletariat as the identical subject-object of history in *History and Class Consciousness*. On the contrary:

> Marx...explicitly characterises capital as the self-moving substance which is Subject. In doing so, Marx suggests that a historical Subject in the Hegelian sense does indeed exist in capitalism, yet he does not identify it

---

38 Christopher J Arthur, *The New Dialectic and Marx's Capital* (Leiden, 2003), pp155, 162, 170. For a detailed critique see Alex Callinicos, 'Against the New Dialectic', *Historical Materialism*, 13:2 (2005).

39 Lucio Colletti, *Marxism and Hegel* (London, 1973), p281. See Riccardo Bellofiore, 'A Ghost Turning into a Vampire: The Concept of Capital and Living Labour', in Bellofiore and Roberto Fineschi, eds, *Rereading Marx: New Perspectives after the Critical Edition* (Basingstoke, 2009), p180.

40 Theodor W Adorno, 'Sociology and Empirical Research', in Adorno et al, *The Positivist Dispute in German Sociology* (London, 1976), p80.

with any social grouping, such as the proletariat, or with humanity. Rather, Marx analyses it in terms of the structure of social relations constituted by forms of objectifying practice and grasped by the category of capital (and, hence, value). His analysis suggests that the social relations that characterise capitalism are of a very peculiar sort—they possess the attributes that Hegel accorded to *Geist*. It is in this sense, then, that a historical Subject as conceived by Hegel exists in capitalism.[41]

So in what sense does Marx understand capital as subject? There is a cluster of remarks at the beginning of the *1861-63 Manuscript* in which capital is treated as a subject. Thus Marx comments on the formula for capital:

> Two points must be stressed here. Firstly, $M—C—M$ is *value-in-process*, exchange-value as a process that takes its course through various acts of exchange or stages of circulation, and at the same time dominates over them. *Secondly*: In this process value is not only preserved, it increases in magnitude, it is multiplied, increases itself, ie it creates in this movement a *surplus value*. It is thus not only self-preserving but self-*valorising value, value that posits value*. (CW30: 12)

Shortly afterwards Marx develops the idea of 'self-valorising value' into subjectivity: 'value as it presents itself here is value-in-process, the subject of a process' (*CW*30: 13). This linking of process and subjectivity is repeated, for example, here:

> Value as capital, self-valorising value, is *value raised to a second power*. Not only does it have an independent expression, as in money, but it compares itself with itself (or is compared by the capitalist), measures itself at one period (the magnitude of value in which it was preposited to the production process) against itself in another period, namely after its return from circulation—after the commodity has been sold and reconverted into money. Value therefore appears as the same subject in two different periods, and indeed this is its own movement, the movement that characterises capital. (*CW*30: 100)

But Marx also seems to suggest that the individual capitalist is a subject:

> It is the money owner...who makes his money, or the value he possesses in the form of money, pass through the process $M—C—M$. This

---

41  Moishe Postone, *Time, Labour, and Social Domination: A Reinterpretation of Marx's Critical Theory* (Cambridge, 1993), p75.

movement is the content of his activity, and he therefore appears only as the personification of capital defined in this way, as the *capitalist*. His person (or rather his pocket) is the starting point of *M*, and it is the point of return. He is the conscious vehicle of this process. Just as the result of the process is the preservation and increase of value, the self-valorisation of value, what forms the content of the movement appears to him as a conscious purpose. *To increase the amount of value he possesses* appears thus as his sole purpose. His purpose is the ever-growing appropriation of wealth in its general form, *exchange-value*, and only in so far as it appears as his sole driving motive is he a capitalist or a conscious subject of the movement $M-C-M$. (*CW*30: 19)

So capital has two subjects, the process of self-valorisation itself and the individual capitalist. This theme is reiterated in the following passage, which has some of the resonances involved in Arthur's assimilation of capital and the Idea:

> in the production process—in so far as this is a valorisation process and hence a process of the self-valorisation of the preposited value or money-value (ie objectified general social labour), past labour, preserves and increases itself, posits surplus-value, through exchange, through the relative appropriation of living labour, an exchange mediated by the purchase of labour capacity. It thus appears as value-in-process, and preserving and maintaining itself in the process. It thus appears as a self—the incarnation of this self is the *capitalist—the selfhood of value*. Labour (living) appears only as the means, the **agency** through which capital (value) reproduces and increases itself. (*CW*30: 95-96)

Marx's treatment of the capitalist here anticipates his famous declaration in the preface to the first edition of *Capital*, I: 'individuals are dealt with here only in so far as they are the personifications of economic categories, the bearers (*Träger*) of particular class relations and interests' (*C*I: 92). The following passage suggests that the status of individual subject is a dependent one, alienated from or subordinated to the objective conditions of production embodied by capital. Marx writes that the worker is

> free, that is, in so far as he, on the one hand, has at his disposal his own labour capacity as a commodity, and, on the other hand, has no other commodity at his disposal, is free, completely rid of, all the objective conditions for the realisation of his labour capacity; and therefore, as a mere subject, a mere personification of his own labour capacity, is a *worker* in

the same sense as the money owner is a *capitalist* as subject and repository of objectified labour, of value sticking fast to itself. (*CW*30: 37-38)

Marx's usage here touches on an ambiguity that is highlighted by Étienne Balibar, between the subject as it is conceived in Roman law and early modern political thought—a person subordinate to another's power, and the philosophical conception of the subject first explicitly formulated in the German idealist tradition but in some way emerging in the 17th century as (in Charles Taylor's words) 'self-defining', the source of epistemic and political authority.[42] Individual workers and capitalists are clearly subjects in the first sense, but what about capital? Marx returns in *Capital*, I, Chapter 4, 'The General Formula for Capital', to the idea of value as 'the subject of a process', or even 'the dominant subject [*übergreifendes Subjekt*] of this process', and declares in the passage stressed by Postone: 'But now, in the circulation M—C—M, value suddenly presents itself as a self-moving substance [*selbst bewegende Substanz*] which passes through a process of its own, and for which commodities and money are both mere forms' (*CI*: 255, 256). We saw in chapter 2 that the problematic of transforming substance into subject is central to Hegel's project. As Dieter Henrich puts it, for Hegel 'this *substance* is an ontological principle that only *underlies* this process... The *subject* for Hegel is, however, nothing but the active relationship to itself'.[43] According to Michael Inwood, for Hegel, 'a substance is in constant activity, generating and dissolving its accidents. Substance appears or "shines" in its accidents and they are its appearance.' Subject, in contrast differentiates itself and restores its unity, in the process developing 'consciousness and agency'.[44] Here we have a paradigmatic case of self-defining subjectivity.

But in *Capital*, I, Marx seems a bit careless of the distinction between substance and subject so important to Hegel, referring to capital or value

42  Étienne Balibar, 'Citizen Subject', in Peter Connor Eduardo and Jean-Luc Nancy, eds, *Who Comes After the Subject?* (New York, 1991); Charles Taylor, *Hegel* (Cambridge, 1977), p6. As Balibar emphasises, initial discussion of the subject in the 2nd sense, above all in Descartes but also in Locke and Hume (as we see below), focuses on an exploration of the concept of substance. See Taylor's detailed genealogy of modern conceptions of subjectivity: *Sources of the Self: The Making of the Modern Identity* (Cambridge, 1989).

43  Dieter Henrich, *Between Kant and Hegel: Lectures on German Idealism* (ed David S Pacini; Cambridge MA, 2003), p290.

44  Michael Inwood, *A Hegel Dictionary* (Oxford, 1992), pp286, 282. Thus the development of substance into reciprocity of action concludes the Doctrine of Essence in the *Science of Logic*, giving way to 'the *self-identical negativity*', 'the *concept*, the realm of *subjectivity* or of *freedom*', *GL*: 505, 506. I am grateful to Enrique Dussel and Emmanuel Renault for drawing my attention to this step in Hegel's argument.

as both. In the French edition he slightly plays down the theme of capital as subject. Thus in the first of the three passages just quoted from *Capital*, I, '*Subjekt eines Prozeßes*' becomes '*une substance automatique*', and in the second '*übergreifendes Subjekt*' disappears in this sentence: 'As value become capital undergoes continual changes in appearance and size, it needs above all its own form in which its identity with itself is affirmed'.[45] It may be helpful to recall some of the classical philosophical discussions of substance. One—a major preoccupation of the British empiricists—concerns the problem of how a substance maintains its identity through the various changes it undergoes. Locke struggles with whether personal identity, which he equates (though not without hesitation) with continuity of consciousness, is dependent on the persistence of a single substance, whether material or spiritual.[46] Hume by contrast deconstructs the very idea of substance, affirming that the self is 'nothing but a bundle or collection of different perceptions, which succeed each other with an inconceivable rapidity, are in a perpetual flux and movement'.[47] Another is provided by Spinoza's analysis of the single substance identical with God and Nature, which he claims is *causa sui*, self-caused: 'By substance I mean that which is in itself and is conceived through itself; that is, that the conception of which is does not require the conception of another thing from which it has to be formed'.[48]

We can see these different meanings of substance in Marx's references to value-in-process. As we have seen, capital is 'self-valorising value' that undergoes a process in which it maintains its identity through the metamorphoses it undergoes from money to commodities and then back to (more) money. It is in *Capital*, II, that Marx examines these metamorphoses in most detail, in his presentation of the three circuits of money, commercial, and productive capital that are integrated as the movement of industrial capital. And it is in this context that we find the following very interesting passage:

> Capital, as self-valorising value, does not just comprise class relations, a definite social character that depends on the existence of labour as wage labour. It is a movement, a circulatory process through different stages [*eine Bewegung, ein Kreislaufsprozess durch verschiedene Stadien*], which

45  Karl Marx, *Le Capital, Livre I* (2 vols, Paris, 1985), I, pp178, 179.

46  John Locke, *An Essay concerning Human Understanding* (Roger Woolhouse, ed; London, 2004), II.xxvii.

47  David Hume, *A Treatise of Human Nature* (Harmondsworth, 1969), I.vi; p300.

48  Baruch Spinoza, *Ethics*, Part 1: Definitions, in *Ethics, Treatise on the Emendation of the Intellect, and Selected Letters* (Seymour Feldman, ed; Indianapolis, 1982), p31.

itself in turn includes three different forms of the circulatory process. Hence it can only be grasped as a movement, and as a static thing. Those who consider the autonomisation [*Verselbständigung*] of value as a mere abstraction forget that the movement of industrial capital is this abstraction in action [*diese Abstraktion in actu*]. Here value passes through different forms, different movements in which it is both preserved and increases, is valorised. (*CII*: 185)[49]

This passage dates from 1877, thereby demonstrating once again that Marx doesn't retreat into a dumbed down version of his value theory in his later years. Here capital is 'abstraction in action', an autonomous movement that is indeed 'in a perpetual flux and movement' but preserves its identity throughout. Given that capital is substance/subject in so far as it maintains itself through these different stages, in what sense can we speak of 'the autonomisation of value'? Marx shortly after this passage makes a crack about Bailey for 'opposing the autonomisation of value which characterises the capitalist mode of production'. In reducing value to contemporaneous exchange value, 'he does not in the least suspect, therefore, that value functions as capital value or capital only in so far as it remains identical with itself and is compared with itself in the different phases of its circuit, which are in no way "contemporary", but rather occur in succession' (*CII*: 186). So here autonomisation is equated with identity-preservation (see *CII*: 233 for a very similar formulation). My guess is that at least two other meanings may be detected here. The first is the idea that we discussed in chapter 3 of capital positing its own presuppositions: capital as *causa sui* functions as a self-reproducing process, the outcome of each cycle of which is the maintenance of the capital/wage labour relationship. The second is the way in which the imperative logic of the process—above all, through the mechanism of the law of value—imposes itself on individual and collective actors.

What is missing here is agency, the idea—central to the German idealist tradition—of the subject as an initiator of action. Marx is not, for example, inviting us to conceive capital-as-subject as itself some kind of collective actor. The strongest proponent of the alternative view is probably Stavros Tombazos, who insists that, for Marx, 'capital is a living

---

49 Harvey glosses this passage thus: 'Contradictions in the overall process of circulation play out autonomously, and by this Marx means in ways that are autonomous from the capital-labour contradiction,' *A Companion to Marx's Capital, Volume 2* (London, 2013), p70. But it comes from *Capital*, II, Chapter 4, 'The Three Figures of the Circuit', which deals with the unity of the three circuits of money, commodity, and productive capital, so 'the capital-labour contradiction' is comprised within this process rather than being separate from it.

social relation endowed with its own will that organises human life according to its own immanent criteria'; it is 'a living organism endowed with a body (use value) and a soul (value), its own will and logic (profit, expanded reproduction, and so on)'. Tombazos is most persuasive when he writes: 'Capitalist reality is a living thing because—among other reasons—it is capable of reacting and defending itself and because it is capable of self-development, whatever the social price might be. It is a human reality that escapes human control; it dominates society, subjecting man to its own purpose, and for these reasons it is a living thing'.[50] What Tombazos is appealing to here is the theme of capital as *causa sui*, positing its presuppositions. Now there is certainly an analogy to life here: chaos and complexity theory emerged precisely to study the way in which systems develop spontaneously in nature with the ability to maintain and sometimes to reproduce themselves. This research has also revealed the sensitivity of such systems to small changes in their initial conditions that can suddenly flip the system from one state to another.[51] Capital as conceptualised by Marx is undoubtedly a complex system in this sense. But the development of self-organised systems in nature is precisely *spontaneous*: no one planned them, and the systems exhibit no 'will' or 'soul'. They are not subjects, and neither is capital.[52]

Another proponent of capital-as-subject, Postone, undermines his own case by effectively denying to capital the properties of consciousness and agency:

Marx's mature critique, therefore, no longer entails a 'materialist', anthropological inversion of Hegel's idealistic dialectic but, in a sense, is its materialist 'justification'. Marx implicitly attempts to show that the

---

50  Stavros Tombazos, [1994] *Time in Marx: The Categories of Time in Marx's Capital* (Leiden, 2014), pp308, 80, 87.

51  For two popular expositions with very different politics, see Ilya Prigogine and Isabelle Stenghers, *Order out of Chaos: Man's New Dialogue with Nature* (London, 1984), and Stuart Kauffman, *At Home in the Universe: The Search for Laws of Self-Organisation and Complexity* (London, 1995).

52  Daniel Bensaïd argues that 'Marx's dynamic economy already presents itself as an unstable system sensitive to initial conditions,' but goes too far in arguing that this implies 'a teleological viewpoint': *Marx for Our Times: Adventures and Misadventures of a Critique* (London, 2002), p305; see generally ch 10. A teleological explanation accounts for phenomena by specifying a goal or goals that they serve, but what chaos and complexity theory do is to provide causal explanations of apparently goal-directed patterns. Capital is not for Marx a subject in the sense in which the term is understood in German idealism, but it is clearly, from the passages cited above, a process, as Emmanuel Renault has stressed in discussion of an earlier version of this paper. I think the way I would put it is that understanding capital as a relation is a prerequisite of conceptualising it as a process. The idea of capital as a complex system is one way of thinking of it as simultaneously relation and process.

'rational core' of Hegel's dialectic is precisely its idealist character: it is an expression of a mode of social domination constituted by structures of social relations which, because they are alienated, acquire a quasi-independent existence vis-à-vis individuals, and which, because of their peculiar dualistic nature, are dialectical in character. The historical Subject, according to Marx, is the alienated structure of social mediation that constitutes the capitalist formation.[53]

So here 'Subject' is reinterpreted as structure. Indeed, the most powerful theme of Postone's interpretation of Marx is that 'capitalism is a system of abstract, impersonal domination.' As he elaborates:

> The system constituted by abstract labour embodies a new form of social domination. It exerts a form of social compulsion whose impersonal, abstract, and objective character is historically new. The initial determination of such abstract social compulsion is that individuals are compelled to produce and exchange commodities in order to survive. This compulsion exerted is not a function of direct social domination, as is the case, for example, with slave or serf labour; it is, rather, a function of 'abstract' and 'objective' social structures and represents a form of *abstract, impersonal domination*.[54]

The account that Postone gives of this form of domination, though couched in more traditional Marxist theoretical terminology, differs little from Brenner's conception of market dependence—the situation that economic actors find themselves in under capitalism where, to reproduce themselves, they must produce for the market and, to maintain their competitiveness, produce as efficiently as possible. The image Postone presents of capitalism is quite close to Althusser's conception of a decentred totality and of history as a process without a subject in which individuals function in the way Marx portrays the capitalists, as 'supports' of the relations of production. Postone complains that 'Althusser transhistorically hypostatised as History, in an objectivistic way, that which Marx analysed in *Capital* as a historically specific, constituted structure of social relations', but Althusser may still capture an important aspect of how Marx understood capital.[55]

Where does all this leave Arthur's and Colletti's theme of capital as '*hypostatisation in reality*'? Perhaps the most useful way to pursue this is

---

53  Postone, *Time, Labour, and Social Domination*, p81.
54  Postone, *Time, Labour, and Social Domination*, pp125, 158-159.
55  Postone, *Time, Labour, and Social Domination*, p77, n 95.

through the theme of inversion. Colletti writes: 'For Marx, capitalism is contradictory not because it is a reality and all realities are contradictory, but because it is an upside-down, inverted reality (alienation, fetishism)'.[56] The theme of the topsy-turvy or inverted world (*auf den Kopf gestellte Welt, verkehrte Welt*) runs through Marx's writing from his letters from the *Deutsch-Französische Jahrbücher* of March 1843 onwards (*CW*3: 139).[57] In the *Economic and Philosophical Manuscripts* of 1844 the inversion now takes a specific historical form—that between labour and capital:

> The more objects the worker produces the fewer he can possess and the more he falls under the domination of his product, of capital... It is the same in religion. The more man puts into God, the less he retains within himself. The worker places his life in the object; but now it no longer belongs to him, but to the object. The greater his activity, therefore, the fewer objects the worker possesses. What the product of his labour is, he is not. Therefore, the greater this product, the less is he himself. The externalisation (*Entäusserung*) of the worker in his product means that not only does his labour become an object, but that it exists *outside him*, independently of him and alien to him, and begins to confront him as an autonomous power; that the life which he has bestowed on the object confronts him as hostile and alien. (*EW*: 324)

The reference to religion highlights a key source of the theme of inversion: Feuerbach's critique of the transposition of subject and predicate involved in Christianity, where all the properties characteristic of human beings and thus constituting their species being are projected onto a deity that is the product of their own imagination. As Colletti and his teacher Galvano Della Volpe stressed, Marx took over this problematic of inversion and applied it to the state and civil society in his *Critique of Hegel's Doctrine of the State*.[58] In doing so he made inversion a tool in what became, starting with the Paris *Manuscripts*, his critique of political economy. Compare the 1844 passage cited above with the following from the *1861-63 Manuscript*:

---

56 Lucio Colletti, 'Marxism and the Dialectic', *New Left Review*, I/93 (1975), p29.
57 There may be an echo in Marx's use of this metaphor of Hegel's discussion of the inverted world of the understanding: see *Phenomenology of Spirit* (Oxford, 1977), §§157-160; pp96-99.
58 Della Volpe's major work is *Logic as Positive Science* (London, 1980). On Feuerbach, see Marx Wartofsky, *Feuerbach* (Cambridge, 1977), and Louis Althusser, 'Sur Feuerbach', in *Écrits philosophiques et politiques* (François Matheron, ed; 2 vols, Paris, 1994, 1995), II.

For labour to be wage labour, for the worker to work as a non-proprietor, for him to sell not commodities but disposition over his own labour capacity—to sell his labour capacity itself in the sole manner in which it can be sold—the conditions for the realisation of his labour must confront him as *alienated conditions*, as *alien powers*, conditions under the sway of an alien will, as alien property. *Objectified labour*, value as such, confronts him as an *entity in its own right*, as *capital*, the vehicle of which is the capitalist—hence it also confronts him as the *capitalist*... Objectified, past labour thereby becomes the sovereign of living, present labour. The relation of subject and object is inverted. If already in the presupposition the objective conditions for the realisation of the worker's labour capacity and therefore for actual labour appear to the worker as alien, independent powers, which relate to living labour rather as the conditions of their own preservation and increase—the tool, the material [of labour] and the means of subsistence only giving themselves up to labour in order to absorb more of it—this inversion is still more pronounced in the result. The objective conditions of labour are themselves the products of labour and to the extent that they are viewed from the angle of exchange value they are nothing but labour time in objective form.

In both directions, therefore, the objective conditions of labour are the result of labour itself, they are *its own objectification*, and it is its own objectification, labour itself as its result, that confronts labour as an *alien power*, as an *independent power*; while labour confronts the latter again and again in the same objectlessness, as mere labour capacity. (*CW*30: 112, 113)

But is the continuity complete? Bidet argues not, distinguishing two forms of inversion in *Capital*, III:

The 'inversion', or something deserving that name, appears only when the categories that characterise this level are applied in an 'essential' sense, ie concerning the production of surplus value. What is then called an 'inversion' is the fact that the non-worker appears as a worker, capital as a thing, etc.

In short, the relation characterises the relationship between the representations inherent to the level of reality of Volume Three and the level of reality of Volume One. It is thus an ideological phenomenon, an inversion in the representation, a discrepancy between this and the reality (of Volume One), but which is supported in the reality (of Volume Three) to which it is in a sense adequate. This use of the theme of inversion is completely coherent with the theory of ideology that Marx offers in Volume Three.[59]

The second form of inversion is that where, as in the passage just cited from the *1861-63 Manuscript*, worker and capital, subject and object are inverted: 'Here the ideological inversion is only the reflection of the inversion in the structure itself,' producing 'the unsustainable paradox that ideology is a true figure of the world as it is'. Bidet argues that 'Marx progressively detaches himself from this [second schema of inversion] as he discovers the necessity for a "fragmented" theory of the ideological corresponding to that of the exposition's process without a subject: this would consist in determining, at each moment of the exposition, the representations that it implies in the agent whose function and practice it defines'.[60] Bidet is right that, as he explains very well, the account of ideology that Marx offers in *Capital* is one that attaches ideological representations to the perspective of agents occupying specific positions in the capitalist production relations (see chapter 3 above). But he is less sure footed than usual in suggesting that Marx distances himself from the theme of real inversion in his later economic manuscripts. Take, for example, this passage from *Capital*, I, which was, of course, written after the *1863-5 Manuscript* from which Engels edited *Capital*, III:

> the worker constantly produces objective wealth, in the form of capital, an alien power that dominates and exploits him; and the capitalist just as constantly produces labour power, in the form of a subjective form of wealth which is abstract, exists merely in the physical body of the worker, and is separated from its own means of objectification and realisation; in short, the capitalist produces the worker as a wage labourer. (CI: 716)

There seems little difference between what Marx says here and the content of the earlier passages cited from the Paris *Manuscripts* and the *1861-63 Manuscript*. Let's consider more fully Marx's great denunciation of the trinity formula towards the end of *Capital*, III, which we touched on in chapter 3:

> Capital-profit (or better still capital-interest), land-ground rent, labour-wages, this economic trinity as the connection between the components of value and wealth in general and its sources, completes the mystification of the capitalist mode of production, the reification [*Verdinglichung*] of social relations, and the immediate coalescence of the material relations of

---

59  Bidet, *Exploring Marx's Capital*, p212.
60  Bidet, *Exploring Marx's Capital*, pp214, 230.

production with their historical and social determination [*geschichtlich-sozialen Bestimmtheit*]: the bewitched, inverted, and topsy-turvy world haunted by Monsieur le Capital and Madame la Terre, who are at the same time social characters and mere things [*die verzauberte, verkehrte und auf den Kopf gestellte Welt, wo Monsieur le Capital und Madame la Terre als soziale Charaktere und zugleich unmittelbar als Bloße Dinge ihren Spuk treiben*]. It is the great merit of classic economics to have dissolved this false appearance and deception, this autonomisation and ossification of the different social elements of wealth vis-à-vis one another, this personification of things and reification [*Versachlichung*] of the relations of production, this religion of everyday life [*diese Religion des Alltagslebens*], by reducing interest to a part of profit and rent to the surplus above the average profit, so that they both coincide in surplus value; by presenting the circulation process as simply a metamorphosis of forms; and simply in the immediate process of production reducing the value and surplus value of commodities to labour. Yet even its best representatives remained more or less trapped in the world of illusion their criticism had dissolved, and nothing else is possible from the bourgeois standpoint; they all fell therefore more or less into inconsistencies, half-truths, and unresolved contradictions [*Widersprüche*]. It is also quite natural, on the other hand, that the actual agents of production themselves feel completely at home in these estranged and irrational [*entfremdeten und irrationellen*] forms of capital-interest, land-rent, labour-wages, for these are precisely the configurations of appearance [*die Gestaltungen des Scheins*] in which they move, and with which they are daily involved. It is equally natural, therefore, that the vulgar economics, which is nothing more than a didactic, and more or less natural translation of the everyday notions [*Alltagsvortstellungen*] of the actual agents of production, giving them a certain comprehensible arrangement, finds the natural basis of its fatuous self-importance established precisely in this trinity, in which the entire inner connection is obliterated. This formula also corresponds to the self-interest of the dominant classes, since it preaches the natural necessity and perpetual justification of their sources of income and erects this into a dogma. (*C*III: 968-969; *M*III: 830; translation modified)

So the assignment of fragments of surplus value to the factors of production is at once 'false appearance and deception', belonging to 'the world of illusion', and 'the religion of everyday life', 'the configurations of appearance' in which 'the actual agents of production' move. Bidet interprets this duality of illusion and actuality thus:

there is a moment indicated here at which appearance (*Erscheinung*) becomes illusion (*Schein*). The categories of competition constitute *Erscheinung*, in the sense that an essential structure is effectively realised in a more concrete structure: the law of value is expressed in exchange at prices of production. This involves a *Schein*, in the sense that this order of expression is mistaken for the inner structure and thus gives a fallacious representation of it. This is why Marx speaks frequently in terms of error, confusion, etc. The illusion is analogous to Kant's transcendental illusion: an illegitimate use of categories that have their proper pertinence elsewhere.[61]

Bidet's argument here is intended to contain Marx's critique of the trinity formula within his first sense of inversion, as an ideological representation. The thought is something like this: economic actors' place in production relations leads them to commit a category mistake, applying concepts that have their validity in a limited domain (roughly speaking that defined by the processes through which different fractions of the capitalist class obtain different portions of surplus value) to the entirety of the capitalist mode of production. But what is the 'illusion' here? It seems best captured by G A Cohen's account of 'capital fetishism': 'First, productivity is separated from its basis in material production, and is attributed to exchange value itself, to capital. Then productivity is referred back to labour power and means of production as physical embodiments of capital, whereas in fact capital is productive in virtue of its embodiment in them'.[62] A looser way of putting this would be to say that capital fetishism involves the transposition of subject and predicate involved in Marx's real inversion. After all, the 'illusion' here is that the value-creating power of living labour is being ascribed to physical objects. But, as Bidet himself acknowledges, the illusion arises from categories that have 'a proper pertinence' in capitalist economic realities. Tombazos makes the point very forcefully:

> ideology and false consciousness are not notions that are subsequently added to the 'reality' of social relations. They form part of these relations, in the same way as surplus value. It is a feature of the nature of surplus value to hide itself in the commodity, to disguise itself in profit, to be confounded with interest, to flirt with the time of circulation; in short, to conceal its origins.[63]

61  Bidet, *Exploring Marx's Capital*, p212.
62  Cohen, *Karl Marx's Theory of History*, pp117-118; see generally ch V.
63  Tombazos, *Time in Marx*, p221.

So it is much harder to separate the two senses of inversion than Bidet suggests. In this respect Colletti, like many other commentators, is right to say that the problematic of alienation informs the whole of Marx's critique of political economy, from the 'Notes on Mill' to *Capital*, I. This continuity, and Marx's associated reliance in *Capital* on the philosophical anthropology developed in the Paris *Manuscripts* indicate the respects in which Althusser's thesis of an 'epistemological break' between the Young and Old Marx is mistaken. But what does change is the status of the problematic of alienation. In the 1844 *Manuscripts* the main explanatory burden is taken by the theory of human nature, which informs a Hegelian dialectic of differentiation (alienated labour under capitalism) and restored unity (communism). This kind of historical dialectic doesn't completely disappear in *Capital*. Towards the end of *Capital*, I, Chapter 32, 'The Historical Tendency of Capital Accumulation', just after Marx predicts that 'the expropriators are expropriated,' he offers this Hegelian triad:

> The capitalist mode of appropriation, which springs from the capitalist mode of production, produces capitalist private property. This is the first negation of individual private property, as founded on the labour of the proprietor. But capitalist production begets, with the inexorability of a natural process [*mit der Notwendigkeit eines Naturprozesses*], its own negation. This is the negation of the negation. It does not re-establish private property, but it does indeed establish individual property on the basis of the achievements of the capitalist era: namely cooperation and the possession in common of the land and the means of production produced by labour itself. (*C*I: 929)

The subject of this process, however, is no longer the human essence, but forms of property, with the transition from initial unity to first negation taking the form of primitive accumulation: 'Private property, which is personally earned, ie which is based, as it were, on the fusing together of the isolated, independent working individual with the conditions of labour, is supplanted by capitalist private property, which rests on the exploitation of alien, but formally free labour' (*C*I: 928). This is a much more narrowly focused dialectic than the one that unfolds in the 1844 *Manuscripts*, and it is undercut by the way in which Marx follows this chapter, which reads like a grand finale, with the bathos of Chapter 33, 'The Modern Theory of Colonisation'. Here Marx focuses on Edward Gibbon Wakefield's *England and America* (1833), a work that fascinated him and to which he returns again and again in his economic manuscripts:

He discovered that capital is not a thing, but a social relation between persons which is mediated through things. A Mr Peel, he complains, took with him from England to the Swan River district of Western Australia means of subsistence and of production to the amount of £50,000. This Mr Peel even had the foresight to bring besides, 3,000 persons of the working class, men, women and children. Once he arrived at his destination, 'Mr Peel was left without a servant to make his bed or fetch him water from the river.' Unhappy Mr Peel, who provided for everything except the export of English relations of production to Swan River! (*C*I: 932-933)[64]

This splendid conclusion underlines Marx's continuing preoccupation with the colonies as exemplifying the general features of capitalist production relations. (He writes elsewhere: '*Ricardo* and other English writers...saw in these colonies, only in more obvious form, *without the fight against traditional relations*, and therefore *untarnished*, the same domination of capitalist production in agriculture as hits the eye everywhere in their own country': *CW*31: 460). But it also relativises the grand Hegelian drama of the preceding chapter. Fredric Jameson has written of 'the two great foreshortened climaxes...: a heroic and a comic one, each in its own way foretelling the end of the system and of the law of value, and the opening on that unforeseeable future which Marx elsewhere calls "the end of pre-history".[65] This double ending of *Capital*, I, underlines how complex Marx's discourse has become—not simply in the different figures he uses and references he makes, but also in the sense of the modes of explanation employed in order to articulate capitalism as a totality (think, for example, of the explanatory importance that, as we saw in chapter 3 above, he gives to competition and to the interests and intentions of individual capitalists when discussing relative surplus value and the tendency of the rate of profit to fall).[66] It has burst the confines of the relatively simple anthropological dialectic that informs the 1844 *Manuscripts*. So the problematic of alienation remains in *Capital*, but no longer does it play the central explanatory role. Of course, labour itself is

---

64  Greg Grandin's wonderful study of Henry Ford's efforts to develop a rubber industry in the Brazilian jungle between the wars shows the same logic at work, since the freely available resources of the jungle gave workers little incentive to stick with Ford: *Fordlandia: The Rise and Fall of Henry Ford's Forgotten Jungle City* (London, 2010), pp150ff.

65  Fredric Jameson, *Representing **Capital**: A Reading of Volume One* (London, 2011), p88. Maximilien Rubel suggests that Marx transposed the order of chapters 32 and 33 to get *Capital*, I, past the Prussian censor: Joseph O'Malley and Keith Algozin, eds, *Rubel on Karl Marx* (Cambridge, 1981), pp222-223 n 57.

66  On Marx's writing, see S S Prawer's superb study, *Karl Marx and World Literature* (Oxford, 1976).

central, but it has itself been differentiated into a set of oppositions—abstract social labour/concrete useful labour, living/dead labour, constant/variable capital, relative/absolute surplus value—that bear the main explanatory burden.

Allen Wood puts it very well:

> Marx's mature theory, then, does not assign to alienation the basic explanatory role projected for it in the early fragment. Yet Marx does not simply abandon the concept of alienation in his mature writings. On the contrary, we find it still used in many places in the *Grundrisse*, *Capital*, and elsewhere. Marx's use of it in these writings, I suggest, is no longer explanatory; rather, it is descriptive or diagnostic. Marx uses the notion of alienation to identify or characterise a certain sort of human ill or dysfunction which is especially prevalent in modern society. The ill is one to which all the varying phenomena exemplifying the images or metaphors of 'unnatural separation' or 'domination by one's own creations' contribute in one way or another.[67]

It seems to me that we need to treat the transposition of subject and object that Marx portrays the capital relation involving as one of these metaphors. Metaphors are false sentences that nevertheless allow us to see the world in a different way.[68] As a result of selling her labour power to capital, the worker loses control of her creative powers (including the power to create value). But what she loses control to is not capital in the sense of an agent, whether we consider this agency spectral or that of some more mundane form of collective actor. The use of the worker's labour power is controlled usually by some kind of managerial hierarchy. But the agents occupying this hierarchy—including the CEO and her minions at the top—do not form an autonomous collective agent. They are themselves subject to the imperative of competitive accumulation. We discussed in chapter 3 some of the problems involved in how Marx conceptualises competition in the *Grundrisse*. This should not allow us to lose sight of the essential truth expressed in formulations such as the following: 'Capital exists and can only exist as many capitals, and its self-determination therefore appears as their reciprocal interaction with one another' (*G*: 414).[69] There is no singular Capital that imposes itself

---

67  Allen W Wood, *Karl Marx* (2nd edn; New York, 2004), p7.

68  Donald Davidson, 'What Metaphors Mean', in *Inquiries into Truth and Interpretation* (Oxford, 1984).

69  Arthur dismisses the significance of such passages: 'for Marx accumulation is not explained primarily by the pressure of competition; this merely ensures that capitalists are forced to conform to the concept of capital.' But his own explanation—'a particular

imperiously on the world. The very alienation that workers and capitalists alike experience consists crucially in their subordination to the competitive logic of an inherently decentred set of economic relationships. Like Walker (Lee Marvin) in *Point Blank*, what we discover as we go deeper into the labyrinths of corporate power is no secret centre from which all power radiates but an impersonal structure staffed by functionaries.

As Tony Smith implies in this excellent dismissal of the subjectivity of capital, politics is at stake here:

> It is not wrong to speak of living labour as capital's 'other', standing 'outside' capital, or to stress how from capital's standpoint living labour is 'nothing'... But it is very misleading to stop here. Living labour is 'inside' capital *all the way down*. There are *no* powers of capital that are not ultimately the collective social powers of labour (or the powers of nature, machinery and science mobilised by collective social labour). On the deepest level of Marx's social ontology it is *capital* that is nothing, a mere 'pseudo-subject'. Capital may be the ruling principle of the social order, subjecting human agents to a discipline that both unleashes and distorts their creative powers, inside the workplace and outside it. But capital has no powers in itself whatsoever, any more than any other fetish object. To think otherwise is fall prey to the very mystification that Marx's concept of capital is meant to dispel.[70]

## The subjectivity of labour

The other side of the pseudo-subjectivity of capital is the potential subjectivity of living labour. If labour ceases to allow capital to use its powers then the limits to capital truly appear. We shall return to this, the core of the politics of *Capital*, in chapter 7. But it is worth stressing here that treating capital as a subject may lead to a devaluation of labour. This is particularly true of the most rigorous attempt to portray capital as a subject, by Postone. He contrasts:

> two fundamentally different modes of critical analysis: a critique of capitalism, *from the standpoint of* labour, on the one hand, and a critique *of*

---

capital never measures up to its concept and is compelled to throw itself into ever more twists of the spiral of accumulation'—both fails to address the indispensable role of competition in Marx's accounts of differential profits and the tendency of the rate of profit to fall (see chapter 3 above) and seems to rely on a mystified essentialism: Arthur, *The New Dialectic and Marx's Capital*, pp152 n 51, 149.

70  Tony Smith, 'The Chapters on Machinery in the 1861-63 Manuscripts', in Bellofiore and Fineschi, eds, *Rereading Marx*, p124.

labour in capitalism, on the other. The first, which is based upon a trans-historical understanding of labour, presupposes that a structural tension exists between the aspects of social life that characterise capitalism (for example, the market and private property) and the social sphere constituted by labour. Labour, therefore, forms the basis of the critique of capitalism, the *standpoint* from which that critique is undertaken. According to the second mode of analysis, labour in capitalism is historically specific and constitutes the essential structures of society. Thus labour is the *object* of the critique of capitalist society.[71]

The latter form of critique is that of Marx in the *Grundrisse* and *Capital*, the former that of what Postone calls 'traditional Marxism', which offers 'not a *critique of political economy* but a *critical political economy*, that is, a critique of the mode of distribution. It is a critique which, in terms of its treatment of labour, merits the name "Ricardian Marxism".' This is a residual category in which Postone dumps virtually every variant Marxism, including (as we have seen) that of Lukács in *History and Class Consciousness*. So 'the idea [central to this text] that the proletariat embodies a possible postcapitalist form of social life only makes sense, however, if capitalism is defined essentially in terms of private ownership of the means of production, and if "labour" is considered to be the standpoint of the critique'. By contrast:

> according to Marx's analysis, the proletariat is an essential element of value-determined relations of production and, as such, is also rendered anachronistic as capitalism develops. Overcoming capitalism, then, must also be understood in terms of the abolition of proletarian labour and, hence, the proletariat. This, however, renders very problematic the question of the relation of working-class social and political actions to the possible abolition of capitalism; it implies that such actions, and what is usually referred to as working-class consciousness, remain within the bounds of the capitalist social formation—and not necessarily because workers have been materially and politically corrupted, but because proletarian labour does not fundamentally contradict capital.[72]

The idea that his critique of political economy committed Marx to denying that the working class is the agent of anti-capitalist

---

71 Postone, *Time, Labour, and Social Domination*, pp5-6.
72 Postone, *Time, Labour, and Social Domination*, pp69, 73, 370-371. In asserting that Marx claims that capitalist development makes the proletariat 'anachronistic' Postone relies on the so-called 'Fragment on Machines' in the *Grundrisse*, discussed in chapter 7.

transformation would have come as a surprise to him. Near the end of his life he wrote with Engels in their famous circular letter to leaders of the German Social Democratic Party (16-18 September 1879):

> For almost 40 years we have emphasised that the class struggle is the immediate motive force of history and, in particular, that the class struggle between bourgeoisie and proletariat is the great lever of modern social revolution... At the founding of the International we expressly formulated the battle cry: The emancipation of the working class must be achieved by the working class itself. (*CW*45: 408)

Nor is it plausible to suggest that Postone (who rather evasively declares that 'I shall not examine the possibility of divergent or contradictory tendencies in Marx's mature works') has, in presenting the two critiques, exposed a discrepancy internal to Marx's theoretical discourse.[73] The confusion is in Postone's own interpretation. One major source lies in his claim that

> Marx now [ie in the *Grundrisse* and *Capital*] implicitly rejects the idea of an immanent logic of human history and any form of transhistorical dialectic, whether inclusive of nature or restricted to history. In Marx's mature works, historical dialectic does not result from the interplay of subject, labour, and nature, from the reflexive workings of the material objectifications of the Subject's 'labour' upon itself; rather, it is rooted in the contradictory character of capital social forms.[74]

This so manifestly contradicts Marx's conceptualisation of the labour process as 'the universal condition for the metabolic interaction (*Stoffwechsel*) between man and nature, the everlasting nature-imposed condition of human existence' (*CI*: 290), that Postone is forced to acknowledge the existence of

> two very different sorts of necessity associated with social labour. Labour in some form is a necessary precondition—a transhistorical or '*natural*' *social necessity*—of human social existence as such. This necessity can veil the specificity of commodity-producing labour—that, although one does not consume what one produces, one's labour is nevertheless the necessary social means of obtaining products to consume. The latter is a *historically determinate social necessity*.[75]

73  Postone, *Time, Labour, and Social Domination*, p19.
74  Postone, *Time, Labour, and Social Domination*, pp139-140.
75  Postone, *Time, Labour, and Social Domination*, p161.

This requires some account of the relationship between transhistorical and historically determinate categories in Marx's critique, but Postone offers none. The distinction in any case undermines the supposedly iconoclastic force of his claim that Marx offers 'a critique *of* labour in capitalism'. Of course, Marx offers a critique of labour *in capitalism*: this is evident from the great chapters 14 and 15 of *Capital* on respectively manufacture and modern industry, and their precursors in the *1861-63 Manuscript* (discussed further in chapter 7). But it doesn't follow that Marx implicates labour as such in this critique, or that he dismisses the bearers of the degraded forms of work under capitalism as incapable of constituting themselves as an emancipatory force. Postone develops his argument for this last claim thus:

> despite the widespread assumption that workers' collective action and bourgeois social forms are opposed, commodity ownership can only be fully realised for the workers in collective form; workers, then, can only be 'bourgeois subjects' *collectively*. In other words, the nature of labour power as a commodity is such that collective action does *not* stand opposed to commodity ownership, but is necessary to its realisation. The historical process of labour power's realisation as a commodity paradoxically entails the development of collective forms within the framework of capitalism that do *not* point beyond that society—rather, they constitute an important moment in the transition from liberal to post-liberal capitalism.[76]

There is a kernel of truth in this argument. Chapter 10 of *Capital*, I, 'The Working Day', portrays collective working class action forcing political reforms that impose on capital the limits to the working day that it is in its interests as a class to introduce to ensure the stable reproduction of labour power but impossible to achieve without state intervention (since otherwise free riders could undercut those individual capitals voluntarily imposing limits). Moreover, the improvements in living standards secured by workers through collective action both give their consumption an enhanced role in the reproduction of capitalism (a theme strongly stressed by Harvey) and facilitate their transformation into the desiring subjects of the society of the spectacle.[77] But improvements in workers' condition—whether through strike action or as a result of political reforms introduced in part as a result of pressure by the workers' movement—have contradictory effects. Thus it is widely acknowledged that the development of the

---

76  Postone, *Time, Labour, and Social Domination*, p275.
77  See, for example, David Harvey, *A Companion to Marx's **Capital**, Volume 2* (London, 2013), chs 8 and 10.

welfare state involves a process of 'decommodification'—in other words, a significant proportion of working class consumption is that of services provided on the basis of entitlement and financed by taxation rather than being purchased by monetary payment derived from wage income or produced by domestic labour within the household. Welfare provision can thus undermine the dominance of capital over labour by making workers less dependent on the labour market; the aim of making the poor accept low-paid employment is therefore one of the most visible aims of neoliberal attempts to restructure the welfare state.[78]

In a striking passage in the *1861-63 Manuscript* Marx argues that the mystified representations of the total process go with the flow of the capitalist's existence, while the workers' conditions of life incite them to reject them and to resist:

> In the capital relation—to the extent that it is still considered independently of its circulation process—what is essentially characteristic is the mystification, the upside-down world, the inversion of the subjective and the objective, as it already appears in money. Corresponding to the inverted relation, there necessarily arises, already in the actual production process itself, an inverted conception, a transposed consciousness, which is completed by the transformations and modifications of the actual process of circulation. However, the capitalist as capitalist is nothing but this movement of capital itself. What he is in reality, he is also in consciousness. Since the positive, dominant side of the relation is expressed in him, he only feels at home precisely in these contradictions; they do not disturb him, whereas the wage labourer, who is trapped in the same inverted notion, only from the other extreme, is driven in practice, as the oppressed side, to resistance against the whole relation, hence also against the notions, concepts and modes of thinking corresponding to it. (*CW*33: 73-74)

Postone ignores what is fundamental to class struggle for Marx, however narrowly distributive its aims, namely how it helps transform the

---

78  This is a huge subject. An authoritative discussion of decommodification is Gøsta Esping-Andersen, *The Three Worlds of Welfare Capitalism* (Cambridge, 1989), ch 2. But the concept precedes this work: see, for example, the subtle Marxist analysis of the interplay of decommodification and 'administrative recommodification' in the modern capitalist state in Claus Offe and Volker Ronge, 'Theses on Theory of the State', in Anthony Giddens and David Held, eds, *Classes, Power, and Conflict: Classical and Contemporary Debates* (Berkeley, 1982). Two pioneering Marxist studies of the welfare state are Ian Gough, *The Political Economy of the Welfare State* (London, 1979), and Norman Ginsburg, *Capital, Class and Social Policy* (London, 1979). For the welfare state under neoliberalism see Ann Rogers, 'Back to the Workhouse', *International Socialism*, 2.59 (1993), and Iain Ferguson, 'Can the Tories Abolish the Welfare State?', *International Socialism*, 2.141 (2014).

working class into a political subject whose collective action tendentially subverts bourgeois ideology. This comes out very strongly in an article in the *New York Tribune* of July 1853, where Marx discusses the mass strikes by textile workers centred on Preston:

> I am…convinced that the alternative rise and fall of wages, and the continual conflicts between masters and men resulting therefrom, are, in the present organisation of industry, the indispensable means of holding up the spirit of the labouring classes, of combining them into one great association against the encroachments of the ruling class, and of preventing them from becoming apathetic, thoughtless, more or less well-fed instruments of production. In a state of society founded upon the antagonism of classes, if we want to prevent slavery in fact as well as in name, we must accept war. In order to rightly appreciate the value of strikes and combinations, we must not allow ourselves to be blinded by the apparent insignificance of their economical results, but hold, above all things, in view their moral and political consequences. Without the great alternative phases of dullness, prosperity, over-excitement, crisis and distress, which modern industry traverses in periodically recurring cycles, with the up and down of wages resulting from them, as with the constant warfare between masters and men closely corresponding with those variations in wages and profits, the working-classes of Great Britain, and of all Europe, would be a heart-broken, a weak-minded, a worn-out, unresisting mass, whose self-emancipation would prove as impossible as that of the slaves of Ancient Greece and Rome. (*CW*12: 169)

Marx's celebration nearly 20 years later of the Paris Commune of 1871—whose aims and leadership he strongly criticised—underlines the extent to which he values working class struggles for 'their moral and political consequences' in transforming those involved into a collective agent of their 'self-emancipation'. He may of course have been wrong about this (a subject I touch on in chapter 7), along with the other 'traditional Marxists' whom Postone consigns to the dustbin of history—not just Lukács, but, for example, such otherwise diverse figures as Rosa Luxemburg, Leon Trotsky and Walter Benjamin. But there seems no doubt about what Marx actually thought.[79]

---

79  For much more on this, see Draper, *Karl Marx's Theory of Revolution*, II, Part I, and Alex Callinicos, *Making History: Agency, Structure and Change in Social Theory* (rev edn; Leiden, 2004), ch 5.

# 6

# Crises

## Crisis and revolution

The question of economic crisis represents a particular point of difficulty for students of *Capital* and its drafts.[1] It was, after all, the outbreak of the crisis of 1857-8—described by Michael Krätke as 'the first world economic crisis, affecting all regions of the world that were in one way or another already integrated in or at least connected to the world market'—that prompted Marx to start on the *Grundrisse*.[2] Moreover, as we saw in chapter 1, the six-book plan that he developed in the course of these studies culminated in a book on the world market and crises. This reflected a conception of crisis as the summation of all the contradictions of the capitalist mode of production. As Marx puts it in the *Economic Manuscript of 1861-63*, 'In world market crises, all the contradictions of bourgeois production erupt collectively' (*CW*32: 163). But, of course, Book 6 was never written, and Part 3 of *Capital*, III, where Marx discusses crises in the context of the tendency of the rate of profit to fall, is clearly a work in progress rather than the presentation of a finished theory. Simon Clarke goes further, arguing that 'Marx's writings on crisis are indeed fragmentary and confused. In isolation from his work as a whole they are not of any great interest, and they certainly do not provide a consistent and rigorous theory of crisis'.[3]

---

1    This chapter developed from a presentation made at the XVII Encontro Nacional de Economia Política, Rio de Janeiro, June 2012. I am grateful to my hosts and to all those who participated in the discussion. In working on this subject, I have also benefitted from supervising Lorenzo Fusaro's PhD Thesis, 'Hegemony and Crisis: On the Relation between World Market Crises and Hegemonic Transitions' (King's College London, 2013), and from his comments on this chapter in draft.

2    Michael R Krätke, 'Marx's "Books of Crisis" of 1857-8', in Marcello Musto, ed, *Karl Marx's Grundrisse* (London, 2008), p174.

3    Simon Clarke, *Marx's Theory of Crisis* (London, 1994), p10. Puzzlingly, despite this pronouncement, Clarke persistently refers to 'Marx's theory of crisis' in his detailed discussions of specific texts.

Clarke has written a valuable and scholarly study of Marx's writing on crisis, but it has a polemical purpose, namely to demolish what Clarke claims is the obsession of 'orthodox Marxism' with 'general crises' and to demonstrate that 'the focus of Marx's work is not the crisis as catastrophic event, but the inherent tendency to crisis that underlies the permanent instability of social existence under capitalism. From this perspective, Marx is the first and most radical theorist of the "postmodern condition".'[4] This unfortunate concession to passing intellectual fashion aside, Clarke's iconoclasm fails both properly to situate economic crises in Marx's thought and to grasp the logic of his analysis in *Capital*. As Daniel Bensaïd puts it in one of the best discussions of Marx on crises, 'Marx produces their determinations at the different logical moments of the process of production, of circulation, and of the reproduction of capital. He doesn't state a positive, coherent and complete theory, but a negative theory, through successive approaches'.[5] Another way of putting it would be to say that we can find in *Capital* not an articulated and finished theory of crisis, but a multidimensional *conception* of economic crises and their place in the capitalist mode of production. In this chapter I identify six determinations of crisis in Marx's economic writings. Two—the formal possibilities of crisis inherent in commodity exchange and the modern capitalist credit system, and the conditions of exchange between the two main departments of production required for the reproduction of the system—are enabling conditions. A second pair—the interaction between fluctuations in wage rates and in the size of the industrial reserve army and the turnover of fixed capital—are conditioning factors. Finally, the interplay between the tendency of the rate of profit to fall and the cycle of bubble and panic on the financial markets constitute the decisive causal mechanisms at work in economic crises.

But what about the place of crises in Marx's thought as a whole? In a recent study of the development of his thinking on the falling rate of profit, Geert Reuten and Peter Thomas argue that in the *Grundrisse*, where Marx first addresses this topic, we find 'a "rhetoric of crisis"' that harks back to the preoccupation with political crisis (specifically of the old regime in Prussia) that he shared with his fellow young Hegelians in the 1840s. Marx in the 1843-44 Introduction to *A Contribution to the Critique of Hegel's Philosophy of Right* discovers in the proletariat the

---

4    Clarke, *Marx's Theory of Crisis*, pp285, 280. For reasons for not considering Marx a postmodern theorist see Alex Callinicos, *Against Postmodernism* (Cambridge, 1989).

5    Daniel Bensaïd, *La Discordance des temps: Essais sur les crises, les classes, l'histoire* (Paris, 1995), p41.

universal class that can carry out a revolution whose aim is not merely political emancipation but 'the *total redemption of humanity*' (*EW*, 256). Reuten and Thomas argue:

> With the failure of the revolutions that coincided with the publication of the *Communist Manifesto*, the defeated '48ers' tried to keep their hopes alive for a revival of this 'world-historical' subject. Fidelity to (the memory of) the theme of crisis, in the midst of widespread abandonment of revolutionary politics by their contemporaries, constituted one of their most potent psychological supports.[6]

So crisis here functions primarily as a political, even psychological concept, and the proletariat as a philosophical category. This interpretation ignores Marx's development from 1844 onwards of a different, more precisely socio-economic conception of the proletariat as part of the formulation of his broader theory of history and revolution.[7] More to the point, Reuten and Thomas fail to appreciate the specific, though still political role that *economic* crises play in Marx's and Engels's thinking after 1848. In September 1850 they broke with the Communist League on the basis of a disagreement starkly stated by Marx:

> The materialist standpoint of the *Manifesto* has given way to idealism, the revolution is seen not as the product of realities of the situation but as a result of an effort of *will*. Whereas we say to the workers: You have 15, 20, 50 years of civil war to go through to alter the situation and to train yourselves for the exercise of power, it is said: We must take power *at once*, or else we must take to our beds. (*CW*10: 626)

A few months later Marx and Engels sought to copper-bottom their political stance by situating the defeat of the revolution in the movements of the economic cycle. Just as the spread of the crisis that broke out in Britain in 1847 to the Continent had helped to spark off the wave of risings in 1848, so the subsequent recovery—made possible by global imperial expansion thanks to the discoveries of gold in Australia and California and Western penetration of China but once again moving across the Channel via Britain—set the seal on their defeat. Rather than put their faith in assertions of revolutionary will or vague democratic

---

6    Geert Reuten and Peter Thomas, 'From the "Fall of the Rate of Profit" in the *Grundrisse* to the Cyclical Development of the Profit Rate in *Capital*', *Science & Society*, 75:1 (2011), p78. This interpretation of Marx's development relies heavily on Stathis Kouvelakis, *Philosophy and Revolution: From Kant to Marx* (London, 2003). For a brief critique, see Alex Callinicos, *The Resources of Critique* (Cambridge, 2006), pp117-119.

7    See especially Michael Löwy, *The Theory of Revolution in the Young Marx* (Leiden, 2002).

phraseology, Marx and Engels argue, real communists must acknowledge their dependence on the movements of the mode of production:

> While, therefore, the crises first produce revolutions on the Continent, the foundation of these is, nevertheless, always laid in England. Violent outbreaks must naturally occur rather in the extremities of the bourgeois body than in its heart, since the possibility of adjustment is greater here [ie London] than there. On the other hand, the degree to which Continental revolutions react on England is at the same time the barometer which indicates how far these revolutions really call in question the bourgeois conditions of life, or how far they only hit their political formations.
>
> With this general prosperity, in which the productive forces of bourgeois society develop as luxuriantly as is at all possible within bourgeois relationships, there can be no talk of a real revolution. Such a revolution is only possible in the periods when *both these factors*, the *modern* productive *forces* and the *bourgeois forms of production*, come *in collision* with each other... *A new revolution is possible only in consequence of a new crisis. It is, however, just as certain as this crisis.* (*CW*, 10: 509-510)[8]

Crises are thus interpreted as both the expression in bourgeois society of the contradiction between the forces and relations of production that Marx in his writings of the mid-1840s identifies as the motor of historical change and the precipitator of 'real revolutions' that 'call in question the bourgeois conditions of life'. A preoccupation with this interplay between economic crises and socio-political revolution is evident in Marx's writings of the 1850s. For example, speculating in the *New York Tribune* in May-June 1853 about the destabilising impact of the Taiping rebellion in China on the world economy, he reaffirms the connection he and Engels had posited in 1850:

> Since the commencement of the eighteenth century there has been no serious revolution in Europe which had not been preceded by a commercial and financial crisis. This applies no less to the revolution of 1789 than to that of 1848. It is true, not only that we every day behold more threatening a conflict between the ruling powers and their subjects, between the State and society, between the various classes; but also the conflict of the existing powers among each other reaching that height where the

---

8 This passage comes from the 'Review May to October' that Marx and Engels drafted for the third issue of the *Neue Reinische Zeitung. Politisch-öknomische Revue*, which never appeared. For background, see Alex Callinicos, *The Revolutionary Ideas of Karl Marx* (4th edn, London, 2010), ch 1, and Jonathan Sperber, *Karl Marx: A Nineteenth Century Life* (New York, 2013), ch 7.

sword must be drawn, and the *ultima ratio* of princes be recurred to...
We may be sure, nevertheless, that to whatever height the conflict
between the European powers may rise, however threatening the aspect
of the diplomatic horizon may appear, whatever movements may be
attempted by some enthusiastic fraction in this or that country, the rage
of princes and the fury of the people are alike enervated by the breath of
prosperity. Neither wars nor revolutions are likely to put Europe by the
ears, unless in consequence of a general commercial and industrial crisis,
the signal of which has, as usual, to be given by England, the representative of European industry in the market of the world. (*CW*12: 99)

Marx's journalism in these years constantly monitors the movements
of the economic cycle to anticipate the onset of the next crisis, which he
had initially predicted for 1852. If Joseph Schumpeter is right in saying
that Britain was in recession by mid-1854, Marx wasn't too far out, but it
took the 1857 financial panic to make the crisis a global one.[9] As we saw
in chapter 2, Marx's economic studies in the early 1850s focus in particular on theories of money and banking, but this preoccupation has a
political dimension as well. Thus in his journalism he pays particular
attention to the pioneering French investment bank the Crédit Mobilier
(*CW*15: 8-24, 130-135). This allows him to develop a critique of the 'system
of fictitious credit' that points towards the much more elaborated analysis of financial markets in *Capital*, III, Part 5 (*CW*16: 33-34). But Marx's
interest in the Crédit Mobilier is inseparable from his and Engels's critique of the regime of Napoleon III, gravedigger of the 1848 Revolution
(most famously developed in *The Eighteenth Brumaire of Louis
Bonaparte*), and their appreciation of the strategic political significance
of France: economic crises may start in Britain (though in 1857 the panic
began in the United States), but they spark revolutions in France. The
Crédit Mobilier, whose Saint-Simonian bosses the brothers Pereire were
closely linked to the regime, in channelling savings to industrial firms
(especially railway companies) practised what David Harvey calls in his
outstanding study of Paris under the Second Empire 'a planned evolution of what we now know as "state monopoly capitalism".'[10] So the end

9   Joseph A Schumpeter, *Business Cycles: A Theoretical, Historical, and Statistical Analysis of
    the Capitalistic Process* (2 vols; New York, 1939), I, p377; see more generally on 1857-8, I,
    pp331-333, and Charles W Calomiris and Larry Schweikart, 'The Panic of 1857: Origins,
    Transmission, and Containment', *Journal of Economic History*, 51:4 (1991).
10  David Harvey, *Paris, Capital of Modernity* (New York, 2003), p119; see generally ch 5, and,
    for an account of the conflicts between the Rothschilds and the Crédit Mobilier (which
    the Rothschilds eventually won), Niall Ferguson, *The House of Rothschild: The World's
    Banker 1848-1998* (London, 2000), Part I.

of 1857 finds Marx invoking the interpenetration of the state and private capital as he gnaws away in both an article for the *New York Tribune* and a letter to Engels written on Christmas Day in order to explain the relatively limited impact of the crisis on France—an empirical variation with political implications (compare *CW*14: 413-418 and 40: 228-232).[11]

Solving this particular puzzle was part of a much larger effort to monitor the course of the crisis. He wrote to Engels a little earlier (18 December 1857):

> I am working enormously, as a rule until 4 o'clock in the morning. I am engaged on a twofold task: 1. Elaborating the outlines of political economy. (For the benefit of the public it is absolutely essential to go into the matter *au fond*, as it is for my own, **individually, to get rid of this nightmare.**)
>
> 2. The *present crisis*. Apart from the articles for the *Tribune*, all I do is keep records of it, which, however, takes up a considerable amount of time. I think that, somewhere **about** the spring, we ought to do a pamphlet *together* about the affair as a reminder to the German public that we are still there as always, and **always the same.** I have started 3 large record books—**England, Germany, France.** All the material on the American affair is available in the *Tribune*, and can be collated subsequently. (*CW*40: 224-225)

So Marx was working on a twin track—writing the *Grundrisse* and assembling the material for an empirical study of the crisis. As Michael Krätke puts it:

> In early October, when he had started writing his first 'Chapter on Money', he began his parallel work on the books of crisis. That was actually another project—the study of the course of the world economic crisis in all details. His work as an empirical researcher, collecting and arranging material on the crisis events in different parts of the world, drawing up statistical tables from various sources, looking for more evidence, kept him busy until the end of January, probably early February 1858—while he was writing the 'Chapter on Capital'. Hence the conventional imagination of Marx, studying first and foremost Hegel's *Science of Logic* while writing the *Grundrisse* manuscript is misguided. At the same time, he was experimenting with the dialectical forms of presentation of the

---

11  See Sergio Bologna's detailed discussion: (1973) 'Money and Crisis: Marx as Correspondent of the *New York Daily Tribune*, 1856-7', http://www.wildcat-www.de/en/material/cs13bolo.htm

basics of political economy and pursuing a full-scale empirical research on the ongoing economic crisis. The books of crisis were not only meant as aid for his work as journalist. They were also important for the theory, the rational explanation of the phenomenon of modern cyclical crises, which Marx regarded as an indispensable part of his systematic critique of political economy'.[12]

Of course, the pamphlet, like so much else Marx planned, never appeared. But the 'Books of the Crisis', when published in *MEGA²*, will amount to 500 pages, bearing witness to Marx's interest in investigating empirically the course of this global economic crisis. The fact that it did not cause the political shock waves implied by Marx's and Engels's post-1848 analysis dampened the hopes expressed by Engels in a letter of 14 November 1857 ('In 1848 we were saying: Now our time is coming, and **so in a certain sense** it was, but this time it is coming properly; now it's a case of do or die' [*CW*40: 203]). But in the very letter (8 October 1858) where Marx acknowledged to Engels 'the optimistic turn taken by world trade **at this moment**', he engaged in a fascinating world-historical speculation:

> There is no denying that bourgeois society has for the second time experienced its 16th century, a 16th century which, I hope, will sound its death knell just as the first ushered it into the world. The proper task of bourgeois society is the creation of the world market, at least in outline, and of the production based on that market. Since the world is round, the colonisation of California and Australia and the opening up of China and Japan would seem to have completed this process. For us, the difficult **question** is this: on the Continent revolution is imminent and will, moreover, instantly assume a socialist character. Will it not necessarily be **crushed** in this little corner of the earth, since the **movement** of bourgeois society is still, in the **ascendant** over a far greater area? (*CW*40: 346, 346-347)

This passage is one of Marx's strongest affirmations of the global character of capitalism as a system whose future lies far from the shores of Europe. His expectations of revolution are at once optimistic—the 'imminent' Continental revolution will 'instantly assume a socialist character' (a prediction for which he would claim the Paris Commune of 1871 as confirmation)—and pessimistic, insofar as such a revolution might be, from a global point of view, a sideshow. But the experience of 1857-8 underlined for Marx the importance of what he called in the 1859

---

12  Krätke, 'Marx's "Books of Crisis" of 1857-8', p169.

*Contribution* 'big storms on the world market, in which the antagonism of all elements in the bourgeois process of production explodes' (*Con*: 182). Hence his decision to conclude the critique of political economy with the world market and crises. He never wrote Book 6, but there are important discussions of economic crises in the *Grundrisse*, the *1861-63 Manuscript* and *Capital* itself. These allow us to identify a more or less coherent multi-dimensional conception of crises and their function within the capitalist system.

### Dimensions of crisis

The multiple dimensions of crisis that Marx discusses reflect, as Bensaïd suggests, their place in the ordering of determinations in *Capital*. In the *1861-63 Manuscript* Marx makes it clear that the analysis of these distinct dimensions must follow his method of rising from the abstract to the concrete:

> The world trade crises must be regarded as the real concentration and forcible adjustment of all the contradictions of bourgeois economy. The individual factors, which are condensed in these crises, must therefore emerge and must be described in each sphere of the bourgeois economy and the further we advance in our examination of the latter, the more aspects of this conflict must be traced on the one hand, and on the other hand it must be shown that its more abstract forms are recurring and are contained in the more concrete forms. (*CW*32: 140)

But Marx's treatment of the different determinations of crises also bears the imprint of the pre-existing understanding of capitalism that he brought to the resumption of his economic studies in the summer of 1857.

### i. *Marx's first theory of crisis: competitive accumulation drives production beyond the limits of the market*

Marx first begins systematically to reflect on the causes of crises in the late 1840s in texts such as the *Communist Manifesto* and *Wage Labour and Capital*. Already here he discovers in bourgeois society a systemic tendency towards overaccumulation and overproduction. Clarke gives an excellent summary of this theory:

> Marx has established that there is a tendency inherent in the capitalist mode of production to develop the forces of production, under the pressure of competition, without regard to the limits of the market, as every

capitalist seeks to increase his profits by introducing new methods of production on an increasing scale. The momentum of the development of production in any branch is determined not by the demand for the product, but by the opportunities for acquiring a surplus profit by advancing the productive forces. The result is that, although the growth of capitalist production at the same time develops the world market, the forces of production develop unevenly and without reference to the requirements of proportionality, so that competition imposes a constant tendency to the disproportional development of the various branches of production.[13]

A version of this explanation of crises had already been developed by Engels before and independently of Marx in *The Condition of the Working Class in England* (1845). Here Engels outlines the nature of a five-to-six year business cycle reflecting

> the nature of industrial competition and the commercial crises which arise from it. In the present unregulated production and distribution of the means of subsistence, which is carried on not directly for the sake of supplying needs, but for profit, in the system under which every one works for himself to enrich himself, disturbances inevitably arise at every moment.[14]

Clarke emphasises the differences between Marx's and Engels's versions of this theory. Engels stresses the uncertainty the manufacturing capitalist struggles with when trying to guess the market for his products, which inevitably leads to gluts and crises:

> Engels's focus on supply and demand implies a focus on the commercial crisis as the decisive moment of the crisis, and also implies that the displacement of competition by planning can eliminate the crisis tendencies of capitalism, and these are preoccupations that recur throughout Engels's work. Marx, on the other hand, was interested not so much in the relation between supply and demand as in the relation between the expenditure of productive labour as the basis of value and the realisation of that value in the form of money. This is reflected in Marx's detailed interest in banking and in financial crises, which was not shared by Engels. Moreover, the implications of Marx's analysis are also much

---

13 Clarke, *Marx's Theory of Crisis*, p143. Clarke here summarises the theory of crisis Marx relies on in the Grundrisse, but he offers a good account of its development in Engels's and Marx's earlier writings: see Clarke, chs 2-4.

14 Friedrich Engels, *The Condition of the Working Class in England: From Personal Observations and Authentic Sources* (Moscow, 1973), p121.

more radical, the elimination of crises requiring the abolition not merely of competition, but of the social form of capitalist production.[15]

However this may be, a broad conception of crisis as a result of the process of competitive accumulation driving production beyond the limits of the market informs Marx's later writings. We find it in his journalism of the 1850s—for example, in the article 'Revolution in China and Europe' that we have already encountered, he writes:

> Amid the most surprising prosperity, it has not been difficult to point out the clear symptoms of an approaching industrial crisis [in Britain]. Notwithstanding California and Australia, notwithstanding the immense and unprecedented emigration, there must ever, without any particular accident, in due time arrive a moment when the extension of the markets is unable to keep pace with the extension of British manufactures, and this disproportion must bring about a new crisis with the same certainty as it has done in the past. (*CW*12: 95-6)

Marx never abandons this conception of capitalism's inherent tendency to overaccumulation and overproduction. Thus it is present in *Capital*, I, in the crucial Chapter 15, 'Machinery and Modern Industry', where he argues that the transformation of the production process required by the hunt for relative surplus value underlies the business cycle:

> The factory system's tremendous capacity for expanding with sudden immense leaps, and its dependence on the world market necessarily gives rise to the following cycle: feverish production, a consequent glut on the market, then a contraction of the market which causes production to be crippled. The life of industry becomes a series of periods of moderate activity, prosperity, overproduction, crisis and stagnation. The uncertainty and instability to which machinery subjects the employment, and consequently the living conditions, of the workers becomes a normal state of affairs, owing to these periodic turns of the industrial cycle. (*CI*: 580-2)

But Marx's fullest exploration of this explanation of crises is during his discussion of Ricardo's theory of accumulation in the *1861-63 Manuscript* (*CW*32: 123-64). In his debates with Malthus, Ricardo endorsed Say's Law, according to which general overproduction (as opposed to the oversupply of some particular product) is impossible since the aggregate production of goods and services generates the income required to purchase them:

---

15   Clarke, *Marx's Theory of Crisis*, p84.

M Say has...most satisfactorily shewn, that there is no amount of capital which may not be employed in a country, because demand is limited only by production. No man produces, but with a view to consume or sell, and he never sells but with an intention to purchase some other commodity, which may be immediately useful to him, or which may contribute to future production. By producing, then, he necessarily becomes either the consumer of his own goods, or the purchaser and consumer of the goods of some other person. (*R*, I: 290)

Ricardo thus assumes that 'productions are only bought by productions, or by services; money is only the medium by which the exchange is effected.' (*R*, I: 291-292) For Marx this argument is a concrete illustration of the damaging effects of Ricardo's failure to grasp the form of value that we discussed in chapter 4:

> If Ricardo thinks that the *commodity* form makes no difference to the product, and furthermore, that *commodity circulation* differs only formally from barter, that in this context the exchange value is only a fleeting form of the exchange of things, and that money is therefore merely a formal means of circulation—then this in fact is in line with his presupposition that the bourgeois mode of production is the absolute mode of production, hence it is a mode of production without any definite specific determination [*Bestimmung*], its determinate traits are merely formal. He cannot therefore admit that the bourgeois mode of production contains within itself a barrier to the free development of the productive forces, a barrier which comes to the surface in crises and, in particular, in *overproduction*—the basic phenomenon in crises. (*CW*32: 156-157; translation modified)[16]

In fact, Marx argues, the possibility of crises is inherent in the basic metamorphosis of the commodity in the simple form of its circulation, C—M—C. Money is more than the means of circulation, and therefore its hoarding or the interruption of the flow of payments through the banking system can disrupt the process of circulation:

> If, for example, purchase and sale—or the metamorphosis of commodities—represent the unity of two processes, or rather the movement of one process through two opposite phases, and thus essentially the unity of the two phases, the movement is essentially just as much the separation of

---

16  Say's Law continues to hold sway in the neoliberal era, as Wolfgang Munchau recently complained: 'The Real French Scandal is Stagnant Economic Thinking', *Financial Times*, 19 February 2014.

these two phases and their becoming independent of each other. Since, however, they belong together, the independence of the two correlated aspects can only show itself forcibly, as a destructive process. It is just the crisis in which they assert their unity, the unity of the different aspects. The independence which these two linked and complementary phases assume in relation to each other is forcibly destroyed. Thus the crisis manifests the unity of the two phases that have become independent of each other. There would be no crisis without this inner unity of factors that are apparently indifferent to each other. But no, says the apologetic economist. Because there is this unity, there can be no crises. Which in turn means nothing but that the unity of contradictory factors excludes contradiction. (*CW*32: 131)[17]

On the basis of this argument, Marx identifies two formal possibilities of crisis: first, that consequent on the separation of sale and purchase inherent in the circulation of commodities, and, secondly, that caused by the disruption of money's function as means of payment within the credit system. He had already analysed the latter possibility in the 1859 *Contribution*, drawing on ideas developed by Sir James Steuart. The function of money as means of payment arises when the transfer of commodity to seller to buyer is separated from the transfer of money—through, for example the issue of a bill of exchange guaranteeing payment at some later date that itself acts as a negotiable instrument that can be presented to bankers for cash at a discount on the price of the commodity representing the interest charged by the accepting house. This form of money develops through horizontal transactions between private actors: 'Just as formerly the value-token as a universal symbol entailed a state guarantee and a legal rate, so now the buyer as a personal symbol gives rise to private, legally enforceable, contracts among commodity-owners' (*Con*: 140). Although money as means of payment is thus a spontaneous effect of commodity transactions, 'the evolution of the credit system, and therefore of the bourgeois mode of production in general, causes money to function increasingly as a means of payment' (*Con*: 143). This generates a new possibility of crisis:

---

17  See also *CI*: 208. Marx's critique of Ricardo is the occasion for a series of interesting remarks on the nature of contradiction, also found in a slightly later discussion of James Mill: *CW*32: 274-98. In a discussion of some of these passages I mistakenly confused Mill with his son John: *The Resources of Critique* (Cambridge, 2006), pp204-205. See also Enrique Dussel, *Towards an Unknown Marx: A Commentary on the **Manuscripts of 1861-63*** (London, 2001), pp114ff, and John Rees, *The Algebra of Revolution* (London, 1998), pp105-107.

When payments cancel one another as positive and negative quantities, no money need actually appear on the scene. Here money functions merely as measure of value with respect to both the price of the commodity and the size of mutual obligations. Apart from its nominal existence, exchange-value does not therefore acquire an independent existence in this case, even in the shape of a token of value, in other words money becomes purely nominal money of account. Money functioning as means of payment thus contains a contradiction: on the one hand, when payments balance, it acts merely as a nominal measure; on the other hand, when actual payments have to be made, money enters circulation not as a transient means of circulation, but as the static aspect of the universal equivalent, as the absolute commodity, in short, as money. Where chains of payments and an artificial system for adjusting them have been developed, any upheaval that forcibly interrupts the flow of payments and upsets the mechanism for balancing them against one another suddenly turns money from the nebulous chimerical form it assumed as measure of value into hard cash or means of payment. Under conditions of advanced bourgeois production, when the commodity-owner has long since become a capitalist, knows his Adam Smith and smiles superciliously at the superstition that only gold and silver constitute money or that money is after all the absolute commodity as distinct from other commodities—money then suddenly appears not as the medium of circulation but once more as the only adequate form of exchange-value, as a unique form of wealth just as it is regarded by the hoarder... This particular phase of world market crises is known as monetary crisis. The *summum bonum* [supreme good], the sole form of wealth for which people clamour at such times, is money, hard cash, and compared with it all other commodities—just because they are use-values—appear to be useless, mere baubles and toys, or as our Doctor Martin Luther says, mere ornament and gluttony. This sudden transformation of the credit system into a monetary system adds theoretical dismay to the actually existing panic, and the agents of the circulation process are overawed by the impenetrable mystery surrounding their own relations. (*Con*: 145-146)

Marx's discussion of money as means of payment and its role in the development of the credit system and of crises underlines the additional intellectual resources he had gained thanks to his critique of the quantity theory (see chapters 2 and 4 above). Nevertheless, in the *1861-63 Manuscript*, he emphasises that both this source of crises and that arising from the separation of sale and purchase 'are merely *forms*, general possibilities of crisis, and hence also forms, abstract forms, of actual crisis' (*CW*32: 142). Marx's subsequent discussion reveals some uncertainty. Thus he writes: 'But now the further development of the potential crisis has to be traced—the real [*reale*] crisis can only be educed from the real [*realen*] movement of capitalist production, competition and credit—in so far as crisis arises out of the form determinations [*Formbestimmungen*] of capital that are peculiar to it as capital, and not merely comprised in its existence as commodity and money' (*CW*32: 143; translation modified). So the explanation of crises depends on the development of the analysis of competition and credit that at this stage Marx had excluded from his theorisation of capital in general (see chapters 1 and 3 above). A couple of paragraphs later, after saying that crises need to be understood at the level, not of production, but of circulation and reproduction, Marx adds: 'the actual [*wirkliche*] movement starts from the existing capital—ie, the actual movement denotes developed capitalist production, which starts from and presupposes its own basis. The process of reproduction and the predisposition to crisis which is further developed in it are therefore only partially described under this heading and require further elaboration in the chapter on "Capital and Profit"' (*CW*32: 143). This chapter is what would eventually become *Capital*, III. The fairly fragmentary draft in the *1861-63 Manuscript* includes a discussion of the tendency of the rate of profit to fall (see below).

In a sense these reflections support Marx's decision to put crises in the final volume of the six-book plan, since they underline the multiplicity of determinations involved. But in the *1861-63 Manuscript* Marx focuses in the rest of his discussion of crises on the problem of overproduction. He is reluctant to characterise it as a consequence of disproportionalities between different branches of production:

> we are not speaking of crisis here in so far as it arises from **disproportionate** production, that is to say, the disproportion in the distribution of social labour between the individual spheres of production. This can only be dealt with in connection with the competition of capitals. In that context it has already been stated that the rise or fall of market-value which is caused by this **disproportion**, results in the **transfer or withdrawal of capital from one trade** to another, the **migration of capital from one trade** to another. This equalisation itself however already implies as a precondition the opposite of equalisation and may therefore comprise *crisis*; the crisis itself may be a form of equalisation. Ricardo etc admit this form of crisis. (*CW*32: 151)

Here disproportionality arises from a lack of correspondence between the amount of social labour allocated to producing a specific commodity and the social need (backed by effective demand) for that commodity. Supporters of Say's Law need not deny the possibility of crises as market prices adjust to changed market values (see chapter 4). But they do deny the possibility of general crises of overproduction, even though for Marx the occurrence of such crises is undeniable. So why do they happen? Marx's response shows him, as so often in his manuscripts, thinking with his pen:

> If one were to answer the question by pointing out that the constantly expanding production...requires a constantly expanding market and that production expands more rapidly than the market, then one would merely have used different terms to express the phenomenon which has to be explained—concrete terms instead of abstract terms. The market expands more slowly than production; or in the cycle through which capital passes during its reproduction—a cycle in which it is not simply reproduced but reproduced on an extended scale, in which it describes not a circle but a spiral—there comes a moment at which the market manifests itself as too narrow for production. This occurs at the end of the cycle. But it merely means: the market is **glutted**. Overproduction is **manifest**. If the expansion of the market had kept pace with the expansion of production, **there would be no glut** in the **market, no overproduction**. However, the mere admission that the market must expand with production, is, on the other hand, again an admission of the possibility of overproduction, for the market is limited externally in the geographical sense, the internal market is limited as compared with a market that is both internal and external, the latter in turn is limited as compared with the world market, which however is, in turn, limited at each moment of time, [though] in itself capable of expansion. The admission that the market must expand if there is to be no overproduction, is therefore also an admission that there can be overproduction. (*CW*32: 153-154)

Marx seems to be acknowledging that merely to point to the process through which the accumulation process drives production faster than the market is a redescription of the problem rather than an explanation. Indeed, Clarke undermines his efforts to play down the significance of the tendency of the rate of profit to fall when he concedes that 'Marx does not offer a simple disproportionality theory of crisis' because 'the problem of crisis comes back to the problem of the fall in the rate of profit that precipitates the crisis by disrupting the relations of proportionality between the branches of production, primarily between those producing means of production and those producing means of consumption'.[18] A little after the passage just cited Marx himself suggests that an explanation of overproduction requires us to look more closely at wages and profits: 'It is the unconditional development of the productive forces and therefore mass production on the basis of a mass of producers who are confined within the bounds of the **necessaries** on the one hand and, on the other, the barrier set up by the capitalists' profit, which [forms] the basis of modern overproduction' (*CW*32: 157-8). This remark points us towards *Capital*, but before we take a look at what he says about crises there, it is worth saying a word about Marx's treatment of equilibrium.

Marx's critique of Say's Law aligns him with those economists—in Ricardo's day Thomas Malthus and J C L Simonde de Sismondi, more recently of course Maynard Keynes—who have argued that capitalism lacks an inherent tendency towards equilibrium (though Marx finds it very hard to find a good word to say about Malthus).[19] As Bensaïd puts it, 'the disjunction of sale and purchase is a principle not of symmetry and equilibrium, but of dissymmetry and disequilibrium'.[20] But Marx does not therefore renounce the concept of equilibrium altogether. Thus in a passage that we cited in chapter 4 when considering his account on the formation of market value, Marx writes: 'The exchange or sale of commodities at their value is the rational, natural law of the equilibrium between them [*das Rationelle, das natürliche Gesetz ihres Gleichgewichts*], this is the basis on which divergences have to be explained, and not the converse, ie the law of equilibrium should not be derived from contemplating the divergences' (*C*III: 289). Equilibrium thus plays a regulative role, holding where the law of value is operative and commodities exchange according to the socially necessary labour time required to produce them:

> On the one hand, every producer of a commodity is obliged to produce a use-value, ie he must satisfy a particular social need...; on the other hand, the law of the value of commodities ultimately determines how much of its disposable labour-time society can expend on each kind of

---

18  Clarke, *Marx's Theory of Crisis*, pp150, 151.

19  According to Enrique Dussel, Marx 'is too negative, too harsh toward Thomas Robert Malthus', *Toward an Unknown Marx*, p90. Marx is considerably more charitable to Sismondi, whom he alleges Malthus plagiarised: see *CW*32: 243-248.

20  Bensaïd, *La Discordance des temps*, p46.

commodity. But this constant tendency on the part of the various spheres of production towards equilibrium comes into play only as a reaction against the constant upsetting of this equilibrium. (*CI*: 476)

Harvey puts it well:

What differentiates Marx from bourgeois political economists (both before or since) is the emphasis he puts on the *necessity* for departures from equilibrium and the crucial role of crises in restoring that equilibrium. The antagonisms embedded with the capitalist mode of production are such that the system is constantly being forced away from an equilibrium state. In the normal course of events, Marx insists, a balance can be achieved only by accident.[21]

So what, according to Marx in *Capital*, are the forces driving capitalism towards disequilibrium? This is best answered by trying to follow the ordering of determinations across the three volumes that provide the context of Marx's treatment of crises.

### ii. *Capital, I: the business cycle regulated by fluctuations in the industrial reserve army*

As we have already seen, Marx argues in the *1861-63 Manuscript* that 'the first section dealing with capital—the direct process of production—does not contribute any new element of crisis' (*CW*32: 143). Here there is a very substantial change in *Capital*, I, where the cycle plays an important role, first in Chapter 15 ('Machinery and Modern Industry') and especially in Chapter 25 ('The General Law of Capitalist Accumulation'), in section 3 of the latter chapter, which Marx significantly augments in the French edition. What he does here is systematically to relate the fluctuations of the business cycle to movements in wages and in the size of the industrial reserve army.[22]

What makes this extension in the scope of Marx's analysis possible is his at least partial abandonment of the six-volume plan, which separated the theory of capital from that of wage labour, and the introduction of Part 6, 'Wages', and in particular Chapter 19, where Marx presents the form assumed by wages as the value of labour as at once 'an expression as imaginary as the value of the earth' and a form of

---

21   David Harvey, *The Limits to Capital* (Oxford, 1982), pp82-83. Harvey refers here to *C*II: 571, cited more fully below.

22   Bensaïd's excellent discussion of Marx on crises in *La Discordance des temps*, ch 2, does not address this particular dimension. Gérard Duménil stresses its importance: *La Concept de loi économique dans 'le Capital'* (Paris, 1978), pp218-220.

appearance of capitalist production relations (*CI*: 677).[23] In Chapter 25 Marx introduces the concept of the organic composition of capital, the relationship between the means of production and labour power reflected in value terms as the ratio of constant capital to variable capital, and argues that, as the process of technical transformation inherent in the capital relation expels living labour from production, the organic composition of capital tends to rise. This in turn leads to a tendency for the industrial reserve army—that is, those layers of the working class that, to differing degrees, are not fully integrated into production—also to rise. But this tendency does not take the form of a continuous trend, but rather that of a cyclical oscillation:

> The path characteristically described by modern industry, which takes the form of a decennial cycle (interrupted by smaller oscillations) of periods of average activity, production at high pressure, crisis, and stagnation, depends on the constant formation, the greater or less absorption, and the re-formation of the industrial reserve army or surplus population. In their turn, the varying phases of the industrial cycle recruit the surplus population, and become one of the most energetic agencies of its reproduction. (*CI*: 785)

The same cyclical movement also regulates that of wages; for Marx, 'the rate of accumulation is the independent, not the dependent variable; the rate of wages is the dependent, not the independent variable' (*CI*: 770). Crucially, the size of the industrial reserve army affects the bargaining power of employed workers, which therefore varies according to the stage of the cycle. Accordingly, 'the general movement of wages is exclusively regulated by the expansion and contraction of the industrial reserve army, and this in turn corresponds to the periodic alternations of the industrial cycle' (*CI*: 790). In a striking passage added in the French edition of *Capital*, I, Marx integrates the cycle, the development of the productive forces, the industrial reserve army, and the globalisation of capitalist production:

> The jerky expansion of production is the primary cause of its sudden contraction; the latter, it is true, in turn causes the former, but would the exorbitant expansion of production, which forms the point of departure,

---

23  See the important discussions of Marx on wages in Roman Rosdolsky, *The Making of Marx's Capital* (London, 1977), pp57-62 and 282-313, and Jacques Bidet, *Exploring Marx's Capital* (Leiden, 2007), ch 4. Given what Part 6 allows Marx to do, Harvey's dismissal ('the ideas are fairly obvious and the writing rather pedestrian') seems rather cavalier: David Harvey, *A Companion to Marx's Capital* (London, 2010), p243.

be possible without a reserve army under the command of capital, without a surplus of workers independent of the natural growth of the population? This increase is achieved by using a very simple process which every day throws workers on the streets, namely the application of methods that, making labour more productive, diminish the demand for it. The conversion, constantly renewed, of a part of the working class who are half occupied or completely idle, thus imprints its typical form on the movement of modern industry.

Just as the heavenly bodies always repeat a certain movement, once they have been flung into it, so too does social production, once it has been flung into this movement of alternate expansion and contraction, repeat it by mechanical necessity. Effects become causes in their turn, and the various vicissitudes, first irregular and seemingly accidental, assume more and more the shape of a normal periodicity. But it is only after mechanical industry has struck root so deeply that it exerted a preponderant influence on the whole of national production; only after, foreign trade began to predominate over internal trade, thanks to mechanical industry; only after the world market had successively annexed extensive areas of in the New World, Asia and Australia; only after, finally, a sufficient number of industrial nations had entered the arena—only after all this can one date the repeated self-perpetuating cycles, whose successive phases embrace years and always culminate in a general crisis, which is the end of one cycle and the starting-point of another.[24]

Marx is not offering here anything like a full explanation of the cycle. More specifically, he is not putting forward a 'wage-push' or 'supply-side' theory of crisis of the kind favoured by Marxists influenced by Ricardo, for whom wage increases, by squeezing profits, precipitate crises.[25] Wages are, as we have seen, the 'dependent variable', responding to the accumulation process mediated by the business cycle. Nevertheless, Marx's analysis of the industrial reserve army underlines the importance to him of the cyclical character of capitalist development—or rather, in a metaphor he takes from Sismondi, its spiral form (CI: 727)—and hence of crises as the turning points of these cycles.

---

24  Karl Marx, *Le Capital, Livre I* (2 vols, Paris, 1985), II, p102 (second para partly translated in CI: 786n).

25  A good statement of the supply-side approach can be found in Philip Armstrong et al, *Capitalism since World War II* (London, 1984); Robert Brenner, *The Economics of Global Turbulence* (London, 2006) is, among other things, a comprehensive critique. More on the industrial reserve army in chapter 7.

### *iii. Capital, II: the turnover and reproduction of capital*

Crises figure twice in Volume II, first positively in Part 2 and then nega-
tively in Part 3. Part 2 is devoted to the turnover of capital. One
determinant of profitability is the length of time it takes for the capital
invested to flow back: in the case of fixed capital, invested in plant and
machinery, this will be spread over several cycles of production, as the
means of production are worn down physically and also suffer what
Marx calls 'moral depreciation' thanks to the development of cheaper
and more efficient replacements.[26] Marx showed a long-standing interest
in the turnover of capital, quizzing Engels in March 1858 about how it
was calculated in Ermen and Engels in Manchester, and in returning to
the subject in the long letter of 30 April 1868 where he set out his plans
for Volume III (*CW*43: 20-26). In *Capital*, II, however, he uses the turnover of capital to help explain the periodicity of crises:

> To the same extent as the value and durability of the fixed capital
> applied develops with the development of the capitalist mode of pro-
> duction, so also does the life of industry and industrial capital in each
> particular investment develop, extending to several years, say an aver-
> age of ten years. If the development of fixed capital extends this life, on
> the one hand, it is cut short on the other by the constant revolutionis-
> ing of the means of production, which also increases steadily with the
> development of the capitalist mode of production. This also leads to
> changes in the means of production; they constantly have to be
> replaced, because of their moral depreciation, long before they are
> physically exhausted. We can assume that, for the most important
> branches of large-scale industry, this life cycle is now on average a ten-
> year one. The precise figure is not important here. The result is that the
> cycle of related turnovers, extending over a number of years, within
> which the capital is confined by its fixed component, is one of the mate-
> rial foundations for the periodic cycle [*Krisen*] in which business passes
> through successive periods of stagnation, moderate activity, over-
> excitement and crisis. The periods for which capital is invested certainly
> differ greatly, and do not coincide in time. But a crisis is always the
> starting point of a large volume of new investment. It is also, therefore,
> if we consider the society as a whole, more or less a new material basis
> for the next turnover cycle. (*C*II: 264)

---

26  For criticisms of Marx for failing to integrate turnover time into his account of the rate of
profit, see Duménil, *La Concept de loi économique dans 'le Capital'*, pp281ff, and Harvey,
*The Limits to Capital*, pp185-188.

But, as Clarke points out, Marx 'never provided even a suggestion of an explanation for crises based on the replacement cycle' of fixed capital. Nevertheless:

> Marx is clearly moving towards a theory of the investment cycle, in which a burst of investment in the boom stimulates inflation and disproportionalities, which in turn provoke speculation and monetary instability, while the crash sees a massive liquidation of fixed capital, which eventually lays the foundation for recovery. However, Marx cannot take the analysis further at this stage, primarily because the problem of fixed capital and the investment cycle is linked to the problem of credit, which he has not yet considered.[27]

This limitation did not prevent Evgeny Preobrazhensky making creative use of Marx's treatment of fixed capital to develop his own original theory of crisis.[28] Indeed, in the history of Marxism it has been *Capital*, II, that has provided the most fertile source of crisis theories by political economists seeking to complete Marx's own work. Rosa Luxemburg even says: '*it is especially important for solving the problem of economic crises*'.[29] Part 3, where Marx seeks to define the conditions of capitalist reproduction by specifying the exchanges required between the two main departments of production (means of production and means of consumption), has exerted to the greatest influence, whether it be on Rudolph Hilferding's attempt to explain crises by disproportionalities between different sectors or Luxemburg's and Henryk Grossman's much more ambitious theories of capitalist breakdown.[30] Rich and complex though the debates provoked by these works are, there is no evidence that Marx himself thought that his analysis of reproduction (a constant preoccupation from the *1861-63 Manuscript* through to his various drafts of *Capital*, II, up to the end of the 1870s) was particularly relevant to explaining crises.

Roman Rosdolsky's discussion of Marx's theory of capitalist reproduction seems to me definitive. He praises Luxemburg for 'her pointing

---

27  Clarke, *Marx's Theory of Crisis*, pp267, 273. See the extensive treatment of fixed capital in Harvey, *Limits to Capital*, ch 8, and *A Companion to Marx's Capital, Volume 2* (London, 2013), ch 3. Schumpeter criticises Marx's attempt to relate the cycle to the turnover of fixed capital in *Business Cycles*, I, pp189-191.

28  E A Preobrazhensky, [1931] *The Decline of Capitalism* (Armonk NY, 1985).

29  Rosa Luxemburg, 'Practical Economics: Volume 2 of Marx's *Capital*', in Peter Hudis, ed, *The Complete Works of Rosa Luxemburg*, I (London, 2013), p421.

30  Rudolph Hilferding, [1910] *Finance Capital* (London, 1981), Rosa Luxemburg, [1913] *The Accumulation of Capital* (London, 1971), and Henryk Grossman, [1929] *The Law of Accumulation and Breakdown of the Capitalist System* (Jairus Banaji, ed; London, 1992).

out of the fact...that Marx's schemes of extended reproduction disregard all those changes in the mode of production which are caused by technical progress—namely, the increasing organic composition of capital, the increase in the rate of surplus value, and the rising rate of accumulation.' Should any of these changes occur, the conditions of equilibrium specified by Marx would break down. But, Rosdolsky continues:

> it cannot be concluded from this 'failure' of the schemes of reproduction (as she supposed), that accumulation is completely 'impossible', but simply that any revolution in the productive forces which takes place on a social scale must bring the given state of equilibrium of the branches of production to an end and lead, via all kinds of crises and disturbances, to a new temporary equilibrium.[31]

In other words, what *Capital*, II, Part 3, does is to specify conditions of equilibrium without implying that these will necessarily be met. This is made clear in a passage that I have already cited in part:

> The fact that the production of commodities is the general form of capitalist production already implies that money plays a role, not just as means of circulation, but also as money capital within the circulation sphere, and gives rise to certain conditions for normal exchange that are peculiar to this mode of production, ie conditions for the normal course of reproduction, whether simple or on an expanded scale, which turn into an equal number of conditions for an abnormal course, possibilities of crisis, since, on the basis of the spontaneous pattern [*naturwüchsigen Gestaltung*] of this production, this balance is itself an accident. (CII: 570-571)

Marx's most famous comment on crises in *Capital*, II, also comes in Part 3. It involves a rejection of the kind of underconsumptionist explanations already developed by Malthus and Sismondi that Luxemburg was greatly to elaborate on the basis of her critique of the reproduction schemes in Part 3:

> It is pure tautology to say that crises are provoked by a lack of effective demand or of effective consumption. The capitalist system does not

---

31   Roman Rosdolsky, *The Making of Marx's Capital* (London, 1977), pp495, 496; see generally Rosdolsky, ch 30, Ernest Mandel, Introduction to Karl Marx, *Capital*, II (Harmondsworth, 1978), Harvey, *A Companion to Marx's Capital, Volume 2*, chs 10 and 11, and, for more introductory treatments, Ben Fine and Alfredo Saad-Filho, *Marx's 'Capital'* (5th edn; London, 2010), ch 5, and Duncan K Foley, *Understanding Capital: Marx's Economic Theory* (Cambridge MA, 1986), ch 6.

recognise any forms of consumer other than those who can pay, if we exclude the consumption of paupers and swindlers. The fact that commodities are unsaleable means no more than that no effective buyer has been found for them, ie no consumers (no matter whether the commodities are ultimately sold to meet the needs of productive or individual consumption). If the attempt is made to give this tautology greater profundity, by the statement that the working class receives too small a portion of its own product, and that the evil could be remedied if it received a bigger share, ie if its wages rose, we need only note that crises are always prepared by a period in which wages generally rise, and the working class actually does receive a greater share of the annual product destined for consumption. From the standpoint of these advocates of sound and 'simple' (!) common sense, such periods should rather avert the crisis. It thus appears that capitalist production involves certain conditions independent of people's good or bad intentions, which permit the relative prosperity of the working class only temporarily, and moreover always as a harbinger [*Sturmvogel*] of crisis. (*CII*: 486-487)

In the background here we see Marx's account of the interrelation between the business cycle and the fluctuations in the size of the industrial reserve army and the level of wages in *Capital*, I, Chapter 25. Commentators often counterpose this passage to an equally famous one, this time in *Capital*, III, Part 6, which can be interpreted as saying the opposite. Marx suggests that, if we conceive society as 'composed simply of industrial capitalists and wage-labourers', and ignore the depreciation of fixed capital, credit, fraud, and speculation,

> a crisis would be explicable only in terms of a disproportion in production between different branches and a disproportion between the consumption of capitalists themselves and their accumulation. But, as things actually are, the replacement of the capitals invested in production depends to a large extent on the consumption capacity of the non-productive classes; while the consumption capacity of the workers is restricted partly by the laws governing wages and partly by the fact they are employed only as long as they can be employed at a profit for the capitalist class. The ultimate reason for all actual [*wirklichen*] crises always remains the poverty and restricted consumption of the masses, in the face of the drive of capitalist production to develop the productive forces as if only the absolute consumption capacity of society set a limit to them. (*CIII*: 614, 615; translation modified)

Marx seems to be returning here to the terrain of the discussion of crises in the *1861-63 Manuscript*, since the two factors he initially cites—disproportionalities and excessive saving—are those used respectively by the Ricardians and Malthus to account for crises. And his own explanation of 'actual crises' (where the conditions he first specifies don't hold) seems is close to passages such as this from the earlier draft:

> *Overproduction* is specifically conditioned by the general law of the production of capital: to produce to the limit set by the productive forces, that is to say, to exploit the maximum amount of labour with the given amount of capital, without any consideration for the actual limits of the market or the needs backed by the ability to pay; and this is carried out through continuous expansion of reproduction and accumulation, and therefore constant reconversion of **revenue** into capital, while on the other hand, the mass of the producers remain tied to the **average** level of needs, and must remain tied to it according to the nature of capitalist production. (*CW*32: 163-164)

The later passage in *Capital*, III, is part of a discussion of the relationship between credit and productive capital in the context of the cycle and is in brackets in the original *1861-63 Manuscript* (*MEGA²* II/4.2: 539-540). It is best taken, in my view, as more an example of Marx continuing to think through his understanding of crises than a considered and settled espousal of underconsumptionism, particularly since the contradictory passage from *Capital*, II, belongs to a considerably later manuscript written in 1878. Maurice Dobb, while making these points, suggests in reconciliation that what 'Marx had in mind in the passage in question was the contradiction between the tendency of capital to expand the productive forces in a way which logically leads to a rise in real wages and its "desire" to restrain wages at a level at which a traditional rate of profit can be maintained'.[32]

### iv. Capital, III: the tendency of the rate of profit to fall and financial boom and bust

We have already started to consider Marx's discussion of crises in *Capital*, III, where it occurs primarily at two levels of determination: Part 3, originally entitled by Marx 'The Law of the Tendential Fall in the Rate of Profit in the Progress of Capitalist Production', and Part 5, 'The Division

---

32  Maurice Dobb, *Political Economy and Capitalism* (London, 1937), p114. Paul Sweezy by contrast uses the passage to crown his argument attributing to Marx an underconsumptionist theory of crisis: *The Theory of Capitalist Development* (New York, 1970), pp172-178.

of Profit into Interest and Profit of Enterprise. Interest Bearing Capital', which contains Marx's most extensive discussion of financial markets.[33] Marx first discusses the tendency of the rate of profit to fall in the *Grundrisse*, and returns to it in both the *1861-3* and the *1863-5 Manuscripts*. In the *Grundrisse* he calls it 'in every respect the most important law of modern political economy, and the most essential for understanding the most difficult relations. It is the most important law from the historical standpoint. It is a law which, despite its simplicity, has never before been grasped and, even less, consciously articulated' (*G*: 748; see also *CW*33: 104). Marx was, of course, perfectly well aware that the idea that capitalist development involved a falling rate of profit long preceded his own theorisation. British economic writers had noticed from the late 17th century onwards the relatively low level of interest rates in the United Provinces, then the most advanced European economy, and the declining trend of interest rates in Britain itself (which was on the way to overtaking Holland). They generally accounted for this by the general increase of wealth in these economies. Adam Smith at once summarised and transcended this discussion by rigorously distinguishing the rate of profit, the return on capital invested in industry or commerce, from the rate of interest on loans, and arguing that both tended to fall as a result of the accumulation of capital and competition among capitalists:

> The increase of stock, which raises wages, tends to lower profit. When the stocks of many rich merchants are turned into the same trade, their mutual competition naturally tends to lower its profit; and when there is an increase of stock in all the different trades carried on in the same society, the same competition must produce the same effect in them all.[34]

By the time of the great debates among British political economists at the end of the Napoleonic Wars, their perception of the problem had changed. They tended now to emphasise low profitability in Britain compared to less developed economies such as the United States and to cite Holland as a case of economic decline (often explained by the overabundance of capital forcing down the rate of profit).[35] Ricardo's explanation for a falling rate of profit was different. As we saw in chapter 2, he uses the labour theory of value to support the assertion that wages and profits

---

33 Engels cut out the final phrase in both titles.
34 Adam Smith, *An Inquiry into the Nature and Causes of the Wealth of Nations* (2 vols, Oxford, 1976), I.ix; II, p105. See generally G S L Tucker, *Progress and Profits in British Economic Thought 1650-1850* (Cambridge, 1960).
35 Tucker, *Progress and Profits in British Economic Thought*, ch VIII.

are inversely related. Wages depend on 'the price of the food, necessaries, and conveniences required for the support of the labourer and his family' (*R*, I: 93). Ricardo accepts Malthus's 'law of population', according to which population tends to rise faster than food production, and he also agrees with Malthus that the operation of this law would prevent wages rises above a minimum of physical subsistence (this is the 'iron law of wages' criticised by Marx in 'Value, Price and Profit'). But Ricardo concludes that the *share* of wages in value newly created tends to rise: 'With the progress of society the natural price of labour has always a tendency to rise, because one of the principal commodities by which its natural price is regulated, has a tendency to become dearer, from the greater difficulty of producing it' (*R*, I: 93). Ricardo follows Malthus in accepting that diminishing returns in agriculture would require over time a larger amount of labour to be devoted to food production. The inescapable corollary, given his theory of value and profits, is that the share of value taken by profits would fall:

> The natural tendency of profits then is to fall; for in the progress of society and wealth, the additional quantity of food required is obtained by the sacrifice of more and more labour. This tendency, this gravitation as it were of profits, is happily checked at repeated intervals by the improvements in machinery, connected with the production of necessaries, as well as by discoveries in the science of agriculture which enable us to relinquish a portion of labour before required, and therefore to lower the price of the prime necessary of the labourer. The rise in the price of necessaries and in the wages of labour is however limited; for as soon as wages should be equal (as in the case formerly stated) to 720*l*., the whole receipts of the farmer, there must be an end of accumulation; for no capital can then yield any profit whatever, and no additional labour can be demanded, and consequently population will have reached its highest point. Long indeed before this period, the very low rate of profits will have arrested all accumulation, and almost the whole produce of the country, after paying the labourers, will be the property of the owners of land and the receivers of tithes and taxes. (*R*, I: 120-121)

This 'stationary state', as later economists such as John Stuart Mill came to describe it, represents, as Marx puts it, 'the bourgeois "Twilight of the Gods"—the Day of Judgement' (*CW* 32: 172). Ricardo may have resituated the problem of the falling rate of profit within the framework of the labour theory of value, but his reliance on the law of diminishing returns exerted a lasting influence that survived the neoclassical 'revolution'. Thus

Stanley Jevons, one of the founders of marginalist value theory, wrote in
1871: 'Our formula for the rate of interest shows that unless there be constant progress in the arts, the rate must tend to sink towards zero,
supposing accumulation of capital to go on. There are sufficient statistical
facts, too, to confirm this conclusion historically. The only question that
can arise is as to the actual cause of this tendency'.[36]

Jevons's remarks are interesting because they underline the extent to
which Marx's own writings on profitability take place against the background of a scholarly consensus that there is a tendency for the rate of
profit to fall. They also give the lie to Jonathan Sperber's suggestion that,
in preoccupying himself with this issue, Marx was constructing 'a back-
ward looking economics, a treatise written in the 1860s, whose central
interests and approaches stemmed from circumstances in the first decades of the 19th century'.[37] This criticism ignores the extraordinary
scientific quality of the political economists' debates in the 1810s and
1820s, and also fails to take into account Marx's very substantial differences with Ricardo. These can be summarised under two headings. First,
in relying on Malthus's theory of population, Ricardo confines his
theory of value and profits within a naturalistic framework. As Marx
puts it, 'he flees from economics to seek refuge in organic chemistry'
(G: 754). Secondly, Ricardo detaches the tendency for the rate of profit
to fall from any account of crises (whose existence as a generalised phenomenon of overproduction he indeed denies). Marx's first account of
the tendency of the rate of profit to fall in the *Grundrisse* already differs
radically from Ricardo's in both these respects. First, it relies, not on the
assumption of falling productivity thanks to diminishing returns in
agriculture, but on *rising* labour productivity, expressed in the rise of
dead labour (constant capital invested in means of production) relative
to living labour (represented by the variable capital invested in employing wage labour). Therefore, while Ricardo's theory of profits presupposes
the absence of technical innovation ('We will assume that no improvements take place in agriculture:' *R*, IV: 12), Marx's makes capitalism's
technological dynamism the source of falling profitability:

---

36   W S Jevons, *The Theory of Political Economy* (Harmondsworth, 1970), pp245-246.
     Maynard Keynes, who never liberated himself from marginalism, argued that investment
     would tend to bring the 'marginal efficiency of capital' (his equivalent to the rate of profit)
     down to the level of the rate of interest: *The General Theory of Employment Interest and
     Money* (London, 1970), pp135-137. See Chris Harman, 'The Crisis of Bourgeois
     Economics', *International Socialism*, 2.71 (1996), http://www.marxists.org/archive/
     harman/1996/06/bourgecon.htm#n 95
37   Sperber, *Karl Marx*, p454.

Presupposing the same surplus value, *the same surplus labour in proportion to necessary labour*, then, the *rate of profit* depends on the relation between the part of capital exchanged for living labour and the part existing in the form of raw material and means of production. Hence, the smaller the portion exchanged for living labour becomes, the smaller becomes the rate of profit. Thus, in the same proportion as capital takes up a larger place as capital in the production process relative to immediate labour, ie the more the relative surplus value grows—the value-creating power of capital—the more *does the rate of profit fall*. (*G*: 747)[38]

Secondly, the tendency of the rate of profit to fall is treated as the expression of the conflict between the forces and relations of production that Marx argues is the motor of historical transformation. It is, moreover, (to put it no stronger) associated with crises, which are themselves interpreted as a symptom of this conflict, reflected particularly in the destruction of capital they involve:

Beyond a certain point, the development of the powers of production becomes a barrier for capital; hence the capital relation a barrier for the development of the productive powers of labour. When it has reached this point, capital, ie wage labour, enters into the same relation towards the development of social wealth and of the forces of production as the guild system, serfdom, slavery, and is necessarily stripped off as a fetter. The last form of servitude assumed by human activity, that of wage labour on one side, capital on the other, is thereby cast off like a skin, and this casting-off itself is the result of the mode of production corresponding to capital; the material and mental conditions of the negation of wage labour and of capital, themselves already the negation of earlier forms of unfree social production, are themselves results of its production process. The growing incompatibility between the productive development of society and its hitherto existing relations of production expresses itself in bitter contradictions, crises, spasms. The violent destruction of capital not by relations external to it, but rather as a condition of its self-preservation, is the most striking form in which advice is given it to be gone and to give room to a higher state of social production. (*G*: 749-750)

Both of these features are preserved in Marx's later discussions of the tendency of the rate of profit to fall in the *1861-63 Manuscript* and

---

38 Hence it is quite nonsensical for Thomas Piketty to assert: 'Marx totally neglected the possibility of durable technological progress and steadily increasing productivity,' *Capital in the 21st Century* (Cambridge MA, 2014), p10.

*Capital*, III. Reuten and Thomas argue that in the *Grundrisse*, 'while he first strongly criticises the "naturalist" presuppositions of classical political economy in his main arguments, his conclusion then problematically transfers a political theory of crisis onto the terrain of political economy'.[39] This seems like an overstatement. Reuten's and Thomas's main evidence for their claim is the following passage:

> These contradictions lead to explosions, cataclysms, crises, in which by momentaneous suspension of labour and annihilation of a great portion of capital the latter is violently reduced to the point where it can go on... Yet, these regularly recurring catastrophes lead to their repetition on a higher scale, and finally to its violent overthrow. There are moments in the developed movement of capital which delay this movement other than by crises; such as eg the constant devaluation of a part of the existing capital: the transformation of a great part of capital into fixed capital which does not serve as agency of direct production; unproductive waste of a great portion of capital etc. (*G*: 750)

The crucial question for our purposes is whether Marx is positing here some economic mechanism that will produce capital's 'violent overthrow'. There is no evidence that he is. On the contrary, in both the passages just cited from the *Grundrisse*, Marx already gestures towards the idea, developed more fully in later manuscripts, that crises, through the 'violent destruction of capital' they involve, allow capitalism to 'go on'—that is, to resume its course of development. Marx never sets out an economic theory of capitalist breakdown of the kind attempted by Luxemburg and Grossman. In an article published in the *New York Tribune* in September 1859, that is, not long after he had written the *Grundrisse*, Marx uses the *Statistical Abstract for the United Kingdom 1844-58* to advance

> a law of production which might be proved with mathematical nicety, by comparing the returns of British exports since 1797. The law is this: That if, by overproduction and over-speculation, a crisis has been brought about, still the productive powers of the nation and the faculty of absorption on the market of the world, have, in the meantime, so far expanded, that they will only temporarily recede from the highest point reached, and that after some oscillations, spreading over some years, the scale of production which marked the highest point of prosperity in one

---

39  Reuten and Thomas, 'From the "Fall of the Rate of Profit" in the *Grundrisse* to the Cyclical Development of the Profit Rate in *Capital*', p85.

period of the commercial cycle, becomes the starting point of the subsequent period. (*CW* 16: 493)

So crises interrupt rather than halt the upward expansion of the productive forces. In an important footnote in the *1861-63 Manuscript* Marx writes: 'When Adam Smith explains the fall in the rate of profit from a **super-abundance of capital**, an **accumulation of capital**, he is speaking of a *permanent* effect and this is wrong. As against this, the transitory **over-abundance of capital**, overproduction and crises are something different. *Permanent crises do not exist*' (*CW*32: 128n*). It is of course true that in the famous Chapter 32 of *Capital*, I, 'The Historical Tendency of Capitalist Accumulation', Marx writes: 'capitalist production begets, with the inexorability of a natural process [*mit der Notwendigkeit eines Naturprozeßes*], its own negation' (*CI*: 929). But the economic dimension of this process is provided, not directly by crises, but rather by the process of centralisation and concentration of capital to which they contribute, which itself acts on political struggles primarily through the polarisation of class relations:

> Along with the constant decrease in the number of capitalist magnates, who usurp and monopolise all the advantages of this process of transformation, the mass of misery, oppression, slavery, degradation and exploitation grows; but with this there also grows the revolt of the working class, a class constantly increasing in numbers, and trained, united, and organised by the very mechanism of the capitalist process of production. (*CI*: 929)

Inasmuch as Marx tends to conceive socialist revolution as inevitable, this is not a consequence of any version of his theory of the tendency of the rate of profit to fall, but rather a reflection of, as Henri Weber puts it, 'the assimilation by Marx and Engels of the constitution of the proletariat as a revolutionary class to a "natural movement", comparable to physical phenomena, which one can hasten or delay, but which must develop in any conditions'.[40] This is undoubtedly problematic, but it is not directly relevant to Marx's theory of profitability and crises.

---

40 Henri Weber, *Marxisme et conscience de classe* (Paris, 1975), p67. See, for further discussion of this problem, Callinicos, *Revolutionary Ideas of Karl Marx*, pp188-201, and for critical reflections on Chapter 32, Bensaïd, *La Discordance des temps*, pp59-61. Marx's position is thus the opposite of that of Luxemburg, who thinks that capitalism has a tendency towards economic breakdown but that whether the outcome is socialism or barbarism depends on the conscious action of the proletariat: see Norman Geras, *The Legacy of Rosa Luxemburg* (London, 1976), ch I.

This is not to say that this theory doesn't develop across successive manuscripts, as Reuten demonstrates in a very important earlier study to which I am indebted.[41] These developments occur in three areas—(i) the organic composition of capital, (ii) the tendency and countertendencies, and (iii) the relationship between the tendency and the business cycle.

(i) In the *Grundrisse* Marx explains the tendency of the rate of profit to fall by dead labour rising relative to living labour. It is only in the *1861-63 Manuscript* that he formulates the conception of the organic composition of capital in the context of the transformation of values into prices of production (see chapter 2). Much later in the manuscript he draws the following crucial distinction:

> The ratio between the different elements of productive capital is determined in two ways. *First*: By the organic composition of productive capital. By this we mean the technological composition. With a *given productivity* of labour, which can be taken as constant so long as **no change** occurs, the amount of raw material and means of labour, that is, the amount of constant capital—in terms of its *material elements*—which corresponds to a definite *quantity of living labour* (paid or unpaid), that is, to the *material elements* of *variable* capital, is determined in every sphere of production...
>
> *Secondly, however,* if one assumes that the organic composition of capitals is given and likewise the differences which arise from the differences in their organic composition, then the *value ratio* can change although the technological composition remains the same. What can happen is: a) a **change** in the value of constant capital; b) a **change** in the value of the variable capital; c) a *change in both*, in equal or unequal proportions. (*CW*33: 305, 306)

Marx is here beginning to distinguish between three kinds of composition of capital—technical, organic and value. As Ben Fine and Lawrence Harris explain:

> The technical composition (TCC) is the ratio of the mass of means of production consumed per production period (ie abstracting from fixed capital) to the mass of wage goods. It is a ratio of physical, material quantities and hence unmeasurable by a single index. The value composition (VCC) is an expression for the same ratio measured in terms of the current values of means of production and wage goods consumed. It is

---

41  Geert Reuten, '"Zirkel vicieux" or Trend Fall? The Course of the Profit Rate in Marx's *Capital* III', *History of Political Economy*, 36:1 (2004).

therefore the ratio of constant to variable capital, C/V. Now for the organic composition (OCC)... It is the C/V where the elements of the means of production and wage goods are valued at their 'old values'. Therefore, changes in the OCC are directly proportional to changes in the technical composition whereas changes in VCC are not.[42]

The passage from the *1861-63 Manuscript* comes a couple of hundred pages after Marx discusses the tendency of the rate of profit to fall. It is only in *Capital*, III, that these concepts are properly integrated. After offering an example where the OCC rises and the rate of profit falls, he writes:

> The hypothetical series that we constructed at the opening of this chapter therefore expresses the actual tendency of capitalist production. With the progressive decline in the variable capital in relation to the constant capital, this tendency leads to a rising organic composition of the total capital, and the direct result of this is that the rate of surplus value, with the level of exploitation of labour remaining the same or even rising, is expressed in a steadily falling general rate of profit. (*CIII*: 318-319)

(ii) It is also only in *Capital*, III, that Marx systematically discusses the factors inhibiting the falling rate of profit. It was common ground among 19th century political economists that there was only a tendency of the rate of profit to fall: thus, as we have seen, Ricardo concedes that technological innovations could counteract diminishing returns in agriculture. John Stuart Mill discusses in some detail the

> counteracting circumstances, which, in the existing state of things, maintain a tolerably equal struggle against the downward tendency of profits, and prevent the great annual savings which take place in this country from depressing the rate of profit much nearer to that lowest point to which it is always tending, and which, left to itself, it would so promptly attain.[43]

In the *1861-63 Manuscript* Marx merely notes:

> If one considers the development of productive power and the relatively not so pronounced fall in the rate of profit, the exploitation of labour must have increased very much, and what is remarkable is not the fall

42 Ben Fine and Lawrence Harris, *Rereading Capital* (London, 1979), p59; compare CI: 762. Alfredo Saad-Filho has a helpful discussion of the three kinds of composition of capital: *The Value of Marx* (London, 2002), ch 6.
43 J S Mill, *Principles of Political Economy with Some of their Applications to Social Philosophy*, in *Collected Works* (ed, V W Bladen and J M Robson, Toronto, 1965), III, p741.

in the rate of profit but that it has not fallen to a greater degree. This can be explained partly by circumstances to be considered in dealing with competition between capitals, partly by the general circumstance that so far the immense increase of productive power in some branches has been paralysed or restricted by its much slower development in other branches, with the result that the general ratio of variable to constant capital—considered from the point of view of the total capital of society—has not fallen in the proportion which strikes us so forcibly in certain outstanding spheres of production. (*CW* 33: 101)

In *Capital*, III, he goes considerably further, perhaps because he is now much less inhibited about considering phenomena arising at the level of competition (see chapter 3 above):

If we consider the enormous development in the productive powers of social labour over the past thirty years alone, compared with all earlier periods, and particularly if we consider the enormous mass of fixed capital in the overall process of social production quite apart from machinery proper, then instead of the problem that occupied previous economists, the problem of explaining the fall in the profit rate, we have the opposite problem of explaining why this fall is not greater or faster. Counteracting influences must be at work, checking and cancelling the effects of the general law and giving it simply the character of a tendency, which is why we have described the fall in the general rate of profit as a tendential fall [*tendenziellen Fall*]. (*CIII*: 339)

Marx then lists six factors—the more intense exploitation of labour, the reduction of wages below their value, the cheapening of the elements of constant capital, the effects of the relative surplus population in forcing down wages, the role of foreign trade in cheapening inputs and of investment in the colonies (where the organic composition of capital is typically lower than in the metropolis), and the increase of share capital where expectations of returns are governed by the rate of interest, which is necessarily lower than the rate of profit. This is plainly a heterogeneous list, which may have been influenced by Mill's discussion of the 'downward tendency of profits' and its 'counteracting circumstances'.[44]

---

44 Fine and Harris claim that 'the list is the same as that proposed by J S Mill', 'Controversial Issues in Marxist Economic Theory', in Ralph Miliband and John Saville, eds, *Socialist Register* 1976 (London, 1976), p162. But this isn't quite right. Very interestingly in the light of the discussion under (iii) in the text, the first of the 'resisting agencies' Mill lists consists in 'the waste of capital in periods of over-trading and rash speculation, and in the commercial revulsions by which such times are always followed;' he adds: 'that such

Nevertheless, as Grossman notes (with the exception of the sixth), 'they are all reducible to the fact that they either reduce the value of the constant capital or increase the rate of surplus value'.[45] Once again Marx is thinking problems through as he writes. But the overall conception of the law of the falling rate of profit as a tendency is deepening:

> We have shown in general, therefore, how the same causes that bring about a fall in the general rate of profit provoke counter-effects that inhibit this effect, delay it and in part even paralyse it. These do not annul the law, but they weaken its effect. If this were not the case, it would not be fall in the general rate of profit that was incomprehensible, but rather the relative slowness of its fall. The law operates therefore as a tendency, whose effect is decisive only under particular circumstances and over long periods. (*C*III: 344)

Fine and Harris offer a persuasive interpretation of how the interaction between tendency and 'counter-effects' is to be understood:

> in considering the counteracting influences, Marx introduces accumulation's effects on distribution and on the value composition of capital. They are at the same level of abstraction as the law as such in the sense that the counteracting influences are not predicated upon the concept of the law—they are not the effects or results of the tendency of the rate of profit to fall. Instead, both the law of the TRPF [tendency of the rate of profit to fall] and the counteracting influences are equally the effect of capitalist accumulation with its necessary concomitant of a rising technical composition (reflected in Marx's analysis by a rising organic composition but a value composition which does not necessarily rise). As Marx puts it 'the *same* influences which produce a tendency in the general rate of profit to

---

revulsions are almost periodical, is a consequence of the very tendency of profits which we are considering,' *Principles of Political Economy*, III, pp741, 741-742. The other counteracting factors are improvements in production, cheap imports, rising population, and the export of capital. According to Grossman, 'even if Marx gave it a much deeper foundation and made it consistent with his law of value, Mill's seminal role is indisputable. In its external structure it shows the same logical construction one finds in Ricardo and in Marx,' *The Law of Accumulation and Breakdown of the Capitalist System*, p74. One of the strengths of Grossman's version of breakdown theory is the much more systematic account that he gives of what he calls 'Modifying Countertendencies' than Marx's: Grossman, ch 3. But he conceives their role somewhat differently from Marx: the countertendencies interrupt the tendency to breakdown that Grossman deduces from the conditions of reproduction, which consequently 'splits up into a series of apparently independent cycles which are only the form of its constant, periodic reassertion', Grossman, p85. The countertendencies thus generate the business cycle.

45  Grossman, *The Law of Accumulation and Breakdown of the Capitalist System*, p133.

fall, *also* call forth counter-effects' (emphasis added). In the light of this we think that the name 'law of the TRPF' is something of a misnomer. The law in its broad definition is in fact 'the law of the tendency of the rate of profit to fall and its counteracting influences'.[46]

One example is provided by the rate of surplus value. As we have seen, Marx's account of the tendency of the rate of profit to fall in *Capital*, III, starts from the assumption of a constant rate of surplus value. But at the end of his discussion of the tendency in the *1861-63 Manuscript* he associates it with a rising rate of surplus value:

> The result of the investigation is this: Firstly, the rate of surplus value does not rise in proportion to the growth in productive power or the decline in the (relative) number of workers employed. The capital does not grow in the same proportion as the productive power. Or, the rate of surplus value does not rise in the same proportion as the variable capital falls in comparison with the total amount of capital. Hence a diminution of the relative magnitude of the surplus value. Hence *a decline in the rate of profit. A constant tendency towards a decline in the same.* (*CW*33: 148)

Similarly, when discussing the counteracting influences in *Capital*, III, Marx shifts from assuming a constant rate of surplus value to positing a rising one:

> the same mode of production that reduces the total mass of additional living labour in a commodity is accompanied by a rise in absolute and relative surplus value. The tendential fall in the rate of profit linked to a tendential rise in the rate of surplus value, ie in the level of exploitation of labour. Nothing is more absurd, then, than to explain the fall in the rate of profit in terms of a rise in wage rates, even though this too may be an exceptional case... The profit rate does not fall because labour becomes less productive but rather because it becomes more productive. The rise in the rate of surplus value and the fall in the rate of profit are simply forms that express the growing productivity of labour in capitalist terms. (*CIII*: 347)[47]

---

46  Fine and Harris, *Rereading Capital*, pp63-64. Dobb offers a similar interpretation of the relationship between tendency and countertendencies in an interesting discussion of Marx's crisis theory that reflects the intense debates among Cambridge economists between the wars: *Political Economy and Capitalism*, pp186-188, and, more generally, ch IV.

47  The relationship between the rate of surplus value and the rate of profit has long been a matter of controversy between critics and defenders of *Capital*. Michael Heinrich has recently argued that Marx fails to show that the rate of surplus value will not rise sufficiently to offset the rise in the value composition of capital: 'Crisis Theory, the Law of the Tendency of the Profit Rate to Fall, and Marx's Studies in the 1870s', *Monthly Review*, 64:11 (April 2113), http://monthlyreview.org/2013/04/01/crisis-theory-the-law-of-the-tendency-of-the-

The result is a much more complex conception of the falling rate of profit than is to be found in Marx's predecessors or in the accounts given by many of his numerous critics. As Fine and Harris put it, he is presenting an 'abstract tendency', ie 'a proposition developed at a certain level of abstraction which by itself yields no general predictions about actual movements in the rate of profit. Actual movements depend on a complicated relationship between the tendency and the counteracting influences which have been abstracted from—their particular balance at particular times'.[48] Where the main work of analysis based on the theory should focus is on the unfolding through time of the interplay between tendency and countertendencies. This is particularly relevant to one of the principal criticisms put forward by economists, Marxist and otherwise, influenced by Piero Sraffa's attempt to rehabilitate Ricardian economics, namely that the same higher productivity that increases the technical composition of capital (the physical ratio of means of production to labour power) will, by making new means of production cheaper, cause the value composition to remain constant or even fall, thereby preventing a fall in the rate of profit. This ignores the organic composition of capital, where, as Fine and Harris put it, 'the elements of the means of production and wage goods are valued at their "old values"'. Since capital accumulation is a dynamic process unfolding in time (and not a succession of instantaneous states each captured in a set of simultaneous equations), when innovation cheapens the elements of constant capital, a divergence opens up between the value at which existing means of production were purchased and the value (increasingly reflecting the

profit-rate-to-fall-and-marxs-studies-in-the-1870s. In rebuttal Guglielmo Carchedi and Michael Roberts argue: 'The interplay between the organic composition of capital and the rate of surplus value co-determines the cyclical fluctuations of the ARP [average rate of profit]. But this does not imply indeterminateness. *In the long run* the ARP must fall through troughs and peaks, ie eventually the rise in the rate of surplus value cannot stop the ARP from falling because it cannot outstrip the rise in the organic composition of capital. But why? The reason is that there is a *socially determined insuperable* limit to the extension of the working day. When that limit is reached, the ARP falls,' 'A Critique of Heinrich's "Crisis Theory, the Law of the Tendency of the Profit Rate to Fall, and Marx's Studies in the 1870s",' *Monthly Review*, 65:7 (December 2013), http://monthlyreview.org/commentary/ critique-heinrichs-crisis-theory-law-tendency-profit-rate-fall-marxs-studies-1870s. I find this argument persuasive (compare Marx's own discussion of the limits to extending the working day: eg *CW*30: 182-185), as I do Carchedi's and Roberts's insistence against Heinrich that a rising rate of surplus value is a countertendency; this is clearly implied by the passage from *Capital*, III, to which this note is appended.

48  Fine and Harris, *Rereading Capital*, p64. The tendency of the rate of profit to fall has been a matter of immense controversy: for an overview, see Stephen Cullenberg, *The Falling Rate of Profit* (London, 1994). Brenner's alternative explanation of the tendency provoked a new wave of discussion: see especially *Historical Materialism*, 4 and 5 (1999).

reduction in costs caused innovation) at which capitalists must now sell their products. John Weeks outlines the consequences:

> During this process, it is the organic composition of capital that is relevant, since the new and lower set of values does not affect capital advanced until the next circuit of capital, when it enters the profit calculation. Even at that point, the new values affect only the increments of fixed capital, for all fixed capital that has been bought at previous values does not circulate in its entirety; part remains fixed in the machines and other equipment. The problem for capital is to realise the existing means of production in the context of the progressive devaluation of those means of production. This problem affects those capitals using new means of production as well as those using socially obsolete ones. For each enterprise means of production and labour power are purchased at one set of values and realised at another. The difference between enterprises is that for those using new means of production the devaluation of advanced capital is offset in part or whole by the reduction in the cost price of the realised commodities.
>
> In this process of accumulation and value formation the rate of profit will fall for some capitals, those using old means of production. As the circuits of capital repeat themselves, each time with technical change reducing the concrete labour consumed in the production of commodities, the stratification of capitals increases. The number of capitals experiencing a fall in the rate of profit depends upon the intensity of the competitive struggle.[49]

(iii) So here a counteracting tendency actually causes the rate of profit to fall, at least for capitals with heavy investments in old means of production. Indeed, Marx argues, the problems caused by the devaluation of capital and the consequent stratification of capitals are most effectively overcome in crises:

---

49  John Weeks, *Capital, Exploitation and Economic Crisis* (London: Routledge, 2010), p135. For good treatments of this issue, see Weeks, *Capital, Exploitation and Economic Crisis*, ch 10, John Weeks, 'Equilibrium, Uneven Development and the Tendency of the Rate of Profit to Fall', *Capital and Class*, 16 (1982), Geert Reuten, 'Accumulation of Capital and the Foundation and the Tendency of the Rate of Profit to Fall', *Cambridge Journal of Economics*, 15 (1991), and Chris Harman, *Zombie Capitalism: Global Crisis and the Relevance of Marx* (London, 2009), ch 3. I offer my own take in 'Capitalism, Competition and Profits: A Critique of Robert Brenner's Theory of Crisis', *Historical Materialism*, 4 (1999). Sraffa's main theoretical work is *The Production of Commodities by Means of Commodities* (Cambridge, 1960). An influential attempt to turn him against Marx is Ian Steedman, *Marx after Sraffa* (London, 1977), and a powerful critique will be found in Pierre Salama, *Sur la valeur* (Paris, 1975). See also Ian Steedman et al, *The Value Controversy* (London, 1981), Ernest Mandel and Alan Freeman, eds, *Ricardo, Marx, Sraffa* (London, 1984), and Ben Fine, ed, *The Value Dimension* (London, 1986).

The means of labour are for the most part constantly revolutionised by the progress of industry. Hence they are not replaced in their original form, but in the revolutionised form. On the one hand, the volume of fixed capital that is invested in a particular natural form, and has to last out for a definite average lifespan within this, is a reason why new machines, etc are introduced only gradually, and hence forms an obstacle to the rapid general introduction of improved means of labour. On the other hand competition [*der Konkurrenzkampf*] forces the replacement of old means of production by new ones before their natural demise, particularly when decisive revolutions [*entscheidenden Umwälzungen*] have taken place. Catastrophes, crises, etc are the principal causes that compel such premature renewals of equipment on a broad social scale. (*CII*: 250)

This argument is part of a much broader understanding of the way in which crises are functional to the process of capital accumulation. Like Schumpeter, Marx believes 'recession is a process that fills a function and not simply a misfortune'.[50] As Grossman puts it, 'in Marx's conception crises are simply a healing process of the system, a form in which equilibrium is again re-established, even if forcibly and with huge losses'.[51] Indeed, what is striking about Marx's treatment of the tendency of the rate of profit to fall in both the *1861-63 Manuscript* and *Capital*, III, is the way in which he seeks to integrate it with the business cycle. In the earlier text he writes:

So where does this tendency for the general rate of profit to fall come from? Before this question is answered, one may point out that it has caused a great deal of anxiety to bourgeois political economy. The whole of the Ricardian and Malthusian school is a cry of woe over the day of judgement this process would inevitably bring about, since capitalist production is the production of profit, hence loses its stimulus, the soul which animates it, with the fall in this profit... But apart from theory there is also the practice, the crises from **superabundance of capital or, what comes to the same, the mad adventures capital enters upon in consequence of the lowering of [the] rate of profit. Hence crises—see Fullarton—acknowledged as a necessary violent means for the cure of the plethora of capital, and the restoration of a sound rate of profit.** (*CW*33: 104-105)[52]

---

50  Schumpeter, *Business Cycles*, I, p143 n 1.
51  Grossman, *The Law of Accumulation and Breakdown of the Capitalist System*, p84.
52  Marx discusses the plethora of capital at an earlier stage in the *1861-63 Manuscript* (*CW*32:

John Fullarton was a leading figure in the banking school, critics of the quantity theory of money whom Marx closely studied in the early 1850s (see chapter 2 above). He argues that the origins of crises lie in the fact that 'the amount of capital seeking productive investment accumulates in ordinary times with a rapidity greatly out of proportion to the increase of the means of advantageously employing it.' Hence the excess capital is splurged on increasingly speculative investment, leading to bubbles, panics and busts. Fullarton concludes, in a passage quoted by Marx:

> From more recent events, indeed, one might almost be tempted to expect, that a periodical destruction of capital has become a necessary condition of any market rate of interest at all. And, considered in that point of view, these awful visitations, to which we are accustomed to look forward with so much disquiet and apprehension and which we are so anxious to avert, may be nothing more than the natural and necessary corrective of an overgrown and bloated opulence, the *vis medicatrix* [healing power] by which our social system, as at present constituted, is enabled to relieve itself from time to time of an ever-recurring plethora which menaces its existence, and to regain a sound and wholesome state.[53]

What Marx does in *Capital*, III, is much more systematically to explore the relationship between the tendency of the rate of profit to fall and the cycle of boom and bust driven by the financial markets. The key locus of this discussion is Chapter 15, named by Engels (who divided what had been a continuous text into separate chapters) 'Development of the Internal Contradictions [*Innern Widersprüche*] of the Law'. Clarke's general description of the *1863-5 Manuscript* is particularly true of this chapter:

> a large number of fragments in which Marx works through his ideas in different ways, sometimes reaching conclusions, sometimes abandoning a train of thought, sometimes losing his way (usually in a thicket of arithmetical examples) without providing any indication of the systematic significance of his observations. Any attempt to present Marx's theory of crises therefore necessarily includes a substantial element of interpretation and reconstruction.[54]

---

128-131), but here there is no consideration of the tendency of the rate of profit to fall.
53  John Fullarton, *On the Regulation of Currencies* (London, 1844), pp162, 165; second passage quoted in G: 849-850.
54  Clarke, *Marx's Theory of Crisis*, pp11-12.

All the same, Chapter 15 shows Marx struggling to integrate all the different aspects of capitalist development—including some of the tendencies that he discusses in *Capital*, I (for example, rising productivity and hence the growth of the relative surplus population, the expansion of the world market, and the concentration and centralisation of capital)—within his conceptualisation of the interplay between the tendency of the rate of profit to fall and the business cycle. This becomes clear in the following, crucial passage, which bears quotation at length:

> Yet these two aspects [rising productivity devaluing capital and thereby slowing down TRPF but also increasing the mass of use values and thereby promoting accumulation] involved in the accumulation process cannot just be considered as existing quietly side by side, which is how Ricardo treats them; they contain a contradiction [*Widerspruch*], and this is announced by the appearance of contradictory [*widerstreitenden*] tendencies and phenomena. The contending agencies function simultaneously in opposition to one another... These various influences sometimes tend to exhibit themselves side by side, spatially; at other times, one after the other, temporally; and periodically the conflict of contending agencies breaks through in crises. Crises [*Krisen*] are never more than momentary, violent solutions for the existing contradictions [*Widersprüche*], violent eruptions that re-establish the disturbed balance for the time being.
>
> To express this contradiction in the most general terms, it consists in the fact that the capitalist mode of production tends towards an absolute development of the productive forces irrespective of value and the surplus value this contains, and even irrespective of the social relations within which capitalist production takes place; while on the other hand its purpose is to maintain the existing capital value and to valorise it to the utmost extent possible (ie an ever accelerated increase in this value). In this it is directed towards using the existing capital value as a means for the greatest possible valorisation of this value. The methods through which it attains this end involve a decline in the profit rate, the devaluation of the existing capital and the development of the productive forces of labour at the cost of the productive forces already produced.
>
> The periodic devaluation [*Entwertung*] of the existing capital, which is a means, immanent to the capitalist mode of production, for delaying the fall in the profit rate and accelerating the accumulation of capital value by the formation of new capital, disturbs the given conditions in which the circulation and reproduction process of capital takes place,

and is therefore accompanied by sudden stoppages and crises in the production process... Capitalist production constantly strives to overcome these immanent barriers [*Schranken*], but it overcomes them only by means that set up the barriers afresh and on a more powerful scale.

The *true barrier* [*Schranke*] to capitalist production is *capital itself*. It is that capital and its self-valorisation appear as the starting and finishing point, as the motive and purpose of production; production is production only for *capital*, and not the reverse. (CIII: 357-358)

We see here very clearly that Marx continues to situate the tendency of the rate of profit to fall as the specifically capitalist expression of the propensity for the productive forces to come into conflict with the relations of production:

economists like Ricardo, who take the capitalist mode of production as an absolute, feel here that this mode of production creates a barrier [*Schrank*] for itself and seek the source of this barrier not in production but rather in nature (in the theory of rent). The important thing in their horror at the falling rate of profit is the feeling that the capitalist mode of production comes up against a barrier to the development of the productive forces which has nothing to do with the production of wealth as such; but this characteristic barrier in fact testifies to the restrictiveness and the solely historical and transitory character of the capitalist mode of production; it bears witness that this is not an absolute mode of production for the production of wealth but actually comes into conflict [*Konflikt*] at a certain stage with the latter's further development [*Fortentwicklung*]. (CIII: 350)

The interesting thing, however, is that, in moving from the transhistorical tendency for the forces to come into conflict with the relations of production, Marx does not treat its capitalist expression as a continuous downward trend in profitability. As Reuten puts it:

In chapter 15...Marx indicates how the tendential decline of the rate of profit is expressed cyclically. Along with the accumulation of capital and the concomitant rise in the organic composition of capital, the rate of profit declines—that is, in the upturn phase of the cycle. This gives rise to an economic crisis, in the process of which the rate of profit is restored, most importantly because of the writing down of capital values ('devaluation of capital') and the scrapping of capital (cf section 3 of chapter 15).[55]

---

55   Reuten, '"Zirkel vicieux" or Trend Fall?', p168.

Indeed, as we have seen, one countertendency, the devaluation of capital caused by rising productivity, is integrated into Marx's account as an important force itself making for crises. But crises themselves help to restore profitability: 'the balance will be restored by capital's lying idle or even by its destruction... All this therefore leads to violent and acute crises, sudden forcible devaluations, an actual stagnation and disruption in the reproduction process, and hence to an actual decline in reproduction' (*CIII*: 362-363). The resulting rise in the relative surplus population brings wages down, thereby increasing the rate of exploitation; this, together with the cheapening of the elements of constant capital achieved by the sudden depreciation of means of production that bankruptcies, write-offs, and takeovers during crises promote, restores the rate of profit: 'And so we go round the whole circle [*Zirkel*] once again. One part of the capital that was devalued by the cessation of its function now regains its old value. And apart from that, with expanded conditions of production, a wider market and increased productivity, the same vicious circle [*Zirkel vicieux*] is pursued once more.' (*MEGA²* II/4.2: 329)[56]

Understanding the tendency of the rate of profit as expressed cyclically is not inconsistent with the idea that capitalism may undergo prolonged periods of relatively high or low profitability. Many Marxist political economists argue that global capitalism has been struggling with chronic problems of low profitability since the late 1960s. The plausibility of such an interpretation depends, of course, in part on the empirical evidence of profit trends, but also on the identification of factors that have prevented the countertendencies from restoring profitability. The most satisfactory explanation to my mind is the effect of the concentration and centralisation of capital in increasing the size of individual units of capital and their interdependence with the state, thereby creating a powerful obstacle to the destruction of capital that Marx identifies as a crucial force pushing the rate of profit back up during crises. The massive bailouts of the US and European banking system in response to the 2008 financial crash provide powerful support for such an analysis.[57]

---

56   In *Capital*, III, Engels replaces '*Zirkel vicieux*' with the weaker formulation '*fehlerhafte Kreislauf*', translated in the Penguin edition as 'cycle of errors' ('dysfunctional circuit' might have been better): *CIII*: 364. See Reuten, '"Zirkel vicieux" or Trend Fall?', p175, and also the discussions of the devaluation and depreciation of capital in Fine and Harris, *Rereading Capital*, ch 5, and Harvey, *Limits to Capital*, pp192-203.

57   See Brenner, *The Economics of Global Turbulence*, Chris Harman, *Explaining the Crisis* (London, 1984) and *Zombie Capitalism*, Parts 2 and 3, Alex Callinicos, *Bonfire of Illusions*

In Marx's own analysis it is the specifically financial cycle of bubble, panic, and bust that acts as a crucial agency for the destruction of capital. Thus he integrates the theme of the plethora of capital that preoccupies the banking school into the theory of the tendency of the rate of profit to fall:

> The so-called plethora of capital is always basically reducible to a plethora of that capital for which the fall in the profit rate is not outweighed by its mass—and this is always the case with fresh offshoots of capital that are newly formed—or to the plethora in which these capitals are available to the leaders of great branches of production in the form of credit.[58] This plethora of capital arises from the same causes that produce a relative surplus population and is therefore a phenomenon that complements this latter, even though the two stand at opposite poles— unoccupied capital on the one hand and an unemployed working population on the other.
>
> Overproduction of capital and not of individual commodities— though this overproduction of capital always involves overproduction of commodities—is nothing more than overaccumulation of capital. (*CIII*: 359)

In the manuscript Marx adds that understanding this overaccumulation 'includes further investigation into considering the *apparent movement of capital* [*erscheinenden Bewegung des Capitals*], where interest-bearing capital etc credit etc are further developed' (*MEGA²* II/4.2: 325). This indicates that there is an integral connection between Part 3 of *Capital*, III, on the tendency of the rate of profit to fall, and Part 5, which

---

(Cambridge, 2010), ch 1, Andrew Kliman, *The Failure of Capitalist Production* (London, 2011), Guglielmo Carchedi, 'Behind and Beyond the Crisis', *International Socialism*, 2.132 (2011), http://www.isj.org.uk/?id=761, and [2014] 'The Law of the Tendential Fall in the Rate of Profit as a Theory of Crises: Twelve Reasons to Stick to It', http:// thenextrecession.files.wordpress.com/2014/04/carchedi-london-11-12-april-2014.pdf,and Michael Roberts, [2012] 'A World Rate of Profit', http://thenextrecession.files.wordpress. com/2012/09/roberts_michael-a_world_rate_of_profit.pdf, and 'From Global Slump to Long Depression', *International Socialism*, 2.140 (2013), http://www.isj.org.uk/index. php4?id=914&issue=140. Naturally this explanation is highly controversial: see David McNally, *Global Slump* (Oakland, 2011), and the exchanges this led to between Joseph Choonara and him in *International Socialism*, 2.132 (2011), 2.133 (2012), and 2.135 (2012).

58  The fact that, Marx argues, typically the mass of surplus value rises as a result of the same factors that cause the rate of profit to fall, thereby permitting accumulation to continue (*CIII*: 225ff.), is used by Grossman to argue that 'breakdown cannot be derived from' the tendency of the rate of profit to fall: *The Law of Accumulation and Breakdown of the Capitalist System*, ch 2 (quotation from p103). Dobb, by contrast, offers arguments why a falling rate of profit 'will have a crucial disequilibrating effect': *Political Economy and Capitalism*, pp103-110 (quotation from p104).

involves Marx's most extensive discussion of the financial system. Clarke dismisses Part 5 as 'rudimentary'.[59] It certainly is a mess. In the overall architecture of *Capital* it functions as part of Marx's exploration of the distribution of surplus value, and more specifically of the fragmentation of surplus value into industrial and commercial profit, profit of enterprise, interest, and rent. The development of the financial market allows holders of idle money (for example, surplus value that has yet to accumulate in sufficient quantity to fund investment on its own: see *CW*33: 165-170 and *C*II: ch 2) to lend it to productive capitalists in exchange for a portion of the surplus value whose extraction the loan will make possible.

Marx, as we have seen, presents interest-bearing capital as the most extreme case of capital fetishism. He also, much more rigorously than his predecessors, distinguishes between the rate of interest and the rate of profit:

> As far as the permanently fluctuating market rate of interest is concerned, this is a fixed magnitude at any given moment, just like the market price of commodities, because on the money market all capital on loan confronts the functioning capital as an overall mass; ie the relationship between the supply of loan capital on the one hand and the demand for it on the other, is what determines the market level of interest at any given time... The general rate of profit, on the other hand, only ever exists as a tendency, a movement of equalisation between particular rates of profit. The competition between capitalists—which is itself this movement of equalisation—consists here in their withdrawing capital bit by bit from those spheres where profit is below the average for a long period, and similarly injecting it bit by bit into spheres where it is above this; or, alternatively, in their dividing additional capital between these spheres in varying proportions. (*C*III: 488-489)

The manuscript then balloons into a massive exploration of both the functioning and the ideological representation of the money market

---

59    Clarke, *Marx's Theory of Crisis*, p273. Good discussions of Part 5 include Martha Campbell, 'The Credit System', in Campbell and Geert Reuten, eds, *The Culmination of Capital: Essays on Volume Three of Marx's* **Capital** (Basingstoke, 2001), and Harvey, *A Companion to Marx's* **Capital**, *Volume 2*, chs 5-7. See also Makoto Itoh and Costas Lapavitsas, *Political Economy of Money and Banking* (London, 1999), chs 2-5. Harvey's decision to integrate his commentary on Part 5 into his book on *Capital*, II, which he justifies by the role the credit system plays in overcoming the necessity of large-scale hoarding to cover the various costs of circulation, has the unfortunate effect of separating Marx's analysis of financial crises from his theory of the tendency of the rate of profit to fall.

(Part 5 sprawls over more than 250 pages in the *MEGA²*). This involves detailed discussion of the relationship between financial and industrial cycles, lengthy extracts with commentary from the parliamentary inquiries into the suspension of the Bank Charter Act in both the 1847 and 1857 crises (headed in the original manuscript 'Confusion'), and critical observations on the theories of money and finance offered by the currency and banking schools (Marx is particularly contemptuous of Samuel Loyd, later Lord Overstone, denouncing 'the "logic" of this millionaire, this **"dung-hill aristocrat"**,' *C*III: 522). As we saw in chapter 1, this part of the *1863-5 Manuscript* caused Engels the greatest difficulty, and in editing *Capital*, III, he extensively rewrote and rearranged text and broke it up into more chapters many of which owe their titles to him. Whatever criticisms we may have of Engels's work, the text with which he struggled cannot be dismissed as lightly as Clarke does.

To begin with, it seems clear that the reason why Marx developed such an extensive discussion of the financial markets reflected, not his undeniable liability to get side-tracked, but a recognition of their importance in completing his analysis of the course of capitalist development. This is perhaps clearest in Chapter 27 of the Engels edition, 'The Role of Credit in Capitalist Production'. Here Marx famously argues that the development of joint stock companies represents the progressive socialisation of production within a capitalist framework as well as the 'transformation of the actual functioning capitalist into a mere manager, in charge of other people's capital, and of the capital owner into a mere owner, a mere money capitalist' (*C*III: 567). He seeks to situate the broader historical significance of this development:

> This is the transcendence of the capitalist mode of production within the capitalist mode of production, and hence a self-transcending contradiction [*die Aufhebung der kapitalistischen Produktionsweise innerhalb der kapitalistischen Produktionsweise selbst und daher ein sich selbst aufhebender Widerspruch*], which presents itself *prima facie* as a mere point of transition to a new form of production. It presents itself as such a contradiction even in appearance. It gives rise to monopoly in certain spheres and hence provokes state intervention. It reproduces a new financial aristocracy, a new kind of parasite in the guise of company promoters, speculators and merely nominal directors; an entire system of swindling and cheating with respect to the promotion of companies, issues of shares and share dealings. It is private production unchecked by private ownership. (*C*III: 569; translation modified)

The latter part of this paragraph makes it clear that (contrary to some social-democratic misinterpretations of Chapter 27) Marx is not proposing that capitalism can render its own overthrow unnecessary through gradually transcending itself. Like the tendency of the rate of profit to fall, the socialisation of production represented by the modern corporation is, as Marx puts it in the *Grundrisse*, a 'form in which advice is given it to be gone and to give room to a higher state of social production'. In the penultimate paragraph of the chapter Marx returns to the relationship between credit and the cycle:

> If the credit system [*Kreditwesen*] appears as the principal lever of over-production and excessive speculation in commerce, this is simply because the reproduction process, which is elastic by nature, is now forced to its most extreme limit; and this is because a great part of the social capital is applied by those who are not its owners and who therefore proceed quite unlike owners who, when they function themselves, anxiously weigh the limits of their private capital. This only goes to show how the valorisation of capital founded on the antithetical [*gegensätzlichen*] character of capitalist production permits actual free development only up to a certain point, which is constantly broken by the credit system. The credit system hence accelerates the material development of the productive forces and the creation of the world market, which is the historical task of the capitalist mode of production to bring to a certain level of development, as material foundation for the new form of production. At the same time, credit accelerates the violent outbreaks of this contradiction [*Widerspruchs*], crises, and with these the elements of dissolution of the old mode of production. (*CIII*: 572)

The more substantive analysis in Part 5 (as opposed to the running commentary on the parliamentary inquiries) largely unfolds with the framework set by this overall understanding of credit as simultaneously accelerating the accumulation process and ensuring that its interruptions in the form of crises take a particularly abrupt and brutal form. This is true, for example, of the discussion (previewed in Chapter 25 of the Engels edition but actually delivered in Chapter 29) of fictitious capital. This is made possible through the use of the interest rate as a means of calculation to capitalise any income, thereby creating markets for securities of different kinds that 'represent nothing but accumulated claims, legal titles, to future production', so that, 'with the development of interest bearing capital and the credit system, all capital seems to be duplicated, and at some points triplicated, by the various ways in which the same capital, or even the same claims, appear in various hands in different guises' (*CIII*: 599, 601).

But although Marx goes on to say that 'everything in this credit system appears in duplicate and triplicate, and is transformed into a mere phantom of the mind [*bloßes Hirngespinst*]' (*CIII*: 603), this analysis of fictitious capital—which, as the role of credit derivatives in precipitating the global economic and financial crisis in 2007-8 shows, has lost none of its relevance—does not imply that the money market is a pure world of illusion.[60] As we should expect from the overall construction of *Capital*, the 'apparent movement of capital' on the financial markets is part of its real functioning. This is particularly clear in the three successive chapters (30-32) Engels carves out from the manuscript under the shared title 'Money Capital and Real [*Wirkliches*] Capital'. Marx here seeks to trace the relationship between the cycles of money and productive capital, at once recognising their specificity and their interdependence. The latter is most strongly asserted in moments of panic and crisis, where the credit system breaks down. He explores here a theme already adumbrated in the *Grundrisse* and the 1859 *Contribution*:

It is the foundation of capitalist production that money confronts commodities as an autonomous form of value, or that exchange value must obtain an autonomous form in money, and this is only possible if one particular commodity becomes the material in whose value all other commodities are measured, this thereby becoming the universal commodity, the commodity *par excellence*, in contrast to all other commodities. This must show itself in two ways, particularly in developed capitalist countries, which replace money to a large extent by credit operations or by credit money. In times of pressure, when credit contracts or dries up altogether, money suddenly confronts commodities absolutely as the only means of payment and the true existence of value. Hence the general devaluation of commodities and the difficulty or even impossibility of transforming them into money, ie into their own purely fantastic form. Secondly, however, credit money is itself only money in so far as it absolutely represents real money to the sum of its nominal value. With the drain of gold, its convertibility into money

---

60 Marxist studies of derivatives include Dick Bryan and Michael Rafferty, *Capitalism with Derivatives* (Basingstoke, 2006), and Tony Norfield, 'Derivatives and Capitalist Markets', *Historical Materialism*, 20.1 (2012). Jairus Banaji offers a suggestive discussion of Marx's concept of fictitious capital and its pertinence to both Britain's colonial opium trade and the crash of 2008: 'Seasons of Self-Delusion: Opium, Capitalism and the Financial Markets', *Historical Materialism*, 21.2 (2013).

becomes problematic, ie its identity with actual gold. Hence we get forcible measures, putting up the rate of interest, etc in order to guarantee the conditions of its convertibility. (*CIII*: 648-649)[61]

Marx subsequently says that this kind of breakdown of the credit system and the resulting flight to cash 'is a regular and necessary phase in the cycle of modern industry' (*CIII*: 708). When Marx returns to the subject of financial panics in *Capital*, I, Chapter 3, 'Money, or the Circulation of Commodities', he offers a vivid sketch of the collapse of credit and the desperate search of every individual capitalist for cash: 'As the hart pants after fresh water, so pants his soul after money the only wealth' (*CI*: 236; compare *G*: 621). But he also refers to 'that aspect of an industrial and commercial crisis which is known as a monetary crisis' (*CI*: 236). As Engels notes, this doesn't mean that all monetary crises are part of larger industrial and commercial crises (*CI*: 236 n 50). Marx emphasises elsewhere that 'a plethora of money capital as such does not necessarily signify overproduction, or even a lack of spheres of employment for capital' (*CIII*: 639). Nevertheless, it is clear the cycle of euphoria and panic made possible by the credit system plays an essential role in Marx's broader understanding of capitalist crises.[62]

**Beyond crises?**

None of the foregoing should suggest that *Capital* contains anything resembling a complete theory of crisis. The unfinished nature of the book is particularly evident in *Capital*, III, above all in Part 5. Nevertheless, it seems to me undeniable that, at successive levels of determination, a conception of capitalist crises is unfolded through *Capital*. This involves (i) the formal possibility of crises arising from the separation of purchase and sale inherent in the circulation of commodities and from the function of money as means of payment; (ii) the interaction between the business cycle and fluctuations in the size of the industrial reserve army and the rate of wages; (iii) the role of the turnover of fixed capital in regulating the length of the business cycle;

---

61  It is one of the strengths of Harvey's outstanding discussion of money and credit in *The Limits to Capital* that he focuses on this 'antagonism between the financial system and its monetary base' (p326): see Harvey, chs 9 and 10.

62  See the detailed discussion of the monetary and financial dimensions of crises in Itoh and Lapavitsas, *Political Economy of Money and Banking*, ch 5, which follows Engels in distinguishing 'between two kinds of monetary crisis: those which form a particular phase of a general industrial and commercial crisis (type 1) and those which appear independently of a general industrial and commercial crisis (type 2)', p124.

(iv) the possibility of disruption inherent in the conditions of exchange between the two main departments of production required for reproduction; (v) the interplay between the tendency of the rate of profit to fall and its countertendencies; and (vi) the function of the cycle of bubble and panic in the financial markets in both, during booms, accelerating the accumulation process and, during crises, effecting the destruction of capital required to restore the rate of profit to a level permitting further expansion.

This would seem to support Ernest Mandel's argument that Marx has a multi-causal theory of capitalist development:

> In fact, any single-factor assumption is clearly opposed to the notion of the capitalist mode of production as a dynamic totality in which the interplay of *all* the basic laws of development is necessary in order to produce any particular outcome. This notion means that up to a certain point *all* the basic variables of this mode of production can partially and periodically perform the role of autonomous variables—naturally not to the point of complete independence, but in an interplay constantly articulated through the laws of development of the whole capitalist mode of production. These variables include the following central variables: the organic composition of capital...distribution of constant capital between fixed and circulating capital...the development of the rate of surplus value; the development of the rate of accumulation...the development of the turnover time of capital; and the relations of exchange between the two Departments.[63]

Mandel is quite right to stress the multiplicity of determinations involved in Marx's conception of crisis. But his own analyses of capitalist development suffer from a failure to specify the relative causal weight of his different 'variables' and therefore to render them open to *ad hoc* adjustment to avoid empirical refutation.[64] We should recall that Marx's own account of his method of rising from the abstract to the concrete involves conceiving the concrete as 'the *concentration* of many determinations, hence unity of the diverse' (*G*: 101; italics added). Marx uses the same term 'concentration' repeatedly in his characterisations of 'world market crises'. Concentration implies that 'the unity of the diverse' has a

63  Ernest Mandel, *Late Capitalism* (London, 1975), p39; see more generally the impressive discussion of Marxist theories of crisis in ch 1.
64  See Alex Callinicos, *Trotskyism* (Buckingham, 1990), pp42-44, and Chris Harman, 'Mandel's *Late Capitalism*', *International Socialism*, 2.1 (1978), http://www.marxists.org/archive/harman/1978/07/mandel.html

specific structure. So, to return to my own list of the determinations of crisis (coincidentally, like Mandel's variables, numbering six), they have different explanatory status. The formal possibilities of crisis (i) and the conditions of exchange between the two departments (iv) are *enabling* rather than playing a directly causal role. The interrelated fluctuations of wages and the industrial reserve army (ii) and the turnover of fixed capital (iii) are *conditioning* factors. The *causality* of crisis for Marx centres on the interplay between the tendency of the rate of profit to fall and the movements of capital on the money market, as I have tried to demonstrate in the preceding section.

This interpretation bears some resemblance to Harvey's suggestion that Marx's 'exposition of the law of falling profits' is 'a "first-cut" statement of his theory of crisis formation under capitalism', with 'a "second-cut" theory of crisis' arising from his analysis of money and credit and offering 'a more integrated view of the relation between financial phenomena and the dynamics of production'. Harvey adds to this his own '"third-cut" theory', the famous 'spatial fix' arising from capital's efforts to escape the infernal cycles of overaccumulation and devaluation by shifting the geographical locus of investment.[65] Whatever its strengths, this argument underplays the tightness of the relationship between the tendency of the rate of profit to fall and the financial cycle that Marx posits in *Capital*, III. No doubt this reflects Harvey's view that 'Marx's falling rate of profit argument is not particularly well honed or rigorously defined even as a purely theoretical argument'; the (in my view) negative consequence of this failure fully to grasp the logic of Marx's theory can be seen in Harvey's more recent espousal of an explanation of crises arising from the possibility of 'blockages' emerging in the different circuits of capital that (to put it charitably) embraces the explanatory looseness already implied in Mandel's version of a multi-causal theory of crisis.[66]

The interpretation of Marx's conception of crises offered in this chapter allows us to put in perspective the claims that various commentators have made that he later retreated from it. On the basis of his own contestable critique of Marx's theory of the tendency of the rate of profit to fall, Michael Heinrich argues that, in revising the *1861-63 Manuscript* in the 1870s, 'presumably, Marx was plagued by considerable doubts

65 Harvey, *Limits to Capital*, pp191, 326, 425.
66 Harvey, *Limits to Capital*, p181. See, for Harvey's more recent views, *The Enigma of Capital and the Crises of Capitalism* (London, 2010), and, for a critique, Joseph Choonara, 'Decoding Capitalism', *International Socialism*, 2.129 (2011).

concerning the law of the rate of profit'.[67] The adverb 'presumably' indicates that Heinrich is riffing; the only evidence he offers—that in 1875 Marx wrote a draft exploring the mathematics of the relationship between the rate of surplus value and the rate of profit—rather suggests his continuing commitment to the theory. As we saw in chapter 1, Heinrich is certainly right when he argues that Marx was preoccupied in this period with deepening his understanding of the credit system. The American journalist John Swinton quotes Marx as saying in an interview in 1878 that *Capital* 'was but a fragment, a single part of a work in three parts, two of the parts being yet unpublished, the full trilogy being "Land", "Capital", "Credit", the last part, he said, being largely illustrated from the United States, where credit has had such an amazing development' (*CW*24: 584). If accurately reported, this remark shows Marx's continual uncertainty about the overall architecture of his critique of political economy; but his interest in deepening his understanding of the financial markets in no way contradicts his commitment to the tendency of the rate of profit to fall given, as we have seen, the role played by bubbles and panics in the interaction of the tendency and its countertendencies.

Clarke is certainly completely mistaken when he asserts that 'the theory of crises plays a rapidly diminishing role in Marx's work after 1868, to be replaced by an emphasis on the secular tendencies of capital accumulation'.[68] Thus in an as yet unpublished notebook dating from the late 1860s (B113), Marx took extensive excerpts from press coverage of the crisis of 1866, focusing especially on the precipitating event, the collapse of the discount house Overend, Gurney & Co, and the speculation and scams driving the preceding boom in railway shares. This study was probably intended to contribute to his revision of *Capital*, III.[69] Marx's

---

67  Heinrich, 'Crisis Theory, the Law of the Tendency of the Profit Rate to Fall, and Marx's Studies in the 1870s'. Heinrich also argues that Marx's treatment of financial markets in *Capital*, III, Part 5, is limited by a failure to take into account the classic analysis of the role of the Bank of England as lender of last resort during financial panics by Walter Bagehot in *Lombard Street*. Bagehot's book was published in 1873, in response to the 1866 crisis, so Marx couldn't have discussed it in the *1863-65 Manuscript*. But he is clear enough that 'the central bank is the pivot of the credit system' (*C*III: 706), and critically discusses the Bank's response to the panics of 1847 and 1857 both in Part 5 and in his earlier journalism of the 1850s.

68  Clarke, *Marx's Theory of Crisis*, p245.

69  João Antonio de Paula, Hugo E A da Gama Cerqueira, Alexandre Mendes Cunha, Carlos Eduardo Suprinyak, Leonardo Gomes de Deus, and Eduardo da Motta e Albuquerque, 'Notes on a Crisis: The *Exzerpthefte* and Marx's Method of Research and Composition', *Review of Radical Political Economics*, 45:2 (2013). See, on the collapse of Overend, Gurney, David Kynaston, *The City of London*, Volume I (London, 1994), pp235-243.

continuing preoccupation with crises is shown, for example, in a letter to Engels of 31 May 1873 where he confesses his hope 'to determine mathematically the principal laws governing crises', though he notes their friend Samuel Moore (one of the 'authorities' to whom Marx deferred on scientific questions) doubted that this was possible (*CW*44: 504). And he writes to Pyotr Lavrov on 18 June 1875: 'One truly remarkable phenomenon is the decrease in the number of years between general crises. I have always regarded that number, not as a constant, but as a decreasing magnitude: what is pleasing, however, is that the signs of its decrease are so palpable as to augur ill for the survival of the bourgeois world' (*CW*45: 78). Nearly four years later, in explaining to another Russian correspondent, Nikolai Danielson, why he had yet to complete *Capital*, he writes (10 April 1879):

> I should under no circumstances have published the second volume before the present English industrial crisis had reached its climax. The phenomena are this time singular, in many respects different from what they were in the past, and this—quite apart from other modifying circumstances—is easily accounted for by the fact that never before the *English crisis was preceded* [sic] by tremendous and now already 5 years lasting crisis in the *United States, South America, Germany, Austria*, etc.
>
> It is therefore necessary to watch the present course of things until their maturity before you can 'consume' them 'productively', I mean '*theoretically*'. (*CW*45: 354)[70]

So, to the end of Marx's career, he continued to attend both theoretically and empirically to the pattern of crises that he was among the first to identify as inherent in capitalist development. Their significance lay in part in how they concentrated and summarised all the contradictions of the capitalist mode of production, and in part because they announced that 'the survival of the bourgeois world' could not be taken for granted. Though they would not eventuate in the economic breakdown of the system, their occurrence would, Marx believed, contribute to its eventual overthrow. This understanding of crisis and revolution is an essential part of the intellectual legacy that Marx left in *Capital*.

---

70  Here, as elsewhere in Marx's and Engels's correspondence, the 'second volume' refers to what was envisaged as the publication of Books II (circulation) and III (the process as a whole) in a single volume. The sheer scale and complexity of the manuscripts that Engels discovered after Marx's death forced him eventually to publish these as separate volumes.

7

# Today

## The modernity of *Capital*

The most boring criticism of Marx—repeated, for instance, in Jonathan Sperber's otherwise scholarly new biography—is that he is an obsolete 19th century thinker grappling with problems of no relevance to the present.[1] As we have seen, Marx strove to make *Capital* a study of capitalism as a global system, and not merely a portrait of the mid-Victorian British economy. This is reflected, for example, in his efforts in the 1870s to ensure *Capital*, II and III, covered the United States and Russia. We can see this effort to establish the generality of the object of *Capital* in the French edition of Volume I. Whereas in the German edition Marx concludes Chapter 26, 'The Secret of Primitive Accumulation', by saying that the expropriation of the peasantry took its 'classic form [*klassische Form*]' in England (CI: 876), in the French he writes:

> Still it is only accomplished in a radical form in England: this country necessarily plays the leading role in our inquiry. But the other countries of western Europe participate in the same movement, although depending on the environment it changes local colour, or tightens into a narrower circle, or presents a less strongly pronounced character, or follows a different order of succession.[2]

Marx's striving to diversify the empirical extension of *Capital* underlines that its object is an abstract one, 'the capitalist mode of production and the relations of production and forms of intercourse (*Verkehrsverhältnisse*)' (CI: 90).[3] What does this imply for efforts to maintain the

1   Jonathan Sperber, *Karl Marx: A Nineteenth Century Life* (New York, 2013). See the assessment of this book by another Marx biographer, David McLellan: http://marxandphilosophy.org.uk/reviewofbooks/reviews/2013/803
2   Karl Marx, *Le Capital, Livre I* (2 vols, Paris, 1985), II, p169. See, on the generality and global character of the object of *Capital*, Lucia Pradella, *L'attualità del Capitale: Accumulazione e impoverimento nel capitalismo globale* (Padua, 2010), and 'Imperialism and Capitalist Development in Marx's *Capital*', *Historical Materialism*, 21.2 (2013).
3   See the discussion in Louis Althusser, 'On Theoretical Work', in *Philosophy and the*

7

actuality of *Capital*? As we saw in chapter 1, Marx told Kugelmann (28 December 1862) that the manuscript he was then working on was 'the quintessence (together with the first part [ie the 1859 *Contribution*])' of his critique of political economy, 'and the development of the sequel (with the exception, perhaps, of the relationship between the various forms of state and the various economic structures of society) could easily be pursued by others on the basis thus provided' (*CW*41: 435). This implies that 'others' continuing *Capital* would involve writing the books of Marx's original 1858-9 plan that he never got round to—on the state, international trade, and the world market and crises. But this wasn't the direction actually taken. Instead to a very large degree the Marxists of both the Second and Third Internationals concentrated on developing an analysis of the new forms taken by capitalist development as a result of what Rudolph Hilferding called the increasing 'organisation' of capitalism—in other words, as a result of the concentration and centralisation of capital, the growth in the size of the individual units of capital and the development of more complex forms of economic coordination, either between sectors (for example, banks and industrial firms) or between private capital and the state. This focus didn't preclude more abstract theoretical developments—thus Hilferding himself paid close attention in *Finance Capital* to integrating an analysis of the financial markets into Marx's value theory. And there were of course debates about *Capital*—above all that provoked by Rosa Luxemburg's critique of the reproduction schemes in Volume II. But informing all this was the effort to understand the current phase of capitalist development; the name the Marxists of the early 20th century gave it—imperialism—underlines the political urgency of this task.[4]

The collective result of these efforts is one of the intellectual glories of the Marxist tradition. Regrettably Michael Heinrich seems to cast it all into a ragbag 'traditional "worldview" Marxism (*Weltanschauungsmarxismus*)' that distorts the meaning of *Capital*; thus he ignores, for example, the theoretical sophistication displayed by thinkers such as Hilferding, Luxemburg, Bukharin, Preobrazhensky, and Grossman.[5] The

---

*Spontaneous Philosophy of the Scientists and Other Essays* (Gregory Elliott, ed; London, 1990).

4   See Alex Callinicos, *Imperialism and Global Political Economy* (Cambridge, 2007), ch 1, and, for an excellent critical survey of early 20th century Marxist political economy, M C Howard and J E King, *A History of Marxian Economics* (2 vols, London, 1989 and 1992), I.

5   Michael Heinrich, *An Introduction to the Three Volumes of Karl Marx's Capital* (New York, 2012), p10. For a much more differentiated view of the development of Marxism, see John Molyneux, *What is the Real Marxist Tradition?* (London, 1985), http://www.marxisme.dk/arkiv/molyneux/realmarx/.

approach they took can be seen as one way of continuing *Capital*, of carrying on the method of 'rising from the abstract to the concrete', by distinguishing different phases of capitalist development and attempting to identify their specific features.[6] But it came at a price. The object of *Capital* tended to be conceived as that of one of these phases of capitalist development—'classical' or 'competitive' capitalism. Apart from misrepresenting how Marx understood his project, this could have negative effects on theorisations of imperialism by, for example, implying that, if 19th century capitalism was 'competitive', 20th century 'monopoly capitalism' had transcended the competition between capitals. Given this premiss, the rejection of Marx's value theory by the *Monthly Review* school made some sense.[7]

This isn't to say that there weren't serious problems to address. One of Bukharin's great achievements was to grasp that the culmination of the tendency for the concentration and centralisation was not, as Karl Kautsky thought, 'ultra-imperialism', in other words the global integration of capital transcending national conflicts, but rather state capitalism, in other words the fusion of private capital in the nation state. But what did this imply for the law of value and what Marx saw as capitalism's inherent liability to crises? Bukharin's answer to the latter question— that the greater the development of state capitalism, the weaker the purely economic contradictions of the system—was badly mistaken.[8] In attempting to grasp the nature and dynamics of Stalinism in Russia, Tony Cliff used the concept of state capitalism more successfully to conceptualise the fusion of economic and political power in the hands of the *nomenklatura* and the resulting separation of the workers from the means of production, but he argued that the law of value continued to operate through the imperative to accumulate imposed by military competition between the Soviet Union and the Western imperialist powers.[9]

---

6   For a defence of this method, see Alex Callinicos, 'Periodizing Capitalism and Analysing Imperialism: Classical Marxism and Capitalist Evolution', in Robert Albritton et al, eds, *Phases of Capitalist Development* (Basingstoke, 2001).

7   Paul A Baran and Paul M Sweezy, *Monopoly Capital* (Harmondsworth, 1968), ch 1.

8   See Callinicos, *Imperialism and Global Political Economy*, pp53-61.

9   See Tony Cliff, *The Nature of Stalinist Russia*, in *Selected Writings* (3 vols, London, 2003), III, ch 7, and, for discussions of the operation of the law of value in the USSR, Chris Harman, 'The Inconsistencies of Ernest Mandel', *International Socialism*, 1.41 (1969-70), http://www.marxists.org/history/etol/writers/harman/1969/12/mandel.htm, Peter Binns, 'The Theory of State Capitalism', *International Socialism*, 1.74 (1975), http://www.marxists.org/history/etol/writers/binns/1975/01/statecap.htm, and Alex Callinicos, 'Wage Labour and State Capitalism', *International Socialism*, 2.12 (1981), http://www.marxists.org/history/etol/writers/callinicos/1981/xx/wagelab-statecap.html.

Both Bukharin and Cliff located competition at the global level. As the 20th century wore on, it became clear that this continued to take economic as well as geopolitical forms. Indeed, one way of thinking about globalisation is that it represents the powerful reassertion of a transnational logic of competitive accumulation to which states and the capitals that in the mid-20th century had been able to gain powerful national perches have had painfully to adapt.[10] The combination of these transformations and of the new era of economic instability that followed the collapse of the long postwar boom in the early 1970s allows us to read *Capital* with fresh eyes.

For example, one feature of the Keynesian economic policy regime that prevailed roughly speaking from the end of the Second World War till the mid-1970s was what neoclassical economists tend to call, in a fine piece of persuasive definition, 'financial repression'. In other words, the Great Depression of the 1930s prompted states to impose tight controls over financial markets and the international mobility of capital. The return of economic instability in the late 1960s and early 1970s was partly a consequence of capital's growing success in throwing off this straitjacket (through, for example, the development of the offshore euro-dollar market), and the neoliberal economic policy regime that took shape during the 1980s notoriously involved the deregulation of financial markets that were becoming increasingly transnationally integrated.[11] As a result, we live in an economic world that in some respects is closer to the one inhabited by Marx 150 years ago than was that of the mid-20th century. Thus the cycle of financial bubble and panic that he studied so closely has come in the neoliberal era to regulate the world economy, with the devastating effects we witnessed in the 2007-8 crash. Indeed, the interplay between the tendency of the rate of profit to fall and this financial cycle that, as I argued in chapter 6, formed the focus of Marx's understanding of crises is of very direct relevance to us as we grapple with the dynamics of the crash and of the slump and recovery that followed it.

This doesn't mean, of course, that the patterns of 21st century crisis are exactly the same as those. First, the process of concentration and

10   See the analysis of these transformations in Chris Harman, *Zombie Capitalism: Global Crisis and the Relevance of Marx* (London, 2009), Parts Two and Three.
11   See, for example, Eric Helleiner, *States and the Reemergence of Global Finance* (Ithaca, 1994), Peter Gowan, *The Global Gamble: Washington's Faustian Bid for World Dominance* (London, 1999), Leo Panitch and Sam Gindin, *The Making of Global Capitalism: The Political Economy of American Empire* (London, 2012), and Costas Lapavitsas, *Profiting without Producing: How Finance Exploits Us All* (London, 2013).

centralisation of capital that led to the structural changes studied by Hilferding and his contemporaries has continued into the neoliberal era. Peter Nolan writes:

> During the three decades of capitalist globalisation, industrial concentration occurred in almost every sector. Alongside a huge increase in global output, the number of leading firms in most industrial sectors shrank and the degree of global industrial concentration increased greatly. The most visible part consists of well known firms with superior technologies and powerful brands. These constitute the 'system integrators' or 'organising brains' at the apex of extended value chains... By the early 2000s, within the high value-added, high-technology and strongly branded segments of global markets, which serve mainly the middle- and upper-income earners who control the bulk of the world's purchasing power, a veritable 'law' had come into play: a handful of giant firms, the 'systems integrators', occupied upwards of 50 percent of the whole global market.[12]

Secondly, the contemporary financial system is decisively shaped by the role played by the state—and particularly by the central banks, reflecting the fact that the dominant form of money is what Costas Lapavitsas calls 'a peculiar hybrid'—credit money generated through the banking system that is underpinned by the authority of the state and by its capacity to appropriate value through taxation. Partly in consequence, but also because of the structural changes that Lapavitsas argues are at the heart of contemporary financialisation, notably the ability of industrial and commercial firms to raise money directly on the financial markets through issuing bonds and commercial paper and consequently the pressure on banks to find other sources of profit than loans to industry, for example by trading on their own behalf and lending to private households:

> the overaccumulation of capital in mature capitalism produces very different financial phenomena to those of Marx's time. Gone is the inability of productive capitalists to honour bills of exchange, gone is also the corresponding impact on relatively small banks specialising in the discount of bills. Overaccumulation now entails vast monetary phenomena, including stock market booms and busts, expanded bank lending that leads to mass insolvency, and state manipulation of interest rates in the money market.[13]

---

12  Peter Nolan, *Is China Buying the World?* (Cambridge, 2012), p17.

13  Lapavitsas, *Profiting without Producing*, pp86, 271. Lapavitsas's book is a most impressive analysis of contemporary financialisation that contains much of value on the Marxist theory of money and finance. Its main weakness lies in his claim that financial profit derives not just from the appropriation of surplus value created in production but also

Thus the global economic and financial crisis that developed in 2007-8 represented a very specific form of the interaction between the tendency of the rate of profit to fall and the financial cycle that is at the heart of Marx's own mature understanding of crises. The neoliberal era saw only a partial reversal of the chronic problems of profitability that had developed in the 1960s: although the rate of exploitation was forced up and a considerable restructuring of capital took place, these were not on a sufficient scale to restore the rate of profit to the levels prevailing during the Long Boom of the 1960s and 1970s. Consequently growth in the advanced economies came to depend increasingly on the development of financial bubbles, notably during the stock-market boom of the late 1990s and the housing bubble of the mid-2000s. Higher asset prices encouraged households to borrow and spend, thereby sustaining effective demand. The collapse of the stock-market bubble in 2000-1 caused only a relatively mild recession centred on the United States, but the way in which the bulk of the Western banking system became sucked into feeding the housing bubble in the US, Britain, and parts of the eurozone precipitated a devastating crisis. The weak recovery in the US and the European Union from the Great Recession of 2008-9 is marked by the deep damage caused to the banking system by the crash (most visible in the eurozone), but has also exposed the underlying weakness of capital accumulation in the advanced capitalist countries.[14]

Nevertheless, the closer one studies Marx's economic writings the greater their actuality seems. This is underlined by the recent appearance

from 'expropriating the income and the money stocks of others through the operations of the financial system' (p145). It is true that, as Lapavitsas points out, Marx noted that 'the working class is swindled in this form too [ie, through 'the renting of houses, etc for individual consumption'], and to an enormous extent; but it is equally exploited by the petty trader who supplies the worker with means of subsistence. But this is a secondary exploitation, which proceeds alongside the original exploitation that takes place directly within the production process itself' (*CIII*: 745). Lapavitsas seems to think of 'financial appropriation' as occurring on a much larger scale than Marx envisages here. Properly to assess this claim would require locating it with respect to Marx's value theory and more particularly the reproduction of labour power (since mortgages, credit cards and the like allow workers to borrow in order to maintain a certain level of consumption). But Lapavitsas completely fails to meet this requirement, despite, for example, Ben Fine's critique of an earlier version of his argument: 'Locating Financialization', *Historical Materialism*, 18 (2010). See also the critical assessments from Tony Norfield, 'Capitalist Production Good, Capital Finance Bad', 6 January 2014, http://economicsofimperialism. blogspot.co.uk/2014/01/capitalist-production-good-capitalist.html, and Joseph Choonara, 'Financial Times', *International Socialism*, 2.142 (2014).

14 Alex Callinicos, *Bonfire of Illusions* (Cambridge, 2010), and 'Contradictions of Austerity', *Cambridge Journal of Economics*, 36 (2012). My understanding of the development of the crisis is heavily indebted to Robert Brenner, *The Boom and the Bubble* (London, 2002).

of a massive study of inequalities in income and wealth by the French economist Thomas Piketty entitled *Capital in the 21st Century*. Although Piketty shows only a limited understanding of Marx's own theory, the title he gives his book is clearly intended to resonate with *Capital*. His main findings—that economic inequality is returning to levels last seen in the early 20th century and that, 'if...the rate of return on capital remains significantly above the growth rate for a significant period of time...then the risk of divergence in the distribution of wealth is very high'—confirm the necessity of a critique of political economy.[15] I have more to say about Marx's writing on labour in the following section, but it is worth stressing here that the process of globalisation would have come as little surprise to him. Already in the *Grundrisse* Marx writes: 'The tendency to create the *world market* is directly given in the concept of capital itself. Every limit appears as a barrier to be overcome' (*G*: 408). This strong sense of the global character of capital comes over very clearly in the earliest part of the manuscript, when Marx discusses the American economist Henry Carey, 'the only original economist among the North Americans'. Carey looks at capitalism from a global perspective—in a brilliant *bon mot* Marx says: 'Carey's generality is Yankee universality. France and China are equally close to him. Always the man who lives on the Pacific and the Atlantic'—in order to argue that the United States needs to protect its developing industries from British competition:

> with Carey the harmony of the bourgeois relations of production ends with the most complete disharmony of these relations on the grandest terrain where they appear, the world market, and in their grandest development, as the relations of producing nations. All the relations which appear harmonious to him within specific national boundaries or, in addition, in the abstract form of general relations of bourgeois society— eg concentration of capital, division of labour, wage labour etc—appear as disharmonious to him where they appear in their most developed form—in their world market form—as the internal relations which produce English domination on the world market, and which, as destructive influences, are the consequence of this domination. (*G*: 885, 886, 888)[16]

On the basis of the much greater development of his value theory in the *1861-63 Manuscript*, Marx is able to deepen his understanding of the relationship between capital and the world market:

---

15 Thomas Piketty, *Capital in the 21st Century* (Cambridge MA, 2014), p25.
16 In the Penguin edition of the *Grundrisse* of the fragment on Bastiat and Carey, the earliest part of the manuscript, is placed at the end.

If **surplus labour** or surplus-**value** were represented only in the national **surplus produce**, then the increase of value for the sake of value and therefore the **exaction of surplus labour** would be restricted by the limited, narrow circle of use-values in which the value of the [national] labour would be represented. But it is foreign trade which develops its [the surplus value's] real nature as value by developing the labour embodied in it as social labour which manifests itself in an unlimited range of different use-values, and this in fact gives meaning to abstract wealth...

But it is only foreign trade, the development of the market to a world market, which causes money to develop into world money and *abstract labour* into social labour. Abstract wealth, value, money, **hence** *abstract labour*, develop in the measure that concrete labour becomes a totality of different modes of labour embracing the world market. Capitalist production rests on the *value* or the transformation of the labour embodied in the product into social labour. But this is only [possible] on the basis of **foreign trade** and of the world market. This is at once the precondition and the result of capitalist production. (*CW*32: 387-388)

It's true that *Capital*, I, Chapter 24, when considering the accumulation of capital, Marx abstracts from national differences:

Here we take no account of the export trade, by means of which a nation can change articles of luxury into means of production or means of subsistence, and *vice versa*. In order to examine the object of our investigation in its integrity, free from all disturbing subsidiary circumstances, we must treat the whole world of trade as one nation, and assume that capitalist production is established everywhere and has taken possession of every branch of production. (*CI*: 727 n 2)

Lucia Pradella argues persuasively that this passage does not imply, as both Luxemburg and Lenin contended, that Marx is here restricting his analysis of accumulation and extended reproduction to 'a "closed national system"'; on the contrary, treating 'the whole word of trade as one nation' allows him to integrate into his analysis the increasing international mobility of both capital and labour already evident in the mid-19th century.[17] This interpretation is not contradicted by the restrictive assumptions

---

17  Pradella, 'Imperialism and Capitalist Development in Marx's *Capital*', pp122-125. In a stimulating essay, Cesare Luporini gives the same passage more significance than it merits, arguing that the assumption Marx makes here 'prevents Marx from explaining conceptually or systematically' the fact that capitalist development simultaneously involves both 'the constitution of a home market' and 'the "global system"', 'Le Politique

Marx makes in his analysis of extended reproduction, as this passage towards the end of the *1861-63 Manuscript* indicates:

> These relations [between departments I and II] could be determined precisely in an enclosed and isolated country. But *foreign trade* allows a part of the *surplus produce* which exists in the form of raw materials, semi-manufactures, accessory materials and machinery, to be converted into the form of *surplus produce* [XXII-1380] of another country, in which it exists in the form of consumable products. It is therefore necessary for capitalist production, which works according to the *measure* of its means of production, without regard to the *satisfaction of a definite given need...* With this the reproduction process is dependent not on the production of mutually complementary equivalents in the same country, but on the production of these same equivalents on foreign markets, on the power of absorption and degree of extension of the world market. This provides an *increased* possibility of non-correspondence, **hence** a possibility of crises. (*CW*34: 221)

Marx does seek in *Capital*, II, to demonstrate the possibility of extended reproduction without invoking foreign trade, but only to simplify the argument:

> Capitalist production never exists without foreign trade. If normal annual production on a given scale is presupposed [*unterstellt*], then it is also supposed [*unterstellt*] together with this that foreign trade replaces domestic articles only by those of other use or natural forms, without affecting value ratios, and therefore without either the value ratios in which the two categories, means of production and means of consumption, mutually exchange for one another, or the ratios between the constant capital, variable capital and surplus value into which the value of the product of each of these categories can be broken down. Bringing foreign trade into an analysis of the value of the product annually reproduced can therefore

---

et l'étatique: un ou deux critiques?', in Étienne Balibar, et al, *Marx et sa critique de la politique* (Paris, 1979), p104. But, as Pradella argues, Marx in *Capital*, I, Part 8, 'analyses the state's fundamental role in generating the capitalist relation, both nationally and internationally, and in reproducing the social order as a whole', 'Imperialism and Capitalist Development in Marx's *Capital'*, p130. Marx didn't develop a more generalised theorisation of this role not because of some conceptual obstacle, but as a result of his more mundane failure ever to write the account of 'the relationship between the various forms of state and the various economic structures of society' he had presumably intended for Book 4 of his original plan. For an extensive discussion of the theoretical issues involved (which is not, as Pradella believes, inconsistent with her argument), see Callinicos, *Imperialism and Global Political Economy*, ch 2.

only confuse things, without supplying any new factor either to the problem or to its solution. (*CII*: 546)

So even when abstracting for specific analytical reasons from foreign trade Marx recognises the indispensable role it plays in capitalist development. And, before the passage from *Capital*, I, cited above, he argues in Chapter 22 that countries where the intensity of labour is relatively high will obtain more value for their products than those where it is low. Moreover, 'the law of value is yet more modified by the fact that, on the world market, national labour which is more productive also counts as more intensive, as long as the more productive nation is not compelled by competition to lower the selling price of its commodities to the level of their value' (*CI*: 702).[18] All this makes it clear how Marx conceives the object of *Capital*, the capitalist mode of production, as developing a global system.

Of course, the formation of this system is, as we have just seen, both 'the precondition and the result of capitalist production'. In the great chapter 'The Genesis of the Industrial Capitalist' in *Capital*, I, Marx shows how the primitive accumulation of capital unfolds amid the colonial conquests and interstate wars of the early modern era. But this supplies the conditions for the dominance of the capitalist mode of production proper, which is what drives the intensive development of the world market that he is trying to conceptualise in the passages cited above:

The development of capital does not begin with the creation of the world, it does not begin *ab ovo* [from the beginning]. Only in the 16th and 17th centuries does it in fact begin to be something which dominates the world and seizes hold of the whole economic formation of society. This is its infancy... The capitalist mode of production in fact only attains a full development with *large-scale industry*, and therefore dates in its totality from the last third of the 18th century (even if it was still only sporadically developed). (*CW*34: 327)

## The relationality of capital

Throughout this book I have defended an interpretation of *Capital* that emphasises Marx's understanding of the capitalist mode of production

---

18  For more on the law of value and international trade, see Anwar Shaikh, 'Foreign Trade and the Law of Value', *Science & Society*, 43:3 (1979) and 44:1 (1980), and Guglielmo Carchedi, *Frontiers of Political Economy* (London, 1991), chs 6 and 7.

as a set of relations constituted by what I call in chapter 4 the two separations—that of workers from the means of production, giving rise to the exploitation of wage labour by capital, and that between capitals, from which arises their competitive struggle. This has involved showing in chapters 2 and 3 how Marx reconstructs the labour theory of value that he had inherited from Ricardo in order to allow him to conceptualise these two separations. Thus the transformation of values into prices of production he develops in the *1861-63 Manuscript* allows him to focus on the first separation in *Capital*, I, before beginning fully to confront the effects of the second in *Capital*, III (though, as we also saw in chapter 3, Marx has to take limited but important account of competition in Volume I when developing his analysis of differential profit and conceptualising the concentration and centralisation of capital). What he takes from Hegel is above all the model of a science that makes this handling of the two separations possible by moving from abstract to concrete through the progressive introduction of ever more complex determinations, though this movement assumes a radically different form from the inwardising (*Erinnerung*) of the diverse shapes of the concept in the *Science of Logic*. The three volumes of *Capital* trace a process of increasing externalisation, as the circulation of capital obscures the extraction of surplus value in production and the fragmentation of surplus value as it is distributed within the capitalist class encourages economic actors to accept partial representations of the totality that can nevertheless effectively orient their calculations and practice. The conception of crises whose development we followed in chapter 6 moves towards (though it never quite achieves) the unity of the total process (*Gesamtprozeß*) that informs this movement, as the growing weight of dead compared to living labour in production finds expression in the tendency of the rate of profit to fall that in turn interacts with the cycle of boom and bust in the financial markets.

The first separation (capital versus wage labour) thus has explanatory priority over the second (competition between 'many capitals'), but what emerges from Marx's constant reformulation of his categories across successive manuscripts is that both are necessary in order to grasp the laws of motion of capitalism. In the flood of interpretations of *Capital* that emerged from the intellectual and political radicalisation of the 1960s and 1970s there was a tendency—encouraged by the ambivalence that, as we have seen, Marx himself displayed—to treat competition as an epiphenomenon of the fundamental antagonism between capital and labour. This was true, for example, of the Italian workerists.[19] Now, as I have already noted in chapter 5, the argument has shifted as sections of the intellectual left seek to write wage labour out of the capital relation. One connection between the debates of the 1960s and 1970s is provided by how the famous 'Fragment on Machines' in the *Grundrisse* has been appropriated. This passage in Marx's extended discussion of fixed capital fascinated the workerists.[20] Marx writes here about:

> the tendency of capital to give production a scientific character; direct labour [is] reduced to a mere moment of this process. As with the transformation of value into capital, so does it appear in the further development of capital, that it presupposes a certain given historical development of the productive forces on one side—science too [is] among these productive forces—and, on the other, drives and forces them further onwards. (*G*: 699)

Marx later elaborates on this:

> The development of fixed capital indicates to what degree general social knowledge has become a *direct force of production*, and to what degree, hence, the conditions of the process of social life itself have come under the control of the **general intellect** and been transformed in accordance with it. To what degree the powers of social production have been produced, not only in the form of knowledge, but also as immediate organs of social practice, of the real life process. (*G*: 707)

This passage is frequently linked to a preceding one:

> The *theft of alien labour time, on which the present wealth is based*, appears a miserable foundation in face of this new one, created by large-scale industry itself. As soon as labour in the direct form has ceased to be the great well-spring of wealth, labour time ceases and must cease to be its measure, and hence exchange value [must cease to be the measure] of use value. The *surplus labour of the mass* has ceased to be the condition for the development of general wealth, just as the *non-labour of the few*, for the development of the general powers of the human head.

---

19  See, for a lucid exposition of the workerist interpretation of Marx, Harry Cleaver, *Reading Capital Politically* (Brighton, 1979), and, for two versions of a critique of Toni Negri's version of workerism, Alex Callinicos, *The Resources of Critique* (Cambridge, 2006), ch 4, and 'Antonio Negri and the Temptation of Ontology', in Timothy Murphy and Abdul-Karim Mustapha, eds, *Antonio Negri: Revolution in Theory* (London, 2007).

20  See especially Toni Negri, 'Crisis of the Planner State: Communism and Revolutionary Organisation', in *Revolution Retrieved* (London, 1988), pp112-118.

With that, production based on exchange value breaks down, and the direct, material production process is stripped of the form of penury and antithesis. (*G*: 705-706)

Large intellectual castles have been erected on the foundations of these rather speculative remarks. For example, Michael Hardt and Toni Negri appeal to 'the Marxian concept of "general intellect"' to justify what they claim to be 'the recent transformations of productive labour and its tendency to become increasingly immaterial. The central role previously occupied by the labour power of mass factory workers in the production of surplus value is today increasingly filled by intellectual, immaterial, and communicative labour power'.[21] The growth of 'immaterial labour' in particular breaks down the boundary between work and personal life. Accordingly, 'we have to revise Marx's notion of the relation between labour and value in capitalist production': 'labour and value have become biopolitical in the sense that living and producing tend to be indistinguishable'.[22] Slavoj Žižek is rather more circumspect, noting that 'the entire discussion of the "general intellect" from the *Grundrisse* belongs to an unpublished fragmentary manuscript—it is an experimental line of development which Marx immediately afterwards discarded, since he quickly saw that it is ultimately incompatible with his new starting point, the analysis of commodities, which focuses on the commodity as a social phenomenon'. But then he throws caution to the winds: 'The problem is that the rise of "intellectual labour" (scientific knowledge as well as practical *savoir faire*) to a hegemonic position (the "general intellect") undermines the standard notion of exploitation, since it is no longer labour time which serves as the source and ultimate measure of value'.[23]

These extrapolations offer a classic illustration of the danger of making the *Grundrisse* the template of Marx's understanding of capitalism rather than a relatively early stage in an extended and complex process of theoretical development. Michael Heinrich is entirely right when he says of the 'Fragment on Machines':

These lines have often been quoted, but without regard for how insufficiently secure the categorical foundations of the *Grundrisse* are. The distinction between concrete and abstract labour, which Marx refers to in *Capital* as 'crucial to an understanding of political economy', is not at

21  Michael Hardt and Toni Negri, *Empire* (Cambridge MA, 2000), p29.
22  Michael Hardt and Toni Negri, *Multitude* (London, 2004), pp146, 148.
23  Slavoj Žižek, *Living in the End Times* (London, 2010), pp192 n 18, 241.

all present in the *Grundrisse*. And in *Capital*, 'labour in the immediate form' is also not the source of wealth. The sources of material wealth are concrete, useful labour and nature. The social substance of wealth or value in capitalism is abstract labour, whereby it does not matter whether this abstract labour can be traced back to labour power expended in the process of production, or to the transfer of value of used means of production. If abstract labour remains the substance of value, then it is not clear why labour time can no longer be its intrinsic measure, and it's not clear why 'production based on exchange value' should necessarily collapse.[24]

Indeed the whole problematic of 'immaterial labour' rests on a misunderstanding of Marx's concept of abstract social labour. Hardt and Negri rely in effect on a substantialist conception of value: if labour has now become 'immaterial' as result of the diminishing weight of manufacturing industry in the advanced capitalist economies, this implies that the kind of labour that Marx had in mind was material—manual labour producing material goods. But this rests on a confusion of abstract and concrete labour. For Marx, *all* labour under capitalism is immaterial insomuch as the different concrete forms of useful labour are, through the processes that we discussed in chapter 4, rendered commensurable and reduced to quantities of abstract social labour. Value, Marx says, has 'a fantastic objectivity [*phantastische Gegenständlichkeit*]—objectivity of abstract human labour, *objective form* of abstract human labour,' (*MEGA²* II/6: 32), 'a ghostly objectivity [*gespenstige Gegenständlichkeit*]' (*CI*: 128; translation modified), arising from the social relations prevailing among producers and their products. It is not some quantity inhering in particular types of physical labour.

Marx's discussion of productive and unproductive labour involves various hesitations and shifts, though he is consistent in saying: '*Productive labour*...is labour which—in the system of capitalist production—produces *surplus value* for its **employer** or which converts the objective conditions of labour into capital, and their owners into capitalists, hence, labour which produces its own product as capital' (*CW*34: 131). But Marx is in general

---

24 Michael Heinrich, 'Crisis Theory, the Law of the Tendency of the Profit Rate to Fall, and Marx's Studies of the 1870s', *Monthly Review*, 64:11 (2013), http://monthlyreview. org/2013/04/01/crisis-theory-the-law-of-the-tendency-of-the-profit-rate-to-fall-and-marxs-studies-in-the-1870s. Tony Smith offers a more sympathetic treatment of the problematic of the general intellect that is, however, distinguished by its in-depth understanding of Marx's value theory and careful analysis of contemporary economic trends: 'The "General Intellect" in the *Grundrisse* and Beyond', *Historical Materialism*, 21.4 (2013).

opposed to identifying productive labour with either manual labour or the production of material goods. For example, in *Capital*, II, he includes the transport industry under productive capital, even though it has no identifiable physical output:

> what the transport industry sells is the actual change of place. The useful effect produced is inseparably connected with the transport process, ie the production process specific to the transport industry. People and commodities travel together with the means of transport, and this journeying, the spatial movement of the means of transport, is precisely the production process accomplished by the transport industry. The useful effect can only be consumed during the production process; it does not exist as a thing of use distinct from the process, a thing which functions as an article of commerce and circulates as a commodity only after its production. However the exchange value of this useful effect is still determined, like that of any other commodity, by the value of the elements of production used up in it (labour power and means of production), plus the surplus value created by the surplus labour of the workers occupied in the transport industry. (CII: 135; see also *CW*33: 41, 145-146)[25]

Marx returns to the topics he broaches in the *Grundrisse* in his very rich and extensive discussion of machinery in the section on relative surplus value in the *1861-63 Manuscript*. This makes it clear that by the 'general intellect' he simply means the sciences as a social practice that has become integrated into the capitalist production process.[26] He suc-

---

25  In my view, the hesitations and inconsistencies in Marx's extensive discussions of productive and unproductive labour, particularly in the *1861-63 Manuscript*, reflect the fact that Marx inherited the problem from the classical economists, who were concerned to differentiate between workers producing profits for capitalists from the servants, retainers and hangers on of the landed aristocracy who consume part of the latter's revenue. This leads Marx often when discussing the provision of services to focus on their purchase with revenues rather than their conditions of production. This is not a helpful framework for addressing productive and unproductive labour in developed capitalist societies where, as Marx himself acknowledges, thanks to technological progress, productive workers are liable to be a shrinking proportion of the workforce but simultaneously the wage form is generalised. For helpful discussion of Marx's shifting and sometimes inconsistent views on productive and unproductive in relation to the development of modern capitalism, see Ernest Mandel, 'Introduction', to Karl Marx, *Capital*, II (Harmondsworth, 1978), pp38-52, and Harman, *Zombie Capitalism*, ch 5.

26  See also Roman Rosdolsky's discussion of the passage on the 'general intellect': *The Making of Marx's Capital* (London, 1977), pp242-244. An interesting passage in *Capital*, III, confirms the interpretation developed in the text: 'We must distinguish here...between universal [*allgemeiner*] labour and communal [*gemeinschaftlicher*] labour. They both play their part in the production process, and merge into one another, but they

cinctly sums up his view of the relationship between the sciences and capitalism slightly before he resumes the analysis of relative surplus value that was interrupted by the long excursus into history of political economy: 'Capitalist production leads to separation of *science from labour* and at the same time to the use of science in material production' (*CW*33: 364). Scientific inquiry simultaneously becomes autonomised and professionalised and is put to the service of capital:

> Just as **machinery** is described here as the '**master's machinery**', and its function is described as *his* function in the *production process* (**The business of production**), so equally is this true for the *scientific knowledge* which is embodied in this **machinery**, or in the **methods of producing**, chemical processes, etc. Science appears as a *potentiality alien* to labour, *hostile* to it and *dominant* over it, and its application—on the one hand concentration and on the other hand the development into a science of the knowledge, observations and craft secrets obtained by experience and handed down traditionally, for the purpose of analysing the production process to allow the application of the natural sciences to the material production process—this, the application of science, rests entirely on the separation of the intellectual potentialities of the process from the knowledge, understanding and skill of the individual worker, just as the concentration and development of the conditions of production and their conversion into capital rests on the divestiture—the separation—of the worker from those conditions. Instead, **factory** labour leaves the worker only a knowledge of certain hand movements; with this, therefore, the laws on **apprenticeship** are done away with; and the struggle of the state, etc, to get the **factory** children at least to learn reading and writing shows how this **application of science upon the process of production** coincides with the suppression of all intellectual development in the course of this process. Admittedly, a small class of

---

are each different as well. Universal labour is all scientific work, all discovery and invention... Communal labour, however, simply involves the direct cooperation of individuals' (*CIII*: 190). Identifying universal with scientific labour represents a shift compared to the 1859 *Contribution* where Marx tends to refer to abstract social labour as universal or general labour. For example: 'Labour which creates exchange-value is thus *abstract general labour* [*abstrakt allgemeine Arbeit*].' (*Con*: 29; in the English edition of the *Contribution* '*allgemeine Arbeit*' is more usually translated as 'universal labour'.) By the time he writes *Capital* Marx has, as so often, clarified and remodelled his categories (though particularly in the first edition of Volume I he sometimes refers to abstract labour as universal labour). Distinguishing abstract from universal labour and restricting the extension of the latter to scientific work avoids the confusion caused by the 'general intellect' passage. I am grateful to Lucia Pradella for stressing the importance of Marx's reconceptualisation of universal labour.

higher workers does take shape, but this does not stand in any proportion to the masses of 'deskilled' workers. (*CW*34: 34)

So far from claiming that the transformation of the sciences into a productive force renders labour no longer the source of value, Marx is concerned about the impact of this transformation on the workers. It is plainly capital that is in command here, and not the 'general intellect'. In a manner that anticipates Harry Braverman's famous study, he explores how the technical transformation of production made possible by the use of the sciences to extract relative surplus value deskills labour.[27] In the following passage he invokes the nickname—the Iron Man—the mill workers gave to Richard Roberts' self-acting mule, introduced in 1830, as the manufacturing capitalists' apologist Andrew Ure explains, 'to restore order among the industrious classes'.[28] According to Robert Allen, Roberts' 'aim was to eliminate the jobs of the high wage spinners who had operated the mules, and in that he succeeded... The mule was the basis of Britain's pre-eminence in cotton production throughout the nineteenth century'.[29] Marx writes:

Here too past labour—in the automaton and the machinery moved by it—steps forth as acting apparently in independence of [living] labour, it subordinates labour instead of being subordinate to it, it is the iron man confronting the man of flesh and blood. The subsumption of his labour under capital—the absorption of his labour by capital—which lies in the nature of capitalist production, appears here as a technological fact. The *keystone of the arch is* complete. Dead labour has been endowed with movement, and living labour only continues to be present as one of dead labour's conscious organs. The *living connection* of the whole workshop no longer lies here in cooperation; instead, the system of machinery forms a unity, set in motion by the **prime motor** and comprising the

27 Harry Braverman, *Labour and Monopoly Capital: The Degradation of Work in the Twentieth Century* (New York, 1974).

28 Andrew Ure, *The Philosophy of Manufactures: or, An Exposition of the Scientific, Moral, and Commercial Economy of Great Britain* (London, 1835), p367. Engels and Marx both first studied Ure (whom they heartily loathed) in the mid-1840s. During his discussion of machinery in the *1861-63 Manuscript*, Marx declares: 'The two books by Dr Ure and Frederick Engels are absolutely the *best* on the factory system, and are identical in the field they cover; the difference being that what *Ure* expresses as the *servant* of the system, a servant whose horizons are confined within the system, is expressed by Engels as a free critic' (*CW*33: 494).

29 Robert C Allen, *The British Industrial Revolution in Global Perspective* (Cambridge, 2009), Kindle loc. 3623. See also 'Roberts, Richard (1789-1864)', *Oxford Dictionary of National Biography*, http://www.oxforddnb.com/view/article/23770?docPos=3.

whole workshop, to which the living workshop is subordinated, in so far as it consists of workers. Their *unity* has thus taken on a form which is tangibly autonomous and independent of them. (*CW*34: 30)

Evidently what Marx is concerned with here is the antagonism between living and dead labour, not the breakdown of the law of value. The preoccupation that he shows in this part of the manuscript with the process of production makes another contemporary attempt to sideline wage labour even more surprising. Fredric Jameson announces at the beginning of his study of *Capital*, I, that it 'is not a book about politics, and not even a book about labour: it is a book about unemployment'. Jameson promises to substantiate this 'scandalous assertion...by way of close attention to its argument and the latter's stages and point-by-point development'. He goes on to offer 'another paradox of *Capital*: for this Bible of the working class scarcely deals with labour at all. The existential experience of labour cannot be reproduced, and leads us in any case outside the realm of capital, which is not interested in the lived qualities of work as such.' The baffled reader is left to wonder what to make of this 'paradox' in the light of the famous Chapter 10 of *Capital*, I, 'The Working Day', and all the torments of over-work that it documents, not to speak of Part 4, 'The Production of Relative Surplus Value', which, after the relatively brief theoretical discussion in Chapter 12, unfolds in three heavily empirical chapters, the third the massive Chapter 15, 'Machinery and Modern Industry', together amounting to over two hundred pages, that seem, to the naïve eye at least, to be all about work. Jameson's only response to this obvious objection looks suspiciously like hand-waving: Chapter 10 'is not about work at all: it is about the impossibility of work in all its extremes, and about the body at the brink of exhaustion. Its deeper subject is not concrete labour but class struggle'.[30]

Yes, indeed, *pace* those who argue there is no class struggle in *Capital*, Chapter 10 is about class struggle, as Marx makes clear near its beginning: the confrontation over the length of the working day of two commodity owners, capitalist and worker, creates

> an antinomy, of right against right, both equally bearing the seal of the law of exchange. Between equal rights, force decides. Hence, in the history of capitalist production, the establishment of a norm for the working day presents itself as a struggle between collective capital, ie the class of the capitalists, and collective labour, ie the working class. (*CI*: 344)

---

30   Fredric Jameson, *Representing Capital* (London, 2011), pp2, 3, 112, 113.

But this doesn't mean that Chapter 10 isn't also about work. Marx added it comparatively late (there is no counterpart in the *1861-63 Manuscript*). He tells Engels (10 February 1866) that, because of his carbuncles, 'I could make no progress with the really theoretical part. My brain was not up to that. I therefore elaborated the section on the "*Working Day*" from the historical point of view, which was not part of my original plan' (*CW*42: 224). But this doesn't mean that it lacks theoretical content. As Harvey says, 'the main thrust of this chapter concerns political force, the capacity to mobilise and to build political alliances and institutions (such as trade unions) to influence a state apparatus that has the power to legislate a "normal" working day'.[31] Here, too, then, the state is present in *Capital*. But this should not be allowed to diminish the sheer power of Marx's descriptions, drawn from the Factory Inspectors' reports and other official enquiries, of concrete instances of over-work. Like any skilful writer, in these Marx acts on the reader's imagination. The account that he quotes, for example, of the interminable working day of the journeyman baker (*CI*: 359-61), may not recapture the baker's 'existential experience' but it does very effectively convey the burden that his specific labour imposes on him. It is rapidly followed by a report of Irish journeymen bakers' agitation against night work and Sunday work (*CI*: 362). Evoking the crucifixion of labour thus leads directly to tracing the development of workers' organisation.

Jameson is on slightly stronger ground when he invokes the general law of capitalist accumulation that Marx presents in *Capital*, I, Chapter 25: 'What is irrefutable is that the general law enunciated here has to do with non-work: not with the production of a working proletariat (let alone its reproduction), but with a "reserve army" which includes people who will never work and who are indeed incapable of working'.[32] Here is what Marx says:

> The greater the social wealth, the functioning capital, the extent and energy of its growth, and therefore also the greater the absolute mass of the proletariat and the productivity of its labour, the greater is the industrial reserve army. The same causes which develop the expansive power of capital, also develop the labour-power at its disposal. The relative mass of the industrial reserve army thus increases with the potential energy of wealth. But the greater the reserve army in proportion to the active labour army, the greater is the mass of a consolidated surplus population,

---

31    David Harvey, *A Companion to Marx's Capital* (London, 2010), p138.
32    Jameson, *Representing Capital*, p70.

whose misery is in inverse ratio to the amount of torture it has to undergo in the form of labour. The more extensive, finally, the pauperised sections of the working class and the industrial reserve army, the greater is official pauperism. *This is the absolute general law of capitalist accumulation.* Like other laws, it is modified in its working by many circumstances, the analysis of which does not concern us here. (CI: 798)

Though this isn't the main point here, this is a somewhat aberrant usage of 'law' by Marx, since he generally uses this term (quite frequently in *Capital*, I, especially) to refer to fairly precise quantitative relationships, which the 'general law' certainly isn't. Is it just about 'non-work'? Not really: in setting out the 'general law' Marx is concerned to draw a contrast between the growth of wealth and of the size and productivity of the proletariat and that of the industrial reserve army with the suffering attendant. More broadly, according to Pradella, 'for Marx, capitalist development itself determines a comprehensive, although differentiated, *impoverishment* of the proletariat on a world scale, which embraces the whole of its existence', spiritual as well as material, and is expressed in a fall in relative (though not necessarily nominal or real) wages.[33] This is as much about employed as it is about unemployed workers. A page after the passage cited from *Capital*, I, just cited, Marx writes:

But all methods for the production of surplus value are at the same time methods of accumulation, and every extension of accumulation becomes, conversely, a means for the development of those methods. It follows therefore that in proportion as capital accumulates, the situation of the worker, be his payment high or low, must grow worse. Finally, the law which always holds the relative surplus population or industrial reserve army in equilibrium with the extent and energy of accumulation rivets the worker to capital more firmly than the wedges of Hephaestus held Prometheus to the rock. It makes an accumulation of misery a necessary condition, corresponding to the accumulation of wealth.

---

33  Pradella, *L'Attualità del Capitale*, p283. See, for detailed studies of the general law of capitalist accumulation and the industrial reserve army that seek to integrate contemporary developments, Pradella, *L'Attualità del Capitale*, esp chs I and VI, and John Bellamy Foster, Robert W McChesney and R Jamil Jonna, 'The Global Reserve Army of Labor and the New Imperialism', *Monthly Review*, 63:6 (November 2011), http://monthlyreview.org/2011/11/01/the-global-reserve-army-of-labor-and-the-new-imperialism. Contemporary Marxists differ about how to understand, within this framework, industrialisation in the South: compare Jane Hardy, 'New Divisions of Labour in the Global South', *International Socialism*, 2.137 (2013), http://www.isj.org.uk/?id=868, and John Smith, 'Southern Labour—"Peripheral" No Longer: a Reply to Jane Hardy', *International Socialism*, 2.140 (2013), http://www.isj.org.uk/index.php4?id=922

Accumulation of wealth at one pole is, therefore, at the same time accumulation of misery, the torment of labour, slavery, ignorance,
brutalisation and moral degradation at the opposite pole, ie on the side
of the class that produces its own product as capital. (*CI*: 799)

Here Marx includes 'the torment of *labour*' in the 'accumulation of
misery' that (this is the 'law') necessarily accompanies the 'accumulation
of wealth'.[34] The presentation of the 'general law' follows Marx's analysis
of the industrial reserve army, whose importance to his overall theory of
capitalist development we already noted in chapter 6. And it is here that
we find the rational kernel of Jameson's claim that *Capital*, I, is a 'book
about unemployment': 'in any contemporary reading, the structural
unemployment in Marx's conception of the "reserve army of capitalism"
[sic], once a secondary feature of this system, moves to the very forefront
of its analysis today.' But look at the slippage that occurs a page later: 'the
fundamental structural centrality of unemployment in the text of
*Capital* itself'.[35] We may have, as Jameson suggests, a particular interest
in what Marx says about the reserve army, but it doesn't follow that this
discussion is 'structurally central' to *Capital*.

All the same, Jameson is right to highlight the actuality of this particular level of Marx's analysis. But, as Roman Rosdolsky insists, 'it is utterly
mistaken to identify the industrial reserve army with "unemployment".'[36]
It is, in the first place, the industrial reserve army of *labour*—in other
words, those layers of the working class that are not fully integrated into
the process of production but whose existence, as Marx's discussion of
how the fluctuations in the reserve army help regulate the business cycle
shows (see chapter 6 above), has definite effects on this process. In Section
4 of *Capital*, I, Chapter 25, which concludes with the 'general law of capitalist accumulation', Marx differentiates between the layers of the reserve
army, which extend well beyond the unemployed:

> The relative surplus population exists in all kinds of forms. Every worker
> belongs to it during the time when he is only partially employed or

---

34  Rosdolsky proposes a narrower reading, arguing that 'the "accumulation of misery"
relates solely to the "Lazarus-layers of the working class",' *The Making of Marx's Capital*,
p303. But Marx's sentence makes no such restriction, assigning 'the accumulation of
misery' to 'the class that produces its own product as capital'. Rosdolsky is so keen rightly
to defend Marx from the charge that he posits the absolute immiseration of the working
class that he misreads him here. But his critique of 'the so-called "theory of immiseration"
is excellent: see pp300-312. See also Gérard Duménil, *La Concept de loi économique dans
'le Capital'* (Paris, 1978), pp173-190.

35  Jameson, *Representing Capital*, pp148, 149.

36  Rosdolsky, *The Making of Marx's Capital*, p302 n 54.

wholly unemployed. Leaving aside the large-scale and recurring forms that the changing phases of the industrial cycle impress on it, so that it sometimes appears acute in times of crisis, and sometimes chronic, in times when business is slack, we can identify three forms which it always possesses: the floating, the latent, and the stagnant. (*CI*: 794)

In fact, Marx differentiates four forms taken by the reserve army: the floating, workers attracted to and repulsed by modern industrial production; the latent, workers in agriculture where low productivity leaves them at least potentially underemployed; the stagnant, 'a part of the active labour army, but with extremely irregular employment'; and, finally, 'the lowest sediment of the relative surplus population [that] dwells in the sphere of pauperism' (*CI*: 796, 797). It is only this last group that, as Jameson puts it, 'includes people who will never work and who are indeed incapable of working'. This differentiated analysis provides a much more helpful framework for analysing the contemporary world of labour rather than, for example, simplistic diagnoses that counterpose precarious workers to those with secure jobs. Marx's account highlights the ways in which the different categories of employed, semi-employed, and unemployed shade off into each other, and also their interdependence. Rosa Luxemburg puts this very well:

The lowest strata of the needy and excluded who are employed only to a small extent or not at all, are not as it were a scum that does not form part of 'official' society, as the bourgeoisie very understandably present them, but are connected with the topmost, best situated stratum of industrial workers by a whole series of intermediate steps. This inner connection is shown itself numerically by the sudden growth in the lower strata of the reserve army that occurs every time that business is bad, and the corresponding contraction at the peak of the business cycle, as well as by the relative decline in the number of those who resort to public assistance with the development of the class struggle and the related rise in self consciousness of the mass of proletarians. And finally, every industrial worker who is crippled at work or has the misfortune of being sixty years old, has a fifty-fifty chance of falling into the lowest stratum of bitter poverty, the 'beggarly stratum' of the proletariat. The living conditions of the lowest strata of the proletariat thus follow the same laws of capitalist production, pulled up and down, and the proletariat, along with the broad stratum of rural workers, the army of unemployed, and all strata from the very top to the very bottom, forms an organic whole, a social class, a class whose varying gradations of need and oppression can only be correctly grasped by the capitalist law of wages as a whole.[37]

Here is another way in which *Capital* today speaks to us more directly than it did in the decades of full employment (in the advanced capitalist societies at least) that followed the Second World War. But the relationship that interests Marx most in his analysis of the industrial reserve army is not that between different layers of workers but that between their entire class and capital. The chapter on the working day is the clearest refutation of the claim put forward, for example, by Michael Lebowitz, that '*Capital* is one-sided and inadequate precisely because the worker is not present as the subject who acts herself against capital'.[38] The significance of Marx's analysis of the interaction between the process of capital accumulation and the fluctuations in the industrial reserve army is that it identifies the mechanisms through which working class collective organisation and action are undermined.

We know that Marx intended that *Capital*, III, would end with 'the *class struggle*, as the conclusion in which the movement and disintegration of the whole shit resolves itself' (*CW*43: 26). It is intriguing to speculate whether this conclusion would have extended to a discussion of the political forms of working class struggle that Marx witnessed, in particular the Chartists, the First International, and the Paris Commune. As it is, the most developed discussion of the strictly economic class struggle that we have by Marx comes not in *Capital*, but in 'Value, Price, and Profit', a report he read to the Central Council of the International in June 1865. Although the occasion for this text was political—a response to the critique of trade unionism offered by the Owenite John Weston, as Marx told Engels (24 June 1865), it 'contains, in an extraordinarily condensed **but relatively popular form**, many new ideas which are anticipated from my book' (*CW*42: 162-163). In fact, 'Value, Price, and Profit' contains much more on trade unions than found its way into *Capital*, and may be seen as a complement to the latter. Rejecting Weston's dismissal of trade union struggles for higher wages, Marx insists on an indeterminacy in the relationship between profits and profits:

37  Rosa Luxemburg, *Introduction to Political Economy*, in Peter Hudis, ed, *The Complete Works of Rosa Luxemburg*, 1 (London, 2013), p289. This comes from an interesting discussion of wages, the reserve army, and trade unions: see pp260-293.

38  Michael Lebowitz, *Beyond **Capital**: Marx's Political Economy of the Working Class* (2nd edn; Basingstoke, 2003), p74.

We can only say that, the limits of the working day being given, the *maximum of profit* corresponds to the physical *minimum of wages*; and that wages being given, the *maximum of profit* corresponds to such a prolongation of the working day as is compatible with the physical forces of the labourer. The maximum of profit is therefore limited by the physical minimum of wages and the physical maximum of the working day. It is evident that between the two limits of the *maximum rate of profit* an immense scale of variations is possible. The fixation of its actual degree is only settled by the continuous struggle between capital and labour, the capitalist constantly tending to reduce wages to their physical minimum, and to extend the working day to its physical maximum, while the working man constantly presses in the opposite direction.

The matter resolves itself into a question of the respective powers of the combatants. (*CW*20: 146)

Marx goes on to explain that the structural balance of forces is weighted in favour of capital, because the tendency for the organic composition of capital to rise as accumulation continues increases the size of the industrial reserve army and thereby weakens the bargaining power of labour. As Rosdolsky comments, 'it is simply not the case that labour and capital represent two autonomous powers, whose "respective shares" in the national product merely depend on their respective strengths; rather, labour is subject to the economic power of capital in capitalism from the outset, and its "share" must naturally always be conditional on the "share" of capital'.[39] Marx's conclusion in the famous peroration to the text is not that the economic class struggle is futile, but that it must develop into a movement for the conquest of political power and the destruction of capitalism:

At the same time, and quite apart from the general servitude involved in the wages system, the working class ought not to exaggerate to themselves the ultimate working of these everyday struggles. They ought not to forget that they are fighting with effects, but not with the causes of those effects; that they are retarding the downward movement, but not changing its direction; that they are applying palliatives, not curing the malady. They ought, therefore, not to be exclusively absorbed in these unavoidable guerrilla fights incessantly springing up from the never ceasing encroachments of capital or changes of the market. They ought to understand that, with all the miseries it imposes upon them, the

---

39   Rosdolsky, *The Making of Marx's Capital*, p284.

present system simultaneously engenders the *material conditions* and the *social forms* necessary for an economical reconstruction of society. Instead of the *conservative* motto, '*A fair day's wage for a fair day's work!*' they ought to inscribe on their banner the revolutionary watchword: '*Abolition of the wages system!*' (*CW*20: 148-149)

Earlier on in 'Value, Price, and Profit', Marx criticises the Malthus-Ricardo 'iron law of wages', according to which population pressure prevents wages from rising above the physical minimum. All the same, he plainly believes that the effect of the accumulation process in swelling the ranks of the industrial reserve army not merely 'rivets the worker to capital' but helps to push wages down. Elsewhere Marx draws distinctions that he doesn't make in 'Value, Price, and Profit', emphasising, for example, in this passage in the *1861-63 Manuscript* that a rising rate of exploitation and falling value of labour power thanks to the extraction of relative surplus value are consistent with increases in real wages made possible by the cheapening of the means of consumption:

> It is clear, further, that the presence and the growth of relative surplus value by no means require as a condition that the worker's *life situation* should remain *unchanged*, ie that his average wage should always provide the same quantitatively and qualitatively determined amount of means of subsistence and no more. This is not the case, although relative surplus value can neither arise nor grow without a corresponding *fall* in the *value of labour capacity* or the *value of wages* (average wages). Indeed, relative surplus value might well rise continuously, and the *value of labour capacity*, hence the value of average wages, fall continuously, yet despite this the range of the worker's means of subsistence and therefore the pleasures of his life could expand continuously. For this is conditioned by the quality and quantity of the *use values* (commodities) he can appropriate, not by their *exchange value* (*CW*30: 245).[40]

Capturing these benefits of their higher productivity would, of course, depend on the effectiveness of workers' organisation. Writing from the perspective of the postwar boom, Rosdolsky comments: 'Marx (and Engels) often overestimated the weight of the factors depressing the condition of the proletariat, and they therefore did not look closely at

---

40  This passage underlines how crass the mainstream economist Brad DeLong is in asserting: 'Marx could not fully grok [sic] that rising real material living standards for the working class might well go along with a rising rate of exploitation and a smaller labour share', http://www.nytimes.com/roomfordebate/2014/03/30/was-marx-right/marx-was-blind-to-the-systems-ingenuity-and-ability-to-reinvent

the possibility of a significant rise in the living standards of the workers, even in the leading capitalist countries'.[41] Here is another case where our perspective on *Capital* may have changed, given the relentless downward pressure on average wages in the advanced capitalist states, especially since the onset of the global economic and financial crisis in 2007-8. In the 'peripheral' eurozone economies such as Greece, Ireland, Portugal, and Spain, absolute immiseration has become an existential reality for large sections of the population.[42] Nevertheless, Marx's analysis consistently identifies workers as active subjects who, if they can organise themselves collectively, can improve, at least temporarily, their material situation and prepare for their ultimate self-emancipation. We can see this as the ultimate implication of the relationality of capital—that the internal dynamics of the capital involve workers actively shaping their destiny in opposition to their exploiters.

## Envoi

Behind these arguments over the interpretation of Marx's *Capital* lie political preoccupations. It's remarkable, for example, how his misreading of the 'Note on Machines' has accompanied Toni Negri through some quite big political and intellectual reversals.[43] More generally, informing the readings of Marx that seek in different ways to repress the relationality of capital by, in particular, marginalising the role of wage labour is the experience of capitalism in the neoliberal era. The Marxist left has had to confront two related questions: has the neoliberal restructuring of capitalism succeeded in setting the system on a new growth path? Has it also so pulverised the working class that it is incapable of acting as a collective subject?

---

41  Rosdolsky, *The Making of Marx's Capital*, p307.

42  See, for example, Ian Traynor, 'Austerity Pushing Europe into Social and Economic Decline, Says Red Cross,' *Guardian*, 10 October 2013, http://www.theguardian.com/world/2013/oct/10/austerity-europe-debt-red-cross, and, on the sharp fall in real wages in Britain since 2008, Richard Blundell, Claire Crawford and Wenchao Jin, 'What Can Wages and Employment Tell Us about the UK's Unemployment Puzzle?', *IFS Working Papers* (2013), www.ifs.org.uk/wps/wp201311.pdf. Rosdolsky himself writes: 'This is not to claim that there are no tendencies towards immiseration in the real capital [sic] world; there are more than enough of them—but one has to know where to look. In fact such tendencies emerge clearly in two spheres: firstly (temporary) in all times of crisis, and secondly (permanent) in the so-called underdeveloped areas of the world', *The Making of Marx's Capital*, p307.

43  See Callinicos, 'Antonio Negri and the Temptation of Ontology', and Maria Turchetto, 'De "l'ouvrier masse" à l' "entrepreneurialité commune": la trajectoire dé l'opéraïsme italienne', in Jacques Bidet and Stathis Kouvelakis, eds, *Dictionnaire Marx contemporaine* (Paris, 2001).

The global economic and financial crisis precipitated by the 2007-8 crash has, to my mind, definitively answered the first question in the negative. It has, however, been harder to get the measure of the changes the past 35 years have brought to the world of labour. Adding to the perplexity has been the predominant form taken by resistance to the effects of the crisis. While there have been very significance cases of working-class collective action, notably in Greece and Egypt, the radi-calisation of the past few years has mainly expressed itself in movements on the streets. The occupation of Tahrir Square in Cairo during the revolution of 25 January 2011 offered a new way of imagining collective self-emancipation that has been imitated in the Puerta del Sol in Madrid, Plateia Syntagma in Athens, Zuccotti Park in Manhattan, Gezi Park in Istanbul, and many other places around the world.

Getting a sense of the strengths and weaknesses of these forms of col-lective action is an urgent political task for anticapitalist activists. They are best understood not simply as particular movements with their own grievances and political bases—though of course they are all that—but as part of the process through which, after the defeats suffered by the workers' movement especially at the onset of neoliberalism in the 1970s and 1980s, new forms of political agency are discovered. It would be an enormous mistake to counterpose them to more 'traditional' forms of working class organisation and struggle. The working class has been restructured in the neoliberal era, as it has at earlier stages in the history of capitalism. As the pattern and locus of capital accumulation change, so too does the configuration of living labour. The resulting restructur-ing does not represent the marginalisation of wage labour or the transformation of capital into a purely parasitic force battening off the commons. If anything, the geographical extension of industrial capital-ism (above all to East Asia) and the restructuring of public and private services in the advanced economies have vastly increased the numbers of those subsumed under the wage form and directly subject to the impera-tives of the law of value.

Of course, all this is a matter of much controversy, and it is not the purpose of this book to address the theoretical and empirical issues involved.[44] But the fact that they seep into the interpretation of *Capital*

---

44  For some contributions focused especially on the British case, see Kevin Doogan, *New Capitalism? The Transformation of Work* (Cambridge, 2009), Neil Davidson, 'The Neoliberal Era in Britain: Historical Developments and Current Perspectives', *International Socialism*, 2.139 (2013), www.isj.org.uk/?id=908, and Jane Hardy and Joseph Choonara, 'Neoliberalism and the Working Class: A Reply to Neil Davidson', *International Socialism*, 2.140 (2013). A much earlier take on these issues is offered by

is yet another indication of how much this is still a living work. As we have seen, Marx struggled with his critique of political economy for more than 20 years, and was in the end defeated by the immensity of the task he had given himself, and by his own frailties and mortality. But what he left behind was more than a melange of unfinished manuscripts. On the contrary, the more we know of these manuscripts, the deeper the understanding we gain of his project—and of his achievement. As I have tried to emphasise, in many ways *Capital*, for all its faults and its incompleteness, speaks to us very directly in the 21st century. This doesn't mean that it should be received uncritically; on the contrary, from the start continuing Marx's analysis of the capitalist mode of production has required a willingness to disagree with him, as Luxemburg did in *The Accumulation of Capital*. This doesn't alter the fact that *Capital* remains indispensable to anyone trying to make sense of the world.

Finally, we should not forget the moral and political passion that informs the work. Near the end of Marx's longest draft, *The Economic Manuscript of 1861-63*, he is working through material on primitive accumulation. He comments on a late 18th century pamphlet demanding measures to impose much stronger discipline on the new workforce being subjected to the rule of capital:

(The flow of Irish people into the industrial districts, etc, since the machine age has fulfilled all this scoundrel's expectations... It is in fact remarkable how all the pious wishes this obsequious sycophant of the industrial and commercial bourgeoisie mechanically reels off—increase in the prices of agricultural products, growth in the national debt, introduction of taxes on **necessaries**, enlistment of foreign workers, depreciation of money, **workhouses** as **houses of terror**, artificial production of a constant 'redundancy of labour'—how all this has become a reality since the arrival of the epoch of large-scale industry in England.) (*CW*34: 296)

Here again we see the actuality of *Capital*: Marx could be discussing some document from the World Bank or the European Commission demanding 'reforms' to increase competitiveness and labour 'flexibility' from some government in the Global South or the eurozone. Marx's world is still our world. He continues working through more of his excerpts till he comes to one describing how at the end of the 18th century 'the **squires of** *Berkshire*', who, 'in their capacity as magistrates...

Alex Callinicos and Chris Harman, *The Changing Working Class* (London, 1987), available at http://www.isj.org.uk/?s=resources#classarticles.

determined the wages of the **agricultural labourers**', set them at starvation levels. Unable to contain his anger, he exclaims: 'Those swine!' (*CW*34: 320).

The solidarity Marx shows here with agricultural labourers who would mostly have been long dead by the early 1860s and his hatred of their masters recalls a passage in Walter Benjamin's 'Theses on the Philosophy of History':

> Not man or men but the struggling, oppressed class is the repository of historical knowledge. In Marx it appears as the last enslaved class, as the avenger that completes the task of liberation in the name of generations of the downtrodden... Social Democracy thought fit to assign to the working class the role of the redeemer of future generations, in this way cutting the sinews of its greatest strength. This training made the working class forget both its hatred and its spirit of sacrifice, for both are nourished by the image of enslaved ancestors rather of liberated grandchildren.[45]

Amid all the debates on *Capital*, it should never be forgotten that Marx wrote it from the perspective of this class and to help its struggle to avenge past sufferings and emancipate itself from the tyranny of the capital relation.

---

45   Walter Benjamin, *Illuminations* (Hannah Arendt, ed; London, 1970), p262.

Appendix

# Althusser's detour via relations

*This Appendix is a lightly edited version of a paper delivered at the International Conference 'Rileggere Il Capitale. La Lezione di Louis Althusser', at the Universita Venezia Ca' Foscari in November 2006. To provide a more detailed philosophical account of the problem of relations in* **Capital** *I am including it here (though it overlaps slightly with the Introduction).*

The title of this session is the same as that of this conference: 'Rereading *Capital*'.[1] It invites us to reflect on the pertinence today of Althusser's own reading of Marx. I want to draw attention to an aspect of this reading that has received little attention but that seems to me of great importance to contemporary debates among critical theorists. I am concerned here with the critique of humanist and historicist Marxism, by which Althusser means the Hegelian Marxism developed by Antonio Gramsci and George Lukács in 'The Object of *Capital*', Part II of the 2nd edition of *Reading Capital*.[2] In developing this critique Althusser puts forward an important philosophical thesis (though not one that he capitalised and numbered): the ontological primacy of relations.

One of the major faults of historicist Marxism, Althusser argues, is how it conceptualises relations. In 'humanist historicism', 'the relations of production, political and ideological social relations, have been reduced to historicised *"human relations"*, ie, to inter-human, inter-subjective relations'.[3] Althusser develops this criticism and his own alternative conception of relations a little later on:

> the social relations of production are on no account reducible to mere relations between men, to relations which only involve men, and therefore to

---

1   My view of Althusser was first presented in *Althusser's Marxism* (London, 1976).

2   There is a large element of caricature in Althusser's portrayal of 'historicism'. For a critique of his treatment of Gramsci, see Peter Thomas, *The Gramscian Moment* (Leiden, 2009), pp24-36, a version of which was presented at the conference at which this paper was given.

3   Louis Althusser, 'The Object of *Capital*', in Althusser and Étienne Balibar, *Reading Capital* (London, 1970), p140.

*variations in a universal matrix, to inter-subjectivity* (recognition, prestige, struggle, master-slave relationship, etc). For Marx, the social relations of production do not bring *men alone* onto the stage, but the *agents* of the production process and the *material conditions* of the production process, in specific 'combinations'.[4]

Here we have a kind of anticipatory condemnation of the entire problematic of recognition that so pervades contemporary social and political theory—Jürgen Habermas, Axel Honneth, Francis Fukuyama, even, in a much more complex and critical way, Pierre Bourdieu. What is Althusser's alternative? Forgive me for quoting at length a justly famous passage:

> the structure of the relations of production determines the places and functions occupied and adopted by the agents of production, who are never anything more than the occupants of these places, insofar as they are the 'supports' (*Träger*) of these functions. The true 'subjects' (in the sense of the constitutive subjects (*sujets constituants*) of the process) are therefore not these occupants or functionaries, are not, despite all appearances, the 'obviousness' of the 'given' of naïve anthropology, 'concrete individuals', 'real men'—but *the definition and distribution of these places and functions. The true 'subjects' are these definers and distributors: the relations of production* (and political and ideological social relations). But since these are 'relations', they cannot be thought within the category *subject*. And if by chance anyone proposes to reduce these relations of production to relations between men, ie, '*human relations*', he is violating Marx's thought, for so long as we apply a truly critical reading to some of his rare ambiguous formulations, Marx shows in the greatest depth that the *relations* of production (and political and ideological social relations) are irreducible to any anthropological inter-subjectivity—since they only combine agents and objects in a specific structure of the distribution of relations, places and functions, occupied and 'supported' by objects and agents of production.[5]

So the real 'subjects'—in the sense of 'constitutive subjects of the process'—are the relations of production, which 'combine agents and objects in a specific structure'. Indeed, the relationality of the relations of production consists in the fact that they combine persons and objects in a definite way. Étienne Balibar in his famous discussion of the 'double articulation of the mode of production' in his contribution to

---

4   Louis Althusser, 'The Object of *Capital*', 174.
5   Louis Althusser, 'The Object of *Capital*', p180.

*Reading Capital*, extends relationality to the productive forces: he argues that both the relations of production and the labour process are to be conceived as forms of appropriation, each involving a specific combination or connexion of labour power and means of production.[6] This idea is reaffirmed by Althusser in in an important slightly later text, *Sur la reproduction*.[7]

Interestingly, however, Althusser corrects the formulation that the relations of production are the 'true "subjects"': 'since these are "relations", they cannot be thought within the category *subject*'. This implies that there is a categorial difference between relations and subjects. Thus relations cannot, as Althusser repeatedly warns, be reduced to inter-subjectivity. But, further, he seems to be affirming that relations not just differ from subjects, but have primacy over them. Thus famously the agents of production are the *Träger* of the production relations, a claim that is greatly developed in 'Ideology and the Ideological State Apparatuses', where Althusser seeks to show how individuals are subsumed under the dominant social relations by being interpellated as subjects. This serves to underpin the primacy of relations over subjects by establishing that ideology functions through subjectivity, thereby contributing to the reproduction of the relations of production.[8]

Althusser returns to the subject in the defence of his *Doctorat d'Etat* in 1975, where he summarises his anti-humanist reading of Marx as follows: 'Marx shows that what in the last instance determines a social formation and allows us to grasp it, is not any chimerical human essence or human nature, nor man, nor even "men", but a *relation*, the production relation, which is inseparable from the base, the infrastructure'.[9] But he adds an intriguing gloss that, as it were, parries in advance Edward Thompson's rhetorically very effective denunciation of his anti-humanism as heartless and cruel:

6   Étienne Balibar, 'On the Basic Concepts of Historical Materialism', in Althusser and Balibar, *Reading Capital*, pp212-216.

7   Louis Althusser, *Sur la reproduction* (Paris, 1995): p50. See also Appendix, 'Du primat des rapports de production sur les forces productives', pp243-252. G A Cohen, who, *contra* Althusser, defends the primacy of the forces over the relations of production in *Karl Marx's Theory of History* (2nd edn, Oxford, 2000), also denies the relationality of the productive forces: for a critical discussion of this denial see Alex Callinicos, 'G A Cohen and the Critique of Political Economy', *Science & Society*, 70 (2006).

8   Louis Althusser, 'Ideology and the Ideological State Apparatuses', in *Lenin and Philosophy and Other Essays* (London, 1971). Warren Montag offers a comprehensive treatment of Althusser on structure and subject in *Althusser and His Contemporaries: Philosophy's Perpetual War* (Durham NC, 2013), Parts I and II.

9   Louis Althusser, 'Is it Simple to be a Marxist in Philosophy?', in *Philosophy and the Spontaneous Philosophy of Scientists and Other Essays* (London, 1990), p236.

If Marx does not start out from man, which is an empty idea—that is, one weighed down with bourgeois ideology—it is in order finally to reach living men; if he makes a detour via these relations of which living men are the 'bearers', it is in order finally to be able to grasp the laws which govern both their lives and their concrete struggles.[10]

Alas, Althusser doesn't seem to have pursued this idea of Marx's 'detour via relations' in any of his later writings.[11] Arguably, it surfaces subliminally when, in defending the thesis that 'the class struggle is the motor of history' against John Lewis, he affirms *'the primacy of contradiction* over the *terms* of contradiction', but this affirmation, hidden in a footnote, goes without development.[12] I shall speculate about the reasons for this failure towards the end of this paper.

For the moment I want instead to extract the philosophical thesis implicit in these discussions, the ontological primacy of relations, and to highlight both its fertility and its relative absence from contemporary debates. Let me stress that acceptance of this thesis does not require one to accept Althusser's functionalist theory of ideology or his effective evacuation of the concept of agency of any content. A critical realist ontology that conceives the real as a nested hierarchy of generative mechanisms can accord causal powers to both relations and agents while attributing to the former a more privileged explanatory role.[13]

A word, then, about the fertility of the thesis, in the first instance with respect to Marx's own development. One way of understanding the trajectory of his critique of political economy is to see it as a movement from substance—not to function (to echo the title of a famous essay of Ernst Cassirer's), but to relation. Marx's writings of the 1840s—*The German Ideology*, for example—often involve, as Derrida points out in *Spectres of Marx*, a substantialist problematic that counterposes to the institutions and ideologies of bourgeois society the struggles of 'real, living individuals'. The formulation of the concept of the relations of production, which first becomes fully visible in *The Poverty of Philosophy*, offered a means of escape, but the refinement of this concept became imbricated in the tortuous process through which Marx painfully constructed, and constantly reconstructed his theory of the capitalist mode of production.

---

10  'Is it Simple to be a Marxist in Philosophy?', p239. See E P Thompson, *The Poverty of Theory and Other Essays* (London, 1978).

11  Althusser, 'Is it Simple to be a Marxist in Philosophy?', p239.

12  Louis Althusser, 'Reply to John Lewis', in *Essays in Self-Criticism* (London, 1976), pp49-50 n 12.

13  Alex Callinicos, *Making History* (2nd edn, Leiden, 2004) and *The Resources of Critique* (Cambridge, 2006), Part II.

Jacques Bidet has shown how in successive manuscripts, from the *Grundrisse* to *Capital*, Marx elaborated and recast his concepts, in the process both relying on and progressively emancipating himself from a Hegelian conception of scientific method that had provided him with an indispensable means of escaping both empiricism and formalism.[14] But one central theme of the final product of this arduous struggle, *Capital* itself, is the way in which capitalist relations of production are systematically occluded by the functioning of the economic system as a whole. Thus, when discussing the Trinity Formula, Marx observes:

> the actual production process, as the unity of the immediate production process and the process of circulation, produces new configurations in which the threads of the inner connection get more and more lost, the relations of production becoming independent of one another and the components of value ossifying into independent forms. (*C*III: 967)

The name that Marx gives for the process through which 'the threads of the inner connection get more and more lost' is, of course, fetishism; the essays making up the first edition of *Reading Capital* and their authors' subsequent reconsiderations were the first to alert us to the extent to which the theory of fetishism is the site of a problem rather than a satisfactory solution.

But there are more as well as less satisfactory statements of the theory in *Capital*: thus Chapter 50 of Volume III, 'The Illusion Created by Competition', offers a fairly detailed examination of what one might call the micro-mechanisms—the incentives available to individual capitals and their calculations—that encourage the fragmentation and naturalisation of economic relations. As Bidet puts it, ideological 'representation is here functionally attached to the activity of the dominant class...as a categorial ensemble implicated in a function defined by the structure, that of the capitalist insofar as acting in the relationship of competition'.[15]

What, in any case, gets lost, Marx claims, is the relationality of capital. And this itself must be conceived as constituted by a double relation—first, the exploitive relationship between wage-labour and capital, and, second, the dynamic, competitive relationship among capitals themselves, which does not simply serve to obscure the 'inner connection' but allows it to function, since it is through the interaction of 'many capitals' in competition that the imperative to accumulate is transmitted.

14  Jacques Bidet, *Que faire du Capital?* (2nd edn, Paris, 2000).
15  Bidet, *Que faire du Capital?*, p182.

Yet if Marx's own discourse in *Capital* gives primacy to relations, it is striking how often in contemporary radical thought it is rather subjects that are given primacy over relations. One example relatively close to both Marx and Althusser is Toni Negri's *Marx beyond Marx*, which uses a particular reading of the *Grundrisse* to reduce the capital-relation to a relationship of force between two subjects—social capital and social labour. At one level, *Empire* and *Multitude* represent a retreat from this position, since capital is dispersed, desubjectified, relativised into the network power of Empire.

But the corollary is to enthrone one 'constitutive subject' of the contemporary capitalist process, the multitude, whose productive vitality simultaneously fuels the machines of Empire and prefigures the liberated 'joy of being communist'. Though Hardt and Negri do occasionally register the interdependence of Empire and multitude, the extent of the disconnect between contemporary labour and capital, as they conceive it, is indicated by their employment of the metaphors of exodus and desertion to evoke the subversion of the capital-relation—as if spatial displacement could somehow substitute for socio-political transformation.

But the prime philosophical example of the privileging of subjects over relations is provided by another theorist, once close to Althusser, now pretty far from Marx—Alain Badiou. In *Théorie du sujet* (1982) he replaces what he calls the 'subjective duel' between proletariat and bourgeoisie with the idea of a discrete subject that subtracts itself from the confining circumstances imposed by socio-historical location. This idea is greatly developed in *L'Etre et l'événement* (1988): here the emergence of a subject is conceived as a rare occurrence defined by fidelity to an event that itself is exceptional, emerging from the void of a situation, from what it excludes.

There is no place for relations in this ontology, whose fundamental constituents are the 'being-multiple' of atomic situations captured by the axioms of set theory and the events and subjects that contingently and exceptionally emerge from them. In response to criticism, Badiou, in the recently published sequel to *L'Etre et l'événement, Logiques des mondes*, develops a 'logic of appearance' that seeks to show how, outside the realm of being itself, relations find their place. But it remains a highly subordinate one: thus 'a relation between two objects is a function that conserves the atomic logic of these objects.' Badiou's concession is merely formal, preserving, as he notes, 'the subordination of the principal properties of appearance [*l'apparaître*] to the more profound determinations of being-multiple'.[16]

16   Alain Badiou, *Logiques des mondes* (Paris, 2006), pp329, 337. See the critique of Badiou's earlier treatment of relations in Peter Hallward, *Badiou: A Subject to Truth* (Minneapolis,

Badiou himself presents Negri as a representative of the 'democratic materialism' to which he counterposes his own 'materialist dialectic'.[17] Certainly there is a systematic philosophical contrast between Badiou's subtractive ontology and Negri's Deleuzian vitalism.[18] But it is important also to see what they have in common in the primacy they give to subjects over relations.

There is, of course, no knock-down way of showing philosophically that Badiou and Negri are mistaken in this. Let me just here offer the pragmatic argument that it is very hard to pursue Marx's critique of political economy without following him in the 'detour' he takes 'via relations'. This is because the main burden of explanation is taken by the capital-relation, conceived, as I indicated above, as dual—as at once the exploitation of wage-labour by capital and the competitive struggle of capitals.

Neither of these dimensions of the capital-relation are intersubjective struggles for recognition; both involve what Althusser calls combinations of agents and material conditions. And both are deeply implicated in the detailed explanations that Marx offers of the functioning of capital economic relations. These explanations are, of course, not complete, and the underlying concepts require in some cases recasting—for example, to take into account the existence of a world system constituted not merely by the movements of capital but by the interactions of a plurality of states.[19] But these and other demands for development, I think it can be shown, do not throw into question, and indeed depend on the kind of primacy given to relations that we find explicitly stated and defended by Althusser in *Reading Capital*.

Why, finally, did Althusser not further develop this insight, whose fertility I have been defending? One guess—but it is only a guess—is that his (tendential) Maoism was a hindrance rather than a help. Thus his discussion of the concept of mode of production in his most Maoist text, the posthumously published *Sur la reproduction*, involves a lengthy treatment of the division of labour in which 'the "technical" division of labour is simply the mask' of managerial power.[20]

Other discussions of the time—for example by Charles Bettelheim and Nicos Poulantzas—similarly tend to privilege the social division of

---

2003), ch 13.

17  Badiou, *Logiques des mondes*, p10.

18  The critical exploration of these ontologies is one of the main themes of my *The Resources of Critique*.

19  See Alex Callinicos, *Imperialism and Global Political Economy* (Cambridge, 2009), ch 2.

20  Althusser, *Sur la reproduction*, p62.

labour (conceived also in hyper-politicised terms) in discussing capitalist economic relations. The issues they raise are real enough, but these discussions failed to capture the complexity of Marx's own evolving analysis of the division of labour and offered a distorted view of capitalist production relations themselves as simply relations of power—a reduction that proved highly vulnerable to the effort, inspired by Foucault, to supplant Marxism with Nietzschean genealogies of power-knowledge.[21]

Whatever the validity of this speculation, it is certainly true that his later writings took Althusser far from the primacy he gave to relations in *Reading Capital*. The 'aleatory materialism of the encounter' taking inspiration from Epicurus that he developed in his years of disgrace isn't in principle inconsistent with this thesis. Indeed, the 1982 text 'Le courant souterrain du matérialisme de la recontre', concludes by returning to Balibar's formulation of 'a mode of production as a double combination' and affirms: 'A mode of production is a combination because this is a *structure* that imposes its unity on a series of elements'.[22] But the text breaks off a few sentences later and it is clear that what captures Althusser's philosophical imagination now is the endlessly restated idea of the encounter as the interference of a plurality of series both the origins and the effects of whose interaction is aleatory.

This idea is the subject of other papers at this conference. Clearly it represents a radicalisation of the anti-teleological conception of Marxism Althusser defended from 'Contradiction and Overdetermination' onwards. The potential of an encounter between Epicurus and Marx has also been identified by Marxists working in other traditions.[23] I have no desire to set myself against explorations of wherever 'aleatory materialism' may take us. But it is perhaps worth saying that this is the aspect of Althusser's thought that, in its celebration of plurality and contingency, is the most congenial to contemporary thought, thanks to the influence of poststructuralism. It may therefore be worth reminding ourselves of other aspects that, though more out of line with the dominant trends, retain their actuality. One of those, I suggest, is Marx's—and Althusser's—'detour via relations'.

---

21  See Alex Callinicos, *Is There a Future for Marxism?* (London, 1982), pp76-78, 149-159, and the outstanding discussion in Ali Rattansi, *Marx and the Division of Labour* (London, 1982).
22  Louis Althusser, 'Le Courant souterrain du matérialisme de la rencontre', in *Écrits philosophiques et politiques* (François Matheron, ed; 2 vols, Paris, 1994, 1995), I, p576.
23  John Bellamy Foster, *Marx's Ecology* (New York, 2000), Andrea Micocci, *Anti-Hegelian Reading of Economic Theory* (Lewiston NY, 2002).

# Index

# Index